Conway

Images of Children in Byzantium

Cecily Hennessy

ASHGATE

Published by
Ashgate Publishing Limited
Wey Court East
Union Road
Farnham
Surrey GU9 7PT
England

Ashgate Publishing Company
Suite 420
101 Cherry Street
Burlington, VT 05401-4405
USA

Ashgate website: http://www.ashgate.com

British Library Cataloguing in Publication Data

Hennessy, Cecily
    Images of Children in Byzantium
    1. Children in art. 2. Art, Byzantine 3. Children – Byzantine Empire - History
    I. Title
    704.9'425'0902

Library of Congress Cataloging-in-Publication Data
Hennessy, Cecily, 1957-
    Images of children in Byzantium / by Cecily Hennessy.
        p.   cm.
    Includes bibliographical references.
    1. Children in art. 2. Art, Byzantine. 3. Children – Byzantine Empire – Social conditions. I. Title.
    N7640.H46 2008
    704.9'425–dc22   2008010398

ISBN 978-0-7546-5631-9

Mixed Sources
Product group from well-managed forests and other controlled sources
www.fsc.org Cert no. SA-COC-1565
© 1996 Forest Stewardship Council
FSC

Printed and bound in Great Britain by
MPG Books Ltd, Bodmin, Cornwall.

Contents

Acknowledgements

In writing this book, I have had the benefit of studying and working at an excellent institution, the use of the finest libraries and generous funding from several sources.

I wish particularly to thank Robin Cormack who supervised my doctoral research at the Courtauld Institute of Art. He was a considerate and expert advisor and has since been encouraging and responsive, and his extensive knowledge and informed approach has contributed greatly to my work. My study of children in Byzantium began under the guidance of Anna Kartsonis at the University of Washington in Seattle, for whose keen direction and warm attention I am very grateful.

It has also been a pleasure to work in the libraries associated with the University of London and particularly in the Warburg library. I am grateful for access to manuscripts at the Bibliothèque nationale, the Vatican, the British Library and the Bodleian Library.

I am deeply indebted to the Arts and Humanities Research Board for a three-year studentship and for additional travel funds enabling research in Greece and in Turkey. I am also grateful to the University of London Central Research Fund for two travel grants for study in Italy, in Greece and at Dumbarton Oaks, and to the Courtauld Institute of Art and to the Society for the Promotion of Byzantine Studies for grants for research in Paris and at the Vatican, and to the Academic Research Board at the Courtauld Institute of Art for further funding.

I am appreciative to Antony Eastmond and to Liz James for constructive suggestions on my work and to Kriszta Kotsis and Kathleen Doyle who both gave detailed and useful criticism as well as to anonymous reviewers who gave valuable recommendations. Many have offered me bibliographic suggestions, advice, discussion, access to unpublished work, photography, hospitality and practical assistance. These include Alixe Bovey, Jas Elsner, John Lowden, Nikos Kalogeras and Rossitza Roussanova.

Thank you all.

List of Illustrations

List of Figures

List of Plates

Illustration Acknowledgements

The following are gratefully acknowledged:
A Turizm Yayinlari figs 2.19, 4.13, 4.14, pl. 14
Athos, Dionysiou figs 2.21, 4.10, 4.11, pls. 1-2
Athos, Iveron fig. 2.20
© Biblioteca Apostolica Vaticana figs 2.17, 5.7, 6.2, pls. 11-12
Bibliothèque nationale de France figs 2.9, 2.11-2.16, 3.3, 5.1-5.3, 5.4, 5.6
Bongers Aurel Verlag fig. 4.12
Karen Boston fig 3.4
British School at Athens fig. 4.1, pl. 9
Robin Cormack fig. 5.9
Courtesy of the Ephoreia of Byzantine Antiquities, Thessaloniki fig. 4.7
Cecily Hennessy figs 2.5-2.7, 3.2, 6.3
Liz James fig. 6.5
London, British Library fig. 5.10
Published through the courtesy of the Michigan-Princeton-Alexandria Expeditions to Mount Sinai figs 4.5-4.6, 6.6-6.7
Moscow, Gosudarstvennyĭ muzeĭ fig. 2.10
New York, Metropolitan Museum of Art figs 4.2, 4.4
Nicosia, Museum of Antiquities fig. 4.3
Oxford, Lincoln College pls. 7-8
Photo RMN/©Caroline Rose fig. 5.11
Photo RMN/© Daniel Arnaut fig. 2.8
© Dr. Ludwig Reichert Verlag figs 4.8-4.9, pl. 10
Károly Szelényi fig. 5.5
Nicole Thierry fig. 6.1
© Copyright The Trustees of the British Museum figs 3.1, 6.4
Turin, University Library fig. 2.18
Vienna, Oesterreichische Nationalbibliothek pls. 3-4 and cover

Abbreviations

ActaNorv	*Acta ad Archaeologiam et Artium Historiam pertinentia, Institum Romanum Norvegiae*
ArtB	*Art Bulletin*
BHG	*Bibliotheca hagiographica graeca*. Edited by F. Halkin. 3 vols. Brussels, 1957.
BHG	*AuctBibliotheca hagiographica graeca*. Edited by F. Halkin. Vol. 4, *Auctarium*. Brussels, 1969.
BMGS	*Byzantine and Modern Greek Studies*
BZ	*Byzantinische Zeitschrift*
CahArch	*Cahiers archéologiques*
CFHB	*Corpus fontium historiae byzantinae*
CHSB	*Corpus scriptorum historiae byzantinae*
DACL	*Dictionnaire d'archéologie chrétienne et de liturgie*. Edited by F. Cabrol and H. Leclercq. 15 vols. Paris, 1907–1953.
DOC	*Catalogue of the Byzantine Coins in the Dumbarton Oaks Collection and in the Whittemore Collection*. Edited by A. Bellinger and P. Grierson. 3 vols. Washington, DC., 1966–1973.
DOP	*Dumbarton Oaks Papers*
JÖB	*Jahrbuch der Österreichischen Byzantinistik*

JWarb	*Journal of the Warburg and Courtauld Institutes*
LIMC	*Lexicon iconographicum mythologiae classicae*. 8 vols. Zurich and Munich, 1981–1999.
ODB	*Oxford Dictionary of Byzantium*. New York, Oxford, 1991.
PG	*Patrologiae cursus completus. Series graeca*. Edited by J.-P. Migne. 161 vols in 166 parts. Paris, 1857–1866.
PL	*Patrologiae cursus completus. Series latina*. Edited by J.-P. Migne. 221 vols in 222 parts. Paris, 1844–1880.
RBK	*Reallexikon zur byzantinischen Kunst*. Edited by K. Wessel. Stuttgart, 1963–.
REB	*Revue des études byzantines*
SC	*Sources chrétiennes*

Chapter 1

Setting

Byzantium, established as the eastern capital by Constantine in the early fourth century, inherited the laws, the societal habits, and the imagery of Rome and included the nascent elements of Christianity. In Constantinople on the shores of the Bosphoros and, at certain points during the 1,200 years of Byzantine culture, as far afield as Egypt and Syria, Sicily and Russia, a complex and fluctuating culture developed which in turn, throughout its history, contributed significantly to the practices and visual ideologies of western society. If not only for its intrinsic value, for its crucial influence on western visual material Byzantium is increasingly seen as a vital region of interest.

Intriguingly, the presence of representations of children in Byzantine art has not attracted much attention. Yet children and childhood are widespread subjects in Byzantine imagery: playful girls pick flowers on mosaic floors, athletic boys perform tricks on manuscript borders and naked infants cavort on ivory boxes. Youthful martyrs stand gracefully on painted icons, devoted children revere saints on church walls and solemn princes hold insignia in illuminated portraits. Children are rarely associated with Byzantine art or history and studies have largely viewed Byzantium as an adult world. Contrary to expectations, children were depicted frequently and sometimes in consequential contexts or locations. That children played a significant role in visual representation suggests that they had a central part in Byzantine life. Why do we not associate them with Byzantium? Ernst Gombrich, writing about the hold of visual records on the imagination and their ability to mythologize the past, commented, 'Who could find it easy, after a visit to Ravenna and its solemn mosaics, to think of noisy children in Byzantium?'[1] Robin Cormack, responding to this, makes the point that art does not necessarily reflect society and that the Ravenna mosaics 'have the apparent "seriousness" of "official" art made for adults'.[2] But, he also counters with the idea that the recognition of the solemnity of Byzantine art is *'our* perception not the Byzantine one'.[3]

---

1   Gombrich (1957) 6.
2   Cormack (1997) 133 for Gombrich quote, 164 for Cormack quote.
3   Cormack (1997) 165.

Similarly, I would suggest that the accepted view that art was made for adults is only our perception and that children's interest in and appreciation of visual material is probably very much at the centre of imagery. Serious art is suitable for adults, but also, as we shall see, for children: both religious and political or official art can be created for children and portrays them in it. Our perception of pre-modern societies is tainted by our own increasingly geriatric culture. In contrast, Byzantium was typical of pre-modern societies in that at least half the population were aged under 20. To what extent does this affect the production and reception of art?

The present book draws on representations from the fourth to the fifteenth centuries, from various parts of the Byzantine empire, and in a wide range of media. The intention is not to provide a chronological survey of the development of art about children, nor to focus on a synchronic selection, nor to take a consciously diachronic view. The aim is to investigate particular images of children, the manner in which they are depicted, with whom they appear, and the contexts in which they are found, with the purpose of determining the place and significance of children in visual representations and, by extension, in Byzantine society at various points in the past. The questions of change over time or of the development of concepts about childhood will not be addressed, since a comprehensive survey of such notions requires extensive work by historians, social historians and literary analysts which remains largely untouched. This does not temper the validity of an art-historical investigation of the ways in which children are portrayed and their place in society at certain moments in time and in key visual sites.

The themes explored arise from the material, with areas of focus and natural groupings in which the images hold related contexts, meanings, or associations. The images themselves are the primary evidence. Each is viewed principally for what it suggests about how children were handled pictorially and how the other figures and settings with or in which the children appear were depicted. The intention is to come to an understanding of three areas of study: the role of art, of children in art and of children themselves in society. Historical, literary and religious texts provide supplementary material and often contribute to these three strands of exploration, adding to an interpretation of an image. Texts can be useful in amplifying perceptions and knowledge of given situations, suggesting layers of meaning to the way an image is portrayed or to the effect it may have had, or to its historical and functional, secular or spiritual context. However, texts do not reveal the actions and beliefs of society any more directly than do pictorial representations; if not applied sensitively, they may distort rather than elucidate the meaning of what is seen.

The terms child and childhood are necessarily used in a broad sense to refer to those people who have not reached maturity: when this occurs and what conditions identify it are complex issues. Contemporary definitions of childhood and adulthood vary, geographically and in a range of contexts, and similarly definitions of different stages in life in Byzantium appear to have fluctuated and to have various interpretations. Our own distinctions between maturity and immaturity are altered in certain legal and moral contexts, as well as societal ones. Contrasting regulations determine this transition from a state of youth, immaturity and lack of responsibility to one of adulthood, maturity and personal responsibility. We are comfortable with this multifaceted view, though it is often discussed, and we have no necessity to perceive childhood as a defined entity. There is a tendency to think that we should be able to make hard and fast distinctions in historical cultures and yet in them we see the same fluctuating use of terminology, regulations and expectations. For the sake of some definition, I apply the term child to those who are generally below the onset of puberty, which in Byzantium was also the marriageable age, that is 12 for girls and 14 for boys, and I apply the term youth or adolescent to those beyond that age. The terms girl and boy are used to refer to children and youth of the respective genders with no specific reference to age. My intention is to use terms such as child, childhood, youth and immaturity in a commonsense way and not one that is bound by strict regulations.

Unlike modern western society, in legal terms, the ancients and the Byzantines recognized that girls matured earlier than boys. Boys from affluent families appear to have had in certain contexts an extended period of what we would call adolescence, during which they were educated, before they assumed full adult responsibility. Girls married young, and they participated in adult life in terms of bearing children. It seems likely that girls did not experience a period of cultural adolescence, a time of preparation before entering the adult world. The lack of records that attest to the emotional state of adolescence in girls that we recognize today, and which is not so dissimilar from the behaviour of boys, may be in part because ancient and Byzantine writers were less interested in female activity. Hormonal changes are biological and perhaps in Byzantium were not so different from those of today, although they may now occur at an earlier age. Girls were most likely controlled by societal pressure to become wives and mothers. Apparently, while boys had an extended period of what we would justifiably call adolescence, girls did not.[4]

An understanding of the representation of childhood and of children in the past requires an awareness of our own perceptions about children today and how they are depicted. As art of the past reveals then contemporary values, so our view is linked to our own time and to our perception of our culture and ourselves. It is tempting, but deceptive, to retroject modern childhood; yet without some understanding of our own assumptions and expectances it is hard to recognize the measure by which we gauge the past. Understanding Byzantine childhood requires examining differences between contemporary and Byzantine approaches to childhood. The past presents both recognizable and unrecognizable precepts and customs, with similarities that seem disarmingly familiar and variances that suggest an entirely different perception

---

4   The issue of adolescence was famously raised by Margaret Mead in Mead (1928); for a critique of her work, see Kleijwegt (1991) 1–11, with references to parallel, but differing studies.

of humanity. The questions discussed and the meanings deciphered may reflect current as well as historical interests and concerns.

Two principal influences, antiquity and Christianity, formed the basis of Byzantine culture. Ancient Greek and Roman culture provided the legal, administrative and social background; Christian doctrine and practice incorporated a new religious framework, fresh concepts and, to some extent, different conduct. Attitudes towards children and childhood derived primarily from the ancient world and were modified and adapted to suit Christianity, which in turn incorporated aspects of Judaism. Studies of Greek, Roman, western medieval, early modern and modern childhood and the family have multiplied in recent years. Less has been written on the visual representation of children throughout western history and very little on Byzantium. Modern studies on childhood usually contain a reference to Philippe Ariès.[5] His review, written in the early 1960s, of childhood in France since the fifteenth century was pivotal in establishing late twentieth-century histories of childhood. He focused on the issue of what childhood is, when, how and why it came into being and attitudes towards it. Any such theory is likely to be controversial, and this is perhaps why Ariès's work has been so central: it begs criticism and contradiction but also raises important methodological and historiographical issues. He premised that childhood, as we know it, did not exist until the seventeenth century, although its emergence began in the fifteenth. Children were then respected for the first time, treated affectionately and seen as entertaining. Adults even aspired to become like them. Rather than entering the grown-up world at the age of seven or so, children started to go through an extended education preparing them for adulthood. Ariès maintains that interest in childhood is an expression of the concept of the family, which prior to this time had not been able to develop due to lack of private space.[6] For him, modern childhood is centred on love within the nuclear family and is a period of psychological and sexual innocence in which the child is educated for life.

Ariès's theory is flawed, in my opinion, in three main respects. First, the nuclear family did not develop in the last 500 years, but has since medieval times formed the basic domestic structure in England and Northern Europe.[7] Second, arguing that childhood became distinct from adulthood in the seventeenth century is perhaps an elitist and narrow view. In the nineteenth century children from poor families were incorporated into the adult world: less than two centuries ago children made up nearly half of the work force, and it was commonly accepted that a ten-year-old would work 12 hours a day.[8] Parents sent their children to work out of necessity rather than choice, yet the practice was sanctioned by society. Only with compulsory schooling

---

5   Ariès (1962, 1996 edn).
6   Ariès (1962, 1996 edn.) 341, 385.
7   On this, see Laslett (1972) 5–9, 126; and for an alternate view, Stone (1977) 21–26.
8   Cunningham (1995) 140. In England, in the 1830s the law was changed so that children under nine could not work in factories and children up to 14 were restricted to eight-hour work days.

for the five to tens, implemented in Britain at the remarkably recent date of 1880, did young children, at least in theory, stop working.[9] However, this is a complex issue, and it is not to say that childhood did not exist in the lower classes of society or that work pre-empts it. Even though children have worked at various times through history in the western world, and do so today as teenagers, the distinction of childhood has existed at least from early antiquity and probably before. Ariès does imply, nonspecifically, that ancient attitudes towards childhood were similar to our own, but fails to trace its continuation and revivals. Third, Ariès's evidence is biased. One of his central claims, that because children died so frequently in medieval times, their parents formed little attachment to them, is based largely on the writings of Montaigne and Molière, who, as childless intellectual men may not reflect general thinking. He fails to show that, in general, medieval parents did not love their children. Similarly, in illustrating the emergence of childhood in the sixteenth century, Ariès depends heavily on the childhood of Louis XIII, as recounted by his doctor, Jean Heroard, who depicted the young prince as an adored and indulged child.[10] This is not sufficient evidence to show a general societal change.

Various authors quickly supplemented Ariès's work. Three major publications in the 1970s represent what has been called the 'sentiments approach' to childhood, which follows Ariès in seeing a major change in attitudes to children, although they disagree as to what these were.[11] Responses in the 1980s have turned to demographics and household economics for evidence to construct a statistics-based understanding of society that includes the poor.[12] Hugh Cunningham identified a transition from the 1960s, when commentators claimed that childhood had progressed historically and was more understood than before, to the 1970s and 1980s, when historians recognized that in the past children had also been brought up in loving nuclear families.[13] Contemporary problems have perhaps raised a greater awareness of positive elements in the past. Over the last 20 years, literature on issues of children and the family has proliferated, with interdisciplinary approaches involving historians, sociologists, psychologists and anthropologists. Certain researchers and commentators have examined current issues of children and the family with a historical approach.[14] Others have discussed children within a broad frame of societal behaviour or the history of emotions.[15] Questions about children and their place in contemporary and historical society are

9   Cunningham (1995) 157.
10   Ariès (1962, 1996 edn) esp. 13–105.
11   On this, see Anderson (1980) 41, 61–64; for summaries, see Cunningham (1995) 8–13.
12   Anderson (1980); Pollock (1983); Goody (1983); Hanawalt (1986); Hanawalt (1993); summarized in Cunningham (1995) 13–17, 38–39.
13   Cunningham (1995) 4–17; also see Cunningham for a survey of the historiography of childhood in the past 500 years, focusing on Locke, Rousseau, the Romantics, particularly Wordsworth, the industrial revolution and nineteenth-century reform (41–162).
14   See, for example, Hardyment (1998).
15   Zeldin (1994).

avidly argued, but not necessarily with much consensus. Collected essays on children or the family, which can present various points of view, often covering a wide span of time, absolve the need for agreement and can present interesting and controversial views.[16]

Several historians, beginning in the late 1960s, but again becoming increasingly popular, have studied childhood in antiquity. Just as Ariès suggested that childhood is peculiar to the early modern and modern eras, Marc Kleijwegt claims that youth did not exist in antiquity, but that Rousseau invented the concept.[17] He sees modern adolescence as a period of adaptation after childhood but before adulthood, which has been lengthened by the complexity of our industrial society. Eyben argues that adolescence in pre-industrial society can be compared with early modern society.[18] Other recent work on ancient childhood includes Mark Golden on Athens and Thomas Wiedemann on Rome.[19]

Further studies have included female children and the family and have tended to emphasize family affections. Suzanne Dixon argues that conjugal love was important in Roman society and Roman mothers had a central role in the moral education of their children, particularly their adolescent sons.[20] Like Dixon, Kate Cooper, discussing virginity, disputes Paul Veyne's view that Augustus's legislation on marriage and the family, not Christianity, turned men towards loving conjugal relationships. However, she agrees that the idea of marital concord, shared by pagans and Christians, stemmed at least from the time of Augustus, and she attributes this to men's self-interest in securing position for themselves.[21]

A collection of essays on the early Christian family, edited by Halvor Moxnes, has looked at both the family as a social institution and at the Christian community as a 'fictive kinship'.[22] The various views, often anthropological in method and using Graeco-Roman and Jewish sources, show the complex range of types of families, and discuss the influence of the familial identities developed by the early church. These are both patriarchal and based on the household, as well as community oriented and based on 'brotherhood'.[23] Another recent book, by Geoffrey Nathan, provides a wider view, follows developments in society up to the sixth century and argues that the effect of church doctrine concerning the family is minimal.[24] He maintains

---

16   See, for example, Burguière (1996); for nineteenth-century attitudes to the family, based on an evolutionary view of the ancient family, see Patterson (1998) 5–43.

17   Kleijwegt (1991), summarized on XII–XV; on cultural primitivism and childhood, see Boas (1966).

18   Eyben (1993) 5–41.

19   Golden (1990); Wiedemann (1989).

20   Dixon (1997) 79–90, esp. 81.

21   Cooper (1996) 1–4; Veyne (1978) 36–63; on women and the family in ancient Rome, see also Hallett (1984); Rawson (1986, 1992 edn); Rawson (1991); Dixon (1988).

22   Moxnes (1997).

23   Karl Sandnes's essay is useful in defining this dichotomy; see Sandnes (1997) 150–165.

24   Nathan (2000).

that the family retained its Roman roots and was not altered by Christianity in terms of composition, living patterns or interfamilial relations. He makes three points. First, societal customs and needs overrode the Christian call for celibacy, and patriarchy remained the norm; second, prior to becoming the state religion, Christianity could accommodate minority interests, but in becoming mainstream it adopted essentially traditional values and so appealed to greater numbers; and third, church authorities often disagreed among themselves, issued canons that contradicted each other and furthermore had little influence on state laws.[25] Nathan reinforces my own sense that in practice church theology and doctrine brought about little fundamental change.

Studies on western medieval children have become comparably popular, both in Europe and in North America. Again, collected essays are favoured, some resulting from colloquia on children or on the family.[26] Shulamith Shahar's work is easily accessible and has similarly shown that mothers and fathers in the middle ages were very attached to their children and mourned deeply at their loss.[27] Sally Crawford has explored the history of Anglo-Saxons and Nicholas Orme, most recently, has given a thorough historical account of children in England focusing on the period 1100–1550.[28]

I have only outlined some of the more influential or relevant studies on children and childhood, but this survey indicates the rapidly growing attention to children in history. This includes an interest in overriding questions, such as defining childhood or adolescence, and in thorough historical interpretations of children's place in society.

As studies on children and childhood have multiplied in the late twentieth century, so have books specifically on children in art, yet these tend to be less scholarly and often very generalized. Some explorations of child iconography have looked to the ancient world, registering children's activities and customs, which are most often recorded in vase paintings or on funerary monuments. Janet Huskinson's catalogue of Roman children's sarcophagi discusses representations of children in detail and raises valuable questions about the interpretation of childhood.[29] Concerning the medieval period, one study was instigated by an exhibition, mainly of manuscript illustrations from the Bibliothèque nationale, Paris. It has lavish illustrations and a notably documentary approach to children.[30] The material is grouped according to social practices, such as the family, stages of life, and education, and the text also summarizes academic interest in children in France during the 1970s and 1980s. Other studies have focused on Dutch and German art, often looking at family or individual portraits and frequently taking the form of catalogues published in association with exhibitions.[31] A more in-depth look

---

25 Summarized in Nathan (2000) 185–188.
26 See, for instance, Itnyre (1996).
27 Shahar (1990, 1992 edn).
28 Crawford (2000); Orme (2001).
29 Huskinson (1996).
30 Riché and Alexandre-Bidou (1994).
31 See, for instance, Kronberger-Frentzen (1940).

at seventeenth-century Dutch art has been made by Mary Durantini, who uses paintings to describe children's position in society, focusing on domestic situations, education and play.[32] She evaluates the place of children in the adult world and their differences from adults, often drawing on intriguing symbolism in the paintings. David Solkin has discussed attitudes towards portrayals of the family in eighteenth-century England.[33] Others have taken a romanticized view of photographs or art about children, frequently using idealized images and sentimentalizing them.[34]

Ann Higgonet's work on current attitudes to children in photography traces what she sees as the development of the image of the innocent child in the eighteenth century by artists such as Reynolds and Gainsborough.[35] She is concerned about the eroticization, either intentional or otherwise, in contemporary photography, but also sees work that attributes 'consciously active minds and bodies' to children as well as innocence.[36] This book raises relevant issues, but her lack of recognition of images of 'innocent' childhood in antiquity and after, as well as her idealization of eighteenth- and nineteenth-century paintings, which display subtly and not so subtly veiled eroticization, needs to be more qualified.

Higgonet raises one point that Ariès also made and which has often been stated: that children throughout medieval times and into the seventeenth century were depicted in art as miniature adults.[37] This ignores both contemporary and historical evidence. Babies and very small children have usually had their own attire, but the creation of special dress for the young, seen as a custom of the twentieth century, even now does not prevail. Today adults and children tend to wear similar clothes on both formal and informal occasions. School uniforms and adult suits are largely interchangeable, as are adults' and children's casual wear, and little girls wear high heels if given the chance. Teenagers may have popularized jeans in the fifties but cowboys wore them long before. To a great extent our children look like us, and we look like them. To say that in a sixteenth-century family portrait the children look like miniature adults shows the adult-centred perception of children: the adults and children look alike since they are wearing the dress of their day. One could equally justifiably say that adults look like overgrown children. However, in depictions of nonspecific children in Byzantine art, small boys are frequently shown in short white tunics, apparently denoting them as children and indicating that they should be viewed as distinct from the adults who are dressed differently. However, in portraits of imperial children and of

---

32   Durantini (1983).

33   Solkin (1992) esp. 86.

34   An example of this, which by current standards is exploitative, is Braun (1925, 2nd edn).

35   Higgonet (1998).

36   Higgonet (1998) 193–225, quote on 12.

37   Higgonet (1998) 8; Ariès (1962, 1996 edn) on children's dress: 48–59, and in art: 31–44.

children of the nobility, they are usually dressed in similar ways to their adult counterparts, indicating that they are wearing contemporary formal dress.

Byzantine children have been the subject of several studies, often in relation to their legal status. This has largely occurred since the 1970s and has coincided with the general rise in interest in children. In the 1973 conference in Paris on children and society, Hélène Antoniadis-Bibicou outlined legislation relating to children from the sixth and seventh centuries, and Evelyne Patlagean, also relying on legal texts, focused on the child as a commodity used to extend family alliances.[38] A further article, by Joëlle Beaucamp, from 1977 placed children in the context of women's legal status.[39] Patlagean also wrote on coming of age and referred to various legal issues, historical examples, and to the story of Digenes Akritas.[40] Her chapter on families and kinship in Byzantium, which is part of the *History of the Family*, again reiterates marriage laws, particularly restrictions on endogamous relationships and village social structures.[41] Ann Moffatt's 'The Byzantine Child' gives a broad overview of childhood, covering marriage, education, children's literature, inheritance and family size, children in monasteries and child abuse, but is minimally referenced.[42] She uses literary and legal texts (which draw on late antique and early Christian models), and biographies, hagiographies and medical texts. A Dumbarton Oaks symposium in 1990 on the Byzantine family and household looks at marriage, adoption, monasteries, hagiography and the contents of the house, but not specifically at children or childhood. It is more concerned with the family as a unit of social organization.[43] Angeliki Laiou's extensive work based on legislation and historical texts also refers frequently to children, although it is primarily centred on women.[44] Timothy Miller has written about orphans from legal, ecclesiastical and monastic standpoints.[45] More recently, Nikolaos Kalogeras has discussed Byzantine childhood and education from the sixth to the ninth centuries, using extensive sources, mostly hagiographic, but also the writings of the church fathers.[46]

While some art-historical studies mention depictions of children, Elias Antonopoulos's work is rare in focusing directly or exclusively on children. He has looked at images in the *Sacra Parallela*, Paris, gr. 923, and in the *Khludov Psalter*, Moscow, State Historical Museum, MS gr. 129, but, as he himself notes, this work is tentative.[47] He has also discussed representations of children with marks of age and wisdom.[48] Other studies have looked at images of Christ and of the Virgin as infants, but these tend to take a standard iconographic

---

38   Antoniadis-Bibicou (1973) 77–83; Patlagean (1973) 85–93.
39   Beaucamp (1977) 145–176.
40   Patlagean (1986) 269.
41   Patlagean (1996) 467–488.
42   Moffatt (1986) 705–723.
43   *DOP* 44 (1990).
44   Of particular interest is Laiou (1992); see also Laiou (1977).
45   Miller (1996) 121–136; Miller (2003).
46   Kalogeras (2000) throughout; Kalogeras (2001).
47   Antonopoulos (1986) 271–287.
48   Antonopoulos (1998) 215–231.

approach and not to look at the images primarily as representations of children.[49]

In discussing images of children in Byzantium, it is helpful to have a sense of children's legal and cultural status. The legal is more straightforward to determine, and the sources reveal an outline of secular and religious authorities' approaches to children, although these changed through time and would not have necessarily been applied homogenously. Certain cases also give complex details about children's behaviour and adults' responses to them and can indicate subtle attitudes in both adults and children. These contribute to the second issue, our sense of children's place in society, but an understanding of children's roles in a nonlegal sense is not easily accessible: the scope is vast and complex in terms of time and geography, and very little research on this topic has so far been undertaken. However, an overview of the legal attitudes to children and a survey of certain religious and cultural approaches to them help create a framework for interpreting Byzantine childhood.

It is pertinent to start with the schematic and pragmatic stages of life in antiquity and in Byzantium and the terminology used in Greek and in Latin to describe children of various ages, both legally and philosophically.[50] However, our translation or understanding of these phases and their terms cannot necessarily be equated with those of Byzantium, and language, as now, was not always consistently applied in all contexts.

In Byzantium, life fell into phases suggested by biological age, educational periods and cultural transitions at times of change, such as marriage, entering military or civil service or opening one's own workshop. This was inherited from antiquity, where the practical division of life into stages was more rigidly defined by the philosophical concept of distinguishing distinct periods of life.[51] Most theories were schematic and adopted the magical number of seven, dividing life into *hebdomades*, or periods of seven years. The Hippocratic school saw life in seven *hilikiai* (age groups) each lasting seven years: *paidion* (birth to six), *pais* (six to 13), *meirakion* (13 to 20) and so on. Varro (117–27 BC) adopted five periods, each 15 years long, beginning with *pueritia*, *adulescentia*, and leading to *iuventus* or adulthood. Others, such as the Pythagoreans, Galen and Plato (who distinguished between levels of intellectual pursuits), all used four stages. Children were separated into age groups, most notably by the Spartans when children were six, but also in Greece in the gymnasium and

---

49   For instance, Nordhagen (1961) 333–337; Lafontaine-Dosogne (1975a) 161–194 and (1975b) 195–241.

50   These laws regarding children are in the *Corpus Juris Civilis*, the *Ecloga* of 726, the *Procheiros Nomos* or *Prochiron* (867–879), the *Epanagoge* (879–886), the *Novels*, as well as commentaries on canon law and patriarchal responses. The *Ecloga* was written under Leo III and Constantine V, the *Prochiron* under Basil I and Leo VI, the *Epanagoge* under Basil I, Leo VI and Alexander, and the *Novels* under Leo VI. The *Ecloga* was a revision of Justinianic law and was an attempt to make it more humane in the light of Christian doctrine. The *Epanagoge* is a synopsis of the *Basilica* which was used until the fall of Constantinople.

51   On this, see Garland (1990) 1–16; Eyben (1993) 6–9, 31–40; Néraudau (1984) 47–49 and for a broader discussion of ages of life, 21–44; Ariès (1962, 1996 edn) 19–20.

agora.[52] Similarly in Byzantium children were educated and trained with their peers, often of the same sex. The artificial, numerically formulated transitions did not reflect actual practice, and in antiquity and in Byzantium, the life span tended to fall into natural periods, encompassing youth, maturity and old age.[53]

The terms used for describing children and adolescents are extensive and varied, although in common language, the Greek *pais* to which the Latin *puer* is comparable had broad use in antiquity and in Byzantium. It applied to both children and slaves, but it should not be assumed that this reflects equivalence in attitude towards them. Common terms used for children in Byzantium include *neognon paidion* and *brephos* for newborn, *nipion* and *paidion* for little child, *pais* and *teknon* for child, boy or girl, *meirakion* for boy and *neaniskos* for youth or young man. As in Roman law, in Byzantium the pre-pubic stage (*anibos, impubes*) for children ended at 14 for boys and 12 for girls. They then entered puberty and were permitted to marry.[54] But children were used as tools for familial alliances and could be engaged at the age of seven, when the male child was able to object if he wished.[55]

Byzantine children had an extended period of legal dependence. Until the age of 25, both male and female were minors (*afilikes, minores*), under the authority of legal guardians, unless made independent (*autexousios* as opposed to *hupexousios*).[56] In Roman law, the guardian was male, normally the father, grandfather or guardian/tutor, but Theodosios made it possible for a woman to be a guardian for her offspring so long as she did not remarry, and Justinian further gave precedence to mothers and grandmothers as legal guardians over male family members.[57] In order to gain independence at a younger age, girls older than 18 or boys older than 20 had to apply to the emperor and, according to a novel of Leo VI, show that they had judgement and intelligence and could be entrusted with their patrimony.[58] Various designations indicate the importance of a child's relation to his parent or guardian. Guardianship was a protective way of caring for orphans, and from the time of Constantine, the rights of adopted children were carefully legislated.[59]

Infanticide and the rejection of children was outlawed in AD 374 and reiterated in Justinian's Code. Some analysts consider that alienation was not widespread, perhaps due to Christian ethics and the assistance provided by the church, although evidence is often hard to interpret.[60] The Code mentions

---

52   Garland (1990) 2–9, with references; Eyben (1993) 6.

53   On this in antiquity, see Garland (1990) 4–5; on old age see Talbot (1984) 267–278.

54   *Codex Justinianus*, V. IV. 24, (dated 530); *Prochiron* IV. 3; some texts, such as *Ecloga* II. 1, state the ages as 15 and 13.

55   *Ecloga*, I. 1, and repeated in the ninth century *Prochiron* I. 7.8; on this, see Patlagean (1973) 87.

56   See Patlagean (1986) 264–265.

57   *Codex Theodos* 3.17.4, *Novels of Justinian*, CXVIII. 5; on this, see Miller (1996) 124.

58   On this, see Antoniadis-Bibicou (1973) 77, with references.

59   On early guardianship laws, see Miller (1996) 121–136, esp. 122–124.

60   *Codex Justinianus*, IV. XLIII. 1; on this, see Patlagean (1973) 85; Moffatt (1986) 714–715; on abandonment, also see Boswell (1988) and, most recently, Miller (2003) 141–175.

brephotropheia, day nurseries set up by the church where abandoned children were fed.[61] Although the Code also forbids selling children, exemptions are made in cases of extreme poverty. In times of hardship, parents might have had no choice but to expose or sell their children, but the buyer had to return the child if he or she were offered a fair price.[62] Children tended to be nursed by their mothers. Some, mostly of the affluent, were fed by wet-nurses although there is little evidence of this after the seventh century.[63]

Children who engaged passively in homosexuality were forgiven if they were aged under 12, according to the *Ecloga* of 726.[64] This suggests the continued practice of pederasty, which was heavily condemned by the Byzantine church, as it was in Judaic custom. The church fathers include pederasty with fornication, adultery, homosexuality and bestiality.[65] Their concerns indicate that the phenomenon existed and posed some threat to current morality, which has perhaps been glossed over in discussions of homosexuality.[66] A Justinianic law against prostitution involving children younger than ten suggests that this was practised.[67] Children could be tortured at the age of 14 and were considered useful as slaves from the age of ten.[68]

Illegitimate children were not able to inherit, but according to Justinianic law, could be legitimized by being offered to the curia, by the father's marriage to the mother, or by the same means that a slave could be freed, such as intervention by the emperor.[69] Under Leo VI, the law was altered so that the father in front of witnesses could declare the child his son or daughter without having to designate them as natural.[70] Illegitimate children were in all strata of society and evidence suggests that they were not estranged or mistreated simply for their birth.[71] These cases show the cultural tendency to legitimize children, which must have been intended to secure care for as many as possible as well as to create inheritors for those who had none. New laws also made it easier to adopt children, even by eunuchs, who were forbidden to marry, and by women who had had none themselves. The adoptive father had to be 18 years older than the child.[72]

After the Council of Trullo in 692, entrance into a monastery was permitted by boys and girls aged ten and above, although Justinian had set the limit at

---

61   Patlagean (1973) 85.

62   *Codex Justinianus*, IV. XLIII. 2 (dated 329); on this, see Patlagean (1973) 86; Antoniadis-Bibicou (1973) 81–82.

63   Moffatt (1986) 713–718, esp. 717; for more on wet-nursing, see Fildes (1988) esp. 1–31 on antiquity to 1200.

64   *Ecloga*, XVII. 38.

65   Laiou (1992) 71 and fn. 15.

66   As by Laiou in a case recorded in the Life of Saint Andrew Salos; *PG* 111:700; *BHG* I, 115z–117k; see Laiou (1992) 78; on homosexuality in Byzantium, see Smythe (1999) 139–148.

67   On this, see Patlagean (1973) 86.

68   On this, see Antoniadis-Bibicou (1973) 78.

69   *Novels of Justinian*, XII; on this, see Antoniadis-Bibicou (1973) 80.

70   On this, see Antoniadis-Bibicou (1973) 80.

71   On this, see Yannopoulos (1975) 232–236.

72   *Novels of Leo VI*, XXVI and XXVII; on this, see Antoniadis-Bibicou (1973) 81.

16 or 17.[73] Leo VI maintained the seventh-century regulation but prevented a child from giving away his or her possessions before being 16 or 17. However, some boys, and girls too, were sent to monasteries at the age of seven to be educated, which in some cases had the same implication as entering a monastery.[74] Precocious young saints are recorded in hagiographic texts as pleading at an early age, some at five or six, to be allowed to join.[75] Girls were also sent when young to convents as related in the Life of Theodora of Thessaloniki (disregarding hagiographic licence perhaps, Theodora's daughter became tonsured aged six).[76] Ten was apparently considered the age of religious maturity, although it was recognized that it varied case by case.[77] Before 12, children were not required to confess prior to taking communion, suggesting that only by that age were they considered morally responsible.[78]

Orphans had varying experiences. Often relatives adopted them, at other times bishops or monasteries cared for them, and occasionally they lived in orphanages.[79] Justinian's laws indicate that orphanages existed in Constantinople and elsewhere and refer to one founded by Saint Zotikos.[80] The most well-known was the orphanage of St Paul in Constantinople, founded in the fourth century and supported by Alexios I.[81] His daughter, Anna Komnene, gives a laudatory account of it, mentioning that refugees were housed there. It was a huge city-like complex, apparently housing thousands of people, and associated with the church of St Paul, a convent and a monastery, and a multiracial school which educated the orphans and children of the poor.[82] The original foundation had included homes for the aged and Anna's account indicates that young, old and infirm shared the space.[83] A sixth-century account by Cyril of Scythopolis suggests that orphanages also might house visiting adults; their function seems to have been quite broad-based, and use indicates that children and adults were not necessarily segregated.[84] The heads of the Orphanage, or *orphanotrophoi*, of St Paul, were often well-educated political figures, and Theodore Prodromos probably lived there, suggesting that the institution was prestigious.[85]

---

73   *Trullo*, Canon 40; *Novels of Justinian* V. V and CXXIII. XXXVIII; on this, see Patlagean (1973) 86, 88; Antoniadis-Bibicou (1973) 78; for girls brought up in a convent, Kecharitomene, see Gautier (1985) 41, lines 369–371; Thomas and Hero (2000) 671, rule 5.

74   On girls, see Talbot (1985), 105–106.

75   For some examples, see Patlagean (1973) 89–90.

76   *BHG* III, 1737, 1739; Talbot (1996) 170–171.

77   On this, see Patlagean (1973) 88, with references.

78   According to Nikolas Grammatikos (1084–1111); for text, see Grumel (1947) n. 995, paragraph 10; Patlagean (1973) 88, fn. 28.

79   Summarized by Miller (1996) 122; on examples of orphans' fates, see 125–127, 132–133; for in depth account, see Miller (2003).

80   On this, see Constantelos (1968) 241–243.

81   On this, see Magdalino (1996) 156–164, with references.

82   *Alexiad*: PG 131:1179–1191; Leib (1937) XV.vii.3–9; Sewter (1969) 492–495; on this, see Magdalino (1996) 156–157.

83   On homes for the aged, see Magdalino (1996) 157.

84   See Constantelos (1968) 242.

85   See Magdalino (1996) 162.

Basil the Great founded a residential school for boys and girls and accepted orphans as part of the monastic community.[86] Other monasteries fed homeless children, while others supported them, such as the Pantokrator, which had eight orphans and four substitutes as candle bearers. They received payment for their work in money and grain.[87] However the presence of children, particularly youths, was problematic, and the children may often have been segregated from the adult population. In his *Testament*, Christodoulos, the founder of St John on Patmos, refers to 'any children I reared from infancy', saying that they can become monks if suited to the life.[88] This suggests that children were nurtured in the monastery, although passages in the *typikon* indicate that originally no 'laymen with women and children might reside on Patmos, nor young men in their boyish prime, before their beard appears, nor eunuchs'.[89] Apparently Christodoulos deviated from this rule and brought up children who presumably were orphaned, abandoned, or given as oblates; they must have been boys as the text states they could become brothers. Later Christodoulos allowed laymen to live in a segregated part of the island.[90] In the Codicil, he states that the monastery's servants may not 'sit at table or drink wine till they get a beard', showing his intention to remove temptation.[91] This ban on youth followed in the tradition of other monasteries and is mentioned in Theodore of Stoudios's Testament for St John Stoudios and in Athanasios the Athonite's Testament for the Lavra monastery.[92] This last, like Christodoulos's, also prohibited eunuchs. Other monasteries took alternative paths to solving the problem, such as pairing older and younger monks or insisting on them all being eunuchs.[93] Lazaros of Mount Galesios mentions the allure of the young as the hardest test.[94] However, the Stoudios monastery had a school for novices, set slightly apart.[95] Clearly certain monasteries took some responsibility for the care and education of homeless children, although their presence raised difficulties, specifically sexual provocation.

---

86   Miller (1996) 127–129; Kalogeras (2000) 150 and, on girls at the school, 222–223.

87   For text, see Gautier (1974) 75–79, lines 783–5, 821; for translation, see Thomas and Hero (2000) 754–755, rules 30, 32.

88   Miklosich and Müller (1860–1890, rep. 1968) VI, 83; Thomas and Hero (2000) B6, 596; this is mentioned slightly misleadingly in Miller (1996) 129.

89   Miklosich and Müller (1860–1890, rep. 1968) VI, 65; Thomas and Hero (2000) A10, 583.

90   Miklosich and Müller (1860–90, rep. 1968) VI, 67; Thomas and Hero (2000) A 13, 584.

91   Miklosich and Müller (1860–90, rep. 1968) VI, 86; Thomas and Hero (2000) C4, 599.

92   Thomas and Hero (2000) 570; Stoudios: *PG* 99:1821, rule 18: You shall not have an adolescent disciple in your cell out of affection; translation in Thomas and Hero (2000) 78; similarly, Athos, rule 34, in Meyer (1894) 102–122; translation in Thomas and Hero (2000) 259. Kalogeras mentions the banning of boys and eunuchs at St Sabas; see Kalogeras (2000) 149.

93   Thomas and Hero (2000) 512; as at Eleousa, rule 5, where old and young monks were paired; see Petit (1900) 73, line 11; translation in Thomas and Hero (2000) 176.

94   Delehaye (1910) 567; Thomas and Hero (2000) 162, rule 196.

95   On the school, see Kalogeras (2000) 151–153, with references.

Byzantine education combined Greek and Roman practices with Christian teaching, which raised certain conflicts, and the degree of ancient influences varied in the monastic, ecclesiastical and secular schools.[96] Although monastic schools did exist from early times in Byzantium, they did not a play large role in education until after the eighth century, when they adopted secular subjects, and then they became more significant in the eleventh and twelfth centuries.[97] Girls also apparently attended convent schools, although less frequently.[98] Since there was no overall state programme, practices varied and children started their education between the ages of four and seven, but most often at seven, and they were often, particularly girls, taught at home.[99] This first stage of education would continue until about the age of 11 and included the three Rs with emphasis on memorization of Homer and the psalms. [100] Training would be in Latin and Greek but primarily Greek from the fourth century, particularly in the provinces. Robert Browning has shown that both the church and the state required literacy for their administration and practice and suggests that the populations of the cities and monasteries were 'functionally literate', indicating that elementary schooling was quite common. He points out the frequency of graffiti and argues that the lack of tomb inscriptions is partly attributable to the overall lack of remaining tombstones.[101] It could be argued that education was not so widespread, but various hagiographic texts indicate that children from poor families, including the son of a prostitute, Saint Theodore of Sykeon, went to school, suggesting that at least primary education was not exclusive to the middle and upper classes.[102]

In the early period secondary schooling diminished and even in Constantinople by the seventh century good teachers were hard to find. Tertiary education had completely disappeared, and would-be scholars learned one-on-one with tutors. This changed in the mid-ninth century, when Caesar Bardas established the Magnaura school, where philosophy, mathematics, astronomy and grammar were taught. Constantine VII later refounded this school. However, sources suggest that secondary education, mostly available in Constantinople, still depended in the tenth century on the student–tutor relationship. By the eleventh and twelfth centuries the University of Constantinople was founded and maintained by the state. The church was influential in education and several schools were linked with monasteries.

---

96   See Kalogeras (2000) 164–168. On education as known from hagiography, see Kalogeras (2000) throughout (up to the ninth century); Harris (1989) esp. 285–321 on late antiquity; Lemerle (1986) throughout (sixth to tenth century); Kazhdan and Wharton Epstein (1985) 120–166 (eleventh–twelfth centuries); Browning (1978) 39–54; Moffatt (1977) 85–92; Speck (1974) (ninth–tenth centuries); Guilland (1953) 63–83; Buckler (1948) 200–220.

97   On monastic schools, see Kalogeras (2000) 145–155, 263.

98   The prohibition by certain convents of female students unless they were taking the veil suggests that others permitted them; see Carr (1985) 105–106.

99   On this, see Antoniadis-Bibicou (1973) 78.

100 See Browning (1978) 53.

101 See Browning (1978) 49.

102 For extensive discussion of these texts, see Kalogeras (2000) 22–60.

During the Latin occupation and afterwards, advanced education was scant.[103] However, after the reclamation of Constantinople in 1261 other schools were founded which concentrated on grammar and the *quadrivium*. Students were unruly in Byzantium as in Rome. For example, two letters, dated to 1080, from Theophylaktos, the archbishop of Ohrid to his pupils defend his disciplinary practice after confrontation in the class.[104]

Children who left school after primary education could become apprenticed, perhaps at the age of 12, as apparently happened with Elias of Heliopolis.[105] He was apprenticed to a carpenter and worked in the workshop or *ergasterion* for which he received a wage. Others did not get a wage during the period of training, which ranged from five to ten years, but received food, and at times, at the end of the contract, the young man would be set up with tools of the trade or some capital.[106] Others, probably the majority, would be trained in the family business and so work at home without a formal contract. Girls also worked but mainly at home, where the traditional skill was spinning. Angeliki Laiou has pointed out that while women worked outside the home for others, this was generally disapproved of and only undertaken by those who had to. Women, and so girls, in rural areas were employed in the vineyards and helped with harvesting and threshing and, in urban environments in the market place, selling what they had made, such as cloth, and food. Women could invest in real estate and own businesses, mostly with other family members.[107]

Laws suggest that children and parents had to make an early decision on the choice between marriage and the monastic life, since the path to each could be established at a young age (however, adults could, and often did, become monks or nuns). As both male and female children could become engaged at age seven, it suggests that they were considered equally mature at this age, though not at puberty. There are frequent cases of girls having intercourse after betrothal but before marriage and therefore at a very young age. This is partly because the two ceremonies were very similar, and often the betrothed girl would live with her fiancé's family from the time of betrothal. Also, parents sometimes misrepresented their children's ages in order to secure an early alliance. For instance, a father betrothed his seven-year-old daughter saying that she was ten, and when the union was blessed a year later it was also consummated.[108] Several such cases are recorded and indicate a tolerance of intercourse in very young girls, although it was known that this could cause physical harm. Other cases indicate that young betrothed girls in the care of their future father-in-laws were voluntarily or involuntarily seduced by the fiancé or sometimes by another member of the household.

103 An example of this is in the autobiography of George of Cyprus, born in 1240/1; see Pelendrides (1993).

104 Mullett (1997) 293; letters in Theophylact (1980–1986 edn) II, G1 and G2.

105 Papadopoulos-Kerameus (1907 edn)

106 Oikonomidès (1979) 73–74.

107 Laiou (2003) 30–31.

108 See Patlagean (1973) 91, with references.

Additionally, exceptions to the age limit could be made by the emperor and were apparently frequently allowed.[109] In several cases the church took what we would consider the more moral stance. A well-known example of this is the church's opposition to the marriage between Simonis, daughter of Andronikos II, and Stefan Uroš II Milutin.[110] Simonis was aged five when wedded in 1299 to Milutin as a diplomatic move to make peace with Serbia. Probably because the marriage was consummated at an early age, Simonis was barren. However, studies indicate that such arrangements were rare.

Another alternative to marriage or the monastery was castration. While some children became eunuchs by accident, others were castrated either by their parents' wish or by force.[111] Paul of Aegina in the seventh century describes the two methods of castration, either by compression or by incision. The former method is used for 'children, still of a tender age', although boys were apparently castrated both before and at puberty.[112] Since those operated on after the onset of puberty would retain characteristics of virility, including ejaculation, the operation was more frequently performed on young children.[113] While eunuchs were generally reviled by society, they were at times extremely popular at court and rose to power. In fact eunuchs could gain a high price and it is part of the complexity of Byzantine society that eunuchs were valued but the act of castration was abhorrent and also outlawed, although the law was poorly enforced.[114] Captured children were castrated and sold as servants or slaves.[115] While a ten-year-old child fetched a price of 10 nomismata, a castrated child of the same age was worth 30, and an adult male fetched 20 while an adult eunuch was worth 50 nomismata.[116]

Such topics necessarily bring up the role of the church. Christianity's approach to childhood engages with two main issues. First, how were Christ's reported attitudes and injunctions about childhood applied and what was the church's apparent doctrine on children regarding both theological and societal matters? And second, to what extent did the church influence common practice, and to what degree did Christianity incorporate Roman or pagan practices, attitudes and morality towards children?[117]

As reported in the gospels, Christ set a small child as an example to his disciples, saying that unless they became humble like little children they would not enter the kingdom of heaven. He also warned them against mistreating children (*Matthew* 18:2–6). On another occasion, he blessed the children surrounding them and said that those in the kingdom of heaven

---

109 *Novels of Leo VI*, CIX; see Patlagean (1973) 88.

110 Ostrogorsky (1968, 1980 edn) 489–490.

111 On eunuchs, see Guilland (1943) 197–238.

112 Aegineta (1844–1847 edn) II, 379–380, cited in Tougher (1997a) 175.

113 Rousselle (1988) 123, cited in Tougher (1997a) 177.

114 *Codex Justinianus*, IV, 42, 1 and 2; on popular literature about eunuchs, see Bréhier (1950) III, 14.

115 Tougher (1997a) 178.

116 Antoniadis-Bibicou (1973) 82.

117 For more on children and the church, see Leloir (1980) 145–152.

were like children (*Matthew* 19:13, 14). The other canonical gospels have corresponding passages placing children in an elevated and paradigmatic position. But as the gospels relate the story, Christ also challenged the role of the family to some extent, asking his followers to put him before worldly ties, which contributed to the rise of monasticism. It is unclear from the gospel accounts what emphasis Christ placed on celibacy, but this certainly became an overriding theme in Christian devotion for both men and women and not only within monastic communities.

The writings of the church fathers show a complex approach to childhood which is beyond the scope of this book to explore thoroughly. I shall only touch on some key features that give an indication of attitudes towards the young. Church teaching was ambiguous regarding children. From the time of the early church, both in the west and in Byzantium, children, perhaps contrary to expectations, were not primarily used as an ideal model. An influential text about childhood was Augustine's *Confessions*, which displays disgust and disaffection for infancy. Grounded in the idea of original sin, he asks, 'Who can recall to me the sins I committed as a baby? For in your sight no man is free from sin, not even a child who has lived only one day on earth'. He only sees a child's innocence in physical terms, for it can be forceful in its dark emotions: 'This shows that, if babies are innocent, it is not for lack of will to do harm, but for lack of strength. I have myself seen jealousy in a baby and know what it means'.[118]

Origen gives a more sympathetic view towards children in the *Commentary on Matthew*, in which he discourses on the gospel references to children. Answering why the great are compared to little children, he refers to their lack of sexual experience and lust; but it is because of their lack of reason that they have not experienced 'infirmities and sicknesses of the soul' and have their passions 'in subjection'.[119] On the positive side, he recognizes that children do not give regard to social standing. He declares that to humble oneself like the child whom Christ placed in front of the disciples is 'to imitate the Holy Spirit, who humbled himself for the salvation of men', but then states that the child was in fact the Holy Spirit.[120] This deflects from the image of a real child as an ideal, and Origen implies that Christ was not using children but rather the spirit as a paradigm, so negating the respect for childhood. In the writings of the church fathers, childhood is often not seen in positive terms, but rather as something to be feared.

While the philanthropy associated with Christianity extended to the treatment of children, they were not necessarily treated in a fundamentally more revered, respected or sensitive way under Christianity than they were under paganism. This is not to say that they were universally cared for in the

118 Augustine, *Confessions*, *Sancti Augustini Confessionum libri XIII* (*Corpus Christanorum* 1981) bk 1, 7.11.

119 Origen, *Commentary on Matthew* XIII.16; Klosterman (1935); *PG* 13:1134–1138.

120 Origen, *Commentary on Matthew* XIII.18 and 19; Klosterman (1935); *PG* 13:1142–1147.

pagan world, but that society as a whole regarded their interests. Children were already treated with legal and private consideration for their rights and needs, as has been demonstrated by Timothy Miller in his discussion of orphans and guardianship.[121] He might argue that Roman laws on guardianship were engineered to protect Roman citizens and wealth, but equally overall legislation led to the protection of children by their seniors.[122] The Byzantine solution to parentless children was to move from the fourth-century practice of entrusting them to widows, to the foundation of orphanages, overseen by bishops, but was this in practice a more compassionate solution?[123] As Ruth Macrides notes, Leo VI (886–912) brought adoption much closer to the concept of baptism by necessitating ecclesiastical blessing in adoption and prohibiting adopted children to marry the children of the family in which they were brought up.[124] We can see this as a tightening of the family unit, and the presence of adopted children within a family.

Sarah Currie, in her thesis *Childhood and Christianity from Paul to the Council of Chalcedon* provides extensive textual evidence concerning the church fathers' views on children, on the family and on alternate celibate life styles and claims that these views deeply affected society.[125] Christ's teaching on children and its incorporation into church theology fundamentally changed the way people saw children and the relationship between adults and children. She concludes that the church held children at the centre of its practice, and this meant that relations between children and adults took on a new sacralized dimension in Christianity. Currie uses a wide range of sources, discusses them in depth, and raises crucial and difficult issues, but, in my view, does not show that the church fathers' teaching on childhood was crucial to Christianity, nor that it largely affected society. She does not sufficiently demonstrate the place of children prior to Christianity, so cannot show a contrast. The church fathers struggled with the notion of childhood and became entangled with the concept of original sin, which, arguably, negates Christ's perspective on children. [126]

Christ attributed innocence to children and urged his followers to become as children, but this was not literally followed by church authorities, nor did they enjoin their flock to do so. Many of Christ's teachings became superseded by more conservative and reactionary stances and by the institution of the church. This, as a governing body seeking to regulate both spiritual and secular life, was more concerned with ritual, doctrine, social taboos and legal and administrative regulation. One could argue that the church fathers largely reacted to societal problems, perceived immoralities and the need to instill consistency and control. They developed a theory of childhood that was both

---

121 Miller (2003) 31.
122 Miller (2003) 30–41.
123 Miller (2003) 108–113.
124 Macrides (1987) 141.
125 Currie (1993).
126 See Currie (1993) 12, for her claim to use both textual and visual evidence, although her approach is heavily weighted on the former: she does use some images, but mostly restricted to sarcophagi, which only minimally support her argument.

largely unrelated to Christ's own teaching and to the common culture and that was sufficiently removed from collective thinking that it did not significantly affect practice. There seems to be little evidence for a cultural break in the treatment of or approaches towards children in the pagan Roman and in the early Christian and Byzantine worlds and established customs prevailed, particularly in rural areas, despite church prohibitions.[127] Similarly, in the west, notions about child sexuality and innocence as preached by the church were not absorbed by the public, partly perhaps because they were inconsistent.[128] It has been noted, however, that among the Orthodox Slavs, society's mores and practice were firmly defined and enforced by the ecclesiastical authorities, so that life was permeated with the expectations of the top end of society.[129] While there is some documentation for this, it remains an issue that is open to debate.

Hagiographic texts perhaps tell more about Christian ideals of childhood, since they reflect believers' expectations about children who grew up to be exemplary. The stories are mostly historically inaccurate and fabricated; they reflect the monastic and probably the public concept of the sanctified childhood.[130] Hagiographies were used to instruct: they gave insight into and direction to religiosity, though they often operated tangentially to the church hierarchy and had a public-driven popularity. Saints gained recognition by miraculous acts and it was only from the thirteenth century that church councils controlled their canonization, so the popularity of saints and the myths associated with them were very much in the people's control.[131]

Saints, even as children, were often on the fringes of society, indulging in asceticism and behaving in unorthodox ways, perhaps living in filth or bodily denial. Theodore of Sykeon, who died in 613, repeatedly refused to eat, got up at all hours of the night, isolated himself for extended periods and lived in abject deprivation for two years. As his biographer, Georgios points out, the *Life* was intended to edify the young so that they might 'emulate his angelic and blameless life'.[132] Yet Theodore's behaviour would wreak havoc on any parent. He is the child genius and the adult child, with maturity and learning beyond his years, but also the rebel against societal norms, and the unnatural misfit who lies and deceives his mother. But this is all praised, for it is done for the glory of God.

The tale can be seen as a measure of the societal tensions caused by precocious children, 'dysfunctional' families and religious fervour. Theodore's grandmother stays with Theodore out of sympathy, but the story illustrates a

127 Levin (1989) gives examples throughout. Judith Herrin is useful in outlining the development of Christianity, particularly on the Christian influence in late antique culture; see Herrin (1987, 1989 edn) 54–89.

128 Shahar (1990, 1992 edn) 102.

129 Levin (1989) throughout.

130 On the social origins of hagiographies, see Patlagean (1968, 1983 edn) 106–126.

131 Cormack (1985a) 17.

132 Theodore of Sykeon: *BHG* II, 1748–1749c; Festugière (1970) I, 19, section 22; Dawes and Baynes (1948) 102–103.

Byzantine generation gap, with a mother who cannot understand her son, and a son bound to break normal convention. Yet the church praises Theodore's faith, and the polarity between mother and son becomes one between the spiritual and the secular. The account shows the societal divisions wrought by spirituality, yet, written by a monk, it confirms the supremacy of faith.

Another saint who is portrayed as precociously intelligent, mature and abstemious is Saint Luke of Steiris, who 'did nothing in childish fashion. Most children enjoy and delight in toys, jokes, games, and lively activities; but for Luke there was none of this, but rather calmness, tranquillity, a steady character, and maturity in all things'.[133] This suggests a lack of appreciation for childish qualities, but also shows those features that the Byzantines associated with childhood. Yet present society also admires child geniuses, gifted children who excel and mature children who take on challenging social or intellectual tasks.

The piety and precocity of religious children are evident in the *Liber Pontificalis*.[134] Like the hagiographic texts, these lives of the popes suggest ideals of childhood. Many of the popes reportedly distinguished themselves as little boys. The earliest childhood record concerns Eugene (654–657), who was 'a cleric from his cradle'. Sergius (844–847) 'had no little contempt for childish amusements' and Nicholas (858–867) 'took no dishonourable delight in any game or anything else that children are wont to do'.[135] Religious leaders and saints alike omitted the stages of childhood, perhaps seen as an unnecessary step towards sanctity. This does not necessarily imply that it was disdained in all children, but does suggest that there was a clear understanding of what it was to be a child. Christianity therefore struggled with an understanding and interpretation of childhood, determining whether it was innocent or flawed, tamed or unnatural, ideal or dispensable.

However, children were integrated into church practice. Infant baptism and confirmation were the norm by the sixth century, after having become widespread in the fourth and fifth centuries.[136] Children were generally baptized after eight days or forty days, although those who were ailing might be baptized in haste.[137] Children would therefore have had access to the main part of the church, even when catechumens were restricted to the narthex, although this latter practice fell into disuse some time after the late seventh century, despite mention of the dismissal of the novices being kept in the liturgy. However, there was as late as the tenth century, as Robert Taft terms it, 'a vestigial catechumenate for children of Orthodox parents and for converts'.[138] The areas of churches accessible to women seem to vary according

---

133 Connor and Connor (1994) 9; this account was written shortly after 961; see ix.

134 Duchesne (1886–1892, 1955–1957 edn); Davis (1989); Davis (1992); Davis (1995).

135 Duchesne (1886–1892, 1955–1957 edn) I, 341; II, 86, 151; Davis (1989) 71; Davis (1995) 75, 205.

136 Wharton (1995) 137 and 191 for ns. 116–117, 81 and 181 for n. 43; also see 121 on Christ depicted as youthful at his baptism; Taft (1998) 62–63.

137 Taft (1998) 61, with references; Baun (1994) 117.

138 Taft (1998) 61, with references.

to practice, although it appears to be largely universal that the sexes were separated.[139] It is not clear at what age the male children would accompany the men rather than the women, but it seems that children were entitled to enter the same areas as other lay adults. Presumably when young the children were with the women, often in one of the aisles or in the gallery, although the eighth-century Saint Stephen is described as a boy accompanying his mother at night vigils and going up close to the chancel to hear better: either she was also allowed in this area or he entered the male areas of the church on his own.[140] Stephen's case highlights an important point: children accompanied their parents to church.

Children were usually brought up in nuclear families, although most households contained various members of an extended family. From the sixth century, families tended to be close social structures.[141] Evelyne Patlagean has done extensive work on the family in Byzantium, which includes issues such as marriage impediments, consanguinity and ritualized parentage.[142] Her essay on the child and the family, focusing on the fourth to twelfth centuries, sets out not to engage with emotional questions but rather to see the place of the child in relation to the interests of the larger society.[143] This is extremely valuable. In her chapter in *The History of the Family*, Patlagean points out that the family household did not normally contain spinsters or bachelors since the unmarried would become monks or nuns, though widows had the choice of entering a convent or staying at home.[144] The modern Greek term for family, *oikogeneia*, does not occur in Byzantium. The *oikos* was the dwelling where up to three generations might live together with servants and slaves. *Syngeneia*, kinship, included direct and collateral relationships and relationships by marriage.[145] Patlagean states that by the ninth century the family had 'begun to emerge as the fundamental socio-political model, with exactly the same associations as in the world of cities of the Roman Empire'.[146] This developed in the thirteenth to fifteenth centuries, during which there is more information. Patlagean uses various rural examples (which give no age of individuals) to show that between one and three generations would live together; particularly popular seems to be sons-in-law living with their mothers-in-law. In other examples the family grouping is further extended with the siblings of a married woman living with her and her husband, along with nephews and nieces. [147]

---

139 On this see Taft (1998) throughout; Gerstel (1998) throughout.

140 The text was written in the early ninth century; *PG* 100:1081; *BHG* II, 1666; Auzépy (1997) 97, 188–199, section 8; in Taft (1998) 31.

141 Kazhdan and Wharton Epstein (1985) 3–4.

142 Patlagean (1966) and (1978a), for instance.

143 Patlagean (1973).

144 Patlagean (1996).

145 Patlagean (1996) 472–473.

146 Patlagean (1996) 474.

147 Patlagean (1996).

Godparents were also a feature of Byzantine life, a practice that creates a spiritual relationship that is envisioned through the language of the family. In this way it is related to monastic vows and to the adoption of a brother.[148] The spiritual relationship of godparenting was necessary at baptism, which introduced ties between the godparent and baptized but also between godparent and natural parent, and even between their children, who called themselves brother and sister. It appears that women were less commonly godparents and that the church preferred one person to act for all the children in a family, so that each child would have only one godparent (excepting imperial children, who could have many). The primary role was to bring the children up in Christian morality, but godparents also acted as advisors or surrogate parents if the need arose and gave gifts. [149] It was obviously judicious, if possible, to choose godparents in good social or financial standing.

The role of imperial children was certainly very closely tied to the church. Political power came through God, often with Christ or the Virgin as mediators. In order to convey this ideology, both privately and publicly, and also to educate the children for future responsibilities, the children were involved in court ritual. This is reflected in literature as well as in visual material. It appears from the accounts given by Constantine Porphyrogennetos in the tenth century that the people held the imperial children in esteem and participated in ceremony at the court. He tells of the public lauding at the birth of a *porphyrogennetos* (that is a child born to the emperor and empress in a special purple chamber in the palace) and recounts the events surrounding the crowning of a junior emperor by the senior emperor, and also the acclamations made to the children born to the emperor: 'let God send fine days to the *augustae* and to the *porphyrogenneti*'.[150]

That the children, particularly the heirs to the throne, were integral to imperial ceremony is apparent from an account given by the daughter of Alexios I (1081–1118), Anna Komnene. She describes little Constantine, the son of Michael VII, who was re-elevated to the status of co-emperor by Alexios in 1081, aged seven:

Later, when Alexios Komnenos was proclaimed emperor, Maria . . . asked for a
written pledge, guaranteed in letters of red and a golden seal . . . that he should be
co-ruler with Alexios, with the right to wear the purple sandals and a crown, and the
right to be acclaimed as emperor with him. Her request was granted in a chrysobull
confirming all her demands. Constantine's woven silk shoes were removed and
buskins wholly of red substituted for them. In the matter of donations or chrysobulls
his signature now appeared immediately after that of Alexios, and in the processions
he followed him wearing an imperial diadem.[151]

---

148 See Macrides (1987) 140–141; on adoption of a brother, see Patlagean (1978a).

149 See Macrides (1987) 143–148 and 155, with full references; Patlagean (1978a).

150 The emperor, receiving his authority from God, is in a position to invest his subordinates: It is he who crowns the *augusta* and the junior emperors, and appoints the patriarch; for *De Cerimoniis*, see Vogt (1935–39) II, chs. 49–52 and for acclamations, Vogt (1935–39) II, ch. 51.

151 *Alexiad*: Leib (1937) III.iv.5; Sewter (1969) 113.

Several examples exist of essays written as advice for young would-be emperors, which articulate the ideal qualities of a ruler, indicating the values and attributes esteemed in emperors.[152] The 'Hortatory Chapters by Basil the Emperor of the Rhomaioi' was probably composed by the patriarch Photios and was dedicated to the young Leo VI (886–912), son of Basil I.[153] Leo was directed to maintain moral principles, virtue and philanthropy; he was to pursue his education, and to maintain an unfailing faith in Christ and love of the church. Emphasis rested on the divine source of the emperor's power and the value of peace. The imperial image of royalty evolved in part through associations made between the emperors and the biblical kings. In the 'Hortatory Chapters' Leo was instructed above all else to read the writings of Solomon to understand the qualities of righteous kingship.[154]

The close conceptual link between the theory of Byzantine rule and biblical precedents is evident in the language used by Constantine VII (945–959) in *De administrando imperio*, written for his son Romanos.[155] He paraphrased excerpts from the psalms and other Old Testament books in his instructions, including lines from Psalm 71 written for Solomon and glorifying his wisdom and fame as well as his bounty and compassion.[156] As can be seen from the writing as a whole, Constantine Porphyrogennetos intended his son to have a sense of integrity, of leadership, and of Christian ethics, with an awareness of the biblical antecedents of the imperial rulers.[157] Constantine was concerned that his son should not only maintain biblical virtues, but should have a practical historical and geographical knowledge of the empire.

The children therefore were given a strong moral foundation. Added to this was political expertise including military knowledge. Michael Psellos, in his history, tells us how Constantine X, in about 1060, tested his young son, Michael, before crowning him:

But, just before he took his seat on the throne, Constantine put him to a severe test, to find out if the young man was really suited to be emperor. The question he asked him concerned political theory. As Michael solved the problem and gave the correct

---

152 A compilation and select translations of these writings are given in Blum (1981); Ernest Barker also provides selected translations and analysis in Barker (1957) esp. 100–104, 120–129, 145–149; Hunger (1978) I, 157–165; for a further summary of the topic, see Anderson (1988) 567–568; and for further comments, see Mullett (1996) esp. 379–384. Their form derived from a collection of Christian precepts written by the deacon Agapetos for Justinian I (527–565) and was based on Greek precedents; on this, see Nicol (1988) 51–79, esp. 56.

153 *PG* 107:XXI–LVI; Kazhdan (1984) 43–57, esp. 43; Blum (1981) 39–41.

154 *PG* 107:LVI; Sansterre (1991) 24.

155 *De administrando imperio*; *PG* 113:157–422; Moravcsik (1967).

156 *De administrando imperio*; Moravcsik (1967) 46, line 46; Sansterre (1991) 25. Another work that draws on biblical analogies is an ode written for Romanos II when he was 12. The young emperor, his father, and mother are likened to the Holy Trinity; see Odorico (1987) 85; Cutler (1995) 610.

157 From the eighth century a prayer was used at the coronation of the sovereign that made an analogy between the new emperor, elevated by God, and King David; see Sansterre (1991) 25.

answer, the emperor regarded it as an omen that he was destined to win great renown in his future reign, and the ceremony of enthronement was at once performed.[158]

The *Paideia Basilike*, written in 1088–89 by Theophylaktos, emphasized military prowess.[159] This was written by a pupil of Psellos, who was later the archbishop of Ohrid, and intended for Constantine, the 14-year-old son of Michael VII. Although piety remained paramount, Theophylaktos also urged military skills and practice in riding and archery.[160] He directed Constantine to obey his mother, Maria, and to receive her blessing as support for both the imperial house and the house of his soul.[161] Military achievements and aristocratic birth had become valued features of the monarchy, with an emphasis on family lineage and duty. Slightly later, Kekaumenos, writing for a son in the late eleventh or early twelfth century, reiterated the traditional imperial virtues of fortitude, righteousness, chastity and intelligence and emphasized faith in God.[162]

Imperial children were seen to be appointed by God and assumed a quasi-divine status that was ritualized in elaborate and mystical court ceremony. The imperial children were trained both intellectually and spiritually to assume power. They were well educated and informed, knowledgeable about history, religion, and politics and expected to participate in public life.

There was no fixed law stipulating when a regent was required, and there is little consistency as to age. Sources are not clear about the age of majority for a sovereign.[163] In 1071 when Michael VII replaced Romanos IV and must have been over 14, there was still question as to whether the regency should be reestablished. Apparently the inauguration of a regency did not just depend on the age of the protégé, but also on his perceived ability to govern, or on the political strength of his protector. Polemis, in discussing the first regency period, suggests that Michael's 'natural powers were less than average', and therefore, although he was of age, the regency was created.[164]

In looking at the other regencies in Byzantium, there is little consistency as to age, and in general it seems that mothers were reluctant to give up power to their children. For instance, Martina ruled with the sons of Herakleios, Constantine and Heraklonas, aged 28 and 15 respectively, although it seems Herakleios wished that Martina rule with the young men, rather than as

158 For *Chronographia*, see Renaud (1928) 7: Constantine X, XXI; Sewter (1953, 1966 edn) 340.

159 *PG* 126:253–286; Kazhdan (1984) 46; Blum (1981) 43–46, 81–98; Barker (1957) 146–149.

160 As discussed by Kazhdan (1984) 46.

161 *PG* 126:285, Ch. XXX; Blum (1981) 96.

162 *Cecaumeni stratigioni*; Wassiliewsky (1896, reprinted 1965); German translation in Beck (1964); Kazhdan (1984) 49; Blum (1981) 42–44; Barker (1957) 125–129.

163 As demonstrated by Yannopoulos, see (1991) 72–73 and fn. 9; Oikonomidès considers 16 to be the age of majority, yet gives no evidence; see (1963) 121. Svoronos also refers to Alexios II's (1180–1183) age of majority as being 16, see (1951) 122; Grierson implies the age of majority was 14; see, for example, *DOC* III/2, 526–527.

164 Polemis (1968) 42.

regent.[165] The first true Byzantine regency occurred in 780 in the time of Constantine VI (780–797) who succeeded his father when he was nine and was dominated by his mother, Irene, for 17 years. Irene banished the young ruler when he was 19 and, although he returned, Irene blinded him when he was 25. Throughout the reign, Irene appeared on all the coins, and Constantine was always depicted unbearded, a sign of minority status.[166] The next regency took place under Theodora, the mother of Michael III (842–867), whose father died in 842 when he was two. Michael's minority was prolonged, according to Grierson, beyond the time allowed by Roman law, and was ended when he was 16 by a coup d'état organized by Bardas. Michael, aged 16, is depicted on the coins with a beard after his mother was removed from power.[167] Constantine VII Porphyrogennetos (913–959) was seven when his uncle Alexander died. Alexander had intentionally removed Constantine's mother, Zoe, from the regency before his death, but she managed to claim power after eight months. However, Romanos Lekapenos married Constantine to his own daughter, Helena, when Constantine was 13½, just before he reached his majority, and Lekapenos made himself co-emperor the following year (920).[168] These examples show that there were no strict rules about a regency; but it is suggested that an heir was considered able to rule in his own name at the age of 14.

Young rulers also play a role in the later years of Byzantium. Just to look at one example, that of John V (1341–1391) in the fourteenth century, we can perhaps get a sense of the youthfulness of the court. John was born in 1332 and only aged nine when his father died, so he ruled under the regency of his mother, Anna of Savoy.[169] John VI Kantakouzenos (1347–1354) reigned for a short period after leading a civil war and married his daughter Helen to John in 1347, when John was 15. John V's first son, Andronikos IV, was born the next year, when John was 16 and he was still only 24 when his son married at the age of eight in 1356.[170] By this time, he had reclaimed the throne from John VI.

This brings us to the important question of the proportion of children and young people in a Byzantine community. We are looking in this book at a broad range of material from different periods and from various locations, but throughout the Byzantine period the population as a whole would have been typical of pre-modern societies. Pre-modern population figures tend to follow largely similar patterns unless affected by disasters such as war or plague, and generalizations about the age of the population can be made.[171] Some research discounts children in life expectancy figures, which

---

165 Ostrogorsky (1956, 1980 edn) 112; Maslev (1966) 321–332.

166 *DOC* III/1, 336–337, pl. XIV, 3; Maslev (1966) 322–323.

167 *DOC* III/1, 452– 460; Maslev (1966) 323–324.

168 *DOC* III/2, 526; Maslev (1966) 324–25.

169 Papadopoulos (1938) n.73.

170 Papadopoulos (1938) n. 81.

171 We can also draw, admittedly broad, analogies with other pre-modern societies. For example, Keith Hopkins looked at Roman funeral markers, recognized their biases, but

gives an inaccurate impression, and shows how young people tend to be excluded from a representative view of society.[172] A useful study has been undertaken by Laiou concerning fourteenth-century Macedonian peasants living on monastic lands.[173] She used census records, which she argued are largely representative in that they do include women and small children, not just working people. However, they are problematic in that they do not give specific ages: these have to be deduced from marital status.[174] For comparative material, she assumed that the population corresponded to a Level 3 mortality table (Model South), with a life expectancy at birth for females of 25, and a few months less for males. She recognized that this choice of model was slightly arbitrary but justified it according to standards in late medieval England.[175] Laiou is probably correct in accepting this age expectancy. She estimated that about half of children died before the age of five, but that if a female child lived to age one, her life expectancy rose to 33, and if she made it to five, she could expect to live to 47. She estimated that a woman would need to bear 12 children if she wanted one female to survive to the age of 30.[176] One sample of her figures shows how very young the population was: for the theme of Thessaloniki for the years 1300–1301, she calculated, while recognizing that the data had some flaws, that of males, 50 per cent were under 20, 43 per cent between the ages of 20 and 45 and 6 per cent older than 45. Of females 46 per cent were under 15, 47 per cent between 15 and 45, and 7 per cent over 45.[177]

While these figures look at a specific area and time period, they give a general indication of what we might expect in other areas and periods. While many children died young, they formed a majority of the population. People who got beyond the dangerous years of childhood could live into old age, although women as young adults had to undergo the hazardous child-bearing years. Contemporary westerners now look towards a society highly populated by the elderly. Byzantine society was heavily weighted towards the young: about half the population were children or teenagers. If the majority of children had only primary education, then by the age of 11 or so they were

estimated according to known demographic models, that is life tables compiled by the UN, that the expectation of life at birth must have been between 20 and 30; see Hopkins (1966) 245–264. Also, Stone estimated from a rare record of population age in England of the 1640s, that one third of children died in their first fortnight, nearly a fifth of the remaining died before the age of five and few lived to old age. This resulted in an 'extraordinarily youthful society'. On this, see Stone (1977) 68–72.

172 As in Talbot (1984) 267–278, esp. 267–268; her figure of a mean age of 35 discounts anyone under '15 or 17.5 years of age' and is deduced from studies on skeletal remains; repeated in the *ODB* under 'Life expectancy', but misleadingly without a note that children are excluded. On life expectancy, see also Patlagean (1977) 95–100.

173 Laiou (1977) 267–298.

174 Laiou (1977) 271–276.

175 Laiou (1977) 276; for life tables, she uses Coale and Demeny (1966). These tables are constructed from nineteenth- and early twentieth-century southern-European evidence. Life tables give the life expectancy and death rates for a population at birth and for subsequent ages.

176 Laiou (1977) 293–294, 296–297.

177 Drawn from tables in Laiou (1977) 277–278.

available for work, and probably helped out with manual labour before then. This makes a large impact on the age of the workforce. The average youth of the population also influences the relative age of the mothers, the temporal and spiritual leaders, the makers of artistic and functional objects and the patrons of the visual material.

The subject of early death brings up the issue of child burial. Burial, regarding the Eastern Roman Empire and Byzantium, has received little attention, and our knowledge remains limited.[178] As with Ariès, the significance of children, particularly in terms of the attachment of parents to children, has often been gauged by the ways their death has been marked. The supposition is that unmarked graves or no grave at all imply little loss. A study by Patlagean highlights these issues. A survey she undertook on fourth-century Asia Minor looks at grave markers, which do not specify age, and finds that families with two, three or four children are most common but that boys' graves exceed those of girls by a ratio of 3:1.[179] It therefore seems that if one assumes, as is reasonable, that the number of female births was comparable to that of male, each family would have had about six children and that four would have survived to the age of two.[180] In order to evaluate the age of children whose graves are marked with epigraphy, she turns to those found between Egypt and the Syro-Palestinian steppe. Here she finds few references to children under 14 years of age, except in one area, that of el-Kerak in Transjordan. Only six children are mentioned under the age of two, compared to 110 between two and 14, of whom 72 are boys and 48 girls. Half of the children alive at the age of two had died by the age of six.[181] These two sets of figures do indicate that both girls and children under two years of age were less likely to be memorialized in death than boys and older children. This implies that girls were less valued and that parents became more attached to their children the older they became, which we should perhaps not find surprising. But one could invert this evidence and argue instead that the presence of these marked graves for children, even if predominantly male and of older children, indicates that their death was considered a great loss.[182] Figures are not proposed for the numbers of adults whose deaths pass without grave markers.

The many laws concerning children suggest widespread cultural concerns over their interests and conditions. These may not coincide with our values, but they show keen interest in childhood rights. Advanced education fluctuated, but basic literacy appears to have been reasonably widespread, including sometimes among the poor. References to Byzantine childhood have failed to emphasize the central role that children had in life, not only just as a societal majority, but also as the focus of familial concerns, educational policies and

---

178 On this, see Ivison (1996) 99.
179 Patlagean (1978b) 180–181.
180 Patlagean (1978b) 182.
181 Patlagean (1978b) 182.
182 For an example of a stillborn child being remembered, born to a 16-year-old who died of the plague, see Schreiner (1985).

financial security. In many cases very young people were societally and financially responsible. They formed the backbone of institutions such as the army and worked in urban centres and in agriculture, being a central component of the workforce. Young girls became mothers, responsible for raising other children. Girls could marry aged 12, and boys went into the army by the age of 16. Small children performed in the circuses, worked as slaves or took monastic vows. But this does not mean that childhood itself did not exist, but rather that children and all the associations surrounding them were important elements integrated into Byzantine life. There is an assumption in modern literature on children and childhood that if children work for a living their childhood has ended. A look at the shoeshine boys on the streets of Istanbul rather suggests that the children maintain their boyish ways while putting their energies to earning money. Adults still treat them as children, pat them on the head, cuff them round the ear and give them direction.

Central to coming to terms with children in Byzantium is the question of the nature of childhood. We have granted that it exists, but beyond this is the question of what generates and delimits it. Can it be perceived in an essentialist or objective manner as a set biological period of life, or should it rather be assessed as a cultural phenomenon, a construction of society and specific to a particular time and place? To what extent does childhood across history and geography have universal factors, shared characteristics, and to what extent is it culturally specific? As we have seen, it has been argued, and rebuffed, that childhood as we know it is a modern occurrence. All people experience a period of immaturity and growth at the beginning of their lives, but was the cultural construct of childhood unknown before the modern era? The present book takes the view that children in ancient Greece and Rome, in Byzantium and in medieval Europe had their own identity as a social group, replete with their own laws, customs, expectations, pastimes and human conditions. Various customs were adopted from other cultures and new innovations developed, but the sense of childhood was a condition which pertained specifically to the young and represented their role in society and society's role towards them, with its own inherent norms and values. However, while a late antique image of a child at play may seem very familiar, the context and associations within which it is set may be quite alien to current notions of childhood and play. Images may record attitudes to children that are both concordant and discordant with our own and which can be interpreted ambiguously.

The problem of the biological/cultural binary in viewing childhood is not dissimilar to the issues that absorbed feminists in the late twentieth century. The current feminist trend is towards gender as a term and concept that focuses discussion on social construction but moves away from the both isolating and personalized focus on 'men' and 'women' and towards the roles of the sexes. Perhaps this is a legitimate way to view childhood: it is biologically determined, and yet its identity, its cultural identity, is performative, fabricated and not essential.[183] Childhood is linked to an anatomical stage, but is not an inherent state. Biologically children universally share distinctive qualities, being physically in transition from immaturity to maturity. Childhood can be defined through biological growth or objective physical characteristics, but is more accurately the perceived characteristics and behaviour of children within their cultural environment. Yet children may be seen both by others and by themselves quite differently within specific historical sites. The fragility and softness of a child may imply innocence in one culture, in another weakness; noisy excitement may mean vitality and promise in one, but aggression and incontinence in another. Therefore, perceptions of performative behaviour are also culturally conditioned.

Perhaps one of the most distinct variances between ancient and modern thinking is the acceptance of pederasty. The model for customary treatment of boys, at least of the upper classes, in ancient Greece would today be classed as paedophilia.[184] This indicates a fundamental difference in approach to childhood and adolescence than our own, and is a measure of how concepts of childhood, education, maturity and so on are culturally dependent. Older men sought after and established reciprocal relationships with boys, usually aged between 12 and 17.[185] The boy received nurture and education, the man fulfilled his sexual desire. These couplings were sanctioned by a minor's father or guardian and were generally accepted in society, although governed by extensive laws.[186] Regarding the biological/cultural binary, David Halperin has applied Foucault's view of sexuality as a cultural production to homosexuality, arguing that all types of sexuality are culture-specific and not 'the basic building-blocks of sexual identity for all human beings in all times and places, but peculiar and indeed exceptional ways of conceptualising as well as *experiencing* sexual desire'.[187] The vast difference between ancient, Byzantine and contemporary approaches to pederasty is one example of the breadth of cultural divergence in attitudes towards children, and this argument encourages us to view children in Byzantium as perceiving and experiencing life in an exceptional way, particular to a given context. Condemnation of pederasty by the church did not necessarily take away the desire for youthful bodies, as is evident today. But this issue has been raised to suggest that behaviour and attitudes towards many areas of life in Byzantium may be fundamentally different in outlook or aspect from what occurred before or since.

---

183 For a summary of gender and feminism, see Liz James's introduction in James (1997) xi–xxiv.

184 Of the many recent books on pederasty, see, for instance, Halperin (1990); Thornton (1997); Garland (1990) 139–141; Dover (1978); also Eyben (1993) 241–246.

185 Stoics allowed boy lovers to be up to 28; see Halperin (1990) 88.

186 See Halperin (1990) 93 with references.

187 Halperin (1990) 9. Halperin emphasizes that the sexual system in ancient Greece was linked to the gender system and that male sexual identity was inseparable from social identity.

Can developments in feminist and gender studies in the past decades apply to studies of children? Children in recent times may form a minority far more marginalized, bereft of power and silenced than women. Our increasing awareness of children's rights echoes the steps taken by feminists throughout the twentieth century, and this is exemplified in historical and art-historical studies of children, which are becoming increasingly popular. Our tendency towards the separation of child and adult spheres perhaps led to the segregation and then lack of recognition of the place of children in history. Only as women's lives came to inhabit the same spaces and follow similar paths to men's did their historical role become recognized. This is not the case with children, who remain societally segregated, though we probably like to think that our society is more sensitive than those of the past to children's interests. But as research in the late twentieth century and now in the early twenty-first century examined and emphasized the previously neglected role of women within society, current concern with children highlights their roles in an adult-dominated world. While feminists adopted and later attempted to reject the practice of reading women into a patriarchal model, the study of children has found no other locus or framework than the adult model. But as women have become a focus of analysis in art-historical and societal discourse, so will children.

Similar to the feminist problem that much of what has been written or visualized about women in the past has been executed by men, we tend to think that most texts, as this one, and images about children are by adults. This is partially true, and children's portrayals of children or childhood are minimal. Our view of children in the past is mainly drawn from adults' views of children. To some extent society is divided, to use James Davidson's term, between them and us, us being the male writers of the texts or creators of the images, and them being women, slaves, barbarians and, although often omitted from consideration, children. But the polarities in this binary view of the world are in flux so no division of society is rigid.[188] In Byzantine society, children are part of the 'them' divide, but we shall find that the interrelation is such that in certain imagery the children are placed in central and significant roles, and that in some cases visual representations were perhaps made by them.

The nature of childhood in Byzantium is not representatively found in the injunctions of the theologians, many of whom did not experience parenthood, nor in the tales of the historians, nor in the laws, which all reflect their own contexts and intentions. But equally one could argue that it is not found in the imagery, since it also does not give an unmediated view of real life. Davidson has summarized this conundrum regarding texts written by Greeks about Greek life. He sees these not as 'windows on a world', but rather as 'artefacts of that world in their own right'.[189] Similarly, images do not present the world

---

188 Davidson (1997) xxv–xxvi.
189 Davidson (1997) xxi.

as it was, but represent a portrayal of an idea, which is specific to the date, the site, the patron and the executor.

Furthermore, while recent studies on childhood have used a variety of social and economic sources providing a view of many levels of society, much in primary and secondary literature about children still concerns well-to-do males. Formerly, and particularly concerning antiquity, studies on childhood, both consciously and unconsciously, used sources written by educated men about boys of their own rank. This is also true concerning imagery. The historical children portrayed are often from affluent backgrounds, and most images of children have a wealthy context: an expensive monumental decoration, a luxury manuscript or a valuable piece of silver. The imagery tends then not only to be focused on the adult and the male, but also on the wealthy.

This chapter has reviewed studies on childhood, social and art-historical, and discussed interpretations of children and the family. It has looked at Byzantine language and laws regarding children, at education, and at the intentions and influences of Christian directives. It has considered problems about the meaning of childhood and concerns about viewing children from the past. These studies on children and the family make it apparent that in ancient, medieval and modern times, childhood was seen as a distinct phase in life. Mothers, fathers, doctors, churchmen and educators all identified it and for the most part were concerned with furthering the welfare of children and responding to needs and interests that are particular to children. Views on childhood reflect the time in which they are written. Ariès, who in the 1960s wrote in a society characterized by nuclear families, looked at the past and deciphered lack of love. Current concerns with high divorce rates, working parents, single-parent or 'blended' families, and children spending long hours at day care or with nannies perhaps make contemporary commentators more sensitive to social and economic pressures as well as to human bonding in less conservative social frameworks. Contemporary problems are not necessarily so new, and nuclear families with at-home mothers may have their own set of problems, suggesting that neither an evolutionary nor a devolutionary model of childhood is accurate.

The definition of terms such as family and childhood are constantly altered and challenged both by specific events and by generalized changing attitudes. S. Dixon writes that 'an appreciation of childhood can change or disappear from a culture and, even when it is found, it can coexist with indifference to the maltreatment of some or all children'.[190] But definitions of what constitutes maltreatment are culturally based. Sending boys aged seven to boarding school might strike one culture as barbaric while to another it is exemplary. Early marriage to a chosen spouse might seem protective and nurturing in one context, but restrictive and disrespectful in another.

And what of emotions towards children in Byzantium? Perhaps rather telling is Patlagean's section titled 'feelings' in her essay on 'Families and

---

190 Dixon (1997) 81.

Kinship in Byzantium', which is less than one page in length. [191] But it does tell us that parents express love for children, they naturally kiss and caress them, and that a father may grieve over a child's illness. A poignant example of this, not mentioned by Patlagean, is given in a funeral oration written by Michael Psellos, the eleventh-century intellectual, politician and philosopher, on the death of his young daughter, Styliane. He admired her greatly, not only for her beauty but also for her character, cheerful and affectionate, and her obedience. He tells us that she was excellent at weaving and that she kept up her studies. [192] The text reads as truly heartfelt and personalized and there is no mistaking grief at her loss. It has been noted that this funeral oration is written in a quite different style from others by Psellos, in which he shows himself in the best light and uses certain *topoi*, which are absent here.[193] One could interpret this as an indication of true feeling. There seems no substantial evidence to suggest that in general emotions towards children were dissimilar from our own.

However, certain issues regarding children are quite different in Byzantium and in the modern era: extended legal dependence, early marriage, strong gender differentiation and, in lower classes, child labour or slavery. Yet, it may be misguided to conclude that overall children were treated less well in Byzantium than they are in contemporary western society. Children were educated, nurtured, respected and cared for. Contrary to the idea that life's transience gave it little value, adults formed strong attachments to their children. Indeed, castration, pre-pubescent intercourse and even early monastic cloistering all seem alien and disturbing to us. Such images come quickly to mind when one thinks of Byzantine childhood, but how representative are they? Legal texts record only deviancies from the norm; judicial proceedings and the history of rulers and aristocracy, just like hagiographic texts and homilies, tell of the exceptions rather than the rule. Front-page news and court transcripts would poorly represent contemporary society. Third-millennium social troubles provoke concern over the breakdown of the family, the disintegration of schooling, increase in youth violence and the loss of childhood to consumerism. However, while not discounting current difficulties, historical sources record similar concerns. Perceptions of Byzantium may well be skewed by the sources, but can visual imagery give a more representative view?

While other disciplines have produced extensive studies on children in history, Byzantine scholars' work has primarily been from the legal standpoint. This is extremely helpful, but children's place in society has been relatively untouched. Similarly, studies of children as subjects of art in Byzantium are minimal; although Antonopoulos has made useful studies of children's images, these are largely in the form of catalogues, rather than questioning or explorative readings of images. It is because so little work has been carried out

---

191 Patlagean (1996) 487–488.
192 Psellos (1876 edn) 62–87; in Laiou (2003) 26–27.
193 Vergari (1989).

on images of children in Byzantium that I chose to cover a wide time span and to select a variety of types of representations and contexts. In this way an initial exploration of the broader subject has been made. But I have also focused in some depth on certain images in order not simply to survey the field, but rather to penetrate the meaning and implications of the representations.

Studies of children in art discuss children as adults perceive them, sometimes in a sentimental or patronizing way, sometimes idealized or symbolized. They tend to romanticize, or simply to group, to list features of childhood, or to illustrate customs. Children are often considered within the context of a family, where the family as a unit or its social position takes prior interest over the children themselves. While this is not necessarily avoidable, this book attempts to also explore imagery and issues it provokes from a child-centred point of view, considering not only children and childhood as the primary subjects, but also how art about children was intended to affect them. We think of ourselves as a society highly conscious of children's interests. But in our public galleries and monuments, statuary and coinage, there are few images of children and relatively less than there appears to have been in Byzantium. Even in the private sphere, few artists choose to portray children. Does this reflect ambiguities in our own approach to them? Are we hesitant to discern or determine their visual presence in the past, just as we are tentative about making contemporary images of them? While this book does not have a social, political or cultural agenda, it attempts to draw attention to children in art history and by extension to children in general in a way that is alert not only to the habitual but also to the unexpected, enigmatic or challenging aspects of childhood.

Several questions will recur regarding the interpretation and understanding of the representations. One concerns the definition of childhood and how we judge the difference between an image of a child and of an adult, and whether there is a stage in between. What is it about a portrayal that tells us that it represents a child rather than an adult, and what aspects of a child are most distinct? Is it dress, size, features, characteristics, behaviour or attitudes? What is explicit or implicit in visual distinctions of different ages, genders and attributes? Do such differentiations tie in with legal, functional or ideal conceptions of childhood? The perception of what constitutes a child and how he or she is defined may be associated with the context of the images and how they were used, whether they were intended for personal and private or general and public use, or perhaps were multifunctional and changed according to situation. Many are found in devotional contexts, and questions arise about the influence of religiosity and spirituality on depictions of childhood. This may also be related to whether children were portrayed as particular historical children or as generalized images and to what extent they were intended to be life-like and realistic or symbolic and referential. They may also represent a concept or abstraction of childhood, or a mythic ideal. Further questions develop about the place of children within the context in which they are imaged: in what sense are the children portrayed in relation to the site where they appear, or perhaps to the adults or other children with whom they are shown, or to themselves? This raises issues about the roles of younger people, including their relation to one another, to their elders, to social communities and to the church.

A recent comment by a Byzantinist states that 'the Byzantines were neither children nor naïve'.[194] He does not, of course, really mean this. The comment is in defence of suggestions that Byzantine art is childish and refers to the artist or possibly to the patron, but also perhaps to the audience, making the assumption that children were neither the creators nor the receivers of visual images. We do tend to assume that visual representations that have survived from Byzantium were not made by children, but are the work of adults, and so images of childhood are not children's but adults' perceptions of childhood. This, however, may be erroneous. We do not know the specific age of artists painting manuscripts or wall decorations or sculptors carving ivory, but since children from less affluent families worked from a young age domestically, agriculturally, or manually as craftsmen, it is probable that some imagery was made by children or by adolescents.

Moreover, a large proportion of the receivers of visual imagery were also children or young people. Our culture, although youth-oriented in many respects, reflects interests and concerns of a mature and ever-ageing population. Although there are many representations of elderly people in Byzantium, and people clearly did sometimes live to advanced age when they would often have had an influential role in society, the average age of the population was much younger than in our own. Byzantium was a paediatric culture, with probably half the population aged under 20. Most children would certainly view imagery, paintings and mosaics in churches, and wealthier children must have had access to illuminated manuscripts. Can we tell if any images were specifically made for children and what makes them distinctive? Or are we mistaken in making a distinction between art made for adults and for children? Is that a modern differentiation that would have been anachronous in the Byzantine world?

The present book will not reveal a consistent view of images of Byzantine children, nor does it intend to portray a tidy or obvious picture of childhood. It draws on a range of visual material that is sometimes perplexing and problematic. Children appear in many contexts, under many guises, with widely differing intentions; each example has its own characteristics and meanings. But viewed in relation to one another, the representations show that, in Byzantium, children were sanctioned subjects for imagery, and youth, in many forms, held appeal and was portrayed in inquisitive and reasoned ways.

Early material is included, since it seems relevant to show briefly some representations and attitudes towards the imaging of children to be found in the late Roman and early Christian periods. Much of the study focuses on Byzantine imagery from the seventh to the thirteenth centuries, but it is

---

194 Maguire (1996) 16.

also appropriate to continue into the fifteenth century and to show portrayals of children directly before the fall of Constantinople. Similarly, while a considerable amount of the art discussed is made in Constantinople, it is valuable to look at other centres of the empire, such as at Thessaloniki and at Cappadocia, but also at areas strongly influenced by the Byzantine church or politics, such as Rome in the early period and Kiev in the middle period. The intention is to be selective, not comprehensive, and to focus on images that highlight or represent primary locations and formats and that characterize major areas of Byzantine life that concerns children. To this end, the material is approached through broad themes: childhood, family, sanctity, power and the representation of Christ and of the Virgin as children. This enables the juxtaposition of otherwise perhaps loosely related images and is intended to contribute to an expansive inquiry into the issues.

The themes grounding the visual material in this study are intentionally broad, and several of them have overlapping functions or meanings. Many of the objects to be discussed are religious, but they are representative of the available material. Secular images of childhood, that is nonspecific children involved in the activities of children, are found on villa and palace floors but also in religious manuscripts. Representations of families are often in depictions of donors in religious contexts. Children joined in family patronage become sanctioned by their shared donation and are closely linked to holy children, who through their own will or fate are deemed sacred. Children with spiritual power are not unrelated to imperial children who have religious and secular authority. Christ and the Virgin share these qualities: depicted as children, they are initially joined to worldly families, elevated as sacred and invested with spiritual power.

The present chapter has raised questions about pertinent approaches to the study of childhood and its meaning in a cultural context and has discussed the definition of terms such as 'child' and 'youth' within Byzantine society. It has questioned when children ceased to be children and became adolescent or adult and how such concepts were perceived and visualized in Byzantium. This is intended to provide a framework, both conceptually and historically, for the exploration of the visual imagery. In addressing the setting, the historical, religious and societal context in which Byzantine children lived, I have highlighted the legal regulations governing children's lives and suggested that their rights were largely respected and protected, even if not compatible with today's mores. A feature of the current literature on children is that it often, as in the work of Evelyne Patlagean for instance, has focused on a series of historical facts about children or, in some cases, about girls in particular, but general conclusions about the place of children in Byzantine society have not been drawn. Our understanding of childhood in Byzantium has still largely not been deepened by the work of social historians, however intriguing the facts may be, and it has not been the intention of this book to fill that gap. However, it does seem entirely valid to look at examples of visual material from Byzantium and to interpret them as evidence of cultural responses and attitudes.

The discussion has introduced a theme that underlies this work: in Byzantium, probably close to half of the population at any given time was under 20. Discounting anyone under 15 or so, life expectancy was about 35, but total life expectancy was closer to 25, since many children died before attaining maturity.[195] Although some people did reach old age, the orientation of life was very different from our own, with experience often condensed into the early years. This means that half the receivers of art were children, adolescents or young adults and, to some extent, the young were also involved in the creation of visual material. Significant numbers of representations must have been intended for the eyes and perhaps touch of young viewers and, since many children started work at a young age, were probably made by them as well. Furthermore, since young people could be placed in positions of responsibility, some of the commissioners of images must also have been youthful. We tend to argue that imagery about children was made by adults, but this may be only half of the truth, and portrayals may reflect the concepts, designs and skill of young people, even of children. Considering all these factors, it should be expected that children are central to Byzantine visual representation. One could argue that children in society formed a silent majority, but the visual representations suggest otherwise, placing children at the core of many images, integrated into family life, spiritually rich and on occasion given secular power. In reflecting on this perspective, how should we determine which imagery was intended for children? It should not be assumed that art depicting children was made for their use or appreciation. However, it is the contention of this book that much more was intended for them than has been recognized.

The second chapter explores issues concerning the identification of images of children in terms of simple issues such as how do we know that a given representation is of a boy, a girl as opposed to a youth or a man or woman? It explores the finding of an interpretation of characteristics of childhood and the various ways children may be used in imagery, for instance portrayed as 'real', 'ideal' or 'conceptualized' children. This questions both how the images were originally intended and how we interpret them. Children appear in many contexts, and they certainly are seen playing, but to a large extent they participate in what we tend to think of as adult activities. This suggests that children were strongly integrated into Byzantine society, but not that they lost their subjective sense of being children: the young are clearly young, signified by size, dress and aspect. We are perhaps misled in referring to an adult society and adult activities, for it seems that the worlds of work, both within the home and outside it, were heavily populated by young people: young rulers, mothers, entertainers, sportsmen, shepherds, soldiers, servants, slaves and saints. The generational division of society is a conception founded on our own experience. Again, it would be delusive to imply that children

---

195 On this, see Chapter 1, fns 172–177.

did not have their own identities and attributes apart from adults. Children are not absorbed or negated within 'adult' activities, but they participate in them. We will see that manuscripts show many and varied uses of images of children. For instance, young people enliven the headpieces and margins of editions of certain sermons. The portrayals indicate that very young children were employed in entertaining, whether as free citizens or as slaves. Children feature in repeated scenes connected with the Old and New Testaments, such as the crossing of the Red Sea and the entry into Jerusalem. In both these cases, they stand out from the crowd, the most noticeable or significant participants, the ones seeing the light in the sky or recognizing Christ's lordship. But children are also used to give a sense of genre, as with the boys who wrestle in scenes of the multiplication of the loaves and fishes, or to make a theological point, as in the *spinario*. Children and adolescent boys are given attributes that indicate their immaturity. However, imagery in consular diptychs indicates the difficulty in distinguishing between children and slaves; yet also many slaves were children. Youthful attributes in Byzantium may not necessarily conform to our ideas about childhood and may have features that expand the meanings of children's identities. This is to be observed in some images of Saint Nicholas and of the Christ child that give them an aspect of age and wisdom. I would argue that the addition of those features that are not realistic in a visual sense, but rather in a symbolic one, further expand the meaning of childhood in Byzantine terms.

The discussion on childhood additionally raises questions about the relation of erotes and children and it is found that the two appear in analogous situations and with related meanings. This suggests that conceptualizations, perhaps idealized ones, about children are associated not only with their physical resemblance to erotes, with their soft, infantile bodies, but also with the connotations held by erotes: fun, mischief and physical pleasure.

The third chapter raises questions concerning the portrayal of apparent family relations. Images of children and young people with parents, siblings and extended family members are used to explore definitions of 'family' and the perception of the nature of family in Byzantium. Many of these are donor portraits and therefore portray historical families, although their tie to physical reality is not always distinct. Other familial representations depict biblical families and so portray alternate ideals or definitions of human relationships. Images of Byzantine families suggest that children were seen to have equal pictorial value to their parents: although the children are often depicted as smaller, presumably realistically reflecting their size, they receive an equal quality of execution and attention to detail as their parents.

The fourth, on sanctity, considers the religiosity of Byzantine life and looks at children who are singled out as sacred, whether identified as saints, as biblical heroes or simply dedicated to the divine. Images representing saintly children sets in the foreground the Byzantine acceptance and propagation of childhood as a facet of sanctity. Furthermore, young saints throughout the Byzantine period, in wall paintings, in icons and in illuminated manuscripts are depicted as youthful and seemingly attractive, suggesting that Byzantine sensibilities were drawn to male youth and its associations of beauty, goodness and closeness to God. Particularly in the eleventh century, this extends to images of the adolescent Christ, highlighting the attraction evidently generated by adolescent beauty and its connotations. However, female saints tend not to be depicted in adolescence. Girls are either small and childlike or young but womanly, which probably illustrates the customs of society, whereby girls were quickly prepared at puberty for marriage and child rearing.

The fifth chapter, on power, turns from the portrayal of sacred to secular authority and explores the depiction of children who have worldly power or who are associated with it, although this is often linked with religious authority. Youthful power is discussed through a series of images of young rulers, generally portrayed in dynastic portraits that focus on male heirs. These images also reveal personal aspects of the subjects' lives and depict the children in ways that reflect their identities, even if conforming to traditional and formal modes of portrayal. The children often hold a central place in the images; they are not relegated to the periphery and, as in the other family portraits, are depicted with equal value as their parents. The images enforce a sense of the children's duties and of their power delegated by the divine.

The sixth chapter, on representations of Christ and of the Virgin as children, focuses on the two most often depicted and most influential children in Byzantium. Their images encase the four themes – childhood, family, sanctity and power – and both reflect and give rise to images of other normal, holy or royal children in individual and in family contexts. The depictions of Christ and of the Virgin emphasize the great popularity in Byzantium of images of children. They demonstrate the multiplication and exaltation of representations of the Christ child in both narrative and symbolic settings. Similarly, the elaboration of the Virgin's story, depicted as a progression through childhood and portrayed in numerous examples, indicates the fascination with and appeal of childhood.

The final chapter looks at conclusions that can be drawn in light of the issues discussed and suggests where they might lead.

Chapter 2

Childhood

This chapter serves to explore some primary questions about the depiction of children and perceptions about them in Byzantium. The aim is to discuss how children were differentiated from adults, in what contexts and with what intentions. The chapter questions distinctions between girls and boys. It addresses the subject and identification of images, including with whom the children are depicted, the activities in which they are portrayed, what they wear and their characteristics. Portrayals of children are sometimes used by historians to determine customs, but the images can also inform on two other closely associated levels. The first concerns the nature of the representation, how the image is handled pictorially and the impression intended by its appearance in relation to its context. The second addresses what the image communicates about children societally, not in terms so much of habits, but society's perception of children, their place in the cultural framework and attitudes towards them. The discussion explores whether the depictions intentionally portray an image of a child or of an adult, or perhaps some other idea or symbol, and the difficulty often encountered in determining the intended identification. It also considers whether the children are visualized within an adult world, where the image principally conveys an adult context, or whether the focus is on children on their own terms.

The chapter questions the expectations we have about the depiction of a child, and whether these are comparable and transferable to Byzantium. Our understanding of childhood is constantly re-evaluated, but there do appear to be certain constants. Children's tastes are surprisingly traditional, despite contemporary western society's warnings against the loss of childhood.[1] We still associate children with particular activities, such as playing games and sports, learning skills, enjoying narrative and fantasy and giving and receiving physical affection. Are these relations equally found in representations in Byzantium, or are children portrayed with a different range of activities and interests?

---

1   As exemplified by the popularity of J.K. Rowling's *Harry Potter* books, which employ traditional settings and narratives; see, for instance, Rowling (1997).

The discussion also focuses on questions about when children cease to be children and become adults, and how their attributes then change. It considers ways in which adolescents may be differentiated from adults or from younger children, and what such distinctions tell us about the framing of attitudes about them. It also discusses what kinds of circumstances in life indicate change.

Children in Byzantium lived in a preponderantly youthful society, in which the majority did not have an extended education but entered the workforce after primary or perhaps secondary education. Children who lived in rural environments were involved in manual labour after leaving school and often had chores at home during their school years; similarly in urban environments, children participated in bread winning. Yet also, in the more affluent classes, children took on responsibility at a young age and, either under the auspices of parents or independently, may have been instrumental in the commissioning of images. We have seen how many rulers came to power when young, even if that power was mediated by a regent. This factor is part of the complexity about when children cease to be children and become adults. We should recognize that images may reflect both adult and child patronage, artistry and perceptions.

Many of the artists or their assistants must have been youthful. This is occasionally indicated in texts. For instance, in the *Life of Saint Pankratios* the painter, Joseph, who made icons for Saint Peter, is referred to as 'the young painter'.[2] As we have seen, children became apprenticed as young as 12, perhaps even younger, although I have found no mention of it, and we do have records of children being placed with artists, as for instance Alimpj, who was 'given by his parents to study icon-painting' and assisted the mosaicists decorating a church of the Dormition in the monastery of the caves at Kiev in the late eleventh century.[3] Byzantine painters are referred to as *zographos* (illuminator as well as painter) or *historiographos*, while illuminators are also called *chrysographos*, one who writes in gold. The *maistor* was the leader of a group of artisans and would train the young in his skills in a structure similar to a guild, a *systima*, but the dominance of these structures and their practices over time seem to have varied.[4] Artists and artisans came from all levels of society, up to the emperor, such as Constantine Porphyrogennetos. Those whose names are recorded (this occurs only rarely prior to the twelfth century), are nearly exclusively male, but this should not rule out the likelihood that girls and women were artists.[5] One is mentioned by John of Ephesos as a 'poor widow woman' in sixth-century Syria, who also gave art classes for a fee, a practice that does not seem to arise later.[6] The standard form of learning seems to be that of being trained when young, and so children

2   *Life of Pankratios, BHG* II, 1410–1412; Usener (1913) 418; Mango (1972) 137; in Maguire (1996) 37–38.

3   A. Cutler in *ODB*, I, 67, 197.

4   Oikonomidès (1979) 108–114.

5   On women artists, see Carr 1985; Carr 1997.

6   A. Cutler in *ODB*, I, 196–197.

were initiated into the arts of painting, illuminating, mosaic work, wood and ivory carving and metalwork from the time they finished elementary schooling, either outside or within the domestic environment. They would start with the basic tasks of preparing tools and materials and undertaking the jobs that required less skill such as painting backgrounds as part of a team. Children could enter monasteries and convents at the age of ten and some period of apprenticeship in scribing and illuminating was practised but still, young monks, perhaps even young nuns too, were probably involved in the production of books (two of the known female scribes in Byzantium were nuns, although evidence for female book production is very scant).[7] Evidence suggests that some monasteries sent manuscripts, sometimes separate quires, to professional illuminators to be decorated, and so we cannot assume that all the decorations were undertaken in a particular scriptorium.[8] Both in the monastic and professional environments, it is hard to say how long a child would have to work learning the skills of book production before being given decorative work. As there were lay illuminators, there were also lay icon painters, who would similarly have been trained from an early age.

In order to explore certain facets of these issues, we will examine examples of children's activities in the light of their locations. The discussion starts with the mosaic floors of the villa at Piazza Armerina in Italy and the floor of the Great Palace in Constantinople and then moves to ivory panels made as consular diptychs. It then turns to manuscript illustrations, first, to the depiction of youth and its transition to adulthood in ninth-century manuscripts: the marginal psalter, known as the *Khludov Psalter*, Moscow, State Historical Museum, MS gr. 129, and a collection of writings by fathers of the church, the *Sacra Parallela*, Paris, gr. 923; then to marginal illustrations in the *Homilies of Gregory of Nazianzos*; and, finally, to children in biblical crowd scenes. A further section investigates the relation between erotes, winged or wingless figures with childlike bodies, and children.[9] The discussion explores similarities and analogies in visual representations and what these might tell us about the intellectual, societal and religious perceptions of childhood, questioning whether there is some conceptual as well as visual relation between the two.

We look then first at a villa belonging to the very beginning of our period, probably datable to 320–340, sited in Sicily at Piazza Armerina.[10] Its owner was most likely closely associated with Rome at the time Constantinople

---

7   Carr (1985) 5–6, 13.

8   Nelson (1987) 58–59, 67, 77.

9   This includes figures variously referred to as putti, erotes, amorini and cupids, as these terms tend to be used interchangeably.

10   For summary, see Dunbabin (1999) 130–142; Wilson (1983) 14; for useful assessment, see Carandini, Ricci and De Vos, hereafter Carandini (1982); for style, see Dorigo (1971) 127–168; for early discussions and theories, see Gentili (1959) (1954); for summary of prior views and North African comparisons, see Dunbabin (1978) 196–212, 243–5; for more North African comparisons, see Salomonson (1965); see also Settis (1975) 873–994; Kähler (1973).

was newly established.[11] The mosaic floors of the villa include numerous representations of children. It serves as an example of late Roman villa culture and of then current ideas about children and childhood both in generalized and in specific terms. In the vast quantity of mosaics, subject matter varies from geometric patterns to elaborate mythological scenes and includes a trans-continental hunting epic and events from the Roman circus as well as analogous portrayals of a local hunt and children sporting in their own microcosmic circus. Individual people, who might be the owner, his wife and members of his immediate or extended family, appear, as do male and female athletes and bathers. Entire floors are given over to erotes involved in fishing and cultivating vines.

The lavish villa has 3,500 square metres of floor mosaic made by several mosaicists, largely from North Africa, perhaps over a period of 50 years.[12] Some of the designs seem particular to this villa, though the craftsmen did not only use unique motifs, but repeated ones found elsewhere.[13] One therefore has to be circumspect in assigning originality and intention to the patron or to the artist. But we can discuss the kind of children depicted, their activities and their placement, as well as the specific and interrelated sense of the imagery in association with the relation of various apartments and rooms to one another and the overall use of the villa.[14]

Images of children occur in three areas: in an entranceway, in a room off the main peristyle and in suites of rooms in the northeast and southeast wings of the house. The first is probably a family portrait and is situated in the vestibule that leads from the peristyle to the palaestra adjacent to the baths; two young people stand on either side of a woman, perhaps their mother (fig. 2.1).[15] I suggest that they are young since their height is less than that of the central figure, and they wear tunics that reveal their calves. As we shall see, diminutive height and short dress are not always indicators of youth and can often suggest low social status. However, in this case the two are dressed in fairly elaborate dress with ample cloaks over their shoulders. The woman lays a hand on the shoulder of the figure to her left, and the figure on her right lays his or her hand on the woman's shoulder. These gestures suggest intimacy and bonding. Furthermore, flanking the three central figures are two women, clearly women from the style of their hair, worn elaborately on their heads, who carry, respectively, a casket and a square pan hanging from a chain. The

---

11   Carandini seconds Cracco Ruggini's theory put forward in 1980 that it was built by Proculus Propulonius; see Carandini (1982) 14, 31, 50–51, 84–86, 92–93. Gentili proposed Maximian Herculeus as the owner, which dates it to the end of the third or the beginning of the fourth century; see Gentili (1954) 32–33; for a resumé of the dating issues, see Dorigo (1971) 129–130 and Dunbabin (1978) 201–202; for geographic and economic situation of Sicily, see Wilson (1990) throughout and on villas, 194–214.

12   For a summary of these views, see Dorigo (1971) 130–132, and on Dorigo's identification of three artistic styles, see throughout.

13   For similarities to African mosaics, see Dunbabin (1999) 130–131, 142–143; Carandini (1982) 281; Dunbabin (1978) 198 and 86, fn. 95; Salomonson (1965) 33.

14   See Carandini (1982) pl. II.2.

15   Carandini (1982) pl. LV.

two younger figures are usually considered to be boys, since they wear knee-length tunics and cloaks. However, their hair is shoulder length, and males in the mosaics, both young and older ones, consistently have short hair. Some, but not all, the girls in the mosaics have their hair up in some arrangement and not free-flowing.[16] Is it possible that these figures are both female and still young enough to wear short garments? This would perhaps explain why one appears to have the cloak draped over the head, and might suggest that the figures are shown with their hair down in preparation for the bath (the bath is after all part of the same building and bathers would not need to leave the house to get to it). Two other portraits are in the frigidarium, each in an alcove of the room, and show two young men, attended by servants, but these appear too old to be considered children.[17] They seem to be mature and affluent young men, well attended and enjoying the luxury of villa life.

Another mosaic that is perhaps also a portrait is in the far wing of the house and is a scene depicting Pan and Eros in a struggle (fig. 2.2).[18] A group of human figures support Eros, on the right, and a group of mythological figures promote Pan, on the left. This image would appear to portray a group of children: they are apparently arranged in order of age, indicated by maturity of features and of dress not by height, with the youngest, a boy,

Fig. 2.1   Mosaic at the Villa Romana del Casale at Piazza Armerina, first half of the fourth century. A woman flanked by two children and servants who appear to be on their way to the adjacent baths

16   The well-known 'bikini' girls have a combination of the two hairstyles. Carandini proposed that the portraits are of Proculus and Aradius Rufinus with their mother Adelphia; see Carandini (1982) 80; Kähler suggested Maxentius and two sons; see Kähler (1973) 48; Gentili proposed Fausta and Maxentius, who had a squint, the children of Maximian; see Gentili (1954) 407–410; Dunbabin also determined both children to be male; see Dunbabin (1978) 202, fn. 28.

17   Carandini (1982) 354, 356, pls LVIII (f), LIX (b^2, with small servant); Kähler (1973) pl. 48.

18   Carandini (1982) pl. XXXIX.

Fig. 2.2   Mosaic at the Villa Romana del Casale at Piazza Armerina, first half of
the fourth century. These are perhaps portraits of some of the children who lived
at the house shown in a fantasy scene supporting Eros who is to fight Pan

given precedence on the same plane as Eros. He is dressed only in a cloak, wrapped across one shoulder, and has short curly hair. Behind him stands an older child, probably another boy, who wears a torque and similarly is bare breasted with a more ample cloak over his shoulder. Behind him stand two figures, apparently girls, and a slightly more mature female further back. The girls wear their hair coiffed on their heads, long-sleeved gowns and cloaks. Compared to the boys, their heads are smaller in relation to their bodies, reducing the impression that they are very young. The maturity of the figure at the back is suggested by her face, which is more oval and less round, and by her hairstyle in which the hair is wrapped around the head and gathered in a bun on top of the head. The two seemingly younger female figures wear their hair up, but it lies loosely on the crown of the head and each has a fringe at the front. The children are encouraging and waving at Eros, who is naked except for bracelets and an armband, and who must represent youth and beauty in contrast to the aged Pan. It seems likely that the children are the offspring of the owner, perhaps attended by a maid. Their alliance with Eros associates them with fun, mischief and perhaps even love. This image does not appear to show the same children as in the other portraits. Are these representations of specific individuals or do they portray children in a generalized sense? I am tempted to think of them as specific children, as their appearance seems to be individualized. If this is the case, several young people were associated with the house, perhaps at one time.[19] Children, one can argue, were significant inhabitants of the villa, and it was thought apt to portray them in daily and imaginary activities.

The children depicted elsewhere may be specific portraits, but this is similarly hard to determine. In one of the two large rooms with figurative decorations to the north of the main peristyle, boys of various ages are included with men in a hunting scene (fig. 2.3). The boys can be differentiated from the men by their reduced height and narrower bodies. One rides a horse, another drives an antelope into a net, and two young men prepare the fire at an altar with a statue of Diana, while two shorter boys approach the scene, one with a horse and one with a dog. Two other small boys put the game into baskets and hold up glasses. They are perhaps servants or slaves preparing the meal. The figures seem young because they wear short tunics that hang to mid thigh and are therefore shorter than those worn by the figures in the vestibule. Our instinct is to read that the shorter boys are younger than the taller ones: the shorter boys also have narrow shoulders and limbs, while the taller figures are broader, suggesting that they are nearly full-grown. This small hunt mosaic contrasts with the epic big game hunting scenes in the long ambulatory to the east of the peristyle, which show hunters, mostly again apparently young, capturing wild animals in exotic lands.[20] The small hunt is different in that it

---

19   R. Wilson, after Dorigo, suggests that one artist made most of the images of children, along with the marine scenes that contain erotes, Orpheus and the kissing couple; see Wilson (1983) 28; Dorigo (1971) 158–163.

20   For a description, see Carandini (1982) 94–104.

Fig. 2.3   Mosaic at the Villa Romana del Casale at Piazza Armerina, first half of the fourth century. Boys of various ages with horses and a dog prepare a sacrifice in the woods after hunting

shows the pleasures and camaraderie of local life, the richness of the hunt in the native vicinity and religious practice at the sacrificial altar. It references Arcadian life, shared male activities and man's control over nature.

The majority of the images of children are in a series of floors in the southeast corner of the complex. The rooms are arranged around a semicircular atrium, flanked by rooms and with an apsidal hall to the east. The floor to the south shows children racing bird-drawn chariots in an arena like the Circus Maximus in Rome, and the one to its east depicts child musicians and actors. The one to the north of the atrium is the one mentioned with Eros and Pan, and to its east is one with further scenes of children hunting.

In the circus scene, all four factions are represented, with each charioteer driving a team of birds and an attendant alongside, one of whom is awarding the victor with a palm (fig. 2.4).[21] This scene has parallels with a large-scale representation of races in the palaestra adjacent to the baths, which illustrates racing quadrigae in the Circus Maximus and includes graphic details of the setting, such as the obelisk of Augustus, viewed from the Palatine (3).[22] The figures appear to be children because they are short in height and wear tunics that barely reach to the knee. Their hair is short and curly, suggesting that they are boys. In room 45, two women make garlands in the apse, and beneath

---

21   Carandini (1982) pl. XLI.
22   See Carandini (1982) 76.

Fig. 2.4   Mosaic at the Villa Romana del Casale at Piazza Armerina, first half
of the fourth century. In a play hippodrome, small boys compete while driving
chariots drawn by large birds, and one is presented with a palm frond in victory

them, in the narrower transition to the main part of the room, baskets and bags of money rest on a bench, probably prizes for the young actors who perform below in three registers.[23] Some of the children play instruments, others appear to be speaking and another holds a whip. In the lower two registers are circular disks with letters of the alphabet protruding from them on sticks, but it is not clear what these signify. The overall mood is good-natured and lively. In another room, a girl and a woman in long dresses gather roses into baskets, while below them older girls weave flowers into garlands. The girl in the top register on the left appears to be younger than the others since her hair is arranged half up and her face is rounder. Below, in the threshold, a boy carries baskets of flowers and small boys are shown in three registers, chasing and being attacked by birds, and catching a hare and a goat.[24] Children also appear in the entranceway to a room in the northeast suite of rooms, forming a transition between the so-called erotic scene in the adjacent room, showing a male and female embracing, and decorative patterns in the room adjoining it to the north.[25] Two boys and two girls are seen playing with balls.

This last image shows girls and boys together, and similarly the actors seem to be of both genders. But largely activities of boys and girls are somewhat differentiated. Young boys are perceived as active, independent, competitive and integrated with the adult domain. Young girls are not portrayed in energetic pursuits and do not participate in the hunt or in the circus. Rather, the daughters of the house stand behind the son as they cheer on Eros, and other girls engage in quiet behaviour, such as weaving flower garlands. Some of these activities seem realistic, while others are clearly imaginary ideals and fantasies.

The variety of sizes of the figures in the mosaics and the distinctions in headdress and clothing suggest that children were depicted with clear differentiations. We determined that boys apparently wear their hair short, while girls, even seemingly young girls, wear it long and up. Boys, both short and tall, can wear tunics that bare their knees, and girls seemingly wear dresses and cloaks, although the figures pictured on their way to the bath present a quandary. Mature men, distinguished by short beards, in the mosaics also can appear in short tunics and women are dressed much as the girls. However, the young are seemingly differentiated from the mature by their rounder faces, their slenderer bodies and their diminished height. This may be stating the obvious, but it serves to present a format for interpreting imagery.

Children play with toys, but also perhaps play at the games of adults: they are shown participating in adult activities or playing with toys that mimic them. Jas Elsner argues that the circus scene parodies the 'very construction of identity'. He sees these scenes as 'humorous asides on the serious themes of the villa's grandest floors', but they also present a 'frame which earths grand

---

23   Carandini (1982) pl. XLII.
24   Carandini (1982) pl. XL.
25   Carandini (1982) pl.XXXVI.

illusions as but the games of children'.[26] In this reading, images of children are relegated to the margins as light comedy, but with an edge which suggests that grand aspirations to power are analogous to play. We cannot necessarily say that the children's circus is a parody of the adult world. Today, children's books and films often place children in adult roles, and a part of childhood practice and fantasy is doing adult things, learning how to behave, aspiring to the future and emulating senior or heroic figures. Childhood is said not to have existed in the past, since children were merely being prepared for adult life; but this is still what parents and educators do today, largely through guiding children to approximate adult activities.[27] Wealthy children in the fourth century perhaps participated in extravagant little races, as today's children ride horses and compete in games. But also children did entertain commercially, and the young actors may have been professionals, a subject to which we shall return. If the imagery was intended for children, it is probably not parody. If it was crafted for adult viewers, then it more likely displays the pride of the adults for the idyllic life of the children. Or perhaps it does present an ironic view of the puerility of extravagant games put on at vast expense, but to my mind this is less convincing and views the images solely from an adult perspective. My sense is that the rooms with depictions of children were in part intended for the use of children, and their presence suggests a sensitivity to children's decorative tastes. Whatever the function of the rooms, or whoever had access to them, the interest in children and their activities intimates that children were central to life in the villa.

Our view of the significance of the mosaics depends on the function of the rooms and who had access to them. In antiquity, villas were emblematic of wealthy rural life, which was revived in Sicily during the fourth century when the island's affluence increased due to its position linking Africa and Italy, and land was bought by Roman aristocracy.[28] The allusions to luxury, to learning, to exotic lands and mythological innuendo exemplify the aspirations and interests of the moneyed and influential classes. While visually and conceptually referencing luxurious splendour, villas were also practical domains in which to live, entertain and fulfil civic obligations. The villa mosaics suggest that children were integral to that life.

The selection of architectural spaces and the layout of the villa are not unlike the larger homes at Pompeii and Herculaneum. Andrew Wallace-Hadrill has highlighted the important public function of the Roman home and the public–private dichotomy that arose when private, domestic needs were fused with public, civic duties. Common rooms, the vestibules and peristyles,

---

26   Elsner (1998) 45–46; the concept of parody had been expressed often in regard to the mosaics, and most recently by Dunbabin (1999) 133; Carandini had a similar response (1982) 75.

27   On the lack of childhood in history, see, most notoriously, Ariès (1962, 1996 edn), as discussed in Chapter 1 above.

28   Carandini (1982) 15; for villa function and use, see Wallace-Hadrill (1994); for connotations and society, see Zanker (1979) 460–523; for villa structure and life, see Percival (1970, 1981 edn).

could be entered by anyone, including the public, apparently without asking, whereas access to bedrooms, dining rooms and baths required an invitation, but still these rooms were not private by today's standards of family privacy.[29] But there was a certain flexibility in the use of space, combining subtle adjustments in the treatment of guests, with a general mobility within the house. Interior decoration offered various ways to establish a deliberate hierarchy within rooms. It was an adaptable tool and was used by patron and artist to manipulate the domestic space and atmosphere. No separate areas for children have been identified in Roman homes, but this is not to say that they did not exist. Our knowledge of what constitutes a bedroom or a living area is so fragile that to determine the gender or age of inhabitants is very tentative. It has been suggested that in wealthy households children slept with nurse slaves, and while this may have been the case, evidence is limited, and probably custom varied.[30] We will look below at scenes of charioteers on children's sarcophagi. There are over forty examples of erotes racing in the Circus Maximus, and apparently no examples of this motif on adult sarcophagi.[31] Could this suggest that the room depicting the children might have been specifically used by children?

If the suites of rooms are public to the extent that the family received personal or honoured guests in them, then adults outside the close family were seemingly receptive to imagery about children. And it is imagery that draws a fine line between depicting them as professional actors, as children playing at acting and as a parody of life that makes it appear as pure enactment. But, similarly, if they were for the private use of adults, then adults within the close family liked to be surrounded by imagery of children and took pleasure in seeing their games, or were intrigued by the interplay of child and adult worlds. In both these cases, the prevalence of imagery of children perhaps seems unusual to us in adult apartments. However, if the rooms were designed for children, then children had wonderfully luxurious quarters, and people had a developed sense of how to decorate a child's room. Does the evidence suggest that the children had their own apartments specifically furnished to represent their interests, ideal activities and mythological fantasies, or at least what the adult patron or designers considered these to be? Or alternatively, were the suites designed for the central core of the family, adults and children, who shared the space? Considering that there is little evidence to suggest that children were segregated and given the imagery of the floors, this seems most likely, since an adult image of a couple embracing is located adjacent to the child imagery. If this is the case, then both adults and children enjoyed the

---

29   See Wallace-Hadrill (1994) 44.

30   On children's space and sleeping arrangements, see Wallace-Hadrill (1994) 9–10, 113, 117; on gender separation and for further bibliography, see 8–9, 218, ns 30–34, 57, 224, n. 40.

31   Huskinson (1996) 46, 79, 106–7; other motifs only found on children's sarcophagi are children's games, marine feasts with cupids, children's death beds and cupids playing in a Dionysiac scene; see Huskinson 46, 106–107.

representations, indicating adult pleasure in portrayals of the young – and not necessarily an ironic pleasure.

Roman households, particularly those of the wealthy and upper middle classes, were large and flexible; the owner and his family shared the dwelling with a fluctuating number of dependants, freedmen, workers, friends and lodgers, and their children.[32] We see a variety of children in the images and from different social levels. In the mosaics, many young boys are engaged in the local hunt, and adolescent boys are involved in ritual worship, obviously mixing freely with the adults; several servants or slaves, who appear very young and may well be children, seem integrated into the day's events. While the children watching Eros and Pan may be members of the family, other children are integrated into the villa's decoration, playing on thresholds, riding on chariots and performing on imagined or realistic stages. Overall, the mosaics at the villa suggest that children were important, even central to the lives of wealthy aristocrats with Roman connections in fourth-century Sicily. Without making any formal distinction between children belonging to the nuclear or extended family or children as servants or dependants, it becomes clear that it was thought valid to depict them on their way to the bath, hunting, playing games, entertaining and participating in the mythological world.

Further early examples of children playing and sporting are found in the pre-iconoclast mosaic floor from the Great Palace in Constantinople. It has been variously dated from the fifth to seventh centuries, but recent excavation suggests it was made at the time of Justinian in the sixth century.[33] The vast palace complex, the centre of Byzantine rule until the twelfth century, lay between the hippodrome and the sea, and the mosaics decorated the colonnade of a peristyle court, which was in front of an apsed hall and appears to have been connected to the hippodrome. Various sections survive, mostly from the north and south colonnades and a little from the west. The outside of the peristyle originally measured 55.5 by 66.5 metres, and at its widest the mosaic extends for 10 metres.[34] The images do not form a continuous narrative or frieze, but they are all on the same scale and are arranged evenly, generally five tiers high, with the figures seen the right way up from the edge of the courtyard. The cameo scenes generally contain from one to four figures and are interspersed with trees that often form part of the composition.

The mosaic features a rather narrow selection of imagery that includes mythological scenes, the hunting of wild and domestic animals, the tending

---

32 Wallace-Hadrill (1994) 116.

33 Jobst, Kastler, Scheibelreiter and Bolognesi Rechi-Franceschini. (1999). See also Mundell Mango (1994) 131–136; Trilling has argued for the reign of Herakleios (610–641); see Trilling (1989) 27–72; Nordhagen favoured the seventh century (first reign of Justinian II (685–695)); see Nordhagen (1963) 53–68; David Talbot Rice gave an overall date of 450–500, but suggested also Justin II (565–578); see Talbot Rice (1958) esp. 148, 167; Mango suggested Marcian (450–457), but later proposed the end of the sixth century; see Mango (1951) 179–186 and Mango and Lavin (1960) 67–73; Brett suggested an early-fifth century dating (Theodosios II (408–450)); see Brett, Macaulay and Stevenson, hereafter Brett (1947).

34 Trilling (1989) 28.

of animals, animals fighting each other and youths sporting. Portrayals of two women have survived, but there are no female children. Boys are depicted in a variety of scenes, tending animals in pastoral settings, hunting and playing sports-like games. From their height, some of the boys are quite young, although they, like the older ones, are muscular. Others appear to be youths, since when they appear with adults, they are about three-quarters their size, and others are young men, characterized by full height, but beardless and with youthful faces. Two of the young boys are seen riding on a camel, two herding geese and one tending a lamb (figs 2.5–2.6). A further image shows a satyr carrying a small boy on his shoulders, which could be Pan with Bakchos.[35] The older boys are also shown tending animals: a boy, dressed in a tunic, assists a goatherd, another boy feeds a donkey and another catches a large hare with a basket.[36] In these examples, the boys are in some sense working, tending or catching animals. In one scene to the lower right of the goat-herding group, boys are involved in playing a game with a wheel and a stick (fig. 2.7). [37] They wear colours on the front of their tunics, showing that they represent factions.

The images fall into two primary contexts, pastoral and sporting. The satyr and child, the lute-playing herdsman, the suckling foal and the grazing sheep emphasize the idyllic, bucolic ambience of peace and plenty. The hunting or sporting scenes can depict violent situations: however, the overall mood is not brutal; the men do not fight each other, and the children are not antagonistic, but rather work in tandem, looking healthy and wholesome. James Trilling has emphasized the violent nature of the images, but they simply reflect daily existence in the country.[38] The boys, numbering nearly as many as the adults, are not spending their childhood in playing games or academic learning, but rather they contribute to pastoral life.

The imagery is essentially naturalistic, with an emphasis on rural rather than urban pursuits, but also on the meeting of the two. The hunting scenes may refer to the *venationes* or simulated hunts in the hippodrome, which took place in an urban setting, when the wild, untamed world was imported into the tamed and controlled world of the auditorium. The boys play and work along with the adults and are in no way separate, suggesting that youths were involved with the festive activities at the hippodrome, or at least in an idyllic description of it. The choice of this imagery in the imperial palace suggests that the emperors, or their families, enjoyed images of the young at work, play and sport: virtually all the figures are young, even the men; an occasional

35   Trilling (1989) figs 19, 25, 28; Brett (1947) pls 31, 52.
36   Brett (1947) pls 28, 30.
37   Brett (1947) pl. 29.
38   Trilling fantasizes that the mosaic shows the emperor Herakleios's struggle for the empire in his inner soul during this 'troubled and heroic period', and has a political and psychological message; equally questionable is his suggestion that the mosaic is based on Vergil's *Georgics*; see Trilling (1989) esp. 31, 60–67. Similarly, S. Hiller's theory that the imagery is Christian in meaning but pagan in presentation seems hard to justify; see Hiller (1969) 275–305.

Fig. 2.5   Istanbul, Great Palace mosaics, first half of the sixth century. Two small boys, one holding a bird, ride a camel led by a burly young man. © Cecily Hennessy

Fig 2.6   Istanbul, Great Palace mosaics, first half of the sixth century. A boy dressed in a short tunic herds geese with a stick, one of several images in the floor mosaic showing boys tending to animals. © Cecily Hennessy

older figure is present, whose receding hairline connotes age, but the prevalent image is one of youth. Children are known to have been enthralled by the races.[39] Many of the charioteers must have been young; for instance, the great sportsman Porphyrius competed from the age of 15 to sixty, and charioteers are often depicted in their youth.[40]

Closely associated with the hippodrome are the consular diptychs, carved in ivory, which were distributed both in Rome and in Constantinople by the consul sponsoring the annual games in order to mark his honour and largesse. These frequently appear to depict youths or perhaps slaves in subsidiary scenes, and our inability to define quite who they are highlights some of the dilemmas in defining age or status.

In the Roman diptych of Consul Basilius, dated to 480, the games are illustrated in the lower register with charioteers racing past the turning posts in the hippodrome.[41] To the right, a small figure, dressed in a tunic to midcalf, stands next to a man in a senatorial toga who is holding his arm up with two fingers raised over him. The small figure would appear to be a boy, although it is not clear what his role is. He apparently had an important place in the festivities and may be a competitor, who is being rewarded for his success. In the diptych of Flavius Clementinus, dated to 513, boys or youths empty moneybags over the floor of the hippodrome in the ritual *sparsio*, when coins were distributed to the people.[42] It is not evident whether these are free young boys, slaves or servants. They are short, but this could be a hierarchical device to indicate their inferiority to the figures in the upper register. Youths tend to be shown as short and slender, but these figures are short and stout. They have round faces, in contrast to those of Clementinus and the personifications of Rome and Constantinople flanking him, which are oval. They have solid, stocky bodies and wear short, sleeveless, midthigh-length tunics, belted at the waist, which are worn by slaves, but also by children. In a diptych of Areobindus, dated to 506, the games are shown below the image of the consul (fig. 2.8). A row of clean-shaven curly-haired spectators watch the contestants, who appear to be young, fighting wild animals.[43] The consul is also clean-shaven but full-faced, with slight lines at the corner of his mouth, which indicate both fleshiness and maturity. The spectators, on the other hand, are slender and although small and therefore lacking in detail, their faces have no lines of age. Yet the portraits of the emperors in the extant sixth-century diptychs tend to be very similar, and they all have round faces, large eyes, heavy rounded fringes and clean-shaven faces, or very short beards that belie any true likeness. The youthful appearance of the viewers therefore negates

---

39   See Huskinson (1996) 113.

40   On monuments, see Vasiliev (1948) 29–49; on Porphyrius, see Cameron (1973) throughout; unfortunately Cameron does not give many details of the age of competitors in Cameron (1976); for representations of charioteers, see Weitzmann (1979b) 93–108, nos 83–99.

41   Weitzmann (1979b) n. 47.

42   A. Eastmond in Buckton (1994) n. 62; Weitzmann (1979b) n. 48.

43   Durand (1992) n. 12.

any attempt to define age. Are they young or just clean-shaven aristocrats? Similarly are the apparently small, lithe bodies of the contestants suggestive of youth or simply a mode of representation?

These examples highlight a frequent difficulty in analysing images of children and young people: how to distinguish between stylistic or iconographic conventions or idiosyncrasies that may or may not indicate youth, but perhaps refer only or also to status or to societal role. When we look at many images of nonspecific people in Byzantium, such as the contestants at the games, or soldiers, shepherds or slaves, we see figures that appear to be young. Is this because the majority of such classes of people were actually young and the artist intended to portray their youth, or is the perception of youth a misapprehension on our part? But also, many slaves were children, so the association of low status, of slavery and of childhood, in some cases, is correct.

In present society, older children and teenagers have, in certain ways, adopted a marked independence, with a culture that is very much their own, a marketplace and entertainments catering to their tastes, their own adapted dialect or vocabulary and, to some extent, habits of behaviour. According to visual representations, what are people in their teens doing in Byzantium? What are their responsibilities, and does society relate to their interests or tastes? Do they have their own milieu or are they simply appendages to the adult world? Are they imaged within an adult sphere and viewed from an adult perspective? Or are they still involved in children's activities, and if so,

Fig. 2.7 Istanbul, Great Palace mosaics, first half of the sixth century. Set as if in the hippodrome, boys play a game of spinning hoops. © Cecily Hennessy

Fig. 2.8   Paris, Musée du Louvre. Diptych of Consul Areobindus, 506. The consul is seated on a throne presiding over fights with wild animals watched by a row of figures in the crowd. © Photo Rmn/© Daniel Arnaudet

are these viewed from an adult's or a child's perspective? Or do we have no way of telling?

In the Great Palace mosaics some of the figures appear to be youths; they are muscular and not as small as the other boys; yet they are playing games, such as spinning wheels around the hippodrome. At Piazza Armerina, quite mature girls weave garlands for the actors imaged below them and they are therefore involved in the child performers' activities. But on the whole, small children play games and larger children are involved in activities that adults also perform. We are perhaps mistaken in calling these adult or mature activities, for if children and teenagers engage in them, they are perhaps more accurately termed serious pursuits. Again, this does not necessarily mean that older children and teenagers did not have their own patterns of behaviour, perhaps unruly, impressionable or immature, but that what we would consider to be the adult world was richly populated with young people.

We have looked at mosaic floors and at ivory diptychs from the pre-iconoclastic period that show children engaged in activities. These all have a secular context and are associated with wealth. We turn now, for contrast, to the post-iconoclastic period and to a religious context, manuscripts.

Manuscripts from the ninth century serve to illustrate the integration of young people into serious pursuits, and we shall focus on two: Paris, gr. 923 and the *Khludov Psalter*, Moscow, Historical Museum, gr. 129. The manuscripts are not similar in style, but do share iconographic motifs and modes of representation.

Paris, gr. 923 contains various biblical extracts and excerpted writings by the church fathers, known as the *Sacra Parallela*, traditionally said to have been compiled by John of Damascus, an eighth-century monk from S. Sabas in Palestine.[44] It is written in uncial letters which date it to the ninth century and is decorated, most frequently, with full-length or bust portraits of saints and church fathers within roundels. Further scenes illustrate the text.[45] The ground of the illuminations is predominantly in gold, the images are outlined in dark ink with occasional features blocked in, details are picked out in red and highlights are in white. Headings and the names of authors in the text are also emphasized with a red-bordered gold bar. Opinions vary as to where the manuscript was made, but most recent views tend towards Constantinople.[46] Elias Antonopoulos has remarked on the frequent appearance of children in the marginal illustrations.[47] Some of the examples he gives of children are certainly valid, such as the child Joseph being hugged by his father, but in others it is questionable whether the artist intended the image to look like

---

44   For illustrations and analysis, see Weitzmann (1979a); for more recent bibliography see Durand (1992) n. 127.

45   On the relation of text and image in the ninth century, see Brubaker (1999) 23–26.

46   References in Brubaker (1999) 25 fn. 29; see, for instance, Wright (1980) 7–8; also see Cormack (1986) 635, n. 39; Grabar suggested Italy, probably Rome; Weitzmann suggested S. Sabas, Palestine, and that it was possibly made during iconoclasm; see Weitzmann (1979a) 20–23, 25.

47   Antonopoulos (1986) 271–287.

Fig. 2.9   Paris, Bibliothèque nationale, gr. 923, fol. 248r, second half of the ninth century. Five herdsmen with crooks watch over their sheep. Are they too young to have grown beards or are their clean shaven faces a simple convention? Bibliothèque nationale de France

a child.[48] Antonopoulos mentions these figures as being young: the three Hebrews in the furnace; angels, who often are of questionable age; shepherds, who are beardless; and soldiers, who again are beardless (fig. 2.9).[49] These figures do form contrasts to the many bearded and longhaired saints and church fathers and to the patriarchs, such as Jacob. They certainly do not appear to be advanced in age; yet equally they do not really have the characteristics of children, neither in their gestures nor in their facial expressions. Taking into account the overall style of the miniatures throughout the codex, which is based on simplistic, stocky, childlike figures, the images might seem to some eyes to represent children when in fact they do not. The bodily forms of those mentioned by Antonopoulos are no different from others in the manuscript.

Similarly, Antonopoulos finds many images of children in the *Khludov Psalter*, Moscow, State Historical Museum, MS gr. 129.[50] Again, he points to beardless Graeco-Roman soldiers and to young martyrs.[51] Antonopoulos suggests that this in part associates them with youths of the antique gymnasium: they are ascetic athletes battling in the struggle for Christ and similarly appear nude. He sees both young and old martyrs, but only young torturers; similarly angels are always young and can look like eunuchs, and allegorical figures are often young.[52] I would disagree with some of his findings: the torturers do not look particularly young, nor do the allegorical figures. On the other hand, James and John are represented as youthful (for John this is not surprising) and there are scenes specifically with children such as boys catching birds and boys dancing around the golden calf (fig. 2.10).[53]

---

48   For Joseph, see Weitzmann (1979a) fol. 344v, fig. 38.

49   See Weitzmann (1979a) three Hebrews, fol. 373v, fig. 385, angels, fols 245r, 214r, 68v, 144v,163v, figs 27, 172, 441, 450, 492, herdsmen, fol. 248r, fig. 22, soldiers, fol. 86r, fig. 167; other examples of young people or children are: Isaac suckled by Sarah, fol. 368v, fig. 31, Joseph in Egypt, fols 387v, 11v, 12r, 377r, 14r, figs 43–47, the daughter of the Canaanite woman, fols 166v, 167r and v, 168r, figs 420–423, and a group of children taught by Basil, fol. 11v, fig. 570 (my fig. 2.44).

50   For facsimile, see Ščepkina (1977); for analysis, see Corrigan (1992).

51   See Ščepkina (1977) for soldiers, fol. 78v, for martyrs, fol. 44r.

52   Antonopoulos (1986) 283–284; see Ščepkina (1977) for angels, fol. 10v, for allegorical figure, fol 88.

53   See Ščepkina (1977) for James and John, fol. 75v, for bird catchers, 107r, for dancers, fol. 108v. Other scenes with young people or children are: boy with birds, fol. 76v, David being anointed, fol. 79r, fol. 89, little boy Christ with Virgin, fol. 79r, young boy with stick, fol. 101v, angels, fol. 102r, crossing the Red Sea, fol. 108r , falling figures, fol. 108v, David with

Fig. 2.10 Moscow, State Historical Museum, gr. 129, fol. 75v, second half of the ninth century. The Apostles James and John, each labeled with his name, appear as young men with beardless faces and haloes

In both these manuscripts, categories of figures seem young, such as soldiers, shepherds and workmen. Their apparent youth might well represent their lack of position in society. We tend to assume that beardless means young, but clearly in the sixth-century consular diptychs this does not necessarily apply. In later periods, when custom changed and mature men characteristically wore beards, often following trends set by the emperors, this deduction may often be accurate. However, lack of a beard may also refer to status or to ethnic origin or may simply be an accepted iconographic mode. For instance, junior emperors were traditionally shown beardless; even Constantine VIII when he was in his sixties, but still second in status to his brother Basil II, was depicted beardless, and specific saints are shown bearded or beardless according to iconographic convention.[54] From the ninth century we consistently see men in power, such as emperors, military leaders, patriarchs, church fathers, bishops and seers as bearded; but their followers, court attendants, some of whom are eunuchs, rank and file soldiers, lay worshippers, servants and slaves are often clean-shaven.

But in addition to being fresh-faced, these figures often wear their hair short and frequently curly, whereas the hair of those with higher status falls to their shoulders. Similarly, they wear clothes that suggest both lack of status and youth. Clean-shaven figures are often shoeless; they wear short tunics and if they have cloaks they are also short. These are features that distinguish children. It may well be that the figures' position in society correlates with their youth, and we would expect that those entering their careers in politics, the military or in the church were young. Also, the depiction of status can be deceptive as to age. For instance, in two examples in the Paris manuscript, a man of wealth and power, the moneylender, is shown much larger than his dependent borrowers (fig. 2.11).[55]

As discussed in Chapter 1, if the average life expectancy in Byzantium was less than 30, the majority of males must have been young. It is therefore

harp, 147v, David with Goliath, fol.148r, Miriam dancing, fol. 148v, Christ presented in the temple, fol. 163v, Zechariah with John, fol. 163v.

54   For Basil II's coins, see *DOC* III/2 pls XLIII–XLVII; on emperors' appearances, see Baldwin (1981) 8–21; Head (1980) 226–240.

55   See Weitzmann (1979a) fols 142r, 142v, figs 560, 562.

hardly surprising that the depiction of a given group of soldiers shows them to be youthful. Boys participated in the adult world at a young age. While the children of the educated classes could, at some points in Byzantine history, carry on their education up to a tertiary stage, perhaps until the age of 19 or 20, many children had either no education or completed only the primary or secondary stages. They would be involved in work of some sort, perhaps tending animals or assisting with chores when very young. A large number of the men depicted in Byzantine images were in fact youthful and had not gained full maturity, so that the images reflect a very young society. Again, this shows how integral youth was to the Byzantine world and the significant role young people played in it.

Just as boys entered into mature activities when young, so did girls. But the depiction of girls or young women is harder to distinguish from their older counterparts, since women's appearances did not change in such a clearly defined way as they grew older and in general women are portrayed in a consistent way, mostly as young, with differentiation of age only perhaps suggested by the covering or uncovering of hair. This also seems linked to morality: loose women show their hair. There are few depictions of females in the *Khludov Psalter*, but they generally show apparently young women, such as the portrayals of the Virgin, who has large eyes and a round face, which suggests youth, the woman at the well, who is depicted as slender and girl-like, the woman with the flow of blood, who has long hair down her back, and Miriam dancing, who also has waist-length ringlets.[56] Similarly, in Paris, gr. 923, age is hard to discern; for instance, Sarah is not clearly old, and Rebecca sending out Jacob could be interpreted to be young.[57] Certain individuals are singled out; for instance, Jezebel has dark lips and displays part of her hair, and the Queen of Sheba has an exotic headdress. However, in general Hebrew women are shown to be slender, but breasted, and with their heads covered.[58] Similarly, in Paris, gr. 510, the women do not seem clearly differentiated in age: Elizabeth and Mary in the visitation, flight and presentation, Jairus's daughter and the woman at the well all appear to be of comparable maturity.[59] Jairus's daughter and the Centurion's son are usually not depicted as children but as adolescents or young adults.[60] There are no parallels to the boys mentioned above, but then there are no comparable biblical or homiletic narratives. Since we do not see images that appear to portray overt adolescence in girls, as they do with boys, it seems that girls passed quickly from childhood to adulthood

---

56   For the Virgin, see Ščepkina (1977) fols 45r, 64r, 79r, 92r, 153r, for the woman at the well, fol. 33r, for the woman with the flow of blood, fol. 84v, for Miriam, fol. 148v.

57   See Weitzmann (1979a) fols 205v, 78r, figs 18, 33.

58   See Weitzmann (1979a) fols 206r, 327v, figs 162, 153.

59   See Brubaker (1999) for Elizabeth and Mary, fol. 3r, fig. 6, fol. 137r, fig. 18, for Jairus's daughter, fol. 143v, fig. 19, for woman at the well, fol. 215v, fig. 25. I do not find, as stated by Brubaker, that women are well-represented in Paris, gr. 510 compared with other ninth-century texts; see Brubaker (1999) 404, fn. 17 and 407, fn. 30; for further discussion of family and women, see also 69–70, and on 'gender balance', 264, 268, 271, 273.

60   For examples of these, see Maguire (1981) figs 75–86.

and, from puberty, are depicted joined to the world of older or mature women. But perhaps youth is shown through bare heads and loose hair, except in the case of the Virgin, where the depiction of modesty required clothing from head to foot. Female protagonists in the gospels are few, but one who is youthful is Salome, and she is often shown bareheaded and slender, though again this may be associated with promiscuity. An early portrayal can be seen in the sixth-century *Sinope Gospels*, Paris, suppl. gr. 1286, where she appears crowned and dressed in a full-length gown.[61] However, again, she is not depicted as a child, but as

Fig. 2.11 Paris, Bibliothèque nationale, gr. 923, fol. 142r, second half of the ninth century. A money lender, seated with his money box, gives a loan to a man, who is depicted as being much smaller, while another begs for help. Bibliothèque nationale de France

a young woman. While adolescent boys are distinguished from their elders and from little boys, girls move quickly from girlhood to adulthood.

A further group of manuscripts contains imagery of children and the young, and one that to me seems unexpected, the marginal illustrations of the *Homilies of Gregory of Nazianzos*. Gregory was a fourth-century bishop of Constantinople who formerly lived as a monk in Cappadocia and returned there in his later years. In addition to his many poems and letters, his homilies, or sermons, became particularly influential. From the eleventh century the so-called liturgical homilies, of which there are 16, were produced in illustrated manuscripts with the homilies arranged according to the liturgical year. Thirty-six illuminated manuscripts appear to have survived, but only 20 of these have illustrations for most of the homilies.[62] While children, such as the Maccabees (the second-century BC Jewish family who were martyred by the Syrians), appear in several codices in the headpieces and principal parts of decoration, nonspecific children involved in daily activities are depicted in some of the decorated initials and margins. These appear in five of the codices, Paris, gr. 550, Turin, Univ. Lib. C. I. 6, Sinai, 339, Vatican, gr. 463, and Athos, Dionysiou, 61, although the first two contain the majority of the

---

61   See Grabar (1948b) 11–12, pl. 1, figs 1–2; for an analysis of Salome in early texts, see Webb (1997) 119–148.

62   These are collectively most accessible in Galavaris (1969); for the Sinai and Turin manuscripts and illustrations reflecting secular life, see Grabar (1960) 123–146, figs 34, 35; on the group of manuscripts, see Galavaris (1969) 13.

images of children. The representations do not directly illustrate Gregory's words, but sometimes embellish his message and can diverge from the textual themes. They are not directly repeated in extant manuscripts, which suggests that the inclusion of child marginalia was an independent choice of the patron or artist and reflected his or her interests.

This is intriguing, since at least two of the manuscripts are associated with monasticism. The twelfth-century Sinai manuscript was dedicated by Joseph Hagioglykerites, the abbot of the Pantokrator monastery, to the monastery of the Theotokos Pantanassa on the island of Glykeria; the Vatican manuscript was written by a monk from the monastery of Galakrinon in Constantinople, in 1062.[63] The Turin and Paris manuscripts may also have had monastic ties: the eleventh-century Turin manuscript is perhaps from Constantinople, and the twelfth-century Paris manuscript was bound in the fourteenth century by a monk, perhaps from Chalkidike.[64] The choice of imagery must have been intended to serve some meaning. The inclusion of unique marginal illustrations suggests the artists freely supplemented their own images. These were often associated with children and games and with fun and entertainment, of which the church ostensibly disapproved and yet to which it could also be receptive. The motifs of youth are light-hearted and full of pleasure, which contrasts with the seriousness of Gregory's texts.

Although Galavaris discusses these illustrations under the heading 'decorative miniatures', the Turin manuscript contains two miniatures where 'decorative' is probably a misnomer, since the images also act metaphorically and didactically.[65] In Gregory's funeral oration for Saint Basil, in which he talks about Basil's ability to give spiritual nurture, the idea that the Logos nourishes mankind is illustrated in the Turin manuscript by a woman helping a small child take its first steps.[66] The child wears a long robe and may be male or female but is clearly very young. In a passage in this same manuscript where Gregory writes about the honour due to parents, this idea is illustrated by two young men, shown with slight bodies and clean-shaven faces, carrying their dead father on a bed.[67]

These are the only examples of parent–child relationships, and otherwise children in the margins are shown alone or with other children. These images do appear to be decorative and have no overt instructional purpose, nor are they required in the overall layout or structure of the illustrations. In two examples in the Paris manuscript, scenes of boys climbing trees supplement the headpieces. At the beginning of the third liturgical homily, the border of the headpiece curves around and up to form the roots and trunk of a tree in which a boy climbs and throws fruit down to his companions below (fig.

---

63   Text of dedication and colophon respectively in Galavaris (1969) 256, 251–252; see also Anderson (1979).

64   Galavaris (1969) 259–260, 242–245.

65   See Galavaris (1969) 166–171.

66   Oration 43, *Oratio in laudem Basilii magni*, PG 36:548; see Galavaris (1969) 167, fol. 83r, fig. 57.

67   Oration 43, PG 36:505; (1992 edn) 132; see Galavaris (1969) 168, fol. 69v, fig. 52.

2.12).[68] At the opening of the twelfth liturgical homily, the central motif shows Gregory meeting Gregory of Nyssa and, in the margin, a boy gives his friend a leg up into a tree.[69] This image of companionship and support may be related to the relationship between the church fathers, who were friends. In the same manuscript, at the beginning of the fifteenth liturgical homily and adjacent to a headpiece, showing Gregory, a monk, and a layman giving alms, boys are shown pushing a little girl, or so it appears, on a rope swing attached to a tree (fig. 2.13).[70] The boys wear breeches and the girl a robe or dress. These three images show clothed children at play, working collaboratively, and apparently happy. We identify them as children

Fig. 2.12 Paris, Bibliothèque nationale, gr. 550, fol. 30r, eleventh century. In this decoration at the corner of a headpiece a boy up a tree throws down fruit to his friends below. Bibliothèque nationale de France

because they are not full height, but also their activities associate them with childhood. We differentiate them as girls or boys according to their dress, which seems viable. In this codex, each headpiece has a marginal illustration of this type on the outer edge of the page. Others include trees filled with birds, and birds or hares frolicking in elaborate ornamented stands. These are associated with nature and liveliness, as are the children.

This Paris manuscript contains several other scenes, which are in the margins but not next to headpieces, portraying naked boys or youths performing. In three separate examples, a single naked boy is seen playing with a dog, standing on a rabbit with a hoop in his hand, and waving a branch.[71] A further image shows a dancing youth holding an elaborate headdress with an animal on top (fig. 2.14).[72] Three more naked boys are involved together: two stand on bird-like animals with their arms around each other's necks while a third smaller boy jumps in the air holding something, perhaps a ball, to his body (fig. 2.15).[73] Again the figures are identified with youth, in some cases by their height, which appears less than that of a man, and by their lack of beards and slender bodies; they are not fully grown men. These scenes are associated more with display than with games: the nakedness of the boys, the animals under

68   Oration 44, *Oratio in novam dominicam*, PG 36:608; see Galavaris (1969) 166, fol. 30r, fig. 409.

69   Oration 11, *Oratio ad Gregorium Nyssenum*, PG 35:832; (1995 edn) 328; see Galavaris (1969) fol. 204r, fig. 416.

70   Oration 14, *De pauperum amore*, PG 35:858; See Galavaris (1969) 167, fol. 251r, fig. 426.

71   See Galavaris (1969) 167, fol. 100r , fig. 420, fol. 6r, fig. 403, fol. 9v, fig. 406.

72   See Galavaris (1969) fol. 99v, fig. 418.

73   See Galavaris (1969) fol. 6v, fig. 404.

Fig. 2.13 Paris, Bibliothèque nationale, gr. 550, fol. 251r, eleventh century. At the side of a headpiece, a small child is pushed on a swing hung from a tree while another looks on. Bibliothèque nationale de France

Fig. 2.14 Paris, Bibliothèque nationale, gr. 550, fol. 99v, eleventh century. In the margin of the manuscript a naked youth performs a dance or acrobatics while holding an elaborate ornament on his head and balancing on a fancy footstool. Bibliothèque nationale de France

their control and their air of exhibition, emphasized by the fact that they tend to stand on animals or decorated pedestals, imply that they are performing. Another image, this one next to a headpiece showing Basil's *koimesis* (dormition) at the beginning of liturgical homily nine, depicts a youth preparing to attack a bear; his stance with foot raised and arm held back holding a stick also suggests performance (fig. 2.16).[74]

Illustrations in the other manuscripts also show children performing; these are not always older children. An image in the Vatican text depicts a very small child doing acrobatics on the head of an adult (fig. 2.17).[75] Similarly, in the Turin codex, a tiny child climbs a pole, apparently held in the mouth or on the head of an adult, while another small child balances a crossbeam; and again, in the Sinai codex, a child hangs from a rope (fig. 2.18).[76] Further images show the public games and dancers, jugglers, acrobats, wrestlers and flute players. In the Turin manuscript, two young snake charmers appear naked, while a naked acrobat arches his body back to form a bridge while balancing on the heads of two comrades.[77] In other cases, the performers are dressed, such as in miniatures showing an acrobat walking on a ball and a juggler.[78] If we read these images as realistic depictions, children apparently performed from a young age, and their work was considered sufficiently morally blameless to be included in a religious book.

None of these portrayals appears directly related to the text, but the frequency of the motifs gives the sense of a secondary visual field running

74   Oration 43, *PG* 36:493; See Galavaris (1969) fol. 94v, fig. 417.
75   See Galavaris (1969) 170, fol. 184r, fig. 84.
76   See Grabar (1960) figs 35a, 34a.
77   See Galavaris (1969) fol. 68r, fig. 51; fol. 67r, fig. 49.
78   See Galavaris (1969) fol. 73v, fig. 54; fol. 72r, fig. 53.

parallel but unrelated to the main imagery.[79] The headpieces concern religious events from the scriptures or from the life of Gregory, and some of the figurative initials show biblical events or church grandees, but many of the marginal illustrations depict apparently nonreligious figures engaged in secular activities. And in the Paris manuscript, these nonreligious scenes all concern young people involved in performance and entertainment of some kind.

The theme of the marginalia is not simply children or childhood, but children and youths as performers. Children associated with their parents appear in relatively prominent places adjacent to headpieces in scenes related to the texts and serve in didactic ways; children picking apples or playing with swings are seen in similar positions; but children as entertainers are marginal in a double sense, pictorially and socially. They appear on the edge of the page, as light-hearted, flamboyant exhibitionists. But also they are professionals and belong to the world of players, working for their livelihood either in family troupes or independently, perhaps as slaves or orphans. How can we explain that the artists of the Gregorian homilies garnished their pages, full of moral reflections and theological maxims, with images of children as public entertainers?

Fig. 2.15 Paris, Bibliothèque nationale, gr. 550, fol. 6v, eleventh century. As a marginal decoration three naked youths perform acrobatic tricks. Bibliothèque nationale de France

Fig. 2.16 Paris, Bibliothèque nationale, gr. 550, fol. 94v, eleventh century. Beside the headpiece and above a decorated initial, a boy draws back his sword as if preparing to fight a bear. Bibliothèque nationale de France

Grabar points out that acrobats, because of their elastic bodies, are suitable material for figurative initials but this can hardly be the only reason for their use.[80] The children fulfil, but perhaps also contravene, our expectations about childhood. They both play games and perform tricks, suggesting various views of childhood. Again, one questions who were the creators and readers

79   On marginalia in medieval art, see Camille (1992); for a critique of Camille, see Hamburger (1993) 319–326.

80   Grabar (1960) 144.

of these manuscripts. Perhaps our initial image of monasteries as childless and celibate leads us to overlook the presence of children in many of them, particularly those which ran schools, but also others which apparently took in orphan children, as, for instance, St John on Patmos.[81] The Pantokrator monastery, where the abbot who dedicated the Sinai manuscript lived, certainly had an orphanage and children were used as candle bearers.[82] There are complicated issues of the associations of these manuscripts to each other and to related manuscripts and the possible use of models.[83] We certainly do not know if any of these manuscripts were intended to be used by children. The corollary is of course, were they perhaps illustrated by young people who incorporated their own imagery? Both these questions will undoubtedly remain unanswered, but whether the books had imperial, aristocratic or monastic patronage we cannot rule out the participation of young people in both their creation and reception.

Another seemingly incongruous site for festive imagery is the tower staircases at S. Sophia in Kiev, dated to the eleventh century, where the wall paintings depict various scenes from the hippodrome.[84] They show the royal family viewing wild animal hunts, acrobats, including a child climbing a pole balanced on an adult's shoulders, and musicians.[85] The towers are separate from the main part of the church; but the north tower does lead directly into the inner gallery on the ground floor, so there is a close tie between the images and sacred space. The paintings demonstrate how the Kievan royalty embraced Byzantine courtly life and were apparently untroubled by its representation close to religious

---

81   Miklosich and Müller (1860–1890) VI, 83; Thomas and Hero, (2000) B6, 596.
82   On issues of where the manuscript was made, see Nelson (1987) 75.
83   On this, see, for instance, Anderson (1979) and Nelson (1987).
84   Discussed in Grabar (1935) 103–117; for bibliography on the church, see Chapter 5, fn. 76 below.
85   See Grabar (1960) figs 22 a, b, c, 23.

practice. Other entertainers decorate an ivory pyxis, probably dated to the fifteenth century, now at Dumbarton Oaks.[86] Here, two imperial children, each flanked by his or her parents, are honoured, while a band of dancers and musicians encircle the back of the container. Nicolas Oikonomidès has suggested that the children are John VIII Palaiologos and Andronikos V, who at the time of their fathers' peacemaking in 1403 would be aged about 11 and perhaps three.[87] Whoever the subjects are, clearly children, even imperial children, could be comfortably associated with such display. And texts also record children performing in the palace. For instance, in the tenth century, Liudprand of Cremona was astonished by a performance given in the *triclinium* of 19 couches, in which two boys, dressed only with a cloth around their bellies, performed on a wooden bar balanced on the head of a man.[88]

Entertainment was associated with imperial patronage through the games in the hippodrome. This influence may have legitimized and sanctioned performance arts in religious contexts. Even though performers were generally considered lower members of society, they had access to the elite. Emperors and the well-born, particularly young men, gave stage performances and competed in the games.[89] And performers and athletes were admired and could be influential.[90] Acrobats, dancers and musicians had a flexible place in the social scale. Imperial and religious ceremony, at the exclusive end of society, was so closely associated that the relation of secular and spiritual contexts was not necessarily strained. Similarly, in the Gregory illustrations, there is no tension between morally religious and playfully nonreligious imagery, although clearly the one is central and the other peripheral. Imperial patronage of festivities was not necessarily highbrow, but designed to give entertainment and pleasure to the populace at large, as well as to the imperial court, who attended in force.

A further area worth exploring is the depiction of childlike figures in certain crowd scenes in illustrations from both the Old and the New Testaments. These are interesting in terms of gauging how children in generalized situations might differ from adults and what is intended by their inclusion. Such representations are often standardized, and similar groupings or gestures are repeated in various manuscripts, showing the recurring use of certain motifs over an extended period of time. The most common scenes with children are the crossing of the Red Sea, the entry into Jerusalem and the multiplication of the loaves and fishes.

The portrayal of the crossing of the Red Sea derives from Jewish art and can be seen in the wall painting from the synagogue at Dura Europos, dated prior to AD 256 and now in Damascus.[91] A very small figure, only about a third as

---

86   Grabar (1960) 123–146; Oikonomidès (1977) 329–339.

87   On Andronikos, see Dennis (1967).

88   Liudprand, *Antapodosis*; for text, see (1998 edn) book VI, 8, 9; and for translation, see (1930 edn) 210; Grabar (1960) 137.

89   On early evidence, see Roueché (1993) 136.

90   On this, see Roueché (1993) 50–53 and appendix 3.

91   Weitzmann and Kessler (1990) 38–39, figs 5, 48, 49; Kraeling (1956) 79–80, l. LII.

tall as the adults, pulls on his parent's right hand, disrupting the orderly line of figures crossing the sea's path. The adults mostly wear white tunics, but he is in a short blue tunic and so stands out. The child is not necessarily male, but I shall refer to him as such. We know that he is a child from his size, his gesture and his dress. A similar image reappears frequently in portrayals of the scene. For example, in the tenth-century *Paris Psalter*, Paris, gr. 139, the child leans his head back, looking at the light in the sky, so that his face is horizontal.[92] This emphasizes his smallness and makes him stand out from the adults, but it is also the child who sees the light of God. The mother holds another child, this one naked, on her shoulders. Another image, showing the continued use of such iconography, is in the fourteenth-century psalter, Dionysiou, 65, in which children reach up to their parents and ride on their shoulders with their heads protruding above the adults (pl. 1).[93] The children stand out visually by breaking the perceptible order of the crowd and draw attention to their presence as individual elements, not as a group of children. But they are also closely integrated with the adults. The children's gestures suggest human ties and give a sense of realism. The action of being carried and turning to the parent emphasizes the children's youth and physical, and perhaps also spiritual or emotional, dependence. Children are not directly recorded in the biblical accounts of the crossing of the Red Sea, although they are mentioned as present in the exodus, and their inclusion refers to future generations of Hebrews (*Exodus* 12:37) and to the admonition to remind children of the exodus during Passover (*Exodus* 13:5–8).

In the entry into Jerusalem, conversely, the children can take on protagonists' roles. They are often standing next to Christ's path, climbing the trees to take a better look at him, or laying their cloaks before him. Again, iconographic elements are often repeated or developed. Early examples are in a fifth-century limestone relief from the church of St John Studios and in the *Rossano Gospels*, where three little children run forward in front of Christ.[94] In a tenth-century ivory in Berlin, two boys straddle a tree, one rides on his mother's shoulders, another grasps his father's hand, two others stretch cloths beneath Christ's donkey, and a final one sits in the foreground pulling a thorn from his foot.[95] In a thirteenth-century example in Iveron, 5, three children are closest to Christ, two at the head of the donkey as if leading it, and one laying his cloak on the ground. A further child sits in his mother's arms.[96] Several examples portray this familial intimacy with parents holding or embracing children. Unusual representations depict all those welcoming Christ as children, as in a wall painting at Karanlık kilise in Göreme, Cappadocia (fig. 2.19).[97] In this scene the children form a group, all looking very similar, ostensibly all male, and

---

92   See Cutler (1984) fol. 419v, fig. 253.
93   *Athos* (1974) I, 421, fol. 202v, fig. 128.
94   Talbot Rice (1959) pl. II.
95   Evans and Wixom (1997) n. 99; on the *spinario*, see Mouriki (1970–1972) 53–66.
96   *Athos* (1975) II, fol. 423r, fig. 37.
97   For Karanlık, see Restle (1967) II, fig. 234. The scroll in Jerusalem, mentioned in Grabar (1954) 175, fig. 14, as having only children, actually includes adults in the initial.

dressed identically, with short dark hair and light robes. Again the children are given simple identification by clear differentiation in size and aspect from the adults: there is no mistaking who are the children.

In the biblical account of the entry, children are not mentioned as present at the city gates, although shortly after they are in the temple crying 'Hosanna to the son of David' (*Matthew* 21:15), an association that is made in the Rossano Gospels and in the psalters. Children perhaps had a role in the Roman *adventus*, to which this scene is probably formally related, although even if iconographically dependent on the Roman precedents, in this new context they took on a Christian meaning.[98] The entry into Jerusalem is also perhaps associated with scenes of the dedication of the temple, such as at Dura. Here, five children are present, and one waves a palm branch, which is also associated with the feast of Tabernacles.[99]

The *spinario* figure in the entry, included after iconoclasm, symbolizes the removal of sin by the coming of Christ.[100] The *spinario* is always young, a reference to children's acceptance of Christ. Homilies glorify the part of children in the events of Palm Sunday, such as one by Cyril of Alexandria, who praises their recognition of Christ, in contrast to the adults' rejection of him, leading to his crucifixion.[101] It appears that children from early times were included in the scene and so we do not know whether theological commentaries, such as Cyril's, were prompted by the visual portrayals or by theological thinking. I suspect that children were typically depicted in crowd scenes, as children were present in crowds, and that the doctrinal commentary followed. The insertion of the *spinario* indicates that the portrayal of a child can have a forceful theological and symbolic meaning. The presence of children in scenes of the multiplication of the loaves and fishes also goes back to early examples, as can be seen in the sixth-century *Sinope Gospels*, Paris, suppl. gr. 1286.[102] Again, in the thirteenth-century Iveron, 5, children also take part (fig. 2.20).[103] A child reaches for food from one of the apostles, and a group of four play in the bottom right, with two children watching while two others wrestle. In the gospel account, the five barley loaves and two fishes belonged to a boy, so the presence of children is not unexpected (*John* 6:9).[104] Other scenes of wrestling occur in the entry to Jerusalem, as in Paris, gr. 54, and were perhaps

---

98   For some discussion of this in relation to Cappadocian wall paintings, see Antonopoulos (1986) 275.

99   Weitzmann and Kessler (1990) 94–98, figs 134–135; Kraeling (1956) 113–117, pl. LVIII.

100 Mouriki (1970–1972) 53–66, with textual references.

101 Homily 13, *PG* 77:1053–1057; Mouriki (1970–1972) 62–63.

102 See Grabar (1948b) 13, fol. 15r, pl. III.

103 *Athos* (1975) II, 298, fol. 63v, fig. 13.

104 See Mouriki (1970–1972) 60, and fn. 49, who refers to wrestling boys in the baptism of the Jews, and the baptism of Christ, as at Kariye Camii; see Underwood (1966–1975) II, pls 214, 243; although, in the second, the boys are playing, perhaps dice, not wrestling. She refers to a child taking off its shoe in Moscow, 146 (State Historical Museum) (Galavaris (1969) fol. 145, fig. 13), but this is not necessarily a child (60–61)0.

Fig. 2.19 Göreme, Karanlık kilise, eleventh century. A painting in the 'dark' church, shows the entry into Jerusalem. One child is climbing a tree to get a better view while a group of children prepare to lay down an elaborate garment for Christ to step on. © A Turizm Yayinlari

'borrowed' from the loaves and fishes scene.[105] To my mind, it is questionable whether portrayals of wrestling children are symbolic of a negative force and it seems more likely that the images simply portray the activities of the young as they pass the day with the adults.

Children also appear in two fourteenth-century baptismal wall paintings, one at the Hodegetria or Aphendiko church in the monastery of Brontocheion

105 Lazarev (1967) fol. 55v, fig. 386; Mouriki (1970–1972) 61, n. 51.

in Mistra, and one at the Old Metropolis in Berroia.[106] Both scenes show children in secondary roles. At Mistra, children, who are now very hard to discern, operate a windlass drawing up a net, a boy holds a rope attached to a net, a naked boy stands on a pillar, two boys sit on the right river bank and a girl is seated picking flowers. At Berroia, a girl and three boys run or dance over a bridge, four youths turn a windlass to haul in a net which contains a chubby naked boy or putto laying on his back, a naked boy sits on a rock on the left bank, another boy sits also on the ground and a woman dips a child upside down into the Jordan.[107] Rebirth is associated with baptism and explicitly so by Gregory of Nazianzos in his homily on baptism.[108] As Doula Mouriki points out, this is highlighted in the opening illustration in the eleventh-century manuscript of the homilies, Moscow, Vlad. 146, where children dive and swim in the river, and a woman dips in her child, holding him by the arms.[109] While the scenes can be attributed to theological meaning, they also refer to daily life in which children have a distinct role, running along to view the special occasion, playing in the water and taking part in fishing activities.

Given that there are iconographic or theological reasons for the inclusion of the children, how are they depicted? On the surface the images present a cross-cut of society; yet they do not portray a naturalistic progression of children of different heights and ages up to adulthood, but rather distinct age groups or phases of life: babes in arms, small children and full-grown adults, some of whom are usually bearded to indicate age. We rarely see older children, or ones whom we would consider adolescent. This suggests that the children are included to give a sense of childhood, as opposed to adulthood, and not to represent a realistic span of life.

The children in the crowd scenes mentioned appear to be all boys in that they have short hair, although this may be a misapprehension. If some are girls, then they are not apparently clearly differentiated from the boys. It is possible that this iconography does not denote sex, and these figures could represent either gender, since small girls and boys appear to have worn the same clothing; though this seems unlikely, and they are probably male.[110] In scenes of Christ teaching, as in the eleventh-century gospel lectionary Dionysiou, 587m, the crowd is entirely male which may indicate that the scene takes place within a male-only area of the temple (pl. 2).[111] Yet in other crowd scenes, women are present. It is not surprising that in biblical scenes there are more images of young male than female protagonists, since men take the prominent roles in the narrative, yet in the crowd scenes where women are

---

106 Mouriki (1983).

107 Mouriki identifies the youths working the windlass as children, but really they must be youths or men since they have distinct muscles and one might even be bald; see Mouriki (1983) 461.

108 *PG* 36:360.

109   Mouriki (1983) 463, 470, fol. 145, fig. 12; Galavaris (1969) 93, fig. 13.

110 On the similarity of male and female clothing, see Kazhdan (1998) 13–15.

111 *Athos* (1974) I, 437, fol. 19v, fig. 203.

ὐ χρείαμ ἐχουσι μαπ6ρθᾶ·

Fig. 2.20 Athos, Iveron, 5, fol. 63v, thirteenth century. In this illustration of the multiplication of the loaves and fishes, a small boy in the centre follows an apostle to get some food while two boys wrestle in the bottom right corner, a scene often included

present, one would expect to see a combination of male and female children. Female children of the upper classes were probably largely secluded within the house, but girls of the lower classes would not have been kept at home since this was not the practice of their mothers.[112] Depictions of crowd scenes make it clear that all women were not secluded in Byzantine society, and clearly some women were well-integrated into everyday life both inside and outside the home. The apparent absence of small girls and the limited age variation suggest that the boy figures are stereotypes that developed in the iconography and therefore that the child's body is largely symbolic of childhood itself and did not necessarily symbolize only male childhood.

112 For the seclusion of women, see Kazhdan (1998), who gives an alternate view to that of Laiou (women had relative freedom in the twelfth century, but otherwise were confined), and finds that practice probably varied; see Laiou (1981) 249–260.

The small children often wear short tunics, usually white or brown, sometimes with coloured borders at the neck and hem. This dress may well portray contemporary custom, but because it is depicted as distinct from the usually brighter coloured garments worn by men and women, it serves to evoke and define the perception of a child. Some adults do wear short tunics, although these usually appear to be those who are poor or slaves. Children within a given scene can all be dressed identically, forming a group among themselves and standing for children as a class, unlike the adults, who are more typically dressed individually. The children in the Berlin panel do not wear apparently contemporary clothing but are dressed in classical-style garments, one of which is tunic-like but tied at the waist, and the others seem to drape around the bodies, often leaving one shoulder bare. The children appear to be derived from classical models, but they are differentiated from the adults.

However, children who are singled out do have differentiated clothing and can be posed and portrayed in isolating and distinctive ways. In the illustration already mentioned in the Dionysiou lectionary, showing Christ teaching, a group of men and three children stand on either side of steps representing a synthronon. The children are all small and dressed in white tunics with green borders elaborated on the shoulders and hems. One sits in a man's arms, another on someone's shoulders, while a third hangs onto an adult's hand. Yet, when in this same manuscript one child is singled out by Christ as an exemplar, he appears in a slightly different costume, perhaps because he is a little older but also to distinguish him (fig. 2.21). [113] His garment is longer, has brown borders and does not have elaborations on the borders down the front, at the shoulders and at the hem. Christ is depicted in the centre of the painting, laying his hand on the child. Men look on from a distance to the right, but the child is very much the focus of the composition. Whereas the children in the crowd scene are normally fleshy, this child looks scrawny and rather overwhelmed. Christ is using him as a symbol of childhood, and it is this that he remains in the image. He contrasts with the children in the former scene, as he stands alone, isolated by the space around him, but protected by Christ's hand on his head and the angel guarding him to the left.

Children in these crowd scenes appear to portray a conventional image of a child, short in stature, affiliated with adults, but also, when perhaps a little older, forming a group amongst themselves. The children are either not gender specific or they are all male; but the single gender appears to convey an image of childhood that has associated with it both dependency on and independence from adults as well as integration with both adults and with peers. Children look to adults for nurture and play robustly with each other yet also stand in relation to Christ or to the sacred.

Children are frequently imaged as small, round-bodied and playful, sometimes grouped together and often in the adult world but not part of it. In certain situations they are visually similar to images of erotes, the pagan

113 See *Athos* (1974) I, fol. 38v, fig. 214.

Fig. 2.21 Athos, Dionysiou, 587m, fol. 38v, eleventh century. Christ places his hand on a child's head, pointing to him as an example for adults

symbols of love and desire, which sometimes have sexual connotations.[114] Erotes are usually depicted as winged figures with childlike bodies, and as children, although some erotes are also wingless, with apparently little difference in meaning. Erotes and children can appear in analogous situations where both are sometimes symbolic of a range of emotions, such as love and desire, playfulness and mischief, purity and eternity. Is there anything this can tell us about the intellectual, societal and religious perceptions of childhood, questioning whether there is some conceptual as well as visual relation between the two?

This is conceptually intriguing, since childhood is, and often has been since antiquity, associated with sexual innocence. This has been emphasized in Christianity, although teachings also suggested that children had eroticized minds and bodies. On the side of innocence, Origen saw the child as a paradigm of sexual abstinence and emotional restraint, and Ambrose identified the child's strength in innocence and renunciation of power.[115] On the other hand, Basil of Ancyra considered all children were sexual after weaning.[116] Similarly,

114 This includes figures variously referred to as putti, erotes, amorini and cupids, as these terms tend to be used interchangeably.

115 Origen, *Commentary on Matthew* XIII; Klosterman (1935); *PG* 13:1134–1138; Ambrose, *De excessu fratris sui satyri*, *PL* 16:1345–1414, esp. 1349–1350; on this, see Currie (1993) 40–41.

116 Basil of Ancyra, *On virginity*, *PG* 30:801 (attributed to Basil the Great); Currie (1993) 119.

Jerome, in Eusebius's *Epistula*, used advice regarding sexuality in talking about the education of a seven-year-old.[117] Clearly, there was no consensus about this. Any perceptible association between children and erotes may be incidental, but it needs investigating. Erotes persisted in Byzantium as part of the classical iconography and style that was continuously re-employed and redefined. The pagan eros visually and conceptually became incorporated into the Christian cherub, and as children appear to be associated with erotes, so are they with cherubs and angels. As Byzantine art integrated imagery from antiquity, so erotes were used in various contexts with a complex series of meanings, some of which are yet to be understood. To what extent do children and erotes have visual similarities and how might any analogy between the two affect our view of childhood in Byzantium?

As the personification of love and desire in Greek mythology, Eros is depicted as a child, both with and without wings, and his characteristic role is to cause mischief and emotional trouble, by inflaming mankind's passions with a torch or arrows.[118] Other gods may grow up and be represented as adults, but in visual representation Eros devolves, in about 300 BC from an adolescent into a child, an attractive, well-rounded little boy, generally with an impish but sensual demeanour, although he is sometimes still portrayed as an adolescent.[119] The relation between childhood and physical love is an ancient association, and although one speculates that it perhaps indicates an elision between fecundity and children, in fact Eros's role is far more closely aligned with Dionysiac pleasure than with fertility. His childlike presence is more probably associated with mischief, but he is also the harbinger of passions, which often cause disruption and suffering. His roles are varied and disparate: he becomes a symbol of free expression, light-hearted frolicking, as well as gratification and erotic fulfilment.

From Eros the single god, signifying love and its pernicious tormenting, its mischievous charm, and its erotic pleasure, erotes, as multiples of an idea, are widely employed. These figures resemble the single Eros, and they carry his associations so that Eros's symbolism becomes multifaceted, nonspecific and broadly implemented. Erotes become allegorized versions of mankind, often seen undertaking human tasks; they become background figures signifying desires or external forces and largely decorative clues to environments and moods. In Christianity they have an ill-defined role that assimilates metaphorical associations of the eucharist, resurrection and eternity, but they never seem to entirely lose their earlier signification.

The surviving wall paintings at Pompeii indicate the variety and popularity of erotes imagery in antiquity. Both Eros as singular deity and erotes as plural

---

117 Jerome, *Sancti Eusebii Hieronymi epistulae*, ed. Hilberg (1912) letter 107: Ad laetem de institutione filiae; Currie (1993) 121.

118 *LIMC* III, 'Eros' 850–942, 'Eros/amor/cupido' 952–1049; Grimal (1991) 143.

119 Stuveras (1969) 7; Stuveras associates this with an increased interest in children, which seems hard to prove; for bibliography and discussion of the various dates for this transition, see Stuveras (1969) 7–12.

allegorizations appear as attendants to Venus.[120] At the House of the Vettii repeated scenes show erotes employed in various scenes of daily life.[121] Full of fun and childish energy, the short, plump figures suggest children at play at adult tasks; tasks become whimsical and appealing, animated with associations of love and humour, although they perhaps good-naturedly mock man's daily toil.

Images of children hunting, riding chariots, and playing games all feature on Roman children's sarcophagi, which are the richest source of imagery associated with children in that period.[122] Adults also appear performing comparable activities, but not as often as children. Erotes are frequently portrayed on sarcophagi for both adults and children.[123] In some sarcophagi, the age of the erotes is possibly related to the age of the human child, and an eros may stand in for the child and become its personification in death.[124] As Janet Huskinson has shown, cupids on children's sarcophagi appear in various settings, both as Dionysos and as part of his *thiasos*, working in the grape harvest, carrying arms or making armour (presumably for Mars), hunting, racing chariots, playing games and in marine settings.[125] They are therefore in scenes very similar to those depicting children, although sometimes children can take their original place, as in a sarcophagus where children, instead of erotes, bring in the harvest.[126] The lack of visual clarity as to the identification of the child or eros figure indicates the lack of fine distinctions between them and suggests not only visual but also conceptual associations.

Huskinson's discussion of cupids raises many pertinent issues, including how cupid imagery 'often deals with the interface of adult and child, of reality and metaphor'. Cupids exist outside the confines of normal life, such as time and gender. She identifies a 'self-irony' that can 'emasculate' what they do and extend to a certain genderlessness.[127] This, in my opinion, is sometimes the case, but the cupids are mostly male and their activities are rather boyish. Importantly, cupids' behaviour is often outside society's norms, and so, as Huskinson states, they can mediate 'between the worlds of adult and child, mortal and immortal, and so embody the complexity of human experience'.[128] Overall the children's sarcophagi suggest a sensitivity and warmth towards children and their interests, as seen at Piazza Armerina. However, the issue of irony recurs, and one has to ask to what extent children and erotes were used

---

120 As in the workshop of Verecundus, and the House of Venus; see Guzzo and d'Ambrosio (1998) 128, 104.

121 See Clarke (1991) 214–218, pls 12, 13, figs 124–128.

122 For specific examples, see Huskinson (1996) 9–10, 15–18; for scenes from everyday life, see for example Amedick (1991) n. 46, pl. 80.1, 2, 3, n. 118, pl. 81. 1, 2, 3, 4.

123 Huskinson (1996) 41–51; for child and adult sarcophagi with grape harvesting, see Bielefeld (1997); for a compilation of erotes and circus-related sarcophagi, see Schauenburg (1995).

124 *LIMC* III, 1043–1044; Huskinson (1996) 41, 105.

125 Huskinson (1996) 41–51.

126 For example, see Bielefeld (1997) n. 140, pls 18–19.

127 Huskinson (1996) 105.

128 Huskinson (1996) 105, 107.

as adult substitutes to take a paradoxical or humorously mocking view at the bitterness or frailty of human life. I do not find conclusive evidence for this.

We can return to Piazza Armerina to explore the depiction of erotes in the floors and to assess further the relation of the imagery of children and of erotes. In a room off the main peristyle and adjacent to the room with the small hunt, cupids are shown in a fishing scene. The erotes are not generalized, but individuated, some naked and some clothed, all with short hair and wings, and all involved in some activity: hauling on the net, riding on a dolphin or rowing. Other scenes of erotes are found off the large open air atrium, the xystus that is to the south of the complex. The erotes are in adjoining rooms on the north and on the south side; on the south they are shown fishing, and on the north they are involved with viniculture: cultivating vines and harvesting and pressing the grapes.[129] The peristyle and the xystus are the grandest spaces in the villa. Guests would have been led aside into the adjacent rooms bordering the colonnades that are decorated with girls dancing and exercising, with men and boys hunting and worshipping, with Orpheus serenading the animals and with the erotes hunting and fishing. The fishing mosaic is one room back from the peristyle and therefore has an aspect of separation and seclusion. The backdrop shows a resplendent villa with a colonnaded walkway, edged with fine trees. It depicts fashionable villa culture and symbolizes the richness of the estate as well as the teeming life of the sea.

The floor with the boys hunting is in an adjacent room. Both these mosaics exemplify an idealized dominance of man over nature, in the countryside and in the water.[130] In the hunt, children tend animals and reap from the land; to a certain extent they behave like the erotes, who are man's agents, but also mythological beings, who cultivate the vine and garner from the waters. The mood of the mosaics of erotes is synchronized with those of children: they are light-hearted and active, with the figures animated and industrious. Although erotes and children are distinct and generally inhabit different worlds, the children operate in the same mode as the erotes: they race after animals, frolic gleefully and work industriously. The two domains intersect when the children, apparently individualized children, enter into the mythological world as supporters of Eros in his battle with Pan. The imagery suggests that children, in terms of what they do, the mood of their lives and the tenor of their activities, are not far from erotes. Just as erotes symbolize love, desire, joy, physical pleasure and are portrayed in industrious activities, particularly reaping the fruits of a luxuriant world, children have the same associations. They enjoy racing the bird-drawn chariots, spearing rabbits, gathering baskets of flowers and performing theatrical pieces, all proto-adult activities, but also the games of children.

Many images were adopted and transposed in Christianity: the sheep bearer became Christ, Nike became an angel, lambs became the apostles, but

---

129 See Carandini (1982) pls XXIII, XLVI, XLVII, XLVIII.

130 On the correlation between Roman culture, nature and its interpretation in painting, see Bergmann (1991) 48–70.

erotes remained erotes, and were accepted into Christian iconography with little change in meaning. Later, the same corporeal form signified cherubs, who are not part of the angelic orders but simply updated erotes transported from a pagan to a Christian context.[131] Confronted with the imagery of new Christianity, the viewer would recognize the familiar erotes and their connotations: the richness of life, pleasure, freedom, food, wine and love, as well as, perhaps, the new Christian gloss of the resurrection, the eucharist and eternal life. Erotes remain omnipresent in the early Christian world and firmly belong in both secular and sacred contexts. Children appear to be allied to these associations. While erotes revel in nature in the half-pagan half-Christian fourth-century world, they reappear in later Byzantine material, the most frequent context being Byzantine ivory boxes from the tenth and eleventh centuries, of which, perhaps the finest is the Veroli casket.[132] The one unifying motif between all but one of the panels on the box is the presence of wingless erotes. The Veroli casket and its close cousins are ostensibly devoid of Christian references, although their owners must have been orthodox Christians.[133] The erotes do not serve a Christian message, but reappear in their own right, sparking with life and revelry, mischievous and promiscuous.

We have seen that children in early domestic mosaics are characterized in daily activities, generally with positive connotations. They do simple rural tasks, such as hunting and tending to animals, but they also play extravagant games, which may or may not reflect reality, although it seems probable that affluent children rode little chariots and other children performed in plays and competed in games. The imagery used to decorate luxurious country villas was not dissimilar to that in Constantinople's finest palace, and the owners of both enjoyed representations of children involved in the concerns of childhood. These activities, perhaps mirroring adult pursuits, are not necessarily parodies of the adult sphere, but realistic or idealized views of children's worlds. Children played, but they also worked, as seen in the marginal illustrations to Gregory's homilies. Childhood was not a distinct phase marked only by activities that are associated with modern childhood, such as playing or learning, but a period in life with many options. Performers, slaves and servants could be young, and their portrayal was deemed valid decoration for luxury floors, religious books and politicized ivory diptychs.

Children could be visualized outside of familial milieux as independent figures and also integrated into a cultural context as well as located in settings associated with myth and fantasy. The erotes form a bridge between childhood and make-believe, but one which is not disassociated from the sacred and draws children into the symbolic vocabulary of Christian belief as insignia of mysterious concepts such as resurrection and eternity. But at the same time,

---

131 For mythological imagery and Christian art, see Huskinson (1974) 68–97, pls 3–6.
132 For recent bibliography, see Cutler in Evans and Wixom (1997) n. 153; Beckwith (1962); Goldschmidt and Weitzmann (1930, 1979 edn) I, 21.
133 On this point, see Cutler (1988) 27.

erotes do not lose their relation with ribaldry, fun and physical pleasure, connotations that cannot be excluded from concepts of childhood.

Our findings suggest that occasionally youths are associated with childish play, but more often they join in mature pursuits such as hunting, shepherding and soldiering. To an extent this enjoins us not to think of these as adult activities, but ones shared by the mature and the youthful alike. In the home, girls similarly took on mature positions at a young age and were involved in responsible activities. But there is nothing to suggest that youth was disregarded and, in the imagery reviewed, youth is for the most part defined and depicted. The portrayals of the young point to the primary place of children in various levels of society and their cohesive integration within it.

The issue of the depiction of childhood and its transition to adulthood will be explored more in the coming chapters. In examining representations of Christ and of the Virgin we shall look further at the portrayal of 'growing up' and the significance of childhood in figures of supreme religious authority. In investigating children and power, we shall question whether a sense of childhood is preserved in images of young rulers, and how secular authority might be associated with youth. In exploring young saints and martyrs, we shall review the childlike characteristics of the young and holy and question the portrayal of youthful adolescence found in many contexts. In the next chapter we shall look at the depiction of childhood in familial contexts, examining children's identities and connections in relation to a social framework and a potentially intimate adult world.

Chapter 3

Family

This chapter explores the cultural and societal context in which Byzantine children grew up and concerns the representation of the identities and relationships of children with their families, most usually with one or more parents or with siblings. It questions how important such ties were and the roles played by each member of the family, as well as the nature of the families. The discussion considers who is included or excluded in family arrangements and whether such groupings portray parents and their shared biological children, or a more limited or extensive and varied selection of people. It explores where such representations are found and what they reveal about attitudes towards the family and familial relationships as well as the role the images may have played in forming or reflecting societal attitudes towards children.

The term family is used to refer to a biological unit, and it is evident that children were typically closely associated with their parents, siblings and extended family members, including those gained through ritual kinship, and that they experienced the emotions and actions of love and responsibility towards one another. However, Byzantine children were also part of the larger 'family' provided by the monastic and secular church, other forms of kinship that offered sometimes physical but also societal and spiritual nurture. Children could leave the enclave of the family and join that of a monastery, thereby removing themselves from an earthly family to join a spiritual one, but one that also worked practically to provide material sustenance and care. This was a commonly accepted alternative for children who were then absorbed into the nonbiological but socially correlative structure provided by monasticism. But nonmonastic children were also obligated to the church, and in this way the Christian community contributed to, or sometimes competed with, the bonds of the institutional family. We shall see examples of children's affiliations with biological, societal and spiritual families.

Our contemporary society is concerned with the state of the family and particularly with rapid changes in perceptions of the nature of families and family life. Sociologists talk about shifts in the family environment, where the nuclear family is exchanged for a varied, perhaps more complex arrangement of people, in which close friends and blended families contribute to a more fluid social grouping. Scientific developments, such as surrogate parenting, raise controversial interpretations of the family. The understanding of parenthood is becoming more ambiguous and yet at the same time the recognition of blood ties is no less strong. Just as it may be hard for us to define our own sense of the family, similarly, it is impossible to determine a simple picture of the Byzantine family, and no attempt is made here to do so. The aim is to explore in what ways it was portrayed or handled, pictorially, looking at what elements within it were stressed, valued or omitted, and what this can tell us about the importance or meaning of the family in certain contexts.

The images are drawn from a wide chronological framework, which encourages a broad view of the questions and gives a range of perspectives. The discussion first examines late antique images in gold-glass portraits and then turns to two folios from the *Vienna Genesis*. Next, it explores ideas about family as presented in three sets of images from the seventh and eighth centuries, all church decorations in Rome and in Thessaloniki. The first portrays individual children in S. Demetrios in Thessaloniki, the second depicts the representation of the Maccabee family, a family of martyrs in S. Maria Antiqua in Rome, and the third presents the portrait of a donor family in the same church. This section also includes a brief look at sixth-century donor portraits in the Basilica Eufrasiana in Poreč and twelfth-century donor portraits in S. Clemente in Rome. The discussion then moves to fourteenth-century Constantinople, to explore the family presented in the *Lincoln College Typikon*, Lincoln College gr. 35, and to discuss some of the changing perceptions but also the persistent features of portrayals of the family in Byzantium. One overriding image of the family in any Christian society is Christ's own worldly family and in particular the nativity.

A group of early portraits, gold-glass medallions, present some views of family life in the first centuries AD.[1] This medium, formed by inserting an image in gold leaf between two layers of glass, is used for a wide range of subjects, both pagan and Christian, such as gods, legends, animals, Christ and the saints, and individual portraits; but the human family is also frequently portrayed. Some images, usually dated between the third and fifth centuries, coincide with the traditional late twentieth-century idea of a nuclear family, showing parents with a small child. While it has been argued that these were originally made as medallions, it seems that some of the portraits were first incorporated into the bottom of vases and were therefore functional in everyday life, although later the base with the image was cut off and used as a marker in the catacombs.

1   A useful catalogue, with bibliographies, remains Morey (1959); for extensive catalogue, see Cabrol and Leclercq (1923) 'Fonds de coupes' II, 1819–1859, esp. 1822, 1853–1856 on families; Garrucci (1857); and more recently, though not fully illustrated, Zanchi Roppo (1969); also Harden (1987) 267.

An example from the British Museum is indicative of this type and shows, apparently, a family group (fig. 3.1).[2] Busts of the parents appear large, while the child is diminutive in size, although portrayed in as much detail as her parents. A chi-rho symbol anointed with oil denotes Christian identity of the figures, and they are all named in an inscription. Another portrait, in the Vatican, depicts a small child, perhaps a boy, in front of his parents; another shows a couple with their children, portrayed in small scale in front of them; and a further rare example of a larger family, now fractured, portrays parents with two older daughters and two younger sons.[3] A particularly fine example is in Brescia. Dated between the third and fifth centuries, it shows the distinguished features, elegant hair and delicately draped clothes of a mother with her son and daughter.[4] Although the mother wears jewels and has an elaborate coiffure, the children are portrayed with equal attention to their appearance. Other glasses show a single parent with one child; for example, one in Paris shows a man with a small son; and a further example, in the Metropolitan Museum, portrays a mother with her son.[5]

The inscriptions often name the figures or wish them good fortune, but others refer to family relationships. In most cases the familial identity is plainly articulated: the busts of the children take the same form as those of the parents and the relationship is defined by the placement of the children between or in front of the parents. These portraits suggest small, intimate families, with sons and daughters figuring centrally. However, the choice of family members may have been selective, with only particular children shown, or, alternatively, others may have been depicted who were adopted or related less closely. The presence of one parent with a child or children may suggest the other parent was no longer living, or it may intentionally single out the relationship between one parent and his or her offspring. Similarly, a single child may denote that he or she is especially favoured, or alternatively the portrait may mark an occasion in the life of one of several children.

The range of subjects used for gold-glass is perhaps surprising. It combines pagan and Christian themes, but also bridges the secular and the spiritual. Some images appear consciously religious, while others embody secular well being. Figures are often blessed by a standing Christ, as in an example from the British Museum showing a married couple flanking Christ, who is himself shown very young. Similarly Christ is often depicted with two saints, such as an example in the Vatican, portraying Peter and Paul.[6] Children also are associated with Christ, as in the glass mentioned previously where the chi-rho denotes the Christian family. But other examples are seemingly devoid of religious meaning and serve to promote an image of secular family values. The gold-glass images had a dual function, with their first meaning imbedded

---

2   Morey (1959) n. 315, with earlier bibliography; most recently, Finaldi (2000) n. 11.
3   Morey (1959) nos. 5 (Zanchi Roppo (1969) n. 88) 59, 97.
4   Morey (1959) n. 237; also see Elsner (1998) 23, fig. 10.
5   Morey (1959) nos. 406, 452.
6   Morey (1959) nos. 310, 66.

in the use of the vessels in a practical world, perhaps as drinking cups. In this mode, the images of the family remind the user of family bonds, obligations or affection, and it seems likely they were made to mark particular successes or moments of transition in family life. Reused as markers for the catacombs, they signify the placement, marking and memory of a familial group, becoming a label or identifier.

While certainly not representative of all late Roman or early Christian families, these images provide exemplars of certain perceptions of family life at the beginning of our period and suggest strong affiliations and the valuing of children in a family setting.

In a related way, images portraying the Joseph story in the sixth-century porphyry manuscript known as the *Vienna Genesis*, Oesterreichische Nationalbibliothek, theol. gr. 31, refute views that families were not close in the medieval world.[7] Here, familial love, particularly fostered between males,

---

7   On the manuscript, see Buberl (1937); Gerstinger (1931); von Hartel and Wickhoff (1895); for a useful summary of Gerstinger, Wickhoff and Buberl, also see Wellesz (1960). The origin of the manuscript is disputed, with suggestions of Italy (Wickhoff) and Alexandria (Gerstinger).

is articulated in expressive terms. Jacob's affection for his youngest sons, Joseph and Benjamin, is accented, while the older brothers, perhaps united in calumny, have a concerted group identity. Granted these elements are in the text: the Hebraic narrative reflects Jewish emphasis on family ties and the customs of nomadic herders who, working and living together in family groups, are integrally dependent on one another. Yet, the illustrator, perhaps influenced by Jewish textual commentary, has emphasized the feeling between Joseph's family and gives attention to Benjamin's infancy and to Joseph's youth, as well as to more generic images of childhood.[8]

The page telling of Joseph's departure to visit his brothers contains four episodes within one illumination, two on both the upper and lower registers (pl. 3).[9] In the upper left, Jacob is seated in an informal setting, in a wooden chair with a round back and curved legs, which establishes a general sense of softness and intimacy in the image. The patriarch leans forward to caress the cheek of Joseph, who bends over taking his little brother, Benjamin, in his arms to bid him goodbye. Benjamin stands close to his father, between Jacob's legs, and raises his cheek to be kissed. All three are dressed in light blue tunics with black ornament, which seemingly identifies their close ties. Benjamin's childishness is emphasized: he looks to be about two or three, with short hair, and a large round head, characteristic of a little child. Joseph is not fully grown but has short, curly hair, a fresh, callow face, and retains youthful grace in his movements. The woman standing behind Joseph is apparently Bilhah, Rachel's maid.[10] In the next image, Benjamin epitomizes childish gestures as he stands crying with one fist in his mouth and the other raised to his cheek. Joseph steps out on the road to Schechem to find his brothers, guarded by an angel. Below he is seen getting directions and walking on, leaning forward in eager expectation of seeing his brothers, who meanwhile sight Joseph and plan to kill him.

The subsequent page tells the story of the attempt made by Potiphar's wife to seduce Joseph (pl. 4).[11] In these scenes, which transgress family mores and in sexual terms show that Joseph, in the eyes of a woman, is no longer a child, the artist is interested in familial imagery and perhaps provides pointers to the married and maternal state of Potiphar's wife and to Joseph's marital future. Adulterous seduction is on the surface, but underlying bonds relate to marriage and the family. In the top left, a lithe Joseph, dressed in a three-quarter-length tunic, black leggings and a purple cloak, tries to make his escape from Potiphar's wife, who grabs at the cloak. In the next episode, Joseph stands thoughtfully, his hand raised to his neck, looking back on the scene, apparently rather mystified and contemplating his escape. The other

---

8   These images insert children into the story where they are not originally part of the text; on the Jewish sources, see Levin (1972) 241–244; Gutmann (1973) 181–185; Gutmann (1966) 39–41 (briefly on the *Ashburnham Pentateuch*); Nordström (1955–1957) 489; also Kraemer (1989) 65–80.

9   See Wickhoff (1895) 15v, page 30; colour pls in Gerstinger (1931) unnumbered.

10   On the possible Midrash source of this figure, see Levin (1972) 242.

11   See Wickhoff (1895) fol. 16r, page 31.

figures in this register and the five beneath, of whom three are children, have not been firmly identified. It is speculated that they derive from Jewish legends or commentary.[12] The figure in the upper right is perhaps a spinning astrologer or fate, while next to Joseph a woman waves a painted rattle above the head of a little child, who sits up in a wooden crib.[13] This is possibly Potiphar's wife with the adopted child, Asenath, who later became Joseph's wife.[14] We therefore see a foretelling of Joseph's sexual or marital life. The other figures, as yet unidentified, show a woman embracing a babe in arms, and two women spinning, one of whom interacts with a small child at her knee. Clearly children, childhood and maternal care are central to the image. These representations show particular focus on familial bonds within a narrative context.

Joseph's story is an illustrative example of family relations and is found in many examples; but, equally, intimations, representations and emblems of family identity are evident in many biblical families from Adam and Eve and their sons, through Isaac, David and Solomon and leading to Christ's own family, a topic to be addressed in a later chapter.

We now turn to the church of S. Demetrios in Thessaloniki. The images here provide a preface to other portrayals of families within church settings, giving an alternate presentation of the depiction of familial and spiritual ties and the various responses such images provoke. In S. Demetrios there were three sets of mosaics that refer to children, but the most elaborate, a series of scenes depicting a young girl, Maria, is lost and now known only from watercolours. These will be discussed in the following chapter on children and sanctity. There are two other panels that portray children in the church, one from the earlier and one from the later part of the seventh century.[15] The first, thought to be prior to a fire ca. 620, is situated on the west end of the south aisle (pl. 5). Demetrios, the patron saint of the foundation, stands to the left in the orant position, while a beardless male and a younger boy, brothers perhaps, move forward in tandem towards the saint with their arms out towards him. They both face the viewer and neither is given place over the other. The older figure is still a youth, with the lack of beard giving him a look of immaturity. He has previously been identified as a woman, but this is not the case.[16] Rather, his fine features connote youth, and his hair can be seen to have the same formation as that of Demetrios. Both he and the smaller boy have short dark hair and covered hands. A further figure formerly stood to the left of the saint,

12   See Weitzmann (1977) 83; Levin (1972) 242–244.

13   Maureen O'Brien has questioned the identity of the astrologer or fate; see O'Brien (2000) 109–110.

14   The Jewish commentaries elide Potiphar with Potiphera, the father of Joseph's wife; on this, see Levin (1972) 243, esp. fn. 25.

15   Soteriou and Soteriou (1952) pls 62, 65 (in colour); Diehl, Le Tourneau, Saladin, hereafter Diehl (1918) I, 61–114, esp. 105–107, II, pl. XXXIII.2; Cormack (1985a) 50–94, esp. 80–83, 92, fig. 23; for extensive bibliography on S. Demetrios, see Cormack (1985b) 121–122; for style and dating issues, see Kitzinger (1958) 20–29 or (1976) 176–185, fig. 22; for S. Demetrios as a pilgrimage site, see Bakirtzis (2002).

16   Influentially, by Diehl (1918); see pl. XXXII.2.

although only the lower legs and bottom half of the robe remain. From the size of the feet it seems this also represented a child. The setting is verdant with trees and shrubs, but with allusions to a sacral landscape given by a vase on top of a column. Demetrios is apparently positioned outside his ciborion. The scene could represent Demetrios in a heavenly garden of paradise, or at home in his church, or a combination of the two.[17] The boys are not marked out as sanctified; in fact they seem like ordinary boys of some wealth, as their garments are richly coloured. The boys approach the saint with veiled hands to honour him and, while showing respect, they do not kneel down in supplication. We clearly see their individualized faces and it seems likely that their identity, although there are no inscriptions, must have been recognizable at the time the mosaic was created.

The children are not with their parents; together, as siblings or as associated young people, they honour the saint. One can speculate that parents of the children paid for the panel, yet it is intriguing that they are not represented, although of course they could have been portrayed in an adjacent image, now lost. Possibly Demetrios was seen to have helped the boys, perhaps to recover from an illness, and they are imaged giving thanks. We have no way of knowing whether their parents lived, or whether the children themselves had died and are shown in paradise, but clearly children's connections with saints could be visualized as independent relationships, apart from the presence of the parents. The biological family is omitted in favour of the association between child and saint.

This is clearly the case in the other extant portrayal of children in the church, which is positioned on the west-facing side of the north pier, one of four piers in front of the chancel (pl. 6). This mosaic is slightly later in date, being made after the ca. 620 fire as part of the reconstruction of the church. The mosaic is therefore facing the viewer entering the church and so appears to be in a prominent location. It is close to the sanctuary and highly visible. A youthful saint is shown between two children. His hair is longer and curlier than in the depictions of Demetrios in the church, and it is more likely that he represents Saint Bakchos, since Saint Sergios is shown as a pendant on the pier on the other side of the chancel.[18] The saint stands dressed in a diamond patterned *chlamys*, similar to Demetrios's costume in other representations in the church, with his right hand raised in prayer. Although the saint is the central and the largest figure, the significance of the image lies in the children at his side. To the left stands a small boy, about five years old perhaps, with short dark hair and veiled hands. To the right stands another child with lighter hair, slightly older and again with covered hands. Bakchos places his hand on his or her shoulder. This is a distinctly intimate construct, the three figures standing close together and the children looking very serious and pious, safe under the saint's protection. All three figures face frontally, with large almond-shaped eyes gazing steadfastly and directly. There is no evidence that the children

---

17   Cormack (1985a) 80–83 suggests the former.
18   See Kitzinger (1958) 25 or (1976) 181.

are related, and it is perhaps incorrect to make that assumption. If they were brothers, one might imagine that the eldest and more important would be on the saint's right, but in fact the younger child takes that place. Perhaps the taller one is a girl, as she might well, although older, take second place to her brother.

It is possible that in this case the parents of the children are shown in nearby mosaics. On the north-facing side of the pier, Saint Demetrios is portrayed with the bishop and the eparch. An inscription below names the men as founders (probably restorers) of the church and records the miraculous protection of the city from barbarians. The bishop is depicted in one of the reconstructed roundels on the north aisle along with a deacon.[19] This deacon also appears on the east-facing wall of the south pier next to Demetrios.

Since bishops were not allowed to be married, one could argue that the children on the pier are most likely those of the deacon or eparch, who was a civil governor with jurisdiction over the diocese. Ernst Kitzinger suggested that the children are the sons of the eparch and that a portrait of the wife of the eparch, the mother of the children, might have been on the south-facing wall of the north pier, where there is now a later mosaic showing the Virgin and a saint, yet there is no evidence to substantiate this.[20] Like priests, deacons were permitted marriage before ordination; but the bishop cannot be entirely excluded, since a bishop could have had children before reaching higher orders.[21] The inscription beneath the bishop and eparch refers to military protection, but the inscription accompanying Demetrios and the deacon asks for another kind of protection: 'Blessed martyr of Christ, friend of the city, take care of citizens and strangers'; the emphasis is on the daily nurturing of the city's inhabitants.[22] We shall see below two donor portraits of children whose fathers held similar positions, and one questions if any connection can be made between the role of a deacon as a provider of care and the importance of his children.

Although we cannot prove that the children at S. Demetrios belong to any of the church officials whose portraits are on the piers, it seems likely. While they could be nonspecific children who represent the saint's largesse and his protection of the young and vulnerable, it is less probable. These children look well dressed, and the attire of the adults on the piers clearly articulates their place in society. Demetrios wears the robe of an aristocratic member of the senate, and the bishop and governor hold their attributes of office, which may suggest that the children are also depicted in a realistic way. If the children were intended to represent the concept of childhood or children in general, they might well have been depicted in more humble attire.

---

19   Cormack (1985a) 90–91.

20   Kitzinger (1958) 25 or (1976) 181.

21   On the three orders in the church, the episcopate, the priesthood and the diaconate, see Duchesne (1903, 1923 edn) 342.

22   Cormack (1985a) 91.

Whether or not these are the offspring of the deacon or founders, it is clear that children, or at least the children of the aristocracy, were valued, even held in esteem by their parents or guardians. The children are placed on the same footing in relation to the saints as the church and civic leaders. The mosaic on the pier is in a highly visible part of the church which, being near to the sanctuary, has holy significance. This is not a private setting, tucked away in an intimate chapel, but one towards which the congregation would face. Although the children are standing alone with the saint, they are not ostensibly holy or monastic, since they have no haloes and wear lay clothes. They appear to be simply the children of wealthy men who paid for the church out of piety and a desire for salvation or to gain political influence and kudos. Like their elders, they too become recipients of the benefits of patronage.

The presence in a church of portraits depicting wealthy patrons and their children was apparently an acceptable choice of imagery for church decoration. The dominant presence of the bishop and dignitaries, displaying their religiosity and their generosity to the church and its congregation, and the presence of the children emphasizes the role of patrons in religious and community life. Did the people of the city and the visiting pilgrims look upon the children as an inspiration to faith, as the prided descendants of city magnates, or as a combination of the two? In what sense were the children seen to inherit the familial piety and largesse? The images suggest that they were closely associated with it.

It might have been more customary, and certainly following in the tradition of imperial dynastic portraiture, to present a family portrait with parents and offspring together. The absence of direct association with the parents in these examples at S. Demetrios shows both the respect and consideration granted to children as individual subjects and recognition of their spiritual independence, since they are imaged with their own relationships to the sacred. These images suggest that, in some cases, children's bonds are not necessarily primarily with the biological family but, within the context of the church, are with a protector saint and the sacred.

A contrasting image of family ties and relations is given in another seventh-century image, the representation of the Maccabees at S. Maria Antiqua in Rome, located in the Roman forum (fig. 3.2). [23] The wall paintings were discovered during excavations in 1900. Probably the church was inaugurated during the first half of the sixth century in a building formerly associated with the Palatine palace; it fell into disuse in the ninth century.[24] This church has several images of children and adolescents, including youthful martyr groups, the Virgin, Christ and John the Baptist as babies with their mothers,

23   Kitzinger (1977) 113–117, pl. VII; Nordhagen (1978) 114–120, pls XXXVIII–XXXIX; Nordhagen (1972) 73; Nordhagen (1962) 62, 71, figs 8–9; Nordhagen (1960) 412–423, pl. LX; Tea (1937) 64 (cult), 91 (dress), 146 (atmosphere), 149 (gesture), 159 (children), 161, 198 (mappa), 289–290 (description), pl. XXX, fig. 19; Wilpert (1917) II.1, 679–680, pl. in IV.1, 163; Grüneisen (1911) 100; Rushforth (1902) 85–86.

24   See Kitzinger (1977) 113. The icons and other possessions of the church were transferred to S. Maria Nova in the Roman forum, now called S. Francesca Romana.

Fig. 3.2 Rome, S. Maria Antiqua, southwest pier, north face, first half of the seventh century. Solomone Maccabee with her seven sons and Eleazar in a family grouping. © Cecily Hennessy

and a child martyr and donor children in the Theodotus chapel, to which we shall turn below.

The Maccabee painting is located on the north face of the southwest pillar in the central nave and is datable to the first half of the seventh century.[25] At the turn of the twentieth century the paintings were photographed and, due to continued deterioration, these records are the most useful, combined with a watercolour superimposed on a photograph done by C. Tabenelli under Wilpert's direction.[26] The painting shows Solomone, the mother, with her sons and Eleazar, an adult male, who is generally considered to be the boys' tutor

25 It measures 172 cm by 174 cm and is 113 cm from the floor; Nordhagen (1978) 114.
26 Nordhagen (1978) pl. XXXIX; Wilpert (1917) IV.1, 163.

or father.[27] When the painting was found, an inscription was visible on the lower frame, which was recorded as ////VMC IIC EPIII//// by Rushforth and as YPI by Wilpert, but no translation has been offered.[28] Solomone and Eleazar are labelled, ΗΑΓΙΑ CΟΛΟΜωΝΕ and ΕΛΕΑΖ[α]Ρ, whereas the seven sons, of whom only six remain, are unnamed. Solomone is the central figure and to her left is Eleazar, who stands, as do all the boys except one, with his head turned to the centre of the group, that is towards her. He holds his right hand to his chest with two fingers pointing towards Solomone. The sons are differentiated in size, in facial features and in dress. The eldest is not yet fully mature as he is beardless, but he has more developed features than his brothers.

The mother is distinctly the focus of the composition. She is dominant both in size and in position. The boys are all visually deferent to her, and all the figures direct their attention towards her as though drawn to her strength or looking towards her for direction. Eleazar has status above the sons, indicated both by his proximity to Solomone and by his inscription, although the boys may not have been individually named at this time.[29] Eleazar is sometimes seen as the boys' teacher and sometimes as their father, though this association is ex-biblical. In the painting, his physical closeness to Solomone, closer than any of the boys, would suggest a marital connection. His advanced biblical age is not depicted. Similarly, Solomone is described as old, but she takes on the appearance of the youthful Virgin. Thus, visually, they appear paired in age.

As in the painting, so in the biblical text the mother emerges as the key devotee and is praised beyond her sons:

The mother, however, was a perfect wonder; she deserves to be held in glorious memory, for, thanks to her hope in God, she bravely bore the sight of seven sons dying in a single day. Full of noble spirit and nerving her weak woman's heart with the courage of a man, she exhorted each of them in the language of their fathers (2 *Maccabees* 7.20–21).[30]

While occurring in an Old Testament setting, the family's martyrdom is seen within the context of the Christian era, and the Maccabees were closely associated with Christ's own martyrdom and Christian sacrifice. Solomone sacrificed her sons presaging the Virgin's sacrifice of Christ, and here Solomone visually signifies her association with the Virgin. Since the Maccabees saved the Jewish tradition into which Christ was born, they are seen as the seed of the church.[31] Ambrose described them as 'the splendid candelabrum of the church, brilliant with seven flames', giving an indication of their Christian

---

27   Kitzinger (1977) 113.

28   Wilpert (1917) II.1, 680; Rushforth (1902) 85; Tea records this inscription as: ///VMC// C ERII////, see Tea (1937) 290.

29   Later, they are named; see Delehaye (1902) 859.

30   Translation in Charles (1913); for commentary and texts for books I–III, see Charles (1913) I, 59–173; for book IV, see II, 653–685.

31   Charles (1913) II, 659.

significance.[32] Gregory of Nazianzos, in particular, in the fourth century, praised the family's martyrdom:

They are worthy to be honoured by all, in that their endurance was in behalf of the law of their fathers. And what would men who were martyred before Christ's passion have achieved if they had been persecuted after Christ and had His death on our behalf to imitate?[33]

He later praises the Maccabees for having lived according to the cross. Eleazar is compared to Stephen, suffering just before Christ as Stephen did just after. The mother is likened to the Mother of Sorrows, while Antiochus plays the role of the devil. Gregory also refers to the mother gathering up and revering the relics of their bodies, clearly placing Solomone in a Christian context.[34] John Chrysostom also wrote about the Maccabees, comparing their struggle with an athletic contest and enjoining believers to follow their example.[35]

In the apocryphal text, Solomone's masculinity is praised, but it appears that visually she is bolstered by a male. She is not referred to as a widow, which would have made her single status acceptable. One speculates that it would be unseemly for a woman to have sons and yet no male partner, and so Eleazar conveniently joins her in an ambiguous role of educator or husband. Yet Solomone's precedence over him is apparent in this early image, a feature that is lost in later manuscript depictions. Her strength and leadership is clearly manifest. This is in part due to the painting's duality in being both a narrative depiction and an icon. The image partially takes the figures out of the narrative context and places them in the position of iconic, devotional saints. However, they maintain their familial identity, although the inclusion of Eleazar, an unrelated member, shows the flexible nature of a biologically framed family.

It is not clear exactly how the paintings functioned in the church and in what sense they are 'icons'. Several of the saints depicted had votive attachments: Solomone had a fibula or brooch at her neck, the Virgin on the northwest pillar apparently held a metal adornment, and Saint Demetrios and Saint Barbara probably had their mouths covered with precious metal.[36] Other paintings, such as that of Saint Anna in the presbytery, had a place for a lamp in the saint's neck so that the child was clearly visible.[37] Therefore a close relation can be drawn between the image of Solomone in a quasi-narrative setting and the

---

32   Ambrose, *De Jacob et vita beata*, ch. XI, *PL* 14:667: quam splendida lucerna Ecclesiae septeno fulgens lumine; mentioned by McGrath (1965) 255–261, n. 40.

33   Oration 15, *Oratio in Macchabaeorum laudem*, *PG* 35:911–934, quote on 912; on this, also see Charles (1913) II, 658; Tea (1937) 64.

34   Summarized in Charles (1913) II, 659.

35   Homily 11, *Homilia de Eleazar et septem pueris*, *PG* 63:523–530.

36   On this, see Belting (1994) 116; Nordhagen (1987) 454; Nordhagen (1978) 141; Kitzinger (1955) 137, fig. 5. The archaeologist Barossi reported that four nails, probably silver, remained in the plaster at Solomone's neck; see Tea (1937) 289; Wilpert (1917) II.1, 680.

37   Nordhagen (1987) 454.

images of the individual saints. This further emphasizes Solomone as the focus of the painting and her frontal pose is suggestive of a single iconic saint. Since the saints' images are not part of an overall programme and they have been adorned with precious metals, Hans Belting argues that they are individual commissions intended for private use within a public church. However, there are no signs of donors in these images, although they are very prominent in the adjacent Theodotus Chapel, which was clearly a personal commission. Surely, images could be adorned without having to be personal investment or property, as is evidenced by icons in the form of panel paintings.[38] The painting seems to straddle the line between iconic portrait and narrative. This is clearly a moment in time and the action is focused on the relation between the characters. Their grouping is natural and suggests human interaction. It seems likely that the three brothers on the left, although their gestures are no longer visible, also had one hand raised in a gesture of speech, like those on the right. They appear to be communicating with Solomone, although equally well the gestures could indicate their united resistance to Antiochus. The closeness of one child with another and the joint focal point within the space of Solomone evoke a sense of communication between the group.

Considering that the biblical Solomone is old, her children must be quite old themselves, although the account of the martyrdom in 2 and 4 *Maccabees* gives no direct information about the age of the sons. They all come forward independently to offer themselves to the authorities and all speak coherently, particularly the youngest. The painting is distinctive in showing the ages of the children in a natural range. Furthermore, each is shown as an individual, both in facial features and in dress. The diversity in the portrayals of the children presents to the viewer a convincing and persuasive representation of a believable family. The grouping of the boys, the younger with the older, is both naturalistic and realistic and suggests familial bonds. That the children are actually too young to take part in the story becomes irrelevant, since their meaning breaks away from the original text. In fact there is little specific connection between the image and the story. This moment is invented and constructed to convey symbolic significance. It is a condensed form of the essence of the narrative, which excludes physical pain and focuses on communion and faith: perhaps qualities more applicable to the seventh-century worshippers.

The story is modified and interpreted to acquire developed meaning in the context of S. Maria Antiqua. A biblical story, channelled by church fathers, is reformulated in the church so that the family as a coherent group is shown together, young and old, in mutual communication with one another. While Solomone could be the generator of this interaction, its focal point is slightly in front of her, and so it could be a figure standing before them, or even the viewer in the space beyond the image. In this way the image invites intimacy, and the presence of the children further enhances this. We get a sense of how sons were visualized as close, supportive and individualized, as well as an

---

38   See Belting (1994) 116.

unconventional version of a marriage or partnership, and the promotion of motherhood and sacrifice. It is apparent that the depiction of the Maccabee children becomes far less particularized in later renditions and this early sensitivity to childhood is intriguing.

No precedents exist for the iconography of the S. Maria Antiqua painting. Prior to the seventh century there is only one, debatable, version, on the Brescia casket from the fourth century, which depicts seven figures being consumed by flames.[39] In later examples illustrating Gregory's homily on the Maccabees, various changes are made to the presentation of the family: Eleazar gains equal authority to Solomone, the boys all tend to be depicted at the same age and often emphasis is on the horrors of their torture. In Paris, gr. 510, a full-page miniature tells the Maccabee story but shows separate scenes focusing on the individual martyrdom of each boy.[40] The images precede the homily, of which the text is on the verso.[41] With nine scenes in a three-row grid, the page has more divisions than all but two in the manuscript: the pages depicting the mission and the martyrdom of the apostles, which are each arranged in a 12-part grid, with the mission having an additional register at the top of the page.[42] The artist has therefore decided not to emphasize continuous narrative, which he does so successfully elsewhere, as in the Joseph page, but rather he separates out the fate of the brothers and places less emphasis on the family and the shared martyrdom. As each apostle undergoes his particular death, so Eleazar, the seven boys and finally Solomone sacrifice themselves one by one. Each is martyred using a different method, which is all graphically depicted. Gregory refers to various instruments of torture, deterrents to the true faith, and the illustrations emphasize physical agony. Eleazar is beaten, the sons are hung upside down from a gallows, flogged, tortured on the wheel, beaten, eyes poked out, burnt alive, and crushed between two blocks, while Solomone throws herself on the fire.[43] In this context, the emphasis in the representation of the Maccabees has become the martyrdom and not the family.

In the later illustrations to Gregory's homilies, there are various ways of representing the scenes, but there are no direct parallels with the S. Maria Antiqua painting. As in Paris, gr. 510, several manuscripts present a selection of individual scenes of each person's martyrdom, while others give conterminous scenes in a landscape setting, but a frequent image is still the family united together.[44] However, the image of the family does not retain

---

39   McGrath (1965) throughout; for pl., see also Kollwitz (1933) pl. 4; the image has a parallel in Athos, Vatopedi, 107, fol. 48r.

40   See Brubaker (1999) 21–22, 257–260, fol. 340r, fig. 34.

41   See Brubaker (1999) 438 for quire diagram.

42   See Brubaker (1999) fol. 32v, fig. 8, fol. 426v, fig. 42.

43   For more description, see Brubaker (1999) 258–259.

44   For examples, see Galavaris (1969): Moscow, State Hist. Museum, 146, fol. 40v, fig. 7 (six separate scenes); Sinai, gr. 339, fol. 381v, fig. 392 (six separate scenes); Paris, gr. 543, fol. 74v, fig. 458 (two registers of landscape scenes with conterminous events); Turin, Univ. Lib. C. I. 6, fol. 29r, fig. 37 (figures in a landscape with conterminous events); Paris, gr. 239, fols 48r, 39v, 40r, 41v, 43v, 44v, figs 207–212 (includes Solomone exhorting her sons). The figures also appear in single initials as, for instance, Solomone and a son in Turin, Univ. Lib.

the individuality of the various members, as seen in S. Maria Antiqua, and no illustration retains the relaxed grouping: the figures stand frontally and regulated on a linear plane. In an eleventh- or twelfth-century manuscript in the Bodleian, Selden B54, the children are as tall as their mother, and nearly as tall as Eleazar, and they are all of equal height and flank the adults in an even row.[45] In a twelfth-century Paris manuscript, gr. 550, the adults stand at either end of the row of sons, who are clearly all children by their height, and all are nimbed.[46] In another instance in a further manuscript in Oxford, Bodleian, Roe 6, from the thirteenth century, the adults have become very large, dominating and protective, each placing a hand on one of the children who appear young and all the same age.[47] In these illustrations, Solomone and Eleazar have equal status and become paired. They may appear to be man and wife and protector of the children. The image of a natural family with children of different ages is no longer important. The united front against sin, visually represented by the line of figures, becomes paramount. However in most cases, the boys are clearly still children, suggesting that youth adds power to martyrdom.

Fig. 3.3   Rome, S. Maria Antiqua, Theodotus chapel, mid eighth century. Theodotus, the chief administrator of the diaconia at S. Maria Antiqua in the Roman Forum is shown with his wife, son and daughter and the Virgin and Child in this painting in the chapel of which he was patron. © Karen Boston

C.I.6; see Galavaris (1969) fols 30v and 31v, figs 40 and 41; in other scenes, they stand before Antiochus, as in Vat. gr. 1947, fol. 30r, fig. 126; Florence, Bib. Laurenziana. Plut. VII, 32, fol. 40r, fig. 264.

45   See Galavaris (1969) Oxford, Bodleian, Selden B. 54, fol. 14v, fig. 288.

46   See Galavaris (1969) Paris, gr. 550, fol. 49r, fig. 411; similarly, London, B.M. Add. 24381, fol. 41v, fig. 95.

47   See Galavaris (1969) Oxford, Bodleian, Roe 6, fol. 159v, fig. 448.

While one can argue that the Maccabee children are viewed with realism, on the other hand they become symbolic of the Christian community. As Solomone is likened to the Virgin, so her sons represent the Christian martyrs and in turn the local community who actually view the image. The church was not one of great wealth or position, and Rome itself at that time was in decline. Pope Martin was not sanctioned by imperial powers, and controversy reigned between Constantinople and Rome, leading to Martin's death in 653. The painting obviously bears no direct relation to this but it can indicate the insecurity of the time, both within the church, politically and militarily. The believers must have been, for the most part, local churchgoers who came to pray. For them the children represent both past and current sacrifice, perhaps the loss of their own children to the continued struggles.[48] But this is an image of a sacred woman surrounded by her supportive sons. The early church was not sympathetic to macabre depictions of death, but rather saw martyrs as blessed and glorified.[49] The image is a source of strength, not of fear or warning, and of strength that comes from a naturalistic depiction of family unity.

The portrayal of a young martyr is paired with portraits of child donors in the so-called Theodotus chapel at S. Maria Antiqua. The chapel is decorated with scenes from the life of Julitta and her son, Quiricus, a three-year-old victim of Diocletian's persecutions as well as with a family portrait including the children of Theodotus, who apparently sponsored the decoration (fig. 3.3). The portraits of the children express the children's relation to their donor parents, to the Virgin who is also in the portrait and to the young martyr in the narrative scenes. The portraits also lead to questions concerning the societal roles of the patrons and their families, who must have held prominent places in the community, and to issues about how the images of the children may have been viewed by less privileged worshippers or by their societal or spiritual superiors.

The barrel-vaulted Theodotus chapel occupies the side chapel or *prothesis* at S. Maria Antiqua.[50] Theodotus was the chief administrator of the *diaconia* based at the church. His decorative plan includes scenes showing the lives of Saint Quiricus and his mother Julitta, who were martyred in Tarsus during the Diocletianic persecution when Quiricus was less than three years old. This choice of subject is not obvious, since although marked in the East by a feast in July, Julitta and Quiricus were not apparently well known in Rome.[51] The choice may be associated with Theodotus's children.

Theodotus is portrayed three times in the chapel, once with the Virgin, the martyrs and the then current pope, once with the Virgin and his family and

---

48   On the history, see Ostrogorsky (1956, 1980 edn) esp. 119–120.

49   Charles (1913) II, 660.

50   Wilpert (1917) II.1, 684–693, pls in IV.1, 166.1, 179, 180, 182.1, 183, 184, 186, 187; description and Latin text in Grüneisen (1911) 118–133, fig. 96, pls IC. LXXVII, IC. LXXVIII; Rushforth (1902) 38–54; Tea (1937) 89–93, 132–133, 324–337, and for a review of paintings under each decorative period, 134–136; Krautheimer (1980) 104, fig. 85.

51   Rushforth (1902) 43–45, and fn. 1.

once alone with the martyrs. The main image in the chapel is that on the far wall, which could be viewed from the entrance although a low marble screen formerly divided the chapel. This shows a representation of the crucifixion, beneath which are seven figures, all frontal, with the Virgin in the centre, dressed in imperial costume, flanked by the saints Peter and Paul.[52] These in turn are flanked by Saint Julitta and the child Saint Quiricus, who is dressed to resemble the apostles. On the far right Theodotus offers a model of the chapel, and on the far left Zacharias, the pope at the time, presents a book. His presence dates the decorations to 741–752.[53] The second portrait, the family portrait, is on the wall between the *prothesis* and the sanctuary, to the left of the doorway into the sanctuary.[54] Theodotus is shown with the Virgin and child, and with a woman, a boy and a girl, who presumably are his wife, son and daughter. Only the lower half of the painting remains, which gives us the faces of the children but not of the adults. On the Virgin's right is a male child in a dark red or brown tunic and leggings, who extends his hands towards her. His expression is serious and his face is bounded by a straight fringe and dark hair lying flatly against his head. To his right is Theodotus. On the Virgin's left is a female child, slightly younger than the boy, whose face is partially lost. Her dress is dark gold or brown with long embroidered sleeves, and she wears a flowered shawl over her shoulders. She has an elaborate beaded necklace and large earrings. Her feet are suspended in air and she stands frontally, holding a flower in her right hand between thumb and forefinger and touches her left thumb with her little finger. Square nimbi frame the heads of both children. On the girl's left is a damaged figure in a red gown, who is probably Theodotus's wife.

A further painting on the back left wall of the chapel shows Theodotus kneeling and presenting two votive candles to Quiricus and Julitta who both stand frontally.[55] Theodotus himself is kneeling and bending over but turns his face directly towards the viewer providing a vivid portrait of a middle-aged man with furrowed brow and thinning hair, framed by a rectangular halo. Again the upper part of the image is damaged and the heads of the saints are lost. On the other side of the door are four saints, three females and one male, named Armentise, who is otherwise unknown.[56]

The martyrdom of Saints Quiricus and Julitta is depicted in the naos area of the chapel in a series of eight scenes on facing walls, starting with two on the

---

52   Grüneisen (1911) pls 36–39; nos 59, 60 on plan at back of book; on the crucifixion iconography, see Belting (1987) 55–69, esp. 58, 68.

53   The dating was disputed, but now seems settled: Grüneisen implies that the two donor images and the narrative scenes were commissioned by Theodotus, but that the altar painting dates to John VII (705–707): Theodotus was said to substitute his own and Zacharias's portraits; see Grüneisen (1911) 118. Rushforth points out that a painted dado with curtain designs runs beneath all the paintings, including the wall behind the altar, which leads him to think they are all of the same date; see Rushforth (1902) 53–54; on this also see Osborne (1979) 57–65; Belting (1987) 56.

54   Grüneisen (1911) 57 on plan.

55   Grüneisen (1911) 58 on plan.

56   Grüneisen (1911) 63 on plan; Rushforth (1902) 53.

left as one enters the chapel.[57] The scenes depicted do not correspond exactly with any known text of the martyrdom, of which the oldest version is in a Justinianic letter, but they do largely conform to the twelfth-century version found in the *Acta sanctorum*.[58] In the upper left, Saint Julitta stands in front of the governor Alexander at the tribunal in Tarsus, having been arrested for her faith. Meanwhile, Quiricus, who was sheltering outside the city, is led in to give his testimony, which he does in the second scene. The third is largely lost, but in the fourth he is flogged. Each of the subsequent methods of torture is labelled, this one being *catomulevatio*. In the fifth scene Quiricus and Julitta are again before Alexander. Quiricus has had his tongue cut out, but he is still able to speak. In the sixth, mother and son appear twice, once at the window of the prison and once below in a caldron consumed by flames (*cacabus*). The story then moves on to the opposite wall and begins on the left by showing the frying pan torture (*sartago*): Christ stands blessing the martyrs as they are laid out on a flat torture device, which must have a fire beneath. In the final scene a man hammers a nail into the child's head, from which blood spurts out (*passio clavorum*). Finally Quiricus is swung in the air by one leg, about to be thrown to the ground.

Closeness between mother and son is apparent throughout the paintings: the boy comes forward to share his mother's fate and they undergo some of the ordeals together, such as lying side by side on the grill and watching together at the window of the prison. The message is clearly one of shared trial, and the boy, although very young, is not in the least dependent on his mother, but stands unmoved in the face of adversity. Family ties, shared hardship and mutual support are evident, but an equally strong theme is the young boy's resilience in the face of persecution. Did eighth-century children appreciate the many episodes of his gory death? It seems bound to impress.

Theodotus's position in society is known by an inscription above his portrait on the east wall, but no longer clearly visible. It read, '(T)HEODOTUS PRIM(ICERI)O DEFENSORUM ET D(ISP)ENSATORE S(AN)C(TA)E DE(E)I GENETRICIS SEMPERQUE BIRGO MARIA QUI APPELLATUR ANTIQUA.[59] As *primicerius defensorum*, Theodotus was responsible for distributing alms to the poor. Historians have assumed that the patron of the chapel is the same man who founded the church of S. Angelo in Pescheria, probably in 755.[60] An inscription recorded with a list of relics refers to this founder as 'THEODTVS HOLIM DVX NVNC PRIMICERIVS SANCTAE SEDIS APOSTOLICAE ET PATER VIVS BENERABILIS DIACONIAE'.[61] John Osborne has shown that the title *primicerius* is different from the term *primicerius defensorum* used to denote Theodotus in his portrait in the Theodotus chapel. The first holds an important clerical position in the papal administration, while the

---

57 Grüneisen (1911) pls 41, 42; nos. 56, 61, 62 on plan.
58 On this, see Rushforth (1902) 50; on texts used by Grüneisen, see (1911) 122, fn. 3.
59 Osborne (1979) 58–59, with references.
60 Krautheimer (1937–) I, 64–74; on dating, see also Osborne (1979) 59.
61 Krautheimer (1937–) I, 67; Osborne (1979) 59.

second distributes alms to the poor. This latter could be clerical but was not exclusively so, which accounts for Theodotus's lack of tonsure.[62] Osborne raises the question of whether these two references to Theodotus refer to the same person.[63] However, they have traditionally been seen to do so and to also refer to the Theodotus who raised the future pope Hadrian. The *Liber pontificalis* tells us that Hadrian was 'brought up and educated by Theodotus, formerly consul and duke, later *primicerius* of our holy church'.[64] However, if Theodotus, the chapel patron, were a dux, that is a military commander, would this title not have been included in the chapel inscription?

Natalia Teteriatnikov has proposed that the boy in the donor portrait is the later pope Hadrian.[65] He became pope in 772 which suggests that he could have been a boy when the chapel was decorated in the time of pope Zacharias, between 741 and 752. I am as yet unconvinced that the Theodotus of the chapel is Hadrian's uncle, but if this were so, we would have an intriguing image showing the integration of an adopted son into a family portrait. But perhaps the point is well taken that we cannot assume that images of adults and children together present a nuclear family and we may be seeing a varied grouping of extended family members, perhaps adopted children, a step-mother, or even an aunt or sister.

Teteriatnikov also proposes that the girl child and the mother have died by the time of the portrait and the paintings are an offering for them. She argues that the girl is dead because her feet do not touch the ground, she holds a rose, and 'her face is still and her hands are not raised toward the Virgin', unlike her brother who has a 'lively expression'.[66] The mother is said to be dead because she is wearing a veil like one used in a funeral context in the catacombs of Commodilla and because, according to the S. Angelo inscription, Theodotus later became a cleric, a move he might have made following his wife's death. Teteriatnikov thinks the boy is slightly younger than the girl, as the girl wears jewellery suitable for someone over 12 years old, but this is perhaps unsubstantiated.

The girl is smaller than the boy, for although their heads reach to about the same height, her feet are not resting on the foreground. Yet are we to interpret that she is not on the same plane as her family and the Virgin? A comparable device has been used in the crucifixion panel, where Longinus and the sponge bearer are depicted as smaller than the Virgin and John and their feet do not touch the foreground on which they stand. Yet they are clearly supposed to be on the same plane, as Longinus's spear is touching Christ. The artist made the figures smaller and suspended them in order to fit them into the composition. All the figures are intended to appear on the same plane and have only been arranged in this way to fit comfortably within the space. The children neatly

---

62   Osborne (1979) 60; noted also in Ladner (1941) I, 105, n. 2.

63   Osborne (1979) 61.

64   For text, see Duchesne (1886–1892, 1955–1957 edn) I, 486; for translation, see Davis (1992) 123.

65   Teteriatnikov (1993) 37–46.

66   Teteriatnikov (1993) 39.

fill the negative space between the adults, and if the daughter were placed in a comparable position as the son, her feet would be confused with the Virgin's footstool.[67] As for facial expressions, assessment of this is challenging, since two-thirds of the girl's face is missing, but the boy hardly has a lively expression. Moving to the mother, her veil is largely lost and, as Teteriatnikov mentions, veils are traditionally used to cover the hands in offerings, which is a much more likely explanation than a funeral context.[68] Furthermore, as mentioned, there is no firm evidence to suggest that this Theodotus is the subsequent cleric at S. Angelo. There is little to substantiate that the mother and daughter are deceased.

One intriguing detail is the square haloes worn by the children and by Theodotus and Zacharias in the panel beneath the crucifixion, and by Theodotus in his image on the back wall. The saints all wear round haloes. It is traditionally held that the square halo represents someone who still lives. In Osborne's discussion of this iconography, he dispels the points made by Tea and Bertelli, who argued that Zacharias was dead at the time of the nimbus portrait, and refers to the earliest textual reference, recorded in the *Life of Saint Gregory the Great* by John the Deacon.[69] Here the nimbus is described not as a halo but as simulating a portrait on a picture panel. This interpretation does not rule out that the nimbus also signifies that the person is living. Square haloes are worn in the mosaic panels at S. Demetrios in Thessaloniki by all three male dignitaries, the bishop, eparch and deacon. It makes sense that the men would want to be recognized and that their features were particularized to allow recognition. Here, the one face of Theodotus that has survived intact, the one on the back wall, is also clearly intended to record specific characteristics. Likewise, Theodotus's children have differentiated features. If we are to accept that the halo indicates portraiture, this suggests that the children were intended to be recognizable by contemporary viewers. As at S. Demetrios, where iconic portraits of the saints are throughout the church, at S. Maria Antiqua images of saints were used iconically in prayer and veneration.[70] The rectangular haloes are perhaps intended to make the viewer aware that these figures are not saints, but mortals, and so should not be the recipients of prayers.

It seems more probable that, rather than commemorating death, the paintings are donations intended to assure the family's salvation and redemption. In his study of Byzantine donor portraits, Henri Franses has

---

67   Teteriatnikov thinks that because the girl's foot touches the stool, she is closest to the Virgin (emotionally), but this ignores the compositional requirements. The rose held by the girl may be a symbol of 'martyrdom and Paradise', but roses are used in many different situations, as indicated by Teteriatnikov's source; see Teteriatnikov (1993) 39 and fns 10–11; Cabrol and Leclercq (1950) 'Rose', XV.1, 9–14.

68   Teteriatnikov (1993) 40; her reference to Duchesne (1903, 1923 edn) 419–427, is not helpful, since this refers to the presentation of virgins.

69   John the Deacon, *S. Gregorii Magni Vita*, PL 75:231; Osborne (1979) 63–64; see also Ladner (1941) 20; Tea (1937) 93.

70   On this, also see Belting (1987) 58.

explored the exchange of gifts (money or buildings in this context) for the afterlife, for absolution from sin.[71] A form of pact is made in which the image becomes part of a system of exchange. Franses takes a structuralist view and sees this practice based in the framework of society: people participate in gift giving as the custom is instilled by society.[72] Theodotus probably was fulfilling societal expectations, but he also hoped to receive salvation. Likewise, in including the children, they are drawn into the educative process of learning about their societal obligations and they receive their own salvation. The children represent Theodotus's future, his familial line, but also perhaps the perpetuation of his life's practice and moral values. In including them he also sanctions their future, probably both financially and morally, for worldly goods are often closely associated with moral or religious worth.

S. Maria Antiqua was by 743 already a *diaconia*.[73] Others in Ravenna and Naples had existed since the sixth century, and derived from Gregory the Great's insistence on tending to the poor. Giving of alms was inherited from civil Roman practice and it was traditional to do so near the forum. The role of the *dispensator* was to attend to the poor and the ill. People would gather at the church to receive bread and wine. Funding for the alms came from lands owned by the church or by gifts from wealthy members, and the *dispensator* would receive these donations on behalf of the church.[74] As both the distributor of food and wine and the recipient of gifts he is a central point of communication in the church. The *dispensator* also distributed the eucharist during the liturgy and so is the human conduit for the communion.

Clearly Theodotus had a highly visible role in the city, giving the people both mundane and sacred food. He was very much in the public eye and his children must have shared some of his renown, even if only through their appearance in church. To what extent may they have been held as exemplars of Christian behaviour? The chapel is usually referred to as a private space, and certainly the iconography is very personal, but it housed an altar probably used, at some point, in the rite of the *prothesis*.[75] It is still disputed as to when a side chapel came to be used as a *prothesis*, though it could have been as early as the eighth century.[76] However, S. Angelo, founded by Theodotus or by his namesake, was apparently the first church in Rome to be built with a triple apse, suggesting there was, at this time, ca. 750, a reason for such architecture.[77] Theodotus's decoration of the chapel might indicate his close liturgical connection with the chapel. If he did prepare the eucharist in the *prothesis*, this area was also the location of his liturgical duties and not an entirely private space.

---

71   Franses (1992).
72   Franses (1992) 148.
73   Tea (1937) 82.
74   Tea (1937) 84–88; Tea, however, confused the two positions.
75   Belting (1987) 69 and 67.
76   Walter summarizes the problems of dating the rite of the *prothesis* in Walter (1982) appendix II.
77   Krautheimer (1937–) I, 73.

The portrait raises questions about the societal roles of the families of prominent members of the community, and how they might have been viewed both by less privileged worshippers and by their superiors. Standing close to the Virgin the children appear central to the image.[78] Theodotus chose to include his children as contributors to the church, and the portrait confirmed them as joint benefactors and recipients of the grace that comes from a religious donation. Their presence also suggests that his gift was given in perpetuity.

As we saw at S. Demetrios, one of the potential fathers of the children depicted on the pier was a deacon, who is shown with Demetrios on the opposite face of the same pier. Another image representing an archdeacon and his son, this time a mosaic from the mid-sixth century, in Poreč, brings up the question of the role of the children of deacons in church life.[79] The basilical church was built by Bishop Euphrasius, who placed his own full-length portrait in the apse along with martyrs and church dignitaries. The Virgin and child are central, seated and flanked by two attendant angels, who look down on the congregation below. On the right stand three unnamed saints, of whom two bear martyrs' crowns. On the left are also three adult figures: the first bishop, Saint Maurus, also carrying a martyr's crown, the current bishop and founder, Euphrasius (543–553), who presents the Virgin with a model of the new church, and the archdeacon Claudius, who bears a book. Standing at his feet is his son, named after the bishop. The boy holds two large candles. Is it just coincidence that the children of those who distribute alms are shown with their parents?

Another image, seemingly related in meaning to the Theodotus chapel portraits, is in the church of S. Clemente in Rome.[80] This painting similarly combines the portrait of a family with images of a saintly child. It shows a miracle experienced by a small boy at Saint Clement's watery shrine beneath the Black Sea, and below this are placed the portraits of Beni and Maria Rapiza, their son, daughter and another female.[81] Inscriptions in this and in an adjacent painting, showing Methodios and Cyrillos bringing the remains of Saint Clement to Rome, record the parents' intention to receive redemption of their souls through patronage.[82]

The inscriptions suggest that the Rapizas decorated the church for their own salvation, but the visual evidence implies that the children were also seen as donors. Osborne comments how infrequent lay patronage was in Rome at this time. It is intriguing that in two of these rare examples, at S. Maria Antiqua

---

78   Rushforth (1902) 52 disagrees.

79   Molajoli (1943, 2nd edn) 41, figs 52–53; Lowden (1997) figs 84–85.

80   Wilpert (1917) IV.1, 540–542, pls IV.2, 240–241; on the church, see Lloyd (1986) 197–223; for a summary of the building and excavations and for further bibliography, see Osborne (1997) 155–157, and on the paintings, throughout; also Osborne (1984); Toubert (1976) 1–33.

81   The miracle depicted in the image was related by Gregory of Tours; see *Liber in gloria martyrum*, *PL* 71:737–738; for translation, see Van Dam (1988) 56–57.

82   Osborne (1997) 159, 162.

in the eighth century and at S. Clemente in the eleventh century, the patrons included their children in the image of giving. While the Theodotus chapel may have had an exclusive audience, the narthex at S. Clemente was highly public. Similarly, the depictions of children in Thessaloniki are in public areas of the church. Situated in a very visible location, they are to be viewed by all worshippers. The combination of family donor portraits and paintings about children at S. Maria Antiqua and at S. Clemente is perhaps coincidental, or can we deduce that benefactors with focused interests in their family are drawn towards stories about children? Was the intention perhaps to enforce the children's sense of belief as much as the parents'? Would the pairing of a child's portrait, pictured as the giver, with the life of a saintly child, pictured as the one revered, affect the sense of duty, obligation and piety of the donor child? Was the intention perhaps as much a moral education to the donor's children as a display of worldly beneficence with spiritual reward?

A further series of donor portraits, this time in a manuscript, shows the detailed and complex representation of an extended family marking patronage amongst the wealthy aristocracy of early fourteenth-century Constantinople. The patron is female, she is named Theodora, and is the founder of the Convent of our Lady of Certain Hope, *Tis Bebaias Elpidos*. The portraits are on 12 folios at the beginning of a copy of the foundation Typikon, Oxford, Lincoln College, gr. 35, now in the Bodleian Library.[83] The folios are illuminated on one side only and provide a series of portraits, perhaps consisting of two sets. The first is a sequence depicting Theodora and her relations with their spouses in lay dress, including her parents, her sons and their wives, and her granddaughters and their husbands. The second is a group of four folios showing the figures in monastic dress and dedicated to God, including Theodora with her spouse and eldest child, Theodora again with the child, the Virgin and the sisters of the community.

The folios have been bound incorrectly, but scholars agree on their original order, which will be described here.[84] The first image on fol. 1v shows Theodora's parents, Constantine Palaiologos, brother to Michael VIII, and his wife, Irene, dressed in aristocratic costume, with their titles inscribed above them; the second, fol. 2r, shows Theodora and her husband, John Synadenos, in a similar presentation; the third, fol. 7r, depicts this same couple in monastic attire with their spiritual names, Theodule (the inscription is lost, but inferred from fol. 11r) and Joachim, with a small female figure between them, dressed in the brown gown of a novice; she must be their only daughter, Euphrosyne (pl. 7). This is followed by a series of six lay portraits of married couples on fols. 8r, 3r, 5r, 6r, 4r and 9v: the only two sons of Theodora and John with their wives, and four granddaughters with their husbands. The women are

83   For the text, see Delehaye (1921); for comment and translation, see Thomas and Hero (2000) 1512–1578; most recently, see Connor (2000) 107–108; for previous analysis, see Hutter (1995) 79–114; for analysis and plates, see Spatharakis (1976) 190–207, pls 143–154; see also Cutler and Magdalino (1978) 179–198; Hennessy 2008.

84   First proposed by Spatharakis (1976) 191–192; and separately by Cutler and Magdalino (1978) 192–194.

depicted in nearly identical guise to that of their elders, showing strict family conformity and close association; the men are also very similarly dressed but with variation in details depicting status. The images are all inscribed with the figures' names and titles. Of the following three folios, 10v, 11r and 12r, the first depicts the Virgin, the second, the founder and her daughter both dressed as nuns, with the daughter appearing smaller and younger than her mother, perhaps in her teens, and the third, the assembled 32 nuns of the community (pl.8).[85]

The dating of the foundation of the convent has been described most persuasively by Irmgard Hutter. She argued that the founder, Theodora, was married in 1281, aged 15, to John Synadenos, a significant member of the nobility, and had three children, of whom the eldest, a daughter, Euphrosyne, was born about 1285 or 1286. At her birth, as recorded in the typikon, Euphrosyne's parents dedicated her to the church and founded the convent for her.[86] Euphrosyne was still at home in about 1295 as she was involved in marriage negotiations with a Bulgarian prince, Theodore Svetoslav.[87] This suggests that although she was dedicated to the church when young, this did not occur directly after her birth as her mother romantically implies, or else that her options were kept open.[88] Hutter surmises that the convent was built between 1285 and 1295 and that community life was established there between 1295 and 1300.[89] However, there is no evidence from the typikon to suggest that Theodora planned the convent prior to the death of her husband, which Hutter estimates to have been in about 1290.[90] At this time, Euphrosyne would have been between ten and 15 years old. Hutter dates the original typikon, therefore, to about 1300.[91] She maintains, I think correctly, that Theodora was responsible for the original text of the typikon, the commemorations, the description of the boundaries, and the miniatures, which were added in about 1330. However, this compilation could have been made as late as 1335, but not later, since Michael Asan, on fol. 9r, was imprisoned and disgraced between 1335 and 1341; similarly Cutler and Magdalino suggest a date between 1327 and 1342, but prefer pre-1335 for the same reason.[92] According to Hutter, Theodora died about 1332, and between then and 1335, Euphrosyne put

---

85 For detailed description of dress and inscriptions, see Spatharakis (1976) 194–199; Cutler and Magdalino (1978) 184–192; Hutter (1995) 82–88; on dress, see Piltz (1994) esp. 18–19; on history of the family members, see Hannick and Schmalzbauer (1976) 125–161, esp. nos 22–25; Polemis (1968) n. 193; Papadopoulos (1938) nos. 11–16.

86 See Hutter (1995) 99.

87 Hutter (1995) 100; Pachymeres (1984 edn) II, L.3. 26, pp. 443–445.

88 Delehaye (1921) section 4; Thomas and Hero (2000) 1524.

89 Hutter (1995) 102.

90 Hutter (1995) 99; see also Polemis (1968) 180, n. 193.

91 Hutter (1995) 102.

92 Hutter (1995) 105; Cutler and Magdalino (1978) 181–184, 198; the *terminus post quem* is 1327 since Andronikos Tornikes is mentioned on the typikon's memorial list and he is elsewhere mentioned as living in this year; on this, see Cutler and Magdalino (1978) 183.

together the revised version of the codex, with an additional typikon written by her.[93]

Hutter argues that the first copy of the typikon, in about 1300, would have only had the image of Euphrosyne as a small girl with her parents (fol. 7r). The other illustrations, the family portraits (fols. 1v, 2r, 8r, 3r, 5r, 6r) and the three images showing the Virgin, Theodora and Euphrosyne and the nuns (fols. 10v, 11r, 12r), would have been incorporated some 30 years later, when Theodora made additions to her typikon and produced a luxury version for her son.[94] These were then all copied (all the portrait illuminations appear to have been painted at the same time and by the same hand) and added to the original codex from 1300, which is the Oxford codex. Hutter's argument is only convincing up to a point. She explains the girlish appearance of Euphrosyne, on fol. 11r, aged about 45 in 1330, as a 'charming compliment'.[95] This interpretation seems very improbable, and it is more likely that the original portrait was made when Euphrosyne was the age at which she is portrayed, as a teenager. She would have been an adolescent at about the time the convent was first functional. Euphrosyne appears less tall than her mother, with a smaller, more youthful face. Her reliance on her mother is emphasized by the way Theodora grasps her wrist, as if leading her forward. Certainly, the lay portraits must be later: the sons were younger than Euphrosyne and by the time of the portraits they both had adult daughters themselves and, as has been shown by others, their titles and status indicate a later date. I would suggest that the figures in monastic costume, that is Euphrosyne as a small girl with her parents, Euphrosyne and her mother, and the sisterhood of nuns, as well as the Virgin, were originally painted at the time of the opening of the convent. These four images combine to form a votive dedication. Furthermore, on fol. 11r, Theodora presents a model of the newly erected building, while Euphrosyne who, after all, was to be entrusted with the foundation, holds a copy of the typikon, presumably the original copy of the typikon used at the inauguration of the foundation.[96] The portrait of Euphrosyne as a small girl presumably records her dedication to the church as a very young girl, an act shared by her deceased father. Her two portraits together indicate that it was important that she was dedicated to the church as an infant and that she entered the community when still a girl. This copy may well have been intended for her personal use. The later lay portraits could have been placed in an earlier version, though not the original, made some time after 1327 and commissioned by Theodora, as suggested by Hutter; it is also possible that all the images were new in about 1335 and that they look retrospectively at Euphrosyne as a small girl and as a teenager, but this seems unlikely. The issue is whether the lay portraits are copies of ones commissioned by Theodora or

---

93   Hutter (1995) summarized on 105; Connor (2000) 108 slightly misrepresents this.

94   Hutter (1995) 108–109.

95   Hutter (1995) 111.

96   On Euphrosyne as heir to the convent, see Delehaye (1921) section 124; Thomas and Hero (2000) 1558.

were originally commissioned by Euphrosyne when she made additions to the earlier copy of the typikon. There is little evidence to support the notion that these portraits are copies and it seems much safer to suggest that they are originals. It is most probable that later lay portraits were added when this copy was made, in about 1335, at the time of Euphrosyne's addition of the second typikon and were therefore the choice of the new patroness of the convent. At the same time she had the original four illuminations copied so that they all appeared uniform.

If I am correct, Euphrosyne would have originally been present in two of the four miniatures and had a justifiably important role in the preface to the typikon: Euphrosyne was integral to Theodora's decision to found the monastery after the death of her husband. Theodora writes of the convent: 'it was also for me and my dearly beloved and most true daughter, whom I consecrated not only from infancy, but almost from the moment of her very birth . . . Like a welcoming harbour [this convent] was to receive her some time later . . . I have now accomplished this task'.[97] Euphrosyne became absolutely central to her life: 'but when my husband died . . . I was left alone in life, anchoring my hopes on one daughter, who is exceptionally dear to me above all others, and on my two young sons'.[98] Part of her intent in founding the convent seems to have been to remain close to Euphrosyne, who otherwise may have married, and to enable Euphrosyne and the nuns to 'live with [Theodora] always'.[99] Furthermore, to keep things in the family, she made her eldest son, who must still have been very young, *ephoros* over the convent.[100] Theodora draws attention to the close relationships within the community, as is often the case, by using metaphors of motherhood: she speaks of the nuns as 'my dear daughters and maidens and brides of Christ', and defines the superior's duties: 'you should care for and watch over these [nuns] as a true mother looks after her own daughters'.[101]

If the four original miniatures were those which are now on fols 7r, 10v, 11r and 12r, this could possibly explain the odd position of the fourth granddaughter on the verso rather than the recto of folio 9. It is plausible that the four original miniatures were arranged as bifolia bound together. When the images were copied and supplemented, the image of the monastic founders with Euphrosyne would have been moved forward to be placed opposite Theodora and John in lay dress, and the final granddaughter portrayed on the verso of folio 9, in their place.

In the lay family portraits, the various relatives are depicted to resemble each other closely in pose and in dress, according to gender distinctions. The inscriptions identify each family member with strict adherence to title, so their individual identities are not hidden, but the overall visual impression is one

97   Delehaye (1921) section 4; Thomas and Hero (2000) 1524.
98   Delehaye (1921) section 8; Thomas and Hero (2000) 1525.
99   Delehaye (1921) section 10; Thomas and Hero (2000) 1526.
100   Delehaye (1921) section 19; Thomas and Hero (2000) 1530.
101   Delehaye (1921) sections 35, 37, and see also 38; Thomas and Hero (2000) 1533, 1534.

of family identity, cohesion and conformism. The lay portraits are markedly different from the religious portrayals, the one lavish and splendid, adorning the body with details of finery, the other dark and simple, blanketing the body to focus entirely on the face. But the two types of portrayals are similar in that they correspond to tradition and uniformity, and the garments reference attachment to a cultural identity and membership of a societal group, one worldly, one spiritual, but both with familial ties. The nuns on fol. 12r are portrayed in a group of about 30, the number originally permitted in the sisterhood, and their entirely monotone bodies form a dark and cohesive cloud from which peep their pale, dedicated faces.[102] In the front row are five young nuns: although they are dressed similarly, they are clearly smaller and wear a different headdress, but were presumably numbered among the 30.[103] Perhaps Euphrosyne and her mother are included in the image, but if this is so, they are not easily distinguishable, and the intention must have been to portray them consistently with their spiritual sisters. Alternatively the sisters are imaged as if grouped behind mother and daughter, seen in the separate miniature, similarly raising their hands towards the Virgin.

Dress and titles are used as definers of two worlds, and Theodora is aligned with both, but Euphrosyne only with the church, since she does not appear in secular dress and only has a spiritual name. However, she did have material wealth, for her mother bequeathed to her the half of the inheritance that she had not already donated to the foundation; this she kept on 'account of the weakness of my human nature' and to care for her daughter's many illnesses.[104] Probably the worldly and the spiritual spheres could intermingle comfortably. However, in the images, prefaced by her splendidly dressed grandparents, parents, brothers and nieces, clearly articulated with societal prestige, Euphrosyne, as child and adolescent, is clearly aligned with the spiritual family. The luxury of patronage allowed her to maintain strong ties with both her biological family and with her sisterhood. In the images she chose to assimilate to the spiritual family.

This chapter has looked at a range of images representing families, from late antique glass to Late Byzantine illuminations, with an emphasis on imagery in Early Byzantium. The gold-glass portraits depict small, closely knit families with children given visually similar value to their parents. In the *Vienna Genesis* the story of Joseph depicts affection and intimacy and gives us a glimpse of Joseph's entry into the adult world. The donor portraits at S. Demetrios suggest children's spiritual independence from their parents and their close affiliation with, and dependency on, young male saints. The Maccabee painting in S.

---

102 Euphrosyne increased the number to fifty, see Delehaye (1921) section 147; Thomas and Hero (2000) 1564. In the illumination there appear to be 32, as counted by Omont; see Omont (1904) 366.

103 The original typikon does not mention the inclusion of children, although Euphrosyne's addition states that lay children should not be educated at the convent, except girls intending to be tonsured; see Delehaye (1921) section 48; Thomas and Hero (2000) 1564.

104 Delehaye (1921) section 124; Thomas and Hero (2000) 1557–1558.

Maria Antiqua shows the partially iconic representation of a sacred family, with individualized sons and the incorporation of a type of father figure, Eleazar. In the Theodotus chapel, the donor children portray family affiliation and the sharing of a dedication and its redemption. Similarly at S. Clemente, the imagery includes children in the donation and joins family portraits with scenes of martyred or miraculous children, perhaps intentionally to impress or to educate the young. The portraits in the *Lincoln College Typikon* show the strong sense of extended family unity and shared redemption in a prestigious fourteenth-century dynasty, with images that emphasize joint identity but give a clear differentiation between secular and spiritual obligations.

All these images suggest strong family ties and concern with the presentation of an articulated familial identity, although this has various permutations. It ranges from a small family, with male and female parents and two or three children, to a multigenerational panoply of relations, who exchange worldly and spiritual connections. Family relations are imaged in terms of physical proximity, usually with the children placed centrally, and with common goals and collective beneficence. Children, for the most part, play at least equal roles to their parents in images of the family, suggesting again the integrated place that children had in Byzantium. An emphasis in this discussion has been religious devotion and the partaking by children of their parents' wealth and generosity. The following chapter will look at how children's sanctity as individuals is depicted in Byzantium.

Pl. 1   Athos, Dionysiou, 65, fol. 202v, fourteenth century. The children stand out amongst the adults as they flee from Egypt with Moses and cross the Red Sea

Pl. 2   Athos, Dionysiou, 587m, fol. 19v, eleventh century. Christ teaches a group of men in the temple. Three small children are also present either on shoulders, in arms or holding hands

Pl. 3   Vienna, Österreichische Nationalbibliothek, theol. gr. 31, fol. 15v, page 30, sixth century. In the upper register, Joseph takes leave of his father Jacob and his little brother Benjamin before being led away by an angel. In the lower register, he finds his brothers and their flocks. A.N.L., picture archives, Vienna

Pl. 4   Vienna, Österreichische Nationalbibliothek, theol. gr. 31, fol. 16r, page 31, sixth century. In the upper register, Potiphar's wife tempts Joseph and grabs his cloak as he leaves. The other scenes with women and children are hard to decipher. A.N.L., picture archives, Vienna

Pl.6   Thessaloniki, S. Demetrios, north pier, west face, seventh century. In mosaic, a saint, probably Saint Bakchos, stands with two children on the pier facing the main part of the nave

Pl. 5   Thessaloniki, St. Demetrios, south aisle, pre 620. In mosaic, Saint Demetrios stands on the left in prayer, while two boys approach him in supplication. A third child is partially lost

Pl. 8   Oxford, Lincoln College, gr. 35, fol. 11r, 1300-1330. The founder, Theodule presenting a model of the church to the Virgin (on the facing page) and holding the hand of her daughter, Euphrosyne. Copyright Lincoln College, Oxford

Pl. 7   Oxford, Lincoln College, gr. 35, fol. 7r, 1300-1330. The founders of the monastery, in monastic dress as Joachim and Theodule, with their daughter Euphrosyne. Copyright Lincoln College, Oxford

Pl. 9   Thessaloniki, S. Demetrios, mosaics of north inner aisle, sixth century.
Watercolour by W. S. George, reference: no. 4, 1908-09. On the left spandrel,
Maria, dressed in a red shawl covering her head and with her mother behind
her approaches Saint Demetrios, while on the right spandrel, the saint stands
frontally in prayer with donors beside him. British School at Athens

Pl. 10   Nerezi, St. Panteleimon, nave, south wall, twelfth century. Saints George, Demetrios
and Nestor stand gracefully in military costume. © Dr. Ludwig Reichert Verlag

Pl.12   Vatican, gr. 1851, fol. 6r, ca. 1179 or ca. 1356. The foreign princess and the daughter of the emperor greet each other in a tent and then sit below chatting on a couch. The tent is pictured from the outside in the top left corner. © Biblioteca Apostolica Vaticana (Vatican)

Pl. 11   Vatican, Slav. 2, fol. 2r, 1344-45. The young heir, Ivan Asen, is lying on his death-bed surrounded by the patriarch of Tŭrnovo, his father the Bulgarian emperor, Ivan Alexander and various family members. © Biblioteca Apostolica Vaticana (Vatican)

Pl. 13   Rome, S. Maria Maggiore, triumphal arch, 432-440. These mosaics show
unusual representations of scenes from Christ's early life. In the upper register, the Virgin
is seated and flanked by angels while another angel in the sky announces that she will
bear Christ. To the right Joseph stands outside the temple. In the register below, the Christ
child is seated on a throne receiving the three magi dressed in Persian costume.

Fig.14   Göreme, Karanlık kilise, eleventh century. Christ Pantokrator appears in the central
dome, and in the drum are six angels in medallions with the young Christ Emmanuel in a
seventh medallion below the gospel held by the mature Christ. In the pendentives are four
youthful disciples, Philip, Judas Thaddeos, Prochoros and Thomas . © A Turizm Yayinlari

Chapter 4

Sanctity

This chapter will look at children who are depicted as specifically and individually sacred, although the representations may imply that they also sacralize those close to them. The images raise questions about the way sanctity in children is portrayed and in what contexts. In what senses are the children perceived as sacred, in what situations do they appear, and what visual tools are used to convey their status, identity and relation to the saints and to the divine? Contemporary culture is largely estranged from the idea of children as purveyors of the sacred, and although children can, in secular terms, be idolized or revered, they may not have the equivalent power and authority they held in Byzantium's religious society. This chapter will explore the nature of that authority, and consider how the representations may have affected or been a result of attitudes towards children and belief and how they may have been integrated into religious or educational practice.

I have selected images or groups of images that address different facets of the Byzantine perception of sanctity in children, both male and female, named and unnamed, individuals that have no known identity and ones familiar from the bible or from hagiography. The first topic concerns the series of mosaics at S. Demetrios, Thessaloniki, showing a little girl's dedication to God, the second focuses on the *David plates*, silver plates depicting the young King David, the third section analyses various depictions of the saintly child, Saint Nicholas, and the fourth explores a group of young male saints who share spiritual and physical ideals. Finally the fifth section looks at youth and age as part of the overall programme of church decoration.

In the previous chapter we looked briefly at the central role of children in S. Demetrios, Thessaloniki, where, in two mosaics, children stand together, perhaps as siblings or peers, honouring Saint Demetrios and embraced and protected by him. The children are imaged physically and spiritually close to the saint, but not necessarily as sacred, since they wear no haloes. In contrast, a series of mosaics on the arcade of the north inner aisle of the same church, now lost, depicted a child who seemed equally intimate with the saint, but who was also marked out as sanctified by the halo she wore.[1] In exploring these mosaics, we see the pivotal place of images of children in the iconography and practice of the church, revealing the strong spiritual ties between the child and the saints, her intermediaries with God. The scenes depict Saint Demetrios and the Virgin with lay figures, of whom the central one is this small girl, named Maria. They portray a series of events in the ritual dedication or supplication of a child to the divine and give us glimpses of the child's relation to her mother, to saints and to her environment. They suggest the central place taken by images of a child's religious experience within the church and by extension the centrality of children's piety within the community.

The church and its decoration is individualized and site-specific, revolving around a local saint and native dignitaries and believers. The congregation had localized lore in the form of the *Miracles of Saint Demetrios*, a collection of accounts of Demetrios's miraculous deeds in Thessaloniki, written by two authors in the seventh century, although the images cannot be specifically linked with any narrative.[2] Maria and the children discussed before were probably local children, closely brought up in faithfulness to the saint. Maria most likely had a distinct relationship to the local church and community, and yet she is depicted in quite generalized terms, which suggests that her images had both specific and universally understood meanings. This perhaps made the representations legible and significant not only to the local people, but also to the pilgrims who came to the site.

The mosaics depicting Maria were destroyed by fire in 1917, but various records made just prior give us a guide as to the appearance of these rare pre-iconoclastic votive images. The mosaics must have been made before 620 when a fire damaged the roof and the ciborion of Saint Demetrios, since mosaics inserted after the subsequent restoration give this year. The original construction of the building was either in or after the second half of the fifth century, and the mosaics are probably datable to the sixth century.[3] Although partially destroyed again, the mosaics were visible in the church and functioning as votive imagery until 1492, when the building became a mosque and the mosaic was covered over. Discovered between December 1907 and February 1908, while the mosque was undergoing repairs, the mosaics were subsequently photographed and copied in watercolour several times, by Russian, French and British scholars, before their destruction less than ten years later. Photographs by N. K. Kluge give an overall view of the mosaics, while M. le Tourneau's photographs are clearer, but not as complete. Le Tourneau's watercolours are impressionistic, but W.S. George's are more accurate and, in colour, provide the most useful record of the mosaics.[4] The

1   Cormack (1985b) nos 30–39, pls 74–77; Cormack (1985a) 87–89; also see Cormack (1969) 17–52.

2   For the text, see Lemerle (1979–1981) I.

3   On this, see Cormack (1985b) 52–57.

4   William Harvey photographed the mosaics in 1907–1908; N.K. Kluge executed watercolours and photographs in the spring of 1908, published with essays by Uspenskij and by Uspenskij and Kluge (1909) 1–61, and 62–67. C. Diehl investigated the mosaics in

mosaics extend over seven of the 12 arches of the arcade. Three of the images in the spandrels portray Demetrios in the orant position, with donors and children, while one shows the Virgin enthroned with angels. The other scenes in the spandrels form a group whose central subject is the little girl. Her name is known from an inscription beneath the final scene of the series. The four scenes featuring Maria are the central focus of the mosaics (pl. 9, fig. 4.1). All the images appear to have been made at the same time; although, since several donors are depicted, they may have been sponsored by various families or by various members of one family, and certainly the Maria scenes were created together as they are bordered by a consistent frame.[5] Repetitions in the patterning of the frames visually link the entire series. In each spandrel appear images of donors, being led or protected by Demetrios or by the Virgin, indicating the links between the divine, the saintly and the laity. The donors may well be members of Maria's family, venerating the saint. The images show an integrated, caring and tactile relation between all elements in the human and divine hierarchy.

Maria's images are in a primary area of the church, and she is clearly the most significant subject of them. Although the mosaics are in a side aisle, Demetrios's ciborion in the nave was probably located in front of the first mosaic depicting Maria. Not only is Maria depicted close to Demetrios's dwelling place, but she is also singled out as especially favoured. In the images of Demetrios and the Virgin with donors, the donors are subsidiary, but in Maria's scenes the relationship between worshipper and saint is developed so that the child is the focus, first presented to the saint, then supplicating herself to him.

In the first scene of Maria's cycle, Demetrios's close relationship with the girl is established. Demetrios receives Maria as a small child, presented to him by a young woman, who scholars concur is probably her mother, although we have no proof of this. In the second scene, the child, ascending the sacred hierarchy, is presented to the Virgin and Child, attended by members of her family, and is blessed by her. The Virgin, flanked again by angels, points to the right, probably towards a now lost image of Christ, and so she also intercedes on behalf of the child. Maria, now older, since she is larger than before, is carried facing forward as if being presented to both the Virgin and to the viewer. The mother's sanctity is inferred through the protection of an angel who places a hand on her shoulder. To the right is another donor, who

---

the summer of 1909 and published his findings, along with watercolours by Le Tourneau and photographs in Diehl and Le Tourneau (1910) 225–247. W.S. George completed comprehensive watercolours sometime in 1908 or before September1909, working under the sponsorship of the Byzantine Research and Publication Fund in association with the British School at Athens. Further photographs were published by Boissonnas in 1919; see also the catalogue of the exhibition at the Royal Academy, *British Archaeological Discoveries* (1936) 102–104; Diehl (1918) I, 61–114, esp. 94–106, pl. XXXI.1 and 2; Grabar (1957) 4–87; Grabar (1978) 64–77; for a summary of this, see Cormack (1985b) 47–52, 58.

5   On this, viewed differently, see Grabar (1978) 67–71; Grabar (1957) 86; and also, Diehl (1918) 95. Grabar seems to have thought that the scenes represented different children, one a boy, and had different patrons.

Fig. 4.1
Thessaloniki, St.
Demetrios,
mosaics of north
inner aisle,
sixth century.
Watercolour by
W. S. George,
reference: no.
2, 1908-09. On
the left spandrel
the baby Maria
is presented by
her mother to
the Virgin, while
on the right,
she is looking a
little older and is
presented to Saint
Demetrios. British
School at Athens

is unusually brought forward into the pictorial space and embraced by an angel; this intimacy may suggest that she is also part of the family. In the following scene, Maria again shows her devotion to Demetrios, accompanied by further family members. She is old enough to walk and comes with her mother bearing gifts of candles for Demetrios. In the final episode, Maria, now older still, again comes with a gift, this time a bird, and with more of her family. She wears a white robe and a red and olive-green shawl over her head, perhaps a sign of increasing maturity. Her mother stands next to a young beardless man with veiled hands, while behind are two pious-looking women with covered and bowed heads. Although the family accompanies Maria, she steps forward on her own, with her mother reaching to catch up with her. The male appears young and smaller than the mother. He could be the father but equally another relative, perhaps a brother. Whoever he is, males are of little significance in these scenes, and particularly in this final image, women are shown to have a dominant role, apparently lauded for their piety within the church. Maria's mother is the child's human protector and nurturer and it is through the mother's guidance that Maria is finally taking her own steps towards the saint. Maria was either fatherless or the father had little role to play in the spiritual upbringing of the child.

Throughout the mosaics, the setting is one of natural vegetation and in this final episode it is elaborated with flowers, leaves, a stream, and a fountain on a stone base. It has been suggested that Maria has died, that this setting represents paradise and that the various buildings refer to funerary monuments [6] Yet this scene is not so very distinct from the others and it would seem odd if she were dead from the beginning and yet grew older. It is more likely that this is an idealized representation of the church and its environment.

She clearly grows older in a family environment and, although she appears to be dedicated to the saint, she does not forsake her relations. If she were given as an oblate to the church, one imagines her attire would indicate this, but even in the final scene she wears bright and rich clothes that suggest worldly wealth rather than asceticism. It has been said that Maria's actions are based on images of the dedication of the young Virgin, but they are only generally similar.[7] However this type of imagery is often repeated in scenes where children are presented to religious authorities, such as in the dedication of the child Samuel and in the presentation of Christ in the temple. It therefore evokes a series of connotations and references.

Although the written accounts do not indicate that Demetrios was particularly accessible to children, the visual material does. Demetrios, young and gentle, invites children to accept and to revere him. All the images of the saints with children in the church promote a sense of guardianship, where the holy figures intercede with God on behalf of individuals or stand with them in solidarity and protection. The children, chief participants, are clearly an important part of the relationships between the viewer, the chosen supplicant, in this case, Maria, Demetrios, the Virgin, Christ and God.

It is clear that the events happened over a period of time, since Maria grows older, but the mosaics were made at one time and look back retrospectively at her childhood. The four scenes within the same border and containing the child are all from the same commission, even if financed by various donors.[8] The individual images of Demetrios and the Virgin at each end of the cycle introduce and punctuate Maria's scenes, which take Demetrios's ciborion as their central axis. The mosaic was costly, took some time to execute and must have been carefully designed in advance. What exactly was the message being conveyed? The episodes are difficult for us to decipher because we expect some kind of narrative, and while the passage of time is indicated by Maria's growth, there is no plot. The child is special, and she is marked by a cross from an early age, which must signify her sanctity, yet the images do not define why she has this distinction. Maria is presented once to the Virgin and three times to Demetrios. As an infant she bears no gifts, but as a girl she offers candles and doves in simple and repeated images of a child offering herself and her tokens to the spiritual leaders of the city.

---

6   See Grabar (1978) 72.
7   On this, see Cormack (1969) 37; for a differing view, see Grabar (1946) II, 92.
8   Observed by Cormack (1969) 23.

Maria is blessed from childhood in the same way some of the saints are marked out from other children, often by extreme piety and behaviour beyond their years. The inscription suggests intervention by Demetrios in Maria's life, and it may be that her birth was exceptional. Hagiographic texts often depict holy children as the much longed-for offspring of barren women. With the production of children being the main goal of marriage, sterility was viewed as a social disgrace, but also as evidence of God withholding his blessing.[9] Children who were born in the face of physical difficulty were seen to be created by miraculous intervention.

The Maria cycle demonstrates the spiritual life of a child, the important role children can have in the community and the perception that they can be inherently blessed. The presentation of the images and their context suggest ways they might affect the religious understanding and experience of worshippers, so children function as transmitters of faith, avenues that offer access to the divine. Similar to the Maccabee painting, the images of a child serve as instigators of belief, tools towards deeper faith and lessons in spiritual strength. But also, in contrast to Theodotus's children who are joined in familial patronage, Maria is the focus of patronage, and her mosaics suggest the individual piety of a child and her ability to draw others with her to the sacred.

In a similar way, imagery of the young biblical King David suggests that he may have been influential as a childhood model. In the Old Testament, there are several young male heroes who grow up from boyhood through adolescence to adulthood, with lives marked by noble deeds and outward recognition of their divine sanctity and authority. These are patriarchs, prophets or kings, such as Isaac, Jacob, Esau, Joseph, Moses, Samuel, David and Solomon. Joseph and David are depicted frequently and are seen in various scenes at different ages, having been singled out by God in their youth. These were very familiar characters in Byzantine belief and, unlike Maria at Thessaloniki, quickly identifiable.

David and Joseph are portrayed in situations related to patriarchal society and nomadic or farming life styles. Joseph becomes a powerful leader and David a king, but when young they were depicted in everyday domestic or rural settings. As mature men, the leaders are clad in imperial costume, but as children and young adults, they appear in common dress, suited to the young. We saw an example of this in the previous chapter in the images of Joseph from the *Vienna Genesis*, where he was dressed in simple tunic and cloak as a boy. One of the clearest images of growing up occurs in Paris, gr. 510. In a page showing scenes from Joseph's life, he moves from childhood to manhood, donning a beard when raised to power (fig. 5.3).[10] This is also the case with David, who usually assumes features of adulthood, perhaps a beard and imperial clothing, only after his crowning.

---

9   For the raison d'être of marriage, see Laiou (1992) esp. 10–11.
10   See Brubaker (1999) fol. 69v, fig. 12.

The *David plates*, now split between the Museum of Antiquities, Nicosia, and the Metropolitan Museum, are a series of nine plates forming a pictorial series of events and encounters from David's boyhood up to his marriage to Michal (figs 4.2–4.4).[11] They reveal concepts and analogies congruent with idealized male adolescence, with the boy faced by and conquering challenges while his life is overseen by God and by destiny. Four small plates show David with one other figure in scenes from his early life as a shepherd, four medium-size plates depict the outward signs of major transitions in his life, and one large plate illustrates the battle with Goliath. The plates are part of a horde found in Cyprus in 1902.[12] Unlike Maria's mosaics, their original function is not clearly religious: neither the patron nor the intended use is known, although Herakleios's imperial patronage has been strongly argued by some and argued against by others.[13] It seems likely that they were used as a deluxe table service, perhaps primarily for display in an opulent setting, although a religious and liturgical function cannot be ruled out. I shall discuss the iconography of the plates before turning to their overall meaning.

The four small plates show David in short tunic and cloak, with a halo. He is depicted killing a lion, killing a bear (*I Samuel* 17:34, 37), being approached by a soldier and speaking with a harpist, or alternatively David as a harpist is approached by a messenger. These last two plates are problematic. The identification of the soldier has been discussed at some length, but the rather confusing iconography of the harpist plate has not been probed. The plate with the soldier will be discussed first.

The soldier has been identified as an unspecified soldier, as Goliath or as Eliab, David's brother.[14] There is little evidence to support Steven Wander's suggestion that he is Eliab, who confronted David on the battlefield (*I Samuel* 17:28–30). The scene does not necessarily depict a confrontation, but it is noticeably similar to the image in the upper register of the largest plate, which has been identified as David confronting Goliath. The soldier is dressed in a comparable way to the military figure in this upper register, to Goliath in the central register of this same plate and to the figure on the far right in the plate portraying the arming of David. It is probable that in this last instance, depicting Saul's court, the figure is Jonathan. Therefore, the small plate may represent the bond between David and Jonathan, described in *I Samuel* 20:16 as a covenant made in the field after the slaying of Goliath. This occurred at the new moon, perhaps indicated in the image by a crescent moon in the half-sphere representing the sky. The two figures in both the upper register of

---

11   Leader (2000) 407–427; Mundell Mango (1994) 122–131; Trilling (1978) 249–263; Spain (1977) 217–237; Wander (1975) 345–6; Wander (1973) 89–104; Weitzmann (1970) 97–111, with earlier bibliography; Dodd (1961) nos 58–66.

12   For a summary of the find, see Leader (2000) 407.

13   See Mundell Mango (1994); also Trilling (1978); Spain (1977); Wander (1973); Leader-Newby (2004) 185–200.

14   Goliath: Smith (1913) 47; a soldier: Dodd (1961) 190; Eliab: Wander (1973) 93; he compares a figure, said to be of Eliab, in the anointing scene with a named figure of Eliab in the same scene in the *Paris Psalter*, Paris, gr. 139, fol. 3v.

Fig. 4.2   New York, Metropolitan Museum of Art, *David plates*, 613-630. The young David, on the left and dressed in a short tunic and cape, appears to be speaking with a soldier in armour whose shield lays on the ground. Metropolitan Museum of Art

the large plate and in the small plate exchange the same hand gestures as in the plate with the harpist. This appears to be a friendly gesture: both figures lift their arms in communication, with the fore and middle fingers raised, as if speaking. In the upper register of the large plate, the military figure is not prepared to fight, since he carries no shield, and David is not armed with his sling, but rather carries what appears to be a spear. If the meeting of the two figures is friendly and not confrontational, then it is hard to justify that the soldier is Goliath. If the subject is Jonathan's and David's covenant, then the events in this register occur after the beheading depicted in the bottom register. Weitzmann identifies the river god between the two figures as a personification of the valley of Elah, and the walled cities on either side as Shochoh and Zekah, features of the site where the battle took place (I *Samuel* 17, 1–2).[15] But, the towns conform to the typical representation of walled cities, and they could indicate just that the men are in a field. The personification may or may not be a river god. The iconography of the small plate with the soldier and of the upper register of the large plate remains uncertain.

---

15   Weitzmann (1970) 103; first noted in Smith (1913) 46.

Fig. 4.3   Nicosia, Museum of Antiquities, *David plates*, 613-630. David, on the left, approaches a harpist surrounded by sheep. Museum of Antiquities, Nicosia

The two small plates showing the military figure and the harpist appear to be paired: both have the same half sphere to denote the sky, with sun and crescent moon, and David has identical dress and gesture.[16] The plate with the harpist was titled by Dodd as 'David summoned to Samuel (?)', and has more recently been labelled 'David approached by messenger while playing the harp', and has been associated with *I Samuel* 16:11, 18–19, when David was called to Saul's court.[17] Although scholars have considered the harpist to be David, David must be the boy on foot, previously said to be the messenger, since he is dressed identically to David talking with the soldier in the other plate. This explains why this figure is nimbed, since David is always shown with a halo. Wander noticed that the 'messenger' was nimbed and thought this to be an iconographical mistake.[18] The harpist is also nimbed, and he may also represent David. However, at the point when Saul summons David, the

---

16   This image of the cities and the firmament, but with no sun or stars, is common later, as in the ninth-century *Cosmas Indicopleustes*, Vatican, gr. 699, fol. 83v; see Stornajolo (1908) fol. 48; Wilpert (1926) 121; Garrucci (1873–1880) III, pl. 153/1.

17   Dodd (1961) 192; Leader (2000) 411.

18   Wander (1973) 96.

Fig. 4.4   New York, Metropolitan Museum of Art, *David plates*, 613-630. This, the largest of the plates, shows the battle between David and Goliath in the central register, while beneath, a detail portrays Goliath's decapitation. Metropolitan Museum of Art

text does not mention a messenger approaching David, but simply states that Saul sent a messenger to Jesse asking for David, and Jesse sent David to the king. If the 'messenger' is not a messenger, but David, as I think he must be, the harpist probably represents Orpheus, or perhaps another incarnation of David, or, possibly Wander is accurate in saying that the iconography is confused. There is no textual reference to David playing the harp in the fields, but only for Saul when he is at court (*I Samuel* 16:13, 18:10), and I know of no equally early depictions of David as the harpist. Although the harpist appears very similar to later depictions of David as the harpist, he does not look like David in any of the scenes in the plates. He appears more mature: while David wears short curly hair, the harpist's locks fall in an elegant florid style, and while David as a shepherd has a short tunic, the harpist wears a long robe with cloth draped across the knee. Wander would explain the differences by saying that the artist used a different model from the other plates, but this kind of argument is unsatisfying.[19]

---

19   Wander (1973) 100, n. 37.

The iconographic type of David the harpist is derived from Orpheus, and it is possible that the artist has confused two images, although still it seems improbable that the likeness of the hero David in one scene could immediately become the lowly messenger in another. Later representations of David playing the harp, as in the ninth-century *Khludov Psalter*, Moscow, State Historical Museum, gr. 129 and in the tenth-century *Paris Psalter*, Paris, gr. 139, are related to portrayals of Orpheus, whose cult was revived in late antiquity.[20] His image is seen in early Christian representations, for instance, in the Domitilla and Calixtus catacombs, and continued to be used to represent the pagan god. A late example of this is in a twelfth-century edition of Gregory of Nazianzos's homilies, Paris, Coislin 239, fol. 122v, where Orpheus sits in a pose similar to that of the figure in the plate.[21] Can the harpist be Orpheus? He was possibly seen as David's inspiration, and it is plausible that the image of Orpheus later became transferred to David, but originated in a scene like this. Sister Charles Murray argues that early images of the Orpheus type do not represent David and that there is insufficient evidence to suggest they existed in Jewish art, a view put forward by Henri Stern. Rather, in early representations, Orpheus was equated with Christ.[22] It is therefore possible that this is a late example of an Orphic-type Christ. The iconography of the plate remains unclear.

Turning to the four medium-size plates, these treat four ceremonial occasions: David's anointing by Samuel (*I Samuel* 16:13), his introduction to Saul (*I Samuel* 16:21, 17:25, 17:31–33, or 17:37), his putting on of arms (*I Samuel* 17:38) and his marriage (*I Samuel* 18:27). Wander argues that David's introduction to Saul refers to *I Samuel* 17:25, but in fact David is not speaking with Saul at this point. Weitzmann suggests that the speaking gestures of the three central figures show David persuading Saul to send him into battle (17:31–33), but the scene more likely represents the moment when Saul sends David to fight, saying, 'Go, and the Lord be with you' (17:37).

The largest plate shows the central event of David's youth, the battle with Goliath, with, as we have seen, perhaps Goliath's challenge or Jonathan and David in the upper register, the fight in the centre and the decapitation in the lower register.

The plates are not grouped chronologically by size, but size seems to accord with the nature of the event depicted. Later events in David's life may have been portrayed in further plates that have not survived, but it seems equally likely that we have a complete set and that the plates focused on David's youth. The traditional connections suggested between the plates and the emperor Herakleios, his identification with King David, his military accomplishments and his imperial gifts, or *largitio*, reflect a tendency to see luxurious objects as

---

20   For the *Paris Psalter*, see Buchthal (1938, 1968 edn) 13–17, fol. 1v, pl. I, and for other examples, pl. XVI; for the *Khludov Psalter*, see Ščepkina (1977) fol. 147v; on David as psalmist, see *RBK*, I, 1158–1161.

21   Buchthal (1938, 1968 edn) fig. 24; for a description of early Christian representations of Orpheus, see Murray, (1981) 37–41.

22   See Murray (1981) appendix to Chapter II, 114–121; Stern (1974) 1–16.

imperial, but may well be correct. Ruth Leader has associated the plates with *paideia*, a term which she does not limit to the classical programme of rhetoric but uses to refer to a 'socially cohesive force', which included both academic and physical education. She argues that the skills constituting *paideia* were mutually recognized by educated people, leading to a shared culture, which was perpetrated through visual material.[23] Leader is insightful in seeing the connection with education and youth but, to my mind, the plates do not bear any direct connection to classical learning or to education; rather, just as the biblical narrative reflects human ideals and exploits, so does the imagery of the plates. More closely, the plates show that knowledge of the bible was central to Christian life and by extension played a large part in education. The focus of the imagery is David's exploits, which could well have served as exemplars for young boys and models of physical prowess and spiritual primacy.

David would not have been shown as an emperor in the plates since he is generally only depicted in imperial garb when mature.[24] Leader is correct in saying that David is portrayed in imperial guise at this time, as in the medallion bust of David in the apse mosaic at St Catherine's Monastery in the Sinai, where he wears a crown and purple *chlamys*.[25] However David is generally not shown in imperial dress as a boy. In the Sinai image, David is not a child, but entering maturity and shown with a light moustache and beard. Typical examples of David when young are in the ninth-century Paris, gr. 510 and in the *Paris Psalter*, Paris, gr. 139: David is shown as a boy at his anointing and, as in the *David plates*, is clad in what Leader calls 'court costume', but this does not seem apt, since Saul is not dressed in this way.[26] David is dressed in the short tunic, which can be associated with both boys and with servants, in the four small plates but later in military garb, when he dons his arms, and in a full-length more formal long cloak, at his marriage. The point of his story is that he is a shepherd boy chosen by God, and so he is shown young and unadorned by power. In the *Paris Psalter*, David is both anointed by Samuel and crowned on the traditional raised military shield as a beardless youth, whereas in the exaltation and the penitence, David is mature and bearded, assuming the crown of the emperor.[27] In the marginal psalters also, such as the *Theodore Psalter*, a clear distinction is maintained between the youthful shepherd and harpist and the mature king and prophet.[28] He is depicted as

---

23   Leader (2000) 421–424; Leader-Newby (2004) 204–206; for an earlier study of paideia, see Jaeger (1961).

24   In the *Rabbula Gospels*, David as the youthful harpist is dressed in a *chlamys*, but the image is not overridingly imperial; see Cecchelli (1959) 56, fol. 4b.

25   The Sinai example is discussed in Kartsonis (1982) 186.

26   Leader (2000) 414–415, 417; for Paris, gr. 510, see Brubaker (1999) fol. 174v, fig. 23; for *Paris Psalter*, see Buchthal (1938, 1968 edn) fol. 3v, pl. 3.

27   Buchthal (1938, 1968 edn) fols 3v, 6v, 7v, 136v, pls 3, 6–8; for bibliography see Cutler (1984) 70–71; on patronage, see Cormack (1986) 616–617; Cormack (1984) 159–160; Buchthal (1974) 330–333. On the inconsistency of beard usages, see Lowden (1988) 57–58.

28   For the *Theodore Psalter*, see Der Nersessian (1970) fol. 28r, fig. 49; fol. 188v, fig. 295; fol. 189v, fig. 296; fol. 37r, fig. 63; fol. 106r, fig. 174; fol. 118v, fig. 196; fol. 190r, fig. 297; fol. 182r, fig. 285; fols 74v, 76r, figs 119, 122; fol. 5v, fig. 9.

a boy who retains his youthful demeanour at his anointing and crowning as well as at his marriage; only later in life does he assume the mantle of imperial authority. Thus, historical accuracy is maintained.

David's representation as shepherd boy contrasts with images of his son Solomon, who is shown in imperial costume as a child. He is depicted so with his father in the ninth-century *Cosmas Indicopleustes* manuscript, Vatican, gr. 699, fol. 63v.[29] Anna Kartsonis has argued that the representation of David as emperor with his son from the ninth century emphasizes the human nature of Christ and the close associations made between the emperor Basil I and David.[30] But while correct, this is not the message of the *David plates*, or of later images of David as a child, which consistently show him accomplishing and being recognized for his own deeds. While the Byzantine emperors were fond of making allusions between themselves and the biblical kings, images of the boy David remained nonimperial.[31]

In this way, he symbolizes the chosen child, favoured by God and raised through his bravery to power. The young David emerges as a sanctified hero, depicted in various stages of his boyhood. He appears as the young boy, nimbed, dressed in tunic and cloak, fending off wild beasts and then going through the process of being chosen, anointed, proven and finally rewarded by marriage. The images show his testing and his maturation, but always as a solitary, encountering each challenge on his own, not nurtured by members of his family, nor by dynastic ties, for he is not portrayed royally when young. He appears as an individual, young, strong, brave and dutiful. Dressed in short flowing tunic with agile limbs and thick curly hair, he epitomizes youthful energy and capability.

Therefore, the emphasis of the plates is on David's youth and his maturation as he takes on the duties of manhood. I have speculated that images of children, like Maria in Thessaloniki, had an impact on children's piety. Similarly, one can imagine that representations of the young David, with his youthful feats of bravery and assumption of responsibility, would have formed an exemplary sequence on which a young boy might meditate. This hypothesis does not imply that we know who used the plates or for whom they were made, but it serves as a reminder that we cannot assume that all art objects were made solely with adults in mind. It is worth mentioning that Herakleios had a son who was named David, and he was made co-emperor under the name of Tiberius.[32] The plates are datable from their stamps to between 613 and 630, but most scholars argue for 629 or 630, linking them to Herakleios's Persian victory. I do not find this argument entirely convincing. However, towards the end of the prescribed period, David/Tiberius was probably a small boy: although his date of birth is not known, his elder brother Heraklonas, known

29   Stornajolo (1908) pl. 26.

30   Kartsonis (1967) 34–39.

31   For recent discussion of David and Basil I, see Brubaker (1999) 185–193, with bibliography; on the relation of Joseph and Basil I, see 173–179.

32   *DOC* II/1, 216, II/2, 390; in part in Mundell Mango (1994) 128.

also as Constantine Herakleios, was born in 625/6, and David was made caesar in 638 and publicly acclaimed in 639.[33] It is conceivable that the plates commemorated his birth, which occurred after several of the children of Herakleios and Martina had been born malformed or died very young.[34] Could the iconography of the boy hero be more suited to the son and namesake than to the father, and therefore suggest that the plates were made for the young prince David?

Like the biblical David, whose heroic actions brought about his rewards, the lives of children who were viewed as saints were enriched in images and in texts by miraculous events that marked them as unique from an early age and which were focused and formalized in selected representations. The inclusion of details about childhood in hagiographies and in images of the lives of the saints suggests a belief in the importance of early life in the formulation of qualities in adulthood. These may be viewed as reflecting aspects of everyday life, but they also present an idealized childhood with impossible features that in some sense, but not entirely, remove it from everyday life. It is in that that their power may lie. Some saints when young rebel against society, while most are paradigms of conformism, intelligent, hard working and holy. The choice of imagery points to expectations about sanctity in the young, while the inclusion of childhood in life cycles may have served to engage young viewers in the imagery on icons and on the walls of churches.

We turn now to look at the portrayal of perhaps the best-known saint whose exemplary childhood became part of popular culture, Saint Nicholas. His story combines the lives of a fourth-century bishop of Myra in Asia Minor and of Nicholas of Sion, co-founder of the monastery of Sion near Myra, who died in 564. The bishop's life is recorded in a sixth-century text, while a monk wrote the abbot's life shortly after his death. The two had been conflated by the tenth century after the cult's expansion in the ninth century, although our earliest images are only from the eleventh century.[35]

The hagiography is a construct, and the choice of scenes from childhood is not based in historical reality, but indicates interests and expectations regarding saintly children. Nicholas, like many other saints, came from humble and normal origins, which contributed to his popularity. He is depicted in typical childhood activities, but his sanctity affects these and so demonstrates his precocity and asceticism. The scenes are both easily recognizable and relate to shared experiences, so the commonplace is combined with the miraculous. Even before he was born, Nicholas was performing unspecified miracles, and at birth stood in the bath for three hours, a symbol of the trinity. He suckled only once on Wednesdays and Fridays, a fast that continued throughout his life. He shone at school, perfected his learning and was said to be impeccable

---

33 *DOC* II/2, 389–390.
34 *DOC* II/2, 289, fn. 4.
35 *BHG* II, 1347–1364n; *BHG Auct*, 1347–1364z; texts are collected in Anrich (1913, 1917); for translation of a Sion version, see Ševčenko and Ševčenko (1984); on texts, see Ševčenko (1983) 18–20, 25–27.

in all aspects.[36] As a child, Nicholas is usually portrayed in two scenes, his first bath and going to school, both events common to most boys. He is not depicted suckling, which was apparently not thought appropriate visual material. However, in certain icons, the Virgin *Galaktotrophousa* is shown nursing the infant Christ, but rarely in a narrative, which suggests perhaps that narrative is thought to draw closer to real life.[37]

In most depictions of Nicholas's bath, he is shown standing up, such as in the later of two twelfth-century icons at St Catherine's monastery in the Sinai and in the mid-thirteenth-century paintings at S. Nicholas, Kastania.[38] In the first, the bath is placed centrally in front of the mother's bed, and the child stands with his arms held up while the midwife to his side also shows her hands raised, demonstrating that he is standing on his own (fig. 4.5). However, the point of the story is sometimes less clearly articulated and Nicholas was not necessarily shown free-standing, but supported by a midwife, as in Prizren, or even lying in a crib, as in the thirteenth-century *Kakopetria* icon.[39] This suggests that the meaning behind the imagery became altered so that original conceptions were subsumed by later interests. [40] The bath scene may then have primarily served to associate Nicholas with other holy children who are depicted in the same way, including Christ and the Virgin. However, most depictions adhere to the original meaning, showing Nicholas as an extraordinary child.

In a subsequent scene, Nicholas is often shown going to school, again an episode in a normal child's life. He is sometimes, though rarely, taken by his father, as in the Sinai icon, by his mother, as at S. George in Staro Nagoričino, dated to 1318, or by both parents, as at Kastania (fig. 4.6).[41] This nurturing attentiveness of parents escorting their children is reminiscent of images of Christ and of the Virgin taken to the temple and, as with the bath scene, viewers would make such associations. The child is sometimes represented as an eager student, shown in the Sinai icon by his quick steps towards the teacher, although in others, such as at Staro Nagoričino, he is encouraged by the tugging hand of his mother. In class, he is occasionally alone with the teacher, but in others, such as in the image from S. Nicholas Orphanos in Thessaloniki, dated 1320–1330, he is joined by schoolmates (fig. 4.7). They sit on a semicircular bench or *synthronon* on either side of the schoolmaster, who presides over them from a raised chair.[42] According to the text, this episode reveals Nicholas's mental brilliance as he excels beyond his peers. His willingness to learn is often indicated by a slate he carries with inscribed

---

36   The texts vary on the details; see Ševčenko (1983) 67.

37   On the *Galaktotrophousa*, see Cutler (1987) 335–350, who gives examples of other suckling children.

38   See Ševčenko(1983) figs 3.1, fig. 7.1.

39   See Ševčenko (1983) 69, figs 20.1, 14.1.

40   On deviation between text and image, see Maguire (1996) 169–186.

41   See Ševčenko (1983) 73, figs 3.2, 21.2, 7.2.

42   See Ševčenko (1983) figs 23.1–23.3.

Fig. 4.5   The Monastery of Saint Catherine at Sinai. Icon of Saint
Nicholas and scenes from his life, detail: baptism of Saint Nicholas
(Saint Nicholas in the bath). Published through the courtesy of the
Michigan-Princeton-Alexandria Expeditions to Mount Sinai

Fig. 4.6   The Monastery of Saint Catherine at Sinai. Icon of Saint
Nicholas and scenes from his life, detail: presentation of Saint Nicholas
(Saint Nicholas going to school). Published through the courtesy of
the Michigan-Princeton-Alexandria Expeditions to Mount Sinai

Fig. 4.7   Thessaloniki, St. Nicholas Orphanos, 1320-30. Nicholas walks into his school accompanied by his mother. The teacher is seated as if in the *synthronon* of a church. Courtesy of the Ephoreia of Byzantine Antiquities, Thessaloniki

letters, or by his pleasure in going to school; but with his peers he is singled out by his halo, not by any show of academic excellence.

Nicholas is depicted as a small child in his youth and as distinctly aged in his adulthood. However, although he looks like a little boy as a child, in some examples, such as at Staro Nagoričino, he already has a receding hairline, which may suggest his spiritual maturity.[43] Although a child, he is old before his time, knowledgeable and ready to accept the rigors of religious life. The imagery suggests that maturity in youth is admirable. Sanctity in childhood actually negates what both then and now is considered childishness. The values we might place on innocence and freedom are forfeited for seriousness and piety. But Nicholas's youth is also emphasized by his depiction as a typical little boy. In the icon, for instance, he wears a simple white tunic with neck and hem borders and bare feet.

The images of Saint Nicholas show him experiencing life in a normal way, but marked out as blessed by his extraordinary precocity and by allusions to maturity. He is clever beyond his years, and this is suggested not only by what he does, standing in the bath or proudly holding up his letters, but also by his body, which is inscribed with his maturity. Sanctity is clad in normalcy, but revealed through abnormality. Nicholas is pictured in a world familiar to most children, but the imagery shows him excelling or undertaking the astounding. In this sense, the representations should not necessarily be

---

43   Ševčenko gives a related interpretation; see Ševčenko (1983) 73; on *puer senex*, see Antonopoulos (1998) 215–231.

interpreted as everyday life but rather as miraculous. They take the viewer beyond the confines of human expectation into a realm where God's power prevails. Furthermore, the viewer perceives Saint Nicholas's sanctity through his halo, but may engage with the details of his life by drawing allusions to other images, such as those of Christ or of the Virgin as children, a topic to which we will return later.

In Saint Nicholas's portrayals, we saw that episodes from childhood were considered important in defining, understanding and in venerating saints, but also that Nicholas's spiritual maturity is conveyed through an appearance of age. There is a group of male saints who are, conversely, portrayed as if embalmed in perpetual youth. They are rarely, if ever, depicted as becoming fully mature but their sanctity is solely portrayed through images of what might justifiably be interpreted as late adolescence. Their images take us towards the boundaries of childhood to explore representations that do not appear to portray children but equally not adults, although the saints were all mature when they died. They are shown to be young, caught between childhood and adulthood, somewhere between men and boys. Several are military saints, but this would not be incongruous, since males served in the military from a young age. Do these saints represent an attachment to youth or suggest that it was particularly appealing in Byzantium, spiritually, aesthetically or even perhaps erotically? How did their youth affect their cults and the way they were venerated?

Saints tend to be depicted consistently at the same age and with uniform features so that they are easily recognizable. Usually martyrs are shown as young, while monks, bishops and church fathers, experienced members of church hierarchy, appear aged. The apostles are differentiated in age: John and Philip are typically young, beardless and boyish; Peter and Andrew are advanced in years, as is Paul. Some of the apostles and a few saints are shown at middle age, with curly, often just greying hair, such as Theodore Teron and Theodore Stratelates, who are remarkably similar.[44]

Both male and female saints are often depicted, at least to the contemporary eye, as physically attractive. Female saints are shown as young women with their heads covered. They are mature in that their bodies are fully grown and they wear adult clothes. An early example is of Saint Barbara at S. Maria Antiqua, who stands with a voluminous stole covering her upper body.[45] Some of the saints are depicted as characteristically old, such as Saint Mary of Egypt, whose age and desiccated body are an indication of her many years of isolation and near starvation in penitence for her youthful folly: she had given herself freely to men since she was 12.[46] Apart from such exceptions, the depictions of female saints are largely consistent and portray young womanhood with attractive features. There do not appear to be cases where

---

44   On the depiction of the Theodores, see Maguire (1996) 21–22.

45   See Nordhagen (1978) 120–121, pls XLV, XLVI.

46   For example at Asinou, Cyprus; see Sacopoulo (1966) pl. XIXa; for *vita*, see *BHG* II, 1041z–1044e; *PG* 87:3697–3726; for English translation, see Talbot (1996) 70–93.

mature female saints are depicted as particularly youthful.[47] This coincides
with findings in Chapter 1, which suggested that girls did not have a period
of adolescence, but moved quickly into adulthood. Numerous texts mention
that outward beauty signifies inner purity, suggesting that this was a common
belief, but it also implies that it was thought appropriate for holy women to be
attractive. This is the case with Saint Thomaïs of Lesbos and with Saint Mary
the Younger, whose 'inner beauty is reflected in the beauty of her body'.[48]
When Theodora of Thessaloniki's portrait was painted after her death at an
advanced age, she was depicted as she looked when young and beautiful.[49]
This perhaps served to portray her as others remembered her, before she went
into the nunnery aged 25, although many who knew her would no longer
have been living. The beauty may have been to emphasize her purity, since,
again, the beauty of her body and her pretty face as a child were associated
with modesty and piety.[50] It may have shown the greatness of her sacrifice
of temporal life, or alternatively perhaps it indicates that people preferred to
revere young and beautiful images.

But similarly, boys are also described in terms of physical and spiritual
beauty, which is often linked with youth. The young Bishop Theodore of
Edessa is described as elegant, with a comely body, cheeks 'just blooming
with down', features that show the beauty of his soul.[51] Alexander Kazhdan
and Henry Maguire have shown that, according to hagiographies, the ascetic
saints are often not physically aesthetic, but, on the other hand, military saints
are 'vigorous and well dressed', with physical health often associated with
round and ruddy cheeks.[52] This may be a rhetorical allusion to beauty as
described in the Old Testament, for David was said also to be ruddy-cheeked
(*I Samuel* 16:12, 17:42), and it certainly applies to some of the military saints,
such as Theodore Stratelates, who is portrayed as strong, mature and manly,
emanating physical and spiritual power. Kazhdan and Maguire argue that
according to hagiographies the 'real value of the image consists of its inner
essence, its spiritual beauty, its relationship with the divine prototype, and
not its accidental qualities – the forms and the colours'.[53] However, the visual
evidence suggests that in many contexts these qualities were conveyed
via what appears to be physical beauty, associated with youth. Many of
the representations of the military saints, such as Demetrios, George and
Prokopios, focus on the elegance and beauty of youth described in relation
to Theodore of Edessa. Considering the existence of texts, it is perhaps not

47   For a recent discussion of female saints, see Gerstel (1998) 89–111.
48   For Saint Thomaïs, see *BHG* III, Supplementum, 2454–2457; *Acta sanctorum novembris*
4, 234–242, esp. 235; for translation, see Talbot (1996) 297–322, esp. 297; in Maguire (1996)
31; for Saint Mary the Younger, see *BHG* II, 1164; *Acta sanctorum novembris* 4, 692–705; for
translation, see Talbot (1996) 254–289, esp. 256.
49   See *BHG* II, 1737–1741, esp. 1737: 31–32; 1738: 32–33; in Kazhdan and Maguire (1991)
6; for translation, see Talbot (1996) 164–237, esp. 210–211.
50   Talbot (1996) 167.
51   See *BHG* II, 1744, 14.11–15, 18.20–23; in Kazhdan and Maguire (1991) 1–2.
52   Kazhdan and Maguire (1991) 3.
53   Kazhdan and Maguire, (1991) 12.

projecting our own ideals of youth to see these men with youthful beardless faces, rosy cheeks and bodies in either weightless or graceful and elegant stances as physically attractive.

Saint Demetrios, in early depictions, such as in his church in Thessaloniki, is not portrayed in military dress but in luxurious courtly robes, tunic and *chlamys*.[54] His face is youthful in that it is unlined and rounded, with large eyes, small lips and full cheeks, and it is topped with thick golden curls. The *Miracles* describe him as ruddy and well dressed, though his ruddiness is only seen in a slight warmth to the cheeks, as his skin is light and delicate.[55] There are many examples of Demetrios depicted as young in icons, for instance a twelfth-century serpentine relief icon from the Xeropotamou Monastery in Mount Athos, where he has a round childlike face and protruding ears.[56] However, this particular form is unusual, since in depictions during and after the tenth century, he is typically shown in military dress, such as in an early fourteenth-century icon from the Vatopedi monastery, which shows a dark-haired boy, pictured from the waist up, wearing green and red military costume.[57] He has full red lips and glazed eyes cast over by a furrowed brow; such interpretations present a typically lyrical and sensual image.

But Demetrios is not alone, for George, Prokopios, Panteleimon, Sergios and Bakchos are shown with similar youth.[58] They were all martyrs, and their immature depiction may serve to emphasize their young lives sacrificed for Christ. All but Panteleimon are military saints, whom the language of hagiography portrays as athletes and soldiers of Christ, engaging in a battle against the evil of the world in which supreme bodily fitness prevails.[59] George's image is very widespread, and in early portrayals he appears as a pale-faced, wide-eyed youth, as in the sixth-century icon of the Virgin from the Sinai (although there is some question as to whether this is George).[60] From the tenth century, like Demetrios, he is shown in military guise on horseback, again elegantly dressed, as in the eleventh- or twelfth-century painting in the north aisle at Hagioi Anargyroi in Kastoria.[61] Images of Sergios and Bakchos are similarly popular, and an early example, a seventh-century icon from Sinai, now in Kiev, demonstrates their identical appearances. This is a curious feature of their representation and serves to show their spiritual

54   For instance Grabar (1953) frontispiece.

55   See *BHG* I, 496–547z; Lemerle (1979–1981) I, sections 161, 275; also in Kazhdan and Maguire (1991) 3.

56   *Treasures* (1997) 6.8.

57   *Treasures* (1997) 2.13.

58   For George, see *BHG* I, 669y–691y; for Prokopios, see *BHG* II, 1576–1584; for Panteleimon, see *BHG* II, 1412z–1418c; for Sergios and Bakchos, see *BHG* II, 1624–25.

59   Sergios and Bakchos are spoken of in these terms; see SS. Sergii et Bacchi (1895 edn) 377, 384; Boswell (1995, 1996 edn) 376–377, 381.

60   See Vassilaki (2000) n. 1; Weitzmann (1976) 18–21, pls 4–6, 43–46; Soteriou and Soteriou (1956–1958) II, 21–22, I, figs 4–7 and colour plate.

61   See Pelekanidis and Chatzidakis (1985) fig. 21.

and emotional closeness.[62] Although historically soldiers, they are depicted in court costume, as in the mid-eleventh- century mosaics at Nea Moni where they appear in the cupola of the inner narthex.[63] The white garments, with richly decorated collars and hems reveal slight bodies and youthful, serious faces. Although they carry swords, they appear defenceless and pure.

It is only in the twelfth century that the images of the young saints take on a more courtly and playful appearance. This can be seen in the church dedicated to Panteleimon at Nerezi, which has several young male saints depicted in the nave. Panteleimon was a doctor, and so not necessarily a figure one would associate with youth, but in his *Life* he is described as young and beardless and having exceeding beauty.[64] Panteleimon appears on the east wall wearing a white robe and carrying a box and scalpel that indicate his profession (fig. 4.8).[65] He has a large gold halo, as do all the saints in the church, and a full head of brown curls, an oval face with a pointed chin, large eyes and a dainty mouth. These features make him appear very young, scarcely more than a boy and very delicate, with pale skin and elegant limbs. On the south wall, George, Demetrios and Nestor stand together (pl. 10).[66] Nestor has tousled, curly hair and a downy beard and moustache, whereas his associates are beardless with shorter hair. All three are dressed in patterned, protective military tunics and carry spears and shields. Demetrios, in the centre, faces frontally, though his right leg is extended giving his body some movement, and his face, like Panteleimon's, is very delicate. George stands with his left hand placed on his hip, his spear held elegantly in his raised right hand and his hips swayed to his right. This graceful pose is exaggerated in Nestor's image: he holds his left arm close to the body, but tilts it outward from the elbow, giving the hand a seemingly effeminate gesture. The other arm is bent at the elbow, so that the hand with the raised sword rests on his hip. Their clothes are colourful and supple, bordered on the hem and flowing over their bodies in undulating folds and, in Nestor's portrait, revealing the line of his thighs. Another early military saint, Prokopios, is displayed on the north wall, pictured with the two Theodores, Teron and Stratelates. He also stands in marked contrapposto, in leggings that reveal his lithesome pose (fig. 4.9). Theodore Stratelates has the same courtly, even perhaps provocative, stance, but his appearance, bearded and with a stronger, more mature face, highlights the seeming youth of his colleagues, providing a clear distinction between the qualities of the youthful and the mature saints.

Other notable examples, among many, of young saints are in Hagioi Anargyroi in Kastoria. In the nave stand Saints George and Demetrios, wearing blue, red and gold military garments, in elegant poses, with George

---

62   Weitzmann (1976) 28–30, B9, pl. XII. Contrary to Boswell, I would not suggest that the evidence indicates a homosexual relationship; for an English translation of their lives, see Boswell, (1995, 1996 edn) 375–390.

63   See Mouriki (1985) I, 140–142, II, pls 58, 60, 196, 200.

64   *PG* 115:448.

65   See Sinkević (2000) fig. 69.

66   See Sinkević (2000) fig. 53.

Fig. 4.8 Nerezi, St. Panteleimon, nave, east wall, twelfth century. The youthful and elegant Saint Panteleimon stands with a box and scalpel, the tools of his trade as a doctor. © Dr. Ludwig Reichert Verlag

in a swirling cape and short tunic and Demetrios in a longer tunic and elaborate armour.[67] They both have wide haloes and face frontally, with finely articulated faces, large eyes, small, pursed lips and rosy cheeks. They are not only youthful, but also exquisitely positioned and dressed in refined clothing. In a further example in Kastoria, in the fourteenth-century paintings in the Taxiarches of the Metropolis, two young male saints, Tryphon and Sozon, are paired.[68] Neither of these saints is military and their smooth faces with longish hair, Tryphon's tousled, Sozon's curled, each with a delicate headdress, could be interpreted to appear gentle and pure. They are placed on the south and north walls of the nave and their images mirror each other, standing in contrapposto pose so that their garments reveal their legs, each holding a cross and wearing a long robe and a swinging cloak with an elaborate lining.

In tandem with the hagiographies, which certainly portray the saints as comely, if not necessarily young, the saints' appearances imply that society favoured images of youth and found spiritual satisfaction or stimulus from them. Their images suggest that the magnetism of youth attracts and stimulates holy fervour, if only in that physical beauty is associated with the beauty of the soul. It may also be that youth was associated with virginity. Regarding the apostle John, Jerome maintained that only he, being a virgin, could look after the Virgin after Christ's crucifixion.[69]

In other cases, also, religious figures are depicted as much younger than indicated in texts. For instance, Moses, when crossing the Red Sea or receiving the tablets of the law, is often portrayed as a very young man, with a hairless face, youthful features and a general air of grace and beauty, as in a twelfth- or early thirteenth-century icon from Sinai.[70] In a twelfth-century Octateuch in Istanbul, Library of Topkapı Sarayı, 8, Moses, nimbed, is dressed in a flowing coral mantle and has short brown hair, a round youthful face and a gentle expression as he stands on the shore of the Red Sea. He is of a similar age when he receives the tablets of the law.[71] In a thirteenth-century gospel book, Dionysiou, 4, Moses kneels before the hand of God, dressed in clinging white robes with dark tousled hair swept from his face and down his back, with a young, intense face.[72] In a twelfth-century gospel book, Florence, Laurenziana VI. 32, the image of Moses receiving the law appears facing one of Christ Emmanuel.[73] The pairing illustrates the concept that the law is given by

67 Pelekanidis and Chatzidakis (1985) fig. 12, nos 59, 60 on plan on 24.
68 Pelekanidis and Chatzidakis (1985) figs 16, 17, nos 35 and 51 on plan on 94.
69 *PL* 40:399; in Cameron (2000) 7.
70 Piatnitsky and others (2000) S–59.
71 See Talbot Rice (1959) fols. 197 v, 257r, figs 20–21.
72 See *Athos* (1974) I, 393–394, fol. 4v, fig. 14.
73 Galavaris (1979) 125, fols 7v, 8r, figs 98–99.

Fig. 4.9   Nerezi, St. Panteleimon, nave, north wall. Portraits
of three military saints, Saints Prokopios, Theodore Stratelates
and Theodore Teron. © Dr. Ludwig Reichert Verlag

Moses but the grace and truth come through Christ. Yet the designers of the manuscript chose to portray Moses as tall, but with a youthful face, and Christ as a boy.

Other Old Testament figures represented as young and attractive are Daniel and Solomon. Daniel is often dressed in Persian costume; he wears tight leggings, a distinguishing Persian cap and has a delicate fine-featured face. Solomon is clad in imperial garb and forms a youthful parallel to the aged David with whom he frequently appears. He is often in identical imperial costume, particularly in representations of the *anastasis*. The emphasis in imagery of David and Solomon seems to be on the relation of father and son, for they look very similar, yet differentiated by age. But Solomon is also depicted alone, as in a full-page miniature in Dionysiou, 65, which shows the young prince dressed in fine regal costume and crowned, but appearing young and graceful (fig. 4.10).[74] Solomon was known for his wisdom, a quality often associated with age, but even in images of him passing judgement over the disputed baby, he can appear young.[75]

In later manuscripts, a popular use of the juxtaposition of youth and age is the portrayal of John the Evangelist and Prochoros. In a psalter from the thirteenth or fourteenth century, Dionysiou, 33, the very young boy sits at the feet of the old man copying down his words, the one bald, wizened and thoughtful, the other young and attentive with youthful face and delicate features (fig. 4.11).[76] A similar image from a fourteenth-century lectionary,

74   See *Athos* (1974) I, fol. 13r, fig. 124.
75   As in Paris, gr. 510; see Brubaker (1999) fol. 215v, fig. 25.
76   See *Athos* (1974) I, 407–408, fol. 104v, fig. 77.

Fig. 4.10 Athos, Dionysiou, 65, fol. 13r, fourteenth century. Pictured against a gold ground, King Solomon appears as a young man, dressed in an irridescent blue silk gown and a shimmering red cloak and red boots

Koutloumousiou, 62, emphasizes the smallness as well as the youth of the boy in contrast to his mentor.[77] This particular image is popular in monastic manuscripts and invites questions to its underlying meaning. It suggests the fondness of aged monks for the company of young assistants, while again indicating an appreciation for the appeal of youth, for Prochoros always appears well formed in body and attractive in features.

---

77   See *Athos* (1974) I, 453, fol. 3v, fig. 306.

Fig. 4.11 Athos, Dionysiou, 33, fol 104v, thirteenth or fourteenth century. Seated in a cave, the aged Saint John the Evangelist receives inspiration from the heavens and dictates his gospel to his young scribe, Prochoros

The textual and visual references in hagiographies to nascent maturity, such as downy cheeks, are reminiscent of ancient Greek cultural values, where young, beautiful boys were esteemed for their physical allure. However, this appreciation was not divorced from spiritual aspirations and the victory of control and chastity over desire, as expressed by Socrates in Plato's *Phaedrus*.[78] An inscription on a set of sixth-century silver spoons found at Lampsakos, Turkey, suggest that in nonreligious contexts, such matters were a source of humour. One, inscribed from Virgil in Latin, reads 'O handsome youth, do not believe too much in beauty', and in Greek, 'You cannot be beautiful

78   For a discussion of pederasty in *Phaedrus*, see Thornton (1997) 206–210.

without money'.[79] Christianity clearly condemned single sex relationships and paedophilia. The existence of laws against homosexuality and pederasty indicate that sex among or with children was an issue, and the prohibition of young boys in certain monasteries points out the fear of the attraction of young males.[80] The images of John and Prochoros may have fulfilled a veiled desire for such company and certainly suggest that relationships between the young and the old, whether platonic or amorous, were valued or emulated. However, it would perhaps be misleading to imply that the youthful saints and biblical figures are a response to male interests alone. Equally the preferences of female patrons and worshippers may influence the choice and slant of representation. Analysis of this issue is beyond the scope of this study. Each case had specific rationale, but the frequency of such imagery suggests a cultural tendency towards the portrayal of male youth.

This awareness of, or sensitivity to, youthfulness is indicated by the conscious balance of youth and age in church decoration. In iconographic programmes the young and the old are often grouped together, with saints of a particular type pictured together in juxtaposition or opposition to an alternate type. The eleventh-century decoration of Karanlık kilise in Cappadocia is an example of this and is of particular interest as the church contains an unusual number of images of the young, both of individual saints and of nonspecified figures in the narrative scenes.[81] The church, part of a monastic complex, is one of three churches which were excavated at about the same time. The other two are Elmalı kilise and Çarıklı kilise. Karanlık kilise is thought to be the earliest, because of the clarity of the painting. The building is a six-domed cave church with a triple apse, narthex and funerary chamber. Four columns support the central dome with another dome to the west of the apse. It is decorated throughout with a combination of scenes from Christ's life and images of saints and prophets.

In order to explain the pattern of youth and age in the church, I shall refer to Restle's numbering system, although he has omitted some figures (fig. 4.12).[82] Entering the church into the narthex, the visitor is facing the southern tympanum and the funeral chamber. Above the funeral chamber Sergios and Bakchos are depicted in medallions, with three male saints, Auxentios, Acindynus and Pegasius below. The military saints George and Theodore flank the entrance to the funerary chamber. On the northern tympanum, Saint Voithus and Sozon are in the medallions, with three male martyrs, Probus, Tarachus and Andronikos in the niches, and four female saints, Barbara, Cyriaca, Mariana and Paraskeve, in parallel iconography to that on the facing tympanum. In the medallions, the figures have beardless, round faces with short hair; in the niches, there are similar-looking figures, flanking a central

---

79   Virgil, *Ecl.* ii.17; Dalton (1901) n. 392; Buckton (1994) n. 133e.
80   For instance, *Ecloga* XVII, 38.
81   Also known as chapel 23; Jerphanion (1925–1942) I.2, 393–430; pls II, 96–110; Restle (1967) I, 128–129, II, figs 218–244; Rodley (1985) 48–56; Jolivet-Lévy (1991) 132–135.
82   Restle (1967) II, n. 22.

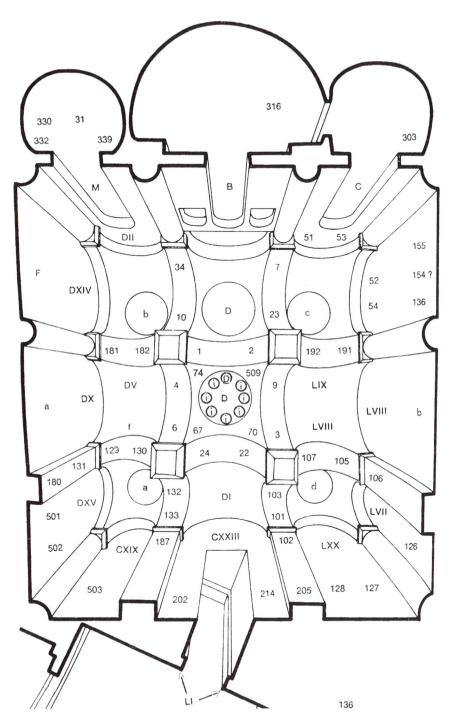

Fig. 4.12 Göreme, Karanlık kilise, eleventh century. A plan of the church showing the location of the paintings, after Restle. Bongers Aurel Verlag

figure who is slightly taller and bearded. In the main part of the church, there are no windows and the space is dark, hence the name of the church, and every corner of wall space, domes and archways is covered in paintings. The space is divided by four central columns which create a central square bay surrounded by eight bays. Over the central bay, the corner bays and the east bay are domes, while the east end has three apses. In the central dome Christ Pantokrator is depicted, surrounded by angels in medallions, by disciples in the pendentives, and by saints in the arches resting on the columns.

On the soffits around the central dome, a young and old figure are paired: to the east of the dome, David (1) and Solomon (2) appear together, each dressed in imperial costume, David, white-haired and bearded, Solomon brown-haired and beardless with a delicate oval-shaped face. To the south are Jeremiah (4), with long grey hair, white beard and a lined forehead, paired with Daniel (6), appearing in Persian costume, with ruddy cheeks and a beardless face. To the north are Isaiah (3), and Habakkuk (9), with long brown hair and oval face. Moving towards the apse, on the southeast soffit Moses (34) appears with long brown hair, ruddy cheeks and beardless, contrasted on the northeast soffit with the balding white-haired Jonah (7). In the north aisle are two young saints, Photios (191) and Aniketos (192), with short hair curled behind their ears and beardless faces. In a corresponding position, on the soffits of the arches in the south aisle are Sergios (181) and Bakchos (182) with very similar appearances, while across the vault from Sergios and Bakchos appear the aged Eustratios (129) and Auxentios (130), depicted with white hair and beard. Across the vault, in parallel position to Eustratios and Auxentios, are two more aged saints, Akepsimas (105) and Aeithaias (107), shown bearded and with white hair and drawn cheeks. On the north soffit at the west end are the very young monk, Abibas (101), and the middle-aged Samonas (103), and to the south a similar pairing of young, Orestes (133), and of middle-aged, Mardarios (132). A further very young saint, Tryphon (187), appears below the west soffit on the south side, another, Joseph (106), on a column on the north wall, and another, Eugenios (131), opposite him on the south wall.

Thus, throughout the church there is a pairing of figures such as Photios, oval-faced, brown-haired and beardless, with those such as Akepsimas, white-haired, perhaps balding, bearded and often with drawn cheeks. It seems apparent that these distinctions must contrast youth with age: soft oval beardless faces must represent a male state of immaturity, compared with the white-haired bearded state of advanced age.

The apostles with Christ in the ascension and in the mission of the apostles are very clearly differentiated, with John and Philip extremely youthful, with short hair and clear round faces. In the last supper, four disciples are young, John, Judas, Thomas and Philip, while Judas, again, is young in the betrayal (fig. 4.13). Thomas, youthful, appears in the raising of Lazaros. John, in the transfiguration, appears as young and, Moses, youthful-looking, is contrasted with the aged Elijah.

Fig. 4.13 Göreme, Karanlık kilise, eleventh century. In the betrayal, the youthful looking Judas embraces Christ while Peter is about to cut off the ear of a small servant. © A Turizm Yayinlari

Other images provide an unusual focus on youth. As already mentioned, in the entry into Jerusalem, all those welcoming Christ are children, while normally there is a combination of children and adults; the shepherd in the adoration of the magi scene is clearly a child, and rather exquisite; another young shepherd with a flute and angels is painted in the nativity in the vault (fig. 4.14). Also, Christ appears as Emmanuel in a central position in the dome in the form of an adolescent surrounded by equally young-looking angels. This is unusual, for the Emmanuel image in monumental painting usually shows Christ, even as an adolescent, with a large head seemingly derived from his portrayal as a baby, but here Christ's face is that of an attractive boy. This will be discussed further in Chapter 6. A further young, pretty angel with curly hair is in the vault above the betrayal (DV). In the pendentives of the dome

Fig. 4.14 Göreme, Karanlık kilise, eleventh century. A youthful
shepherd dressed in a short tunic plays a flute in the nativity.
Above, the three magi offer gifts. © A Turizm Yayinlari

below the Emmanuel are four disciples, Philip, Judas Thaddeos, Prochoros
and Thomas, who are all young and beardless, appearing like boys.[83] On the
southeast wall is also a depiction of the three Hebrews in the fiery furnace (F),
where the Hebrews are, as typically, very young.

There are few images of both female saints and of what one might think of
as middle-aged men in the main part of the church. Those of women are all at
the west end, somewhat separate from the pattern devised for the males. They

---

83   Restle (1967) II, fig. 220.

are Helena (502), who appears with Constantine (501), Irene (503), Catherine (202), Eudokia (205) and Paraskeve (214). They are depicted as young women, but not extremely youthful. The examples of middle age, that is bearded but before grey hair sets, are the evangelists Mark and Luke, who are paired with the older John and Mathew.

Many of these iconographic elements must have been intentional. The pairing and contrasting of aged and youthful saints was clearly designed, indicating that at least pictorially the depiction of age was significant. But the inclusion of so many young saints, the many images of children, the emphasis on the young Christ and his youthful followers, and the very young angels point to a focus of interest on youth, its sanctity and its role in worship. Perhaps the most fruitful avenue in exploring the reasons for this apparent emphasis on youth and age is to look at the donors of the church. However, it is not known who the principal donor was, nor to what extent he and his associates may have influenced the iconographic programme of the church. While the church is apparently part of a monastic complex, it had originally portraits of eight donors, or at least eight figures who may well be associated with the patronage of the church.[84] Of these, seven survive, and of those seven all are male, only one has a religious title, and most appear to be young.

One image, showing two of the donors, would appear to be the most important: it appears in the apse.[85] Christ is seated flanked by the Virgin and by John the Baptist, while two small figures kneel at his feet. Two inscriptions by these figures read 'Entreaty of the servant of God, Nikephoros the Presbyter' and 'Entreaty of the servant of God, Basil'. The figure on the left, the presbyter, is clearly not an old man, although the youngest age at which one could become a priest was 30, and he is clearly beardless.[86] Is he perhaps a eunuch? He wears priestly vestments – a plain *phenolion* (a cape worn by priests and bishops) over a long robe, with an *epitrachelion* (a band) falling in front and ending with geometrical, fringed embroidery in black and white and a smaller vestment around the neck).[87] His companion, as far as one can see, also had short hair and was beardless.

Another donor portrait appears in the narthex, where two men are integrated into the scene of the Blessing of the Apostles (DXIX). This is on the west vault, opposite the entrance to the naos. The inscription on the left reads, 'Entreaty of the servant of God, John Entalmatikos', and on the right, 'Entreaty of the Servant of God, Ge[neth]lios'. Entalmatikos does not seem to be a title, either civil or religious, although it may be associated with *entalma*, a word used, according to a recent publication on this church, 'for certain letters of patriarchal authority'.[88] There was formerly an inscription over the doorway leading from the naos to the narthex, but this is no longer legible.

---

84   On this, see Wharton (1988) 45–46.
85   Yenipinar and Şabin (1998) 60 and figs on 61–62.
86   Justinian, Nov. 123, Trullo, canon 14.
87   Yenipinar and Şabin (1998) 60.
88   Yenipinar and Şabin (1998) 31.

There are two more donor images, each depicting a donor flanking the archangels Gabriel and Michael, who are represented in the centre of the north and south walls. The one with Gabriel, on the north wall, now only shows the small beardless head of a figure, with very short hair, perhaps a boy. Presumably there was originally another figure on the left. The one with Michael, on the south wall, shows two figures with short hair and at least the one on the left appears to be beardless.

We therefore have seven, perhaps eight male donors, one with an ecclesiastic position. They do not have apparent familial links, such as might be indicated by a family grouping. However, a child's grave was found in the narthex, which does suggest that the church could have been used in some way as a burial area by a local family. Whoever the donors were, the intention of the iconographic programme was to include many young male saints and biblical heroes and to highlight their youth by contrasting them to a largely equal number of older saints and prophets. The consistency of the juxtaposition of the imagery suggests an organized programme and cannot be put down to pure coincidence. Perhaps the most likely explanation, although it must remain purely hypothetical, is that the imagery was intended to reflect to some degree the audience, in part made up by the young men of the donor portraits.

These examples show the emphasis on the sanctity of children and the young as participants in worship and the object of devotional practice. We explored the representation of a young girl dedicated throughout her early life to Saint Demetrios, of a biblical hero, the young David, of the exemplary childhood of Saint Nicholas, and of young male martyrs. The design of the paintings at Karanlık kilise suggest that age distinctions were clearly important. These disparate images, decorating luxury silver plates, mosaics and wall paintings in churches, and panel paintings in monasteries, suggest the significance attached to prodigious children, chosen by God and held up as subjects and models of devotion.

Chapter 5

Power

Images of imperial children correlate with a visual language with which we are familiar in Byzantium: frontality, hierarchy and formality; the representations of the children appear, on the surface, to fall obediently into such conformity. This chapter explores to what extent this is accurate. In depictions of children who appear to hold power or the potential for power, children are often linked with their parents, though not exclusively so. The term power is used specifically to refer to worldly power; however this, as in depictions of adult rulers, is often linked with spiritual authority: young rulers are imaged as sharing religious power, usually delegated to them by Christ or by the Virgin. We will look at what kind of familial or political connections are portrayed in these images, how the correspondent positions of imperial family members give information about formal or familial relations, and in what way the two are interrelated. To what extent are private relationships revealed in the portraits? The study questions how far representations of children in power reflect an individual appearance, not so much in terms of their physical characteristics (of which we know very little), but in terms of differentiation and individualization. Can we detect any reference to the children's psychological or inner qualities? The discussion focuses on whether these children were always presented in an official capacity or whether there were situations in which they appeared less formally, perhaps revealing more about them as children (and hence the cultural take on childhood), or as members of a family (and hence the cultural concept of the family), or as individuals. It questions to what extent these images were seen by the public and whether any differentiation in representations was dependent on the context or function of the image or the object on which it appears.

Dynastic portraits appear in a variety of manuscripts, in both those for the private use of the imperial family and those for more general use. Portraits of the imperial children have traditionally been seen as presenting a purely institutionalized programme, spelling out constitutional theory and upholding the line of succession. While this is evident, a closer look at the portraits also indicates variances and suggests subtle distinctions in individual cases. The discussion opens with the children of Basil I, moves to Constantine VII's son,

Romanos II, and then to the sons of Constantine X and of Alexios I. The next section turns to paintings outside the Byzantine centre, looking at portrayals of the children of Yaroslav in S. Sophia in Kiev, and is followed by a return to Constantinople to explore a portrait of Manuel II's sons. The most public, and the most frequently found, representations of children in power appear on the coinage, where imperial children were portrayed with their father and sometimes their mother. Usually it is only the children associated with the throne who are shown and these are exclusively male. One possible exception is Thecla's appearance with Michael III (842–867) during the regency of his mother, Theodora, suggesting that Thecla, his sister, also had some claim to the throne.[1] In manuscripts, also, the children depicted in family portraits are most usually those elevated to the crown, co-emperors ruling with their father or young emperors ruling in conjunction with a regent, most often their mother. The representations are therefore not strictly familial, but rather dynastic portraits. They serve to show the succession of power and not the family as a social group. Girls are therefore noticeably absent, as well as the boys, usually the younger ones, who were not groomed for succession.

However, both male and female children of Basil I (867–886), were portrayed in a mosaic in the *Kainourgion*, part of the imperial palace decorated by the emperor, which is known only from a written account by Constantine Porphyrogennetos (945–959), Basil's grandson, in the *Vita Basilii*.[2] The ceiling of the bedchamber was said to be designed by Basil and decorated with images of Basil and his wife Eudokia, both enthroned and dressed in imperial regalia, while 'round the building like shining stars' the children they had in common were depicted, similarly attired. The mosaic showed all the children, male and female, apparently on equal footing.

The account gives some clues to Basil's ideals regarding his children. Sons and daughters were all educated in the scriptures, since the boys carried codices of the divine commandments, while the girls held books of the divine laws. Constantine Porphyrogennetos points out that the painter wanted to show the equality of religious education given to both girls and boys. Even though Basil himself was untaught, he had all his children educated. The entire family was said to be giving thanks, to God and to the cross depicted in the centre, for all the goodness in their reign. The children and parents expressed gratitude to God for each other and asked for protection. Basil emphasized the unity of his family, their devotion to God and their literacy. Basil himself was illiterate, a fact mentioned in this account, and began life in the court as a stable hand.

It is not possible to establish to which of Basil's and Eudokia's children the *Vita* refers. The children represented in the mosaic are described as 'the children they had in common'. Cyril Mango comments that this is possibly a reference to the illegitimacy of some of the children. Not only were Leo and

---

1   *DOC* III/I, 454, pl. XXVIII, nos 1a–1d.4; other sisters also appeared on one coin; see *DOC* III/1, 407.

2   *PG* 109:348–352; Constantine Porphyrogennetos (1838 edn) bk V, section 89, pages 333–335; for translation, see Mango (1972) 197–8.

Stephen said to be Michael's, but also a daughter, Anastasia, was possibly not Eudokia's. Therefore, only four children, Alexander, Anna, Helena and Maria, were apparently the shared progeny of the imperial couple.[3] We shall return to this topic below.

It is not clear how secluded this bedchamber was, but one imagines it was only semi-private and served some function in public life, even if only to receive more intimate guests.[4] Constantine VII was obviously struck by this room's decoration since he spends quite some time describing it. Considering that the *Vita* was apparently written to extol the strength and virtues of the Macedonian dynasty, this is perhaps not surprising, and certainly the dynastic element is present, but not in a conventional way. The writer describes the representation of a family as much as a dynasty. Basil's family was evidently fractured, himself a usurper and his children of questionable parentage, and perhaps the mosaic attempts to cover over real life divisions. But importantly it suggests that within certain settings, and here as interior decoration, girls were imaged on equal terms with boys.

The mosaic also shows the close association seen between worldly and religious power and the respect given to learning. God and Christ in the form of the cross are the generators of the family's good fortune. This emblem is consistently repeated in the dynastic portraits, but it is notable here in that Christ blesses the family as a whole, and each child draws its strength from a spiritual foundation. Religious devotion is gained or demonstrated through books and knowledge, which indicates the emphasis given to education. Young rulers were often taught by the most learned men of the court, and Basil designated the patriarch Photios, who was a leading religious, intellectual and political figure, to instruct his children.[5] We shall look below at a book written by Photios for the eldest son, Leo, and at the values held appropriate for future emperors.

The mosaic makes an interesting comparison with a portrait of Basil I and his wife and sons in Paris, gr. 510, a large and luxurious copy of the *Homilies of Gregory of Nazianzos* (figs 5.1–5.2).[6] The manuscript is dated between 879 and 883.[7] The portraits appear on two folios, which would originally have faced

---

3   Mango (1972) 198, fn. 73. N. Adontz argued that all the children after Constantine were born of Basil and Eudokia: Michael was sterile, since he had no children either from his relationship with his concubine Eudokia Ingerina, who became Basil's wife, or from his marriage with Eudokia; see Adontz (1933) esp. 502–510; for further discussion, see Kislinger (1983) esp. 128–136, and for a view arguing for Basil's fathering of all the boys, see Tougher (1997b) 42–45.

4   For the use, in general, of private space in Byzantium, see Patlagean (1987) 567–590.

5   On this, see, for example, Vryonis (1992) 682–683; and on Basil's own education, see 681–682.

6   On this, see Brubaker (1999) with full bibliography; Durand (1992) n. 258; Der Nersessian (1962) 197–228; Maguire (1995) 63–71; Spatharakis (1989) 89–93; Spatharakis (1981) n. 4; Spatharakis (1976) 96–99, figs 62–65; Bordier (1883) 62–89; Omont (1929) 10–31, pls XV–LX.

7   Basil's eldest son, Constantine, must have died by the time of this portrait, indicating it is dated post 879 but pre 883, the year of Eudokia's death.

Fig. 5.1   Paris, Bibliothèque nationale, gr. 510, fol. Cv, 879-883. As a frontispiece to this manuscript, the emperor Basil I stands in the centre in imperial dress flanked by the prophet Eliah and Gabriel. Bibliothèque nationale de France

Fig. 5.2   Paris, Bibliothèque nationale, gr. 510, fol. Br, 879-883. Facing the portait of Basil I is this formal representation of the empress Eudokia and two of her sons, Leo and Alexander. Bibliothèque nationale de France

one another.[8] On the left folio Basil is joined by his spiritual protector, Elijah, who hands him a *labarum*, a symbol of his office, and by the archangel Gabriel who signifies his power from God.[9] The image therefore emphasizes Basil's position as ruler.[10] The inscription around the three reads, 'Clearly Elijah records a victory over your enemies, while Gabriel announcing the joy, oh Basil, crowns you protector of the world'.[11] In the other half of the portrait, Eudokia Ingerina, Basil's wife, stands in the centre with Leo, the elder son, on the left, and Alexander, the younger, on the right. Eudokia, with the title *augusta*, stands flanked by Leo on the viewer's left and Alexander on the right, each named despot, indicating that they both share the status of co-emperor.[12] Similarly, an inscription encircles the miniature of Eudokia: 'Basil, king of the Romans, elevated you, a well-branched vine bearing as the grapes of sovereignty the serene *despotai* with whom you shine, oh light-bringing Eudokia'.[13] The inscription indicates that Eudokia received her power from Basil. The boys are dressed similarly to their parents, in a *skaramangion* and geometrically patterned *loros*, and they each wear a diadem and carry an orb and *akakia* (a pouch containing dust held ceremonially by members of the imperial family). Leo, the elder, became despot in 870 and Alexander only shortly before or at the time of the making of the portrait, sometime before mid-November 879. Differences in status are subtly indicated. Leo, for instance, has three rows of pearls on his boots while his brother Alexander has only two, but both the boys' feet are placed in front of their mother's suggesting that they have a more exalted position than she does.

The portraits appear traditional and have always been considered so. But while presenting a standard dynastic portrait, they also offer a nuanced representation of sensitive familial relationships. The arrangement of the imperial sons in this portrait is unusual: they flank their mother, not their father, as was customary in the coinage, or both parents, as is seen in later imperial portraits. This arrangement elevates Eudokia's importance, yet it might also suggest factors regarding the boys' relations with Basil. Leo, the elder son shown here, probably aged about 14, was generally thought at the time to be the son of Basil's predecessor, Michael, Eudokia's long-time lover, whom Basil murdered in order to seize power.[14] The choice of this particular and unusual composition of mother and sons was perhaps intended to emphasize the boys' relationship with their mother, while separating them from Basil, who apparently hated Leo and was not fond of Alexander. Alexander was quickly crowned after the

---

8   Fols. Br and Cv; on the ordering of the pages, see Brubaker (1999) 5–7; Der Nersessian (1962) 198.

9   On Basil and Elijah, see Brubaker (1999) 159, 161.

10   See Brubaker (1999) fol. Cv, fig. 5.

11   See Spatharakis (1976) 97. On Basil and Elijah, see Moravcsik (1961) 90–91.

12   Kalavrezou-Maxeiner showed that Spatharakis, after Omont, misread Alexander's title as *Adelphos*; see Kalavrezou-Maxeiner (1978) 21.

13   See Spatharakis (1976) 98; also see Brubaker (1999) 5.

14   Mango considers Stephen to be older than Alexander and also the son of Michael; see Mango (1973) 23–24.

death of Basil's eldest and favourite son, Constantine, perhaps in the hope that he would one day supplant Leo.[15] Constantine was probably born from a prior marriage, further complicating familial tensions.[16] After Constantine's death, Basil virtually never minted coins depicting his other sons, but was portrayed on his own on the coinage. Alexander does not appear on the major coins, and Leo is removed after the death of Constantine. The boys only appear on ceremonial coins minted for Alexander's coronation.[17] More normally, and in previous centuries, dynastic strength was emphasized by the presence of co-emperors on the more important coins.

The portraits arguably provide a personalized impression of court relationships, and this reading suggests that whoever conceived of the arrangement of the figures was giving primary consideration to Basil's wishes. In Leslie Brubaker's recent book on this manuscript, she reiterates that Photios, the book lover and imperial tutor, commissioned this volume as a gift for Basil and perhaps his family, although she indicates that Photios and Basil alone were the audience for some parts of the book.[18] Brubaker demonstrates that Photios's thinking is reflected in the choice of illustrations to the text of the book but, I would suggest, the volume and the design of the portraits could have been commissioned by Photios, by another courtier or by the emperor himself. Whoever selected the visual vocabulary was most likely intent on culling the emperor's favour and took care to generate precisely the right imperial response. The ruler himself may have chosen a visual discourse suited to his own self-image. The presence of the portraits and the particular arrangement of the figures in the portraits do indicate that the book was intended for the private use of the emperor and/or his family, although the size of the volume does not suggest frequent personal reading: it is not easily portable nor easy to handle.[19]

However, aspects of the images accompanying the text can be read to suggest that the book was intended for the use of the sons imaged in the portrait as much as for their father. Leslie Brubaker suggests in her conclusions that the book was made for Basil and his family, although her arguments rest largely on Basil's interests.[20] But perhaps the key recipients were Leo and Alexander as much as, or rather than, their father. They were under the instruction of Photios, who prepared educative texts for Leo, giving moral guidance, such as the 'Hortatory Chapters', attributed to Basil, the emperor of the Romans.[21]

---

15   Vogt (1908) 61.

16   S. Tougher views this differently; see Tougher (1997b) 43–44.

17   *DOC* III/2, 477–488. However, Constantine, Basil's son, does appear on a coin with Eudokia, a fact which further leads Grierson to consider Constantine to be Eudokia's child; see *DOC* III/2, 474. It was possibly a memorial mint issued after their deaths, which, to my thinking, does not necessarily mean they were related by blood.

18   Brubaker (1999) esp. 411–412.

19   It measures about 410 mm by 300 mm; see Brubaker (1999) 2.

20   Brubaker (1999) xvii, 412, 414: 'we can even speculate that Paris.gr.510 was directed to Photios's pupil Leo as well as to Leo's father Basil'. Mango has suggested that the book was rather given to the Nea Ekklesia; see Mango (2000) 280.

21   *PG* 107:XXI–LVI; on this, see Kazhdan (1984) 43–57, esp. 43; Blum (1981) 39–41.

Basil, however, was illiterate and, as Brubaker states, we have no evidence that the writings of Gregory of Nazianzos interested him.[22] The adult Leo, on the other hand, was educated, erudite and interested in scriptural and theological thinking. His funeral oration for Basil demonstrates his familiarity with Gregory's writings.[23] Children learn faster than adults, which is perhaps why Basil remained illiterate and Leo became a scholar.

The images are narrative and didactic, as well as detailed and demonstrative. The purpose of the images appears to be not only to illustrate the given texts but to elaborate on their significance and implications. Images harmonize with text to give context, accent and peculiarity to Gregory's homilies. The representations are imaginative and graphic, but also educational. They would serve well as instructional tools. Brubaker shows that the images provide lessons on good rule and respect for church authority.[24] Would Photios have taken an audaciously instructive approach to Basil, or was the instruction intended for the young princes?

The argument for the boys as recipients of the book is strengthened by the references in the images to youthful heroes. Brubaker has drawn attention to the frequent depictions of women and familial situations in Paris, gr. 510. The nature of the texts, being commentary rather than narrative, allows for visual excursions.[25] She suggests that Photios's thinking is exemplified in the particular choice of imagery in the book's illustration. If the concept of family is emphasized in the images, this implies that Photios had a special interest in the family. Was he particularly concerned with such issues? I would suggest that he is more interested in the education of the young princes under his tutelage. Brubaker argues that women are shown more often that one would expect in the manuscript and calculates that families appear in 29 of the 46 miniatures, while women appear in 27 of them.[26] In listing the women included, Brubaker cites frequent images of the Virgin, Gregory's mother and sister, Solomone Maccabee, Helena and Paraskeve, Justina, Job's wife, and Mary and Martha, who are said to be depicted larger than usual.[27] However, comparisons with other ninth-century manuscripts do not appear to show that Paris, gr. 510 has an overriding number of images of women or families. For instance, women often appear in crowd scenes, such as the crossing of the Red Sea, the loaves and fishes and the entry into Jerusalem. In Paris, gr. 510 there is an image of

---

22   Brubaker (1999) 412.

23   Brubaker suggests that evidence of Photios's teaching can be seen in Leo's funeral oration for Basil I, which is based on Gregory's for Saint Basil; see Brubaker (1999) 414; on Leo's use of this and of Gregory's oration for his brother, see Adontz (1933) 507.

24   Brubaker (1999) 413.

25   First shown in Der Nersessian (1962) 197–228; further demonstrated in Brubaker (1999) throughout.

26   Brubaker (1999) 403–405, fn. 17 and 407, fn. 30; for further discussion of family and women, see also 69–70, and on 'gender balance', 264, 268, 271, 273.

27   Brubaker (1999) 405–406. However, the Virgin's presence at the deposition parallels ninth-century theological developments in recognizing Mary as the mother of god and emphasizing Christ's humanity; see 405.

Miriam dancing, but this is also in the *Khludov Psalter*.[28] But also the presence of women and families is not unexpected. It seems erroneous to view normative Byzantine visual culture as solely reflecting a patriarchal hegemony in which women and children do not usually figure. The patron or illuminator used scenes from the bible and from history and hagiography. These stories feature women, in both the Old and New Testaments, and in stories about saints they feature in major and minor roles, because the narratives tell us about life as integrally lived by men and women, and by children, who are normally generated in familial contexts.

However, the manuscript is perhaps notable for the frequent representations of young male biblical heroes: there is an exceptional number of images of adolescent boys, sometimes in contexts in which they are not likely to be found. The 12-year-old Christ is pictured among the doctors in the temple; he appears with round face and short hair, clearly young, and kisses his mother goodbye in a tender fashion.[29] An entire page is given to Joseph's youth; he is shown growing up, first as a boy with his father and brothers, and donning a beard and the *chlamys* of authority when appointed by the pharaoh (fig. 5.3).[30] The young Isaac, Jacob and David all appear on one folio and, unusually, Jacob dreaming is portrayed as a boy, with features not unlike those of Christ with the doctors.[31] This youthful image of Jacob is repeated in the twelfth-century Vatican, gr. 746, but an earlier representation in the Via Latina catacomb shows a bearded and aged Jacob.[32] Joshua, shown stopping the sun and meeting an angel, and Moses, on the same folio, both appear youthful.[33] Moses is again depicted as young when he crosses the Red Sea and defeats the Amalekites.[34] Likewise, Samson and Gideon wear short tunics and have round youthful faces.[35] Jonah also, though dressed in a full-length robe, has a similar face.[36] Daniel and the three Hebrews in the furnace are also shown young, apparently not quite fully grown, and with fresh faces; however, this is how they are normally depicted.[37] Some of these figures are often portrayed as young, such as Moses (as discussed in the previous chapter), the three Hebrews and Daniel. Early representations in the sixth-century *Rabbula Gospels*, Plut. I, 56, and in the sixth-century Syriac bible, Paris, syr. 341 show Habakkuk as both youthful and mature, but in both these manuscripts Joshua is depicted as bearded and Jonah

---

28   Moscow, Historical Museum, 129, fol. 148v; see Brubaker (1999) fig. 143.
29   See Brubaker (1999) fol. 165r, fig. 21.
30   See Brubaker (1999) fol. 69v, fig. 12.
31   See Brubaker (1999) fol. 174v, fig. 23.
32   Vatican gr. 746, fol. 97r, illustrated in Brubaker (1999) fig. 101; also Hesseling (1909) fig. 99; for Via Latina, also mentioned by Brubaker; see Ferrua (1990) fig. 48, Ferrua (1960) pl. XCVII.
33   See Brubaker (1999) fol. 226v, fig. 26.
34   See Brubaker (1999) fol. 264v, fig. 28, fol. 424v, fig. 41.
35   See Brubaker (1999) fol. 347v, fig. 35.
36   See Brubaker (1999) fol. 3r, fig. 6.
37   See Brubaker (1999) fol. 435v, fig. 43.

Fig. 5.3   Paris, Bibliothèque nationale, gr. 510, fol. 69v, 879-883. In a full page illumination, Joseph's life from the Old Testament is told in a series of narrative images. Bibliothèque nationale de France

as mature.[38] Similarly, in the ninth-century Paris, gr. 923, Samson is depicted as mature.[39] Such examples suggest that this number of youthful representations was not typical.

It is not possible to prove that the book was intended for the sons, but a case may be made for this. I would suggest that the repeated appearance of the young heroes is designed to provide models for the boys to emulate and with which to identify. It seems plausible that the portraits were made and the book designed on the occasion of Alexander's elevation to the throne in 879. This followed the death of the eldest son Constantine and signified Basil's restatement of dynastic power. Perhaps the book was given to both sons to mark their joint role as junior emperors and heirs to their at least nominal father.

It is possible that Leo's son, Constantine VII, gave a similarly luxurious book, the *Paris Psalter*, Paris, gr. 139, to his son Romanos II. This has been suggested by Hugo Buchthal, although he argued that the gift must have been an earlier version of the manuscript and that the extant volume is a later copy.[40] The text in the book held by David in the image known as the exaltation of David is from Psalm 71, which was written by David for his son, Solomon.[41] Constantine gave Romanos *De administrando imperio*, which was written for him, on the occasion of his 14th birthday. The opening of this text includes quotes from this same psalm.[42] Buchthal argues, convincingly, that it is likely that the psalter was presented to Romanos on the same occasion as the text. He also maintains that the first image in the manuscript was David portrayed as a harpist and that this faced the exaltation.[43] Versions of these miniatures are arranged in this way in two thirteenth-century psalters, one of which is the Vatican, Palat. gr. 381.[44] Therefore the opening images would be of the young chosen boy and the mature crowned leader, alluding to father and son. One could argue that several of the extant images in the *Paris Psalter* refer to youthful power, such as the elevation of David on the shield.[45] It would seem a probable hypothesis that luxurious illustrated books would be presented by emperors to their sons, particularly if the imagery enforced dynastic goals. The *Barberini Psalter*, to be discussed below, almost certainly was presented to the young prince depicted in the opening miniature.

---

38   On Habakkuk, who appears as both young and old, see Brubaker (1999) 285, fn. 24, with examples; for the *Rabbula Gospels*, see Cecchelli (1959) fol. 7b (Habakkuk, youthful), 6a (Jonah), 4a (Joshua) and for the Syriac bible, see pl. 5, fig. 5 (Joshua), pl. 7, fig. 4 (Jonah); for the Syriac, also see Sörries (1991) fols. 52v, 178v, 180v, fig. 7 (Joshua), fig 15 (Jonah), fig. 18 (Habakkuk, mature).

39   Full pages illustrated in Brubaker (1999) fols 246v, 161v, figs 90–91.

40   Buchthal (1974) 330–333, pl. 72.

41   Fol. 7v; Buchthal (1938, 1968 edn) pl. VII.

42   *De administrando imperio*; *PG* 113:157–422; for text and translation, see Moravcsik (1967) 46–47.

43   Fol. 1v, Buchthal (1938, 1968 edn) pl. I.

44   Buchthal (1974) 333; *Miniature* (1905) fols. 1v, 2r, pls 19, 20.

45   Buchthal (1938, 1968 edn) pl. VI.

The proposed recipient of the *Paris Psalter*, Constantine VII's only son, Romanos, is depicted with his wife in the *Romanos ivory*, a carved plaque, perhaps originally part of a triptych (fig. 5.4).[46] Christ stands centrally on a raised *suppedion*, flanked by the couple on whose crowned heads his hands rest. Dressed in ceremonial costume, with their hands gesturing towards Christ, the emperor and empress appear young, yet their height suggests that they are fully grown. Each bears an engraved inscription, together naming them Romanos and Eudokia, emperor and empress of the Romans.[47]

The relief has been used as a fundamental tool to assess the development of ivory carving from the ninth century. Although it was traditionally held to depict Romanos IV (1068–1071) and Eudokia Makrembolitissa and dated between 1068 and 1071, Hayford Peirce and Royall Tyler re-evaluated its origin and concurred that it represents Romanos II (959–963) and was made between 945 and 949.[48] They claimed that since the eighth century the emperor was always shown bearded, whereas the emperor's sons were beardless.[49] Therefore, this ivory could not depict Romanos IV, a full emperor, but rather Romanos II, a junior emperor. In 945, Romanos, aged six, married the daughter of Hugh of Provence, Bertha, who was four and renamed Eudokia on her marriage. Bertha-Eudokia only lived four more years. Therefore, at the oldest, the children could be aged ten and eight. Goldschmidt and Weitzmann corroborated the view of Peirce and Tyler, which remained largely unchallenged until 1977. Ioli Kalavrezou-Maxeiner then assigned the ivory to Romanos IV, basing her argument primarily on the status and title of Eudokia as compared to that of little Bertha. Weitzmann, in 1979, affirmed this revised identification and agreed with Kalavrezou-Maxeiner largely due to her discussion of the figure style.[50] More recently, Anthony Cutler, in one case with supporting evidence from Philip Grierson, has refuted Kalavrezou-Maxeiner's position.[51] A further study by Maria Parani approves the tenth-century date.[52] These arguments will not be reviewed here, but I would accept that the ivory portrays the earlier Romanos as a boy and his child-wife Eudokia, in about 945.

It is likely that this ivory was a formal gift representing the union of the young couple. The children were, therefore, not shown at their real ages, but as they would appear in the future. The image belies the transgressions of the marriage, for children were not legally able to marry before the ages of 14 (for the groom) and 12 (for the bride). Though approved by a dispensation from the

---

46   Durand (1992) n. 232, with bibliography; Cutler (1995) 605–610; Goldschmidt and Weitzmann (1930, 1979 edn) II, n. 34; Kalavrezou-Maxeiner (1977); Peirce and Tyler (1927) 129–136; Peirce and Tyler (1941) 15–16.

47   ΡΩΜΑΙΟC ΒΑCΙΛΕΥC ΡΩΜΑΙΩΝ and ΕΥΔΟΚΙΑ ΒΑCΙΛΙC ΡΩΜΑΙΩΝ.

48   The earliest attribution is in Du Cange (1680) 162, with illustration; Peirce and Tyler (1927) 129–136 surmised that it predates the ivory of Otto II and Theophano, thinking it unlikely that this latter image of Christ blessing the emperor and empress would arise in the west.

49   Peirce and Tyler (1927) 130; on this, see also *DOC* III/1, 143.

50   Goldschmidt and Weitzmann (1930, 1979 edn) 45; Kalavrezou-Maxeiner (1977).

51   Cutler (1995) 605–610; Cutler (1998).

52   Parani (2001).

Fig. 5.4   Paris, Bibliothèque nationale, cabinet des médailles, 945-949. The *Romanos ivory* probably commemorates the marriage of the young junior emperor Romanos II, aged about six, and his four-year-old wife, Eudokia. Bibliothèque nationale de France

emperor, in this case the most interested party, the marriage was unorthodox and may have caused some concern. The couple are portrayed as young, for Romanos remains beardless, but fully grown, as if at a more conventional age of marriage.

The function of the ivory carving would affect the manner in which the royal couple was depicted. Until the eighteenth century the ivory was inlaid in the wooden binding of an eleventh-century western gospel book, which suggests the ivory was in the west from an early date.[53] It is quite possible that the *Romanos ivory* was intended as an official representation, possibly made as an ambassadorial gift, and it therefore replicated the kind of image that one sees on the official coinage, where young emperors are portrayed as older than they really were. Romanos was depicted as youthful on the coinage.[54] Coins dated between 945 and 959 show a junior emperor of significant stature, but smaller than Constantine VII.[55]

A similar lack of attention to specific age, but probably for different reasons, is found in the imperial Crown of Hungary, which was clearly an imperial gift. As it is now, the crown is a piecemeal assemblage from various sources. The enamels were presented in 1075 to Géza I (1074–1077), the King of Hungary, as an official offering by the Byzantine emperor Michael VII.[56] Depicted in enamel, Michael takes the place of honour in the centre and on his right, our left, is Constantine, his one-year-old son. Géza, a poor cousin in the Byzantine family of nations, is on the right (fig. 5.5).[57] The message of the crown is the unity of the Byzantine commonwealth, supremely ruled by Michael with Constantine as his heir. Constantine is depicted as symbolically young but mature enough to fulfil his role as junior emperor, and beyond his one year. The crown therefore shows us, as did the *Romanos ivory*, that in public art, imperial children were not necessarily depicted at their real age, a maxim often repeated in discussions of young Byzantine rulers. Yet this precept has perhaps biased us to ignore the realistic portrayal of children in other contexts.

Michael is also depicted in a manuscript portrait, which was made some years before the enamel just discussed, when he was in his late teens and at the centre of a rather complex power arrangement. The manuscript, Paris. gr. 922, was, like Paris, gr. 510, apparently made for members of the imperial family

---

53   D. Gaborit-Chopin in Durand (1992) n. 148.

54   Grierson dates a coin showing Romanos as a large child to 945, when the boy was six, although he does not explain the specificity of the date; see *DOC* III/2, pl. XXXVII, 14.1.

55   *DOC* III/2, pl. XXXVII, 15.9–15.33.

56   Wessel (1969) n. 37, figs 37a–g; Bárány (1961) esp. 34–41; on dating, see Polemis (1968) 63. Kelleher argues the date to have been after 1074: see Kelleher (1951) 57. Some scholars speculate that the crown was intended for Géza's wife. For an appraisal of the various views, see Twining (1960) 387–398.

57   The inscription reads ΚΩΝ(CTANTINOC) ΒΑCΙΛΕΥC ΡΩΜΑΙΩΝ Ο ΠΟΡΦΥΡΟΓΕΝΝΗΤΟC. Kelleher (1951) 36. For the political background of this gift, and the articulation of the 'Family of Kings' in the iconography of the crown, see Obolensky (1971b, 1974 edn) 213–214.

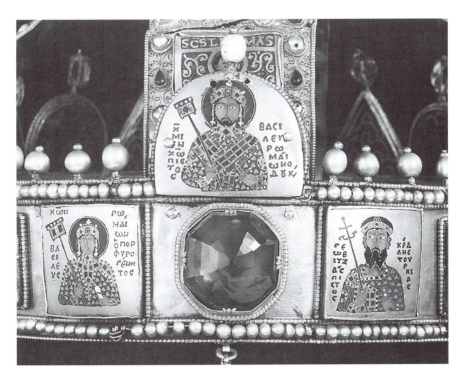

Fig. 5.5   Budapest, Hungarian National Museum, enamels 1074-77. The *holy crown of Hungary* contains enamels showing Michael VII in the centre, with Géza, the Hungarian ruler to the right and Michael's infant son, shown
as a boy, to the left. Károly Szelényi

and similarly contains a dynastic miniature (fig. 5.6).[58] In contrast, however, this manuscript is small, minimally illustrated and clearly for personal use. The portrait, as in Paris, gr. 510, seems traditional in form, but portrays a specific situation. This manuscript was made for Michael's mother, the empress Eudokia Makrembolitissa, wife of Constantine X Doukas (1059–1067). The book contains writings of the church fathers and opens with a so-called 'magic square' with the inscription 'this book belongs to Eudokia Augusta' repeated in a pattern.[59] The same words designating ownership appear in an acrostic

58   Fol. 6r; see Spatharakis (1981) n. 71, fig. 126, with bibliography; Spatharakis (1976) 72, 102–106, 181, 242, 251–252, 356, fig. 68; Wessel, (1970) 344, fig. 199; Anderson, (1979) 229–238; Kalavrezou-Maxeiner (1977) 317; *RBK* I, 768, III, 473, 750, 752, 783; Lazarev (1967) 250, n. 35; *Byzance* (1958) n. 28; Jerphanion (1930) 71–79, 71, 73; Grabar (1936) 118, fn. 1; Diehl (1925–1926, 2nd edn) II, 631; Ebersolt (1926) 37, 46–47, 65; Omont (1892) 14; Omont (1886–1898) 176–177; Bordier (1883) 126–128; Montfaucon (1708) 51, 295–298; Hennessy (1996) 74–107.

59   Fol. 4r; reproduced and discussed in Montfaucon (1708) 295–298; for further comment on this type of square patterned dedication, see Dimitrova (1994) frontispiece, 26–27. Dimitrova is apparently unaware of the Paris manuscript, since she claims that the 'magic square' in B.M. Add. MS 39627 (a fourteenth-century Bulgarian manuscript made for the Tsar Ivan Alexander) 'provides a unique example' of such a device. She suggests that the scribe Simeon, who calligraphed the manuscript, was the inventor of the magic square. The form of the Tsar's square, bearing the inscription 'Io Alexander Tsarya Tetravaggel', is identical to that of Eudokia. The Tsar's gospel contains a double-page family portrait, and it

Fig. 5.6   Paris, Bibliothèque nationale, Paris, gr. 922, fol. 6r, ca. 1067.
The family of Constantine X. Bibliothèque nationale de France

dedicatory poem that faces the portrait and reads ΕΥΔΟΚΙΑC Η ΔΕΛΤΟC
ΑΥΓΟΥCΤΗC ΠΕΛΕΙ. [60] In the portrait, the central figure is the Virgin, who
crowns the empress on the right, and a male figure on the left, who has always
been said to be Constantine X, the emperor. Flanking them are two children.
Angels in blue gowns fill the upper left and right corners and are leaning down

---

seems highly likely that the combination of the portrait and the 'magic square' was derived
in some fashion from Eudokia's *Sacra Parallela*.
    60   Fol. 5v (fols 4v and 5r are blank).

to place crowns on the heads of the children. All the figures face frontally and are dressed in imperial regalia. The Virgin and the empress both stand on rhomboid-shaped *suppedia*, whereas the three male figures stand on rounded ones, which suggests a certain equality of status between them. The bearded figure is full-grown and wears a red *loros* and holds the *akakia*. The child to the left is the size of a young adolescent. He has short brown hair and wears a blue *chlamys* over a red tunic. The figure to the right is smaller and appears to have blond hair and is dressed in red in a full length, long-sleeved tunic.

Constantine X acceded to power on 24 November 1059, accompanied by his second wife Eudokia Makrembolitissa.[61] Constantine and Eudokia, according to most sources, had a total of seven children, four of them boys, of whom one died in infancy. Michael, Andronikos, Anna and Theodora were born prior to Constantine's accession, while Konstantios and Zoe were *porphyrogenneti*. Konstantios, according to Psellos, was born within a year of Constantine's accession and immediately given the imperial title.[62] Shortly afterwards, Michael, the eldest (probably in 1060), received the same honour, but Andronikos was not crowned until the reign of Romanos IV (1068–1071).[63] Constantine ruled for seven years and died in May 1067, when Eudokia became regent for two of the sons, Michael VII and Konstantios. The regency lasted seven months and six days and ended on 1 January 1068, when Romanos Diogenes married Eudokia and became emperor. Romanos IV ruled for less than four years, being defeated and captured at Manzikert on 26 August, 1071.[64] Eudokia then resumed joint rule as regent with her sons. Psellos's version claims that Michael was prepared to abdicate if his mother wanted, so anxious was he not to contravene her wishes. However, Michael soon asserted himself and Eudokia was exiled to a monastery by late October 1071.[65] The first regency, therefore, lasted for seven months (May 1067–1 January 1 1068), and the second for about one month (September–October 1071). It is to this first period of the regency, I suggest, that the *Sacra Parallela* portrait illumination belongs.

Eudokia became regent for two of the sons, Michael, the eldest and Konstantios, the third son. Konstantios took precedence over the second son, Andronikos, since he was born a *porphyrogennetos*, that is during his father's reign.[66] The dedicatory poem is the key to the actual meaning of the image, which rather than representing the parents and two of their sons, depicts Eudokia and her three sons, Michael, Andronikos and Konstantios, during the period of her regency. The poem is addressed to Eudokia and opens by proclaiming Eudokia's power through Christ and continues (from line seven):

---

61 Polemis (1968) 29.

62 For *Chronographia*, see Renaud (1928) II, 7: Constantine X, XXI; Sewter (1953, 1966 edn) 340.

63 See *DOC* III/2, 779, fn. 4.

64 *DOC* III/2, 780; also see Gautier (1966) 156–59.

65 *DOC* III/2, 780.

66 On the term porphrogennetos, see Dagron (1994) 105–142.

> Now then, carrying out sensibly so many things,
>   you have really found an immaterial inheritance
>   by denying every earthly desire.
> For this reason you are now adorned with the crown of power
>   in all the hymns and holy books
>   together with the children, resplendent in the crown,
>   the light-bearing branches of the purple.[67]

The denial of earthly desire probably refers to a vow Eudokia made to Constantine shortly before his death, in which she promised that she would not remarry.[68] She would not bear the crown of power if Constantine still lived, and she is pictured in this very book ruling together with her children. A further line (18), 'Dissolve, oh queen, the darkness of grief', presumably refers to her husband's recent death.

The implications of this poem, that Constantine is dead and Eudokia rules with her children, have perhaps been overlooked because it has always been assumed that the eldest son, Michael would be depicted beardless. In the coinage, junior emperors and young men ruling under a regent were depicted with a fresh face, while the senior emperors wore beards. Michael's exact age is not known, but as his parents probably married before 1050 and the children's tutor and court historian Psellos described him as 'long past his boyhood and able to think for himself', or as someone who is of age (between about 17 and 45), at the time of his father's death, he could well have been 17 or more.[69] Eudokia is slightly larger than Michael, showing her precedence over her son, who was treated as a minor. He was apparently not very intelligent and quaked in his shoes at the sight of his mother.[70] As we have seen, there was no fixed law for imperial 'coming of age'. In general, as in this case, mothers were reluctant to give up power to their children.

Whereas his mother and her advisors did not consider Michael old enough, or wise enough, to rule, the illuminator, or whoever prescribed the portrait, showed him as a man. Legally he was a child, but visually an adult and permitted in this private context to appear so. In relation to this, it is worth mentioning Alexios II's mosaic portrait in the south gallery at S. Sophia, which depicts him individualized and at a particular time in his youth, indicated by a downy moustache (fig. 5.7).[71] The portrait was perhaps made at the time of his coronation in 1122 at the age of 16. This area of the church was used primarily by the imperial family and therefore was, in some sense, private.

In the Paris manuscript, made for the empress's own private use, public and traditional iconography was adapted to show a regent with her sons. It is notable how similar the image is to other dynastic portraits. Little has changed

---

67   Text and translation in Spatharakis (1976), 103–104.

68   On this vow, see Oikonomidès (1963) 101–128.

69   For *Chronographia*, see Renaud (1928) 7: Eudokia II; Sewter's translation (1953, 1966 edn) 345.

70   For *Chronographia*, see Renaud (1928) 7: Eudokia I; Sewter (1953, 1966 edn) 345.

71   Whittemore (1942) 26–28, 84–86, pl. 20; Mango (1962) 28–29; Cormack (1994) esp. 242.

except Michael's appearance as a man, but otherwise the traditional formula of frontality, signs of office, and ceremonial costume are all present. Eudokia and her sons take up and maintain the reins of power, using visual means to reinforce their own sense of continuity. There is no reason why manuscripts as private gifts or intended for personal use cannot contain political messages. Individuals need assurance of their right to rule and religious supremacy, so that political messages cannot all be seen as intended for public viewing.

Fig. 5.7   Istanbul, S. Sophia, gallery, ca. 1122. This mosaic in the imperial area of the gallery shows Alexios II probably at the time of his coronation at the age of sixteen. His parents are shown on the adjacent wall with the Virgin and Child

Another, apparently formal but evidently private, portrait is in the *Barberini Psalter*, Vatican, Barb. 372, which contains in a straightforward way many dynastic elements of imperial children's portraits (fig. 5.8).[72] The manuscript was probably given to the young boy shown standing between his parents beneath an enthroned Christ in a mandorla. An angel crowns each figure, and the boy holds a book in his left hand. Scholars have disputed the identity of the figures shown, and overpainting complicates the issue, as does the place of the *Barberini Psalter* in relation to comparable psalters. It seems most likely, as argued by Jeffrey Anderson, that the emperor is Alexios I (1081–1118) with the empress Irene and their first son John.[73] John was born in 1088 and probably elevated to the throne in 1092, aged four. Anderson, however, does not think John is the recipient of the psalter. He proposes political and doctrinal motives in Alexios's commissioning of the manuscript connected with his stance against iconoclasm. This was taken up to defend Alexios's purloining of liturgical implements in order to fund battles between 1081 and 1091.[74] Anderson shies from recognizing a private function for the book, writing that 'manuscripts, it might be argued, are not an ideal means of influencing public opinion, an observation seriously flawed by its avoidance of the issue of the nature and size of the audience in cases such as that of the *Barberini Psalter*'.[75] He does not, however, indicate that the psalter had widespread use or a public function, merely that it was made at the Studios monastery. The centrality of the boy and the clear message of his coronation seem to indicate his primary role. While adult imperial portraits usually indicate that political power comes through Christ, that the leaders are anointed from on high and rule with God's sanction, the same is so for children's portraiture. The children, by court practice and by education, were

---

72   Fol. 5r; Spatharakis (1981) n. 312, with bibliography; Anderson (1983) 35–67; Spatharakis (1976) 26–36; Bonicatti (1960) 41–61; De Wald (1944) 78–86.

73   First proposed in Jerphanion (1930) 71–79; see also De Wald (1944) 78–86; Anderson (1983) 35–67.

74   See Anderson (1983) 56–57.

75   Anderson (1983) 59.

Fig. 5.8   Vatican, Barb. gr. 372, fol. 5r, ca. 1092. This frontispiece miniature probably depicts the emperor Alexios I with his young son John, perhaps at the age of four when he was crowned, and the empress Irene. © Biblioteca Apostolica Vaticana (Vatican)

instilled with these concepts. The portrait was surely intended as educative, graphically demonstrating political and religious constitutional theory for the prince.

Just as Basil's daughters were not shown in Paris, gr. 510 manuscript, Alexios's daughter Anna is not in the portrait. The image clearly emphasizes Alexios's worldly power and religious authority. Presented to the boy, the image is clearly intended to impress upon him his future role, which until his birth had been invested in Anna and her betrothed, Constantine, the son of Michael VII. The image emphasized the altered political situation, and perhaps additionally warded off any aspirations to power that Anna and a future husband might have had.

Byzantine dynastic portraiture was taken up with enthusiasm by satellite rulers, clearly desiring to emulate Constantinopolitan practices. One distinctive example is in S. Sophia in Kiev, built between 1036 and 1047 by Yaroslav, Grand Prince of Rus'.[76] The church, a huge and elaborate building, signified both his powerful rule and dedication to Christianity, but also his simultaneous dependence on but independence from Byzantium. Central to the decoration of the church were three walls in the nave devoted to paintings of Yaroslav's family with Christ. Of the dynastic portraits from Byzantium, either surviving or known from texts, the example most similar to Yaroslav's family portrait was that designed by Basil I for his *Kainourgion* palace mentioned above.[77] Perhaps Yaroslav was directly influenced by Basil's mosaic, showing all Basil's children, boys and girls alike, wearing crowns and praising God. It has been suggested that S. Sophia in Kiev was influenced by the *Nea Ecclêsia*, which was, like the mosaic, erected within the palace by Basil I, and was dedicated by Photios in 881.[78] Although painted some 150 years after the installation of Basil's mosaics, it is quite possible that the paintings identify Yaroslav's own prodigious family with that of Basil, founder of the Macedonian dynasty. The childless Zoe (1028–1050 – with husbands/sister/adoptee), then ruling in Constantinople, endeavoured to perpetuate the faltering and infertile dynasty, but her problems must have been apparent to Yaroslav. His prolific family formed a marked contrast with that of Zoe's third husband, Constantine IX Monomachos (1042–1055), against whom Yaroslav's eldest son Vladimir led an attack in 1043. It was probably about this time that the paintings were executed. While using Basil's iconography to associate himself with a great emperor, Yaroslav was perhaps highlighting his own advantage over the emperors in Constantinople.

Yaroslav began building the church in 1036, less than fifty years after his father Vladimir had officially adopted Christianity.[79] The political and religious union with Byzantium was both driven and sealed by Vladimir's marriage with Basil II's sister, Anna, in 989.[80] As a condition of the nuptial agreement,

76   Kämpfer (1992) esp. 77–87; Poppe (1981) esp. 38–41, figs 6, 7; Lazarev (1971) esp. 236, figs a, h; Lazarev (1966) 47–48, fig. 30; Logvin (1971) esp. 37–38, figs 13, 125 (in colour); Powstenko (1954) esp. figs on 138, 139, 141 and figs 149, 153–160 (before and after cleaning); Kämpfer (1978) 111–116, figs 60–63; Poppe (1968) (French summary, 28–29). I do not have access to the Russian and Ukrainian texts by Vysockij, Lazarev and Karger, whose views have been assimilated through the synopsis and critique of others.

77   *Vita Basilii*, PG 109:348–352; Mango (1972) 197–198.

78   Cross and Conant (1936) 494; the church is described in the *Vita Basilii*, PG 109:341–345; Mango (1972) 194–195.

79   For a comprehensive explanation of the dating for the construction, see Poppe (1981) 39, 48–49. Poppe argues, convincingly, that the stone work was begun in 1038 and completed by 1045 when S. Sophia in Novgorod was begun by the same craftsmen. The church was probably consecrated close to 1046. On Lazarev's hypothesis that the church was consecrated on 11 May 1046, see Poppe (1981) 39, with references; also Kämpfer (1978) 111, fn. 41.

80   Meyendorff (1981) 4.

Vladimir converted and made Christianity the official religion. It seems that in adopting Christianity and in joining and conceding to the Byzantine family of nations, the emperor embraced a set of beliefs, but also a conceptual and visual language encapsulating political power and religious faith, as well as a prescription for dynastic portraiture in which children played a significant role.

The church has nominal and visible links with S. Sophia in Constantinople and therefore gave Yaroslav, in emulating the Byzantine emperor and his church, both concrete and evocative associations as worldly ruler and divinely appointed delegate of the church. Yaroslav's fresh self-image, surrounded and supported by his children, enunciated secular and sacred power. While familial power was well known to the Russians, to the faithful in Kiev worshipping in S. Sophia the imperial portraits, showing Yaroslav and his family with Christ, must have represented a new and potent ideal. At that time, S. Sophia was the grandest church built outside Constantinople and much larger than anything being constructed in Constantinople at the time. Designed with five main aisles and 13 domes, the interior was decorated with a complex series of mosaics and wall paintings. The portraits of Yaroslav and his family approaching Christ were set centrally in the church on the north, west and south walls of the nave. They were designed to be optimally seen from the east end of the church. Yaroslav emphatically articulated his own place with his wife and offspring next to Christ, closer to God than the religious leaders, who were often appointed by Byzantium and with whom there was a continual power struggle.[81]

The restorations and recordings of the imperial portraits reflect various cultural concerns in the past. The royal portraits were probably painted in three seasons between 1043 and 1046.[82] Only six figures remain, four on the south wall and two on the north (fig. 5.9). The west wall has been destroyed. The wall paintings have been considerably altered over time: in the seventeenth century, major restorations and alterations were done to the west wall, and in 1858, the four figures on the south wall were changed into representations of Wisdom, Faith, Hope and Charity.[83] The two remaining on the north wall are apparently in their original state. New plaster was laid over the adjacent north-wall figures and repainted.[84] A programme to clean all the church decorations began in 1936 and was completed by the 1950s.[85] However, the portraits on the south wall may not have been restored correctly.

The most useful record of the paintings, though not in their original state, is a copy of a drawing made by the Dutchman A. van Westerveldt, the court

---

81   On this, see Cross and Conant (1936) esp. 477–486; Obolensky (1957, in 1971a) 23–78; Meyendorff (1981) esp. 14–15.

82   Poppe (1968) 28.

83   Powstenko (1954) 132.

84   Powstenko maintains this was done in the fourteenth and fifteenth centuries when, probably, Lithuanian princes were painted; but this seems unlikely, since they do not appear in Westerveldt's drawing; see Powstenko (1954) 132.

85   Lazarev (1971) 221.

Fig. 5.9   Kiev, S. Sophia, nave, south wall, 1043-1046, heavily restored. The church has royal portraits showing the king Yaroslav and his children, both boys and girls. Robin Cormack

painter to the general of the Duchy of Lithuania, J. Radziwill. Westerveldt made the original drawings in 1651. They were destroyed in 1812, but only after a copy had been made for the last Polish king, Stanislaw August Poniatowski, which was found in 1904 and published in 1908.[86] In 1634–1646, prior to Westerveldt's drawing, the paintings had been altered under the metropolitan Peter Mogyla.[87] The records therefore bear witness not only to the eleventh-century paintings, but also to Mogyla's changes, Westerveldt's interpretation and the interpretation of the copyist at the Polish court. Another watercolour exists from 1845/47, executed by F. Solncev. This shows the painting on the south wall before it was repainted in 1858.[88]

In Westerveldt's drawing the symmetrical composition centres on the figure of a ruler, who is flanked on the left by a princely donor, followed by four children of various ages, and on the right by an adult princess and four additional children. The various endeavours to explain the wall paintings have unanimously held that Westerveldt omitted two of the figures in the composition. As can be seen from the drawings, he did not distinguish between the three walls on which the paintings lie, but rather presented the figures as if placed on a single surface. The central figure is frontal and bearded with a crown and halo, holding a sceptre. Under Mogyla's restoration of 1634, the figure of Christ was replaced with one of Saint Vladimir, on whom Mogyla founded a cult at S. Sophia. At this time, the adult prince and his wife, Yaroslav and Irene, were given crowns and Yaroslav a moustache. According to Andrzej Poppe, the figures to the left and right of them, which were nearly

---

86   On this, see Powstenko (1954) 56.
87   Kämpfer (1978) 111; Poppe (1968) 6–11, 28.
88   Poppe (1968) 28, fig. 3b.

completely destroyed, were not repainted. This is why they were not included in Westerveldt's drawing.[89] Yaroslav holds a model of a church in his left hand, which he presents to Christ. Behind him in a row, and decreasing regularly in size, are four figures in full-length garments, of whom the first two carry candles in their left hands. On the other side, Irene, his wife, is followed by four other figures who decrease in size like those on the other flank, but the last two figures are smaller than the last figure on the other side. The figures without candles have their arms raised out towards Christ and all are seen from three-quarters view. They do not appear to be wearing shoes but rather are in stockinged feet, with one foot placed in front of the other.

Many scholarly interpretations rest on the gender of the children, arguing that the female children are in the south, standing behind their father, and the male in the north, standing behind their mother, and therefore in the suitable place in the church for male and female worshippers. H. Logvin suggested that the figures on the north wall were female, arguing that women worshipped in the north part of the church. Therefore the sons, on the south wall, were wrongly restored.[90] While it has been suggested that women in general were confined to the galleries, this would mean that they were excluded from communion, which was not the case. Thomas Mathews has traced various records which suggest that in earlier times women worshipped in one aisle of the church, but were also present in the galleries, as were men too.[91] Recently, Robert Taft has provided more evidence to suggest that practice varied.[92] Art historians have interpreted the Kievan paintings in a very literal way, assuming that the figures must be standing in the location allocated to them for worship, so that the women would be in the south gallery above the image of female children.

There is, I would argue, no evidence from the drawing to suggest that the children are either male or female. There appears to be no gender distinction in dress: Yaroslav and Irene both wear a very similar robe tied at the waist and have a *chlamys* draped over the left arm. In the other figures, the dress shows variations of pattern and decoration within two basic designs. Three of the children wear the *chlamys*, the second and fourth on the south wall and the first on the north wall. The remaining children wear unbelted, full-length robes, with ornate trim down the centre and borders around the lower hem. There is also no distinction in dress due to age, since the smallest child on the south wall is wearing a *chlamys* like the parents.[93] Comparing the photographs of the present-day wall paintings with Westerveldt's drawings and Solncev's watercolour, the portrayal of the clothes seems largely consistent. However, changes may well have been made in the ca. 1634 restorations, which are recorded in both.

---

89   Poppe (1968) 28.
90   Logvin (1971) 37.
91   Mathews (1971) 129–133.
92   Taft (1998) 27–87; on women's areas of churches see also Gerstel (1998) 89–111 (though, I would suggest, rather problematic); Teteriatnikov (1993) 44 and fn. 45.
93   Poppe debates that the second and fourth figures on the south wall are boys, and that the first might also be; see Poppe (1968) 29.

Yaroslav, as patron, and the Byzantine artists, or artists highly influenced by Byzantine masters, were apparently not concerned to show distinctions between male and female, neither in dress nor in status. This equality between male and female may in part derive from the influence of Yaroslav's mother, Anna, the sister of Basil II, a woman who played an important religious and political role. Coming to Kiev to marry Vladimir in 989, she had brought with her the trappings of her own culture: clothes, books, religious paraphernalia and also craftsmen who had set about building the Church of the Tithe under Vladimir's direction. The new visual language of Kievan rule was therefore dependent on a woman, and implemented through her lens. Perhaps in deference to his wife's lineage and in recognition of the crucial role that women can play, Yaroslav gave the females visual equality. Furthermore, Yaroslav recognized the diplomatic value of girls and used his daughters to great political advantage, making alliances in the Christian world by marriages between his daughters and the rulers of Norway, France and Hungary.[94]

Can we determine the identity of any of the children? Yaroslav and Irene had six sons and three, possibly four, daughters. They were all alive in 1043–1046, since the eldest son Vladimir died in 1052. He was born in 1020 and the third son, Svyatoslav, was born in 1027.[95] The *Primary Chronicle* does not mention the birth of the second son, Izyaslav, who inherited the kingdom, nor of any of the daughters. The fourth son (Yaroslav's favourite), Vsevolod, was born in 1030, and the fifth/sixth, Vyacheslav, between 1034 and 1036.[96] Another son, Igor, appears to have been born before Vyacheslav, although Poppe maintains Igor was born after Vyacheslav, who was born in 1036, and that the daughters were married between 1043 and 1049.[97] Therefore, if the paintings were completed in, say, 1045, the eldest of the six sons would be 25 and the youngest about nine. The eldest daughter would be married and have left home, although she might well be still included in the portrait. Of course her husband could be present also, but this does not seem to be the case. It is unclear whether the second and third daughters were married at this time. I have found no evidence to substantiate that there was a fourth daughter, which may suggest that the children are not separated by gender. Ten children were portrayed and so perhaps one or more may have been a grandchild.

In interpreting these paintings, we are faced with many layers of restoration and interpretation. Certainly, the iconography as presented by Westerveldt is rather different from that described in the account of Basil's mosaic in the *Kainourgion*. Westerveldt showed the Russian children walking in a solemn procession with two of them holding candles. But the emperors and their children in Westerveldt's drawing appear rather unusual: their bodies have solid, volumetric shapes and their headdresses do not conform to Byzantine

---

94   Meyendorff (1981) 15.

95   Cross (1953) 222–225, 231.

96   Cross (1953) 225, 232. Vsevolod married a Byzantine princess, who bore a son in 1053; on this, see Cross (1953) 231; Obolensky (1971b, 1974 edn) 294. She was probably the daughter of Constantine Monomachos.

97   Cross (1953) 232; Poppe (1981) 40.

custom. It seems likely that the images were noticeably changed in the 1634–1646 renovations, or that Westerveldt made a loose interpretation of what he saw. Perhaps the original, as apparently glimpsed in the smallest figure on the north wall, was more similar to the portrayal of Basil's children, standing frontally with raised arms. According to Poppe the portraits on the north wall are in their original unrestored state. [98] They have uncovered heads, as can be seen from a close-up of the second figure from the right, and may suggest the original appearance of those on the south wall.[99] This raises questions about the restoration of the figures on the south wall who are standing, as in the drawing, turned towards the west. Logvin may well be right in saying that the white handkerchiefs on the heads on the south wall are a nineteenth-century addition.[100] Poppe also questions the accuracy of the present-day restoration of the figures on the south wall, particularly in light of the Westerveldt drawings and the Solncev watercolour.[101] But he also suggests that the girls were given their royal hats with sable borders in 1634, as seen in the drawing.[102] Apparently, in 1935 the nineteenth-century layer of oil paint was removed without taking into account that during the 1843–1853 renovation the painter, having removed the eighteenth-century layer of roughcast, changed the paintings, particularly the heads. He is said not to have altered the clothes so much.[103] My sense is that Westervedlt's drawing shows us more of a seventeenth-century restoration, or a seventeenth-century view of an already distorted image, than has so far been admitted. However, the concepts behind Basil's palatial mosaic and Yaroslav's church wall painting correspond: an expression of dynastic rule under God, and a celebration of the children with their parents.

Yaroslav's family portrait is one example of the many dynastic images articulated by rulers of Byzantium's allies and dominions. In the most thorough study of this type of portraiture, focusing on Georgia, Antony Eastmond has explored the meanings entailed in depictions of royal children, particularly in the portraits of Queen Tamar and her son Giorgi Laša, the future Giorgi IV. The two are shown with Tamar's second husband, Davit Soslan, at the Monastery of Natlismcemeli; with her father Giorgi III, shortly after Laša's coronation at Q'inc'visi and at Betania; and mother and adult son together are shown together at the monastery of Bertubani.[104] These examples highlight the importance of strengthening the seeming insecurity of a female ruler through depictions of her male offspring. As so often in dynastic portraits from Constantinople, the royal daughter is not included.

---

98   Poppe (1981) fn. 91.

99   Lazarev (1966) fig. 30; Kämpfer (1978) fig. 60.

100 Logvin (1971) 37.

101 Poppe (1968) 29.

102 Poppe (1968) 28.

103 Poppe (1968) 29.

104 Eastmond (1998) 124–141, 144–149, 161–164, 169–178, figs 62–64, 69–70, 74–77, 81, 83–85; Velmans (1977) fig. 17.

Other examples of the embedding of future political control through images of children are found in Balkan, particularly Serbian, wall paintings.[105] Of particular interest is a portrait of Milutin and his very young wife Simonis, the daughter of Andronikos II, in the Church of Joachim and Anna at Studenica.[106] It is probably dated to 1314, when Simonis was ten. Placed on the south wall and facing portraits of saints and of the Virgin and Child, the painting invokes Milutin's sainted connections. Simonis was only five when she married; the union broke with Byzantine ideas of childhood and sexuality: political expediency ruled over conventional morality. Simonis is portrayed as a woman, fully grown. Clearly, in this case, childhood became masked by proprietary.

Further examples come from Bulgaria, including two manuscripts from the rule of Tsar Ivan Alexander. In B.M. Add. MS 39627, dated in a colophon to 1356, the Tsar is depicted with the principal members of his family in a double page portrait (fig. 5.10).[107] The manuscript was probably copied from Paris, gr. 74 or a very similar Byzantine manuscript. On the left page stand his three daughters and the elder daughter's husband. On the facing page, Ivan Alexander stands with his second wife, Theodora, with the eldest son, Ivan Šišman, between them, and the second son, Ivan Asen, to Ivan's left. The boys are small and clearly not yet in power, but their important place in the dynasty is shown through positioning. The second manuscript is Vatican, Slav. 2, a translation of the history of the Chronicle of Constantine Manasses, which also contains portraits of Ivan Alexander and his family.[108] This manuscript is dated to 1344–1345 and was made about ten years prior to the other.[109] In one image, the young heir, Ivan Asen, is lying on his death bed surrounded by the patriarch of Tŭrnovo, Ivan Alexander, one of the emperor's sons, the Tsarina Theodora, Ivan Asen's wife (who was the daughter of Andronikos III Palaiologos and who married aged nine in 1336) and two of Ivan Alexander's daughters (pl. 11). A further miniature depicts Ivan Asen arriving in heaven, and a third shows Ivan Alexander with his sons.[110] Ivan Asen stands to the right of his father, with an angel beside him, indicating that he has died. The two other sons, Michael and Ivan Stratsimir are next to their father.[111] The two scenes of Ivan Asen's death and arrival in heaven are different from the other imperial portraits. No longer a frontal ceremonial portrait, the image tells the

---

105 Velmans (1977) 62–74; figs 23, 25, 30, 31, 32.

106 Velmans (1977) fig. 24; Hamann-MacLean and Hallensleben (1963) fig. 246.

107 Fols 2v–3r; for good reproductions, but an unsatisfactory discussion of the manuscript, see Dimitrova (1994) 35–36, figs 11, 29; see also Bakalova (1986) esp. 19–21, 37, 47, 48, 52, figs 15–16; Filov (1934) esp. 14–18, pls 1–2, 135–136, Spatharakis (1976) 69–70; Der Nersessian (1927) esp. 9.

108 Dujčev (1963) esp. figs and text 2, 3, 69; Spatharakis (1976) 160–165, figs 103, 105; Filov (1927) esp. 30–32, 77, figs 2, 3, 69; Bakalova (1986) 21–32, figs 3, 4, 5.

109 Filov (1927) 10–15; Dujčev (1963) 32; Spatharakis (1976) 164 says Ivan must have died during its execution, but he could have died before. According to Papadopoulos, Ivan died shortly after his marriage; see Papadopoulos (1938) n. 77.

110 See Dujčev (1963) fols 2r, 2v, 205r, figs 2, 3, 69.

111 On this, see Spatharakis (1976) 163–164.

Fig. 5.10 London, B.M. Add. 39627, fols 2v, 3r, 1356. This double page portrait shows the emperor of Bulgaria (second from the right) with his wife Thamara and their two small sons, while on the facing page are his three daughters and the eldest daughter's husband. Copyright British Library

narrative of these idealized historical events. The participants display their relationships and their own involvement in the scenes.

Conversely, a slightly later manuscript illumination maintains the traditional form of dynastic portraiture. A portrayal of Manuel II and his family was used as a frontispiece to a copy of the writings of Saint Dionysios the Areopagite, Paris, Louvre, MR 416, which was probably made between 1403 and early 1405

(fig. 5.11).[112] Displaying the legendary prestige of Byzantium, it reiterates the strength of Manuel's protection through Christ and his role as religious leader. It is an image of idealized order, with anointed power and familial unity. The portrait gives quite different impressions from those that recent historical

112 Fol. 2r; Durand (1992) 356; Spatharakis (1981) n. 278, figs 492–494, with bibliography; Lowden (1992a) 249–260; Wessel (1975) 219–229; Beck (1976) 184. As a fourth son was born in 1404 or early 1405, it is thought this portrait predates his birth.

Fig. 5.11 Paris, Louvre, MR 416, fol. 2r, 1403-05. The eldest son of the emperor Manuel II stands close to his father and dressed alike. The family, including the empress Helena and Theodore and Andronikos, are being protected by the Virgin and Child. © Photo Rmn/© Caroline Rose

realities might suggest, with Manuel plagued by hostilities between members of the imperial family and the imminent threat of subjection to the Turks. John, co-emperor and future John VIII, stands next to his father, dressed identically to him, and visually sharing his power, while the younger sons in the centre,

Theodore and Andronikos, are ostensibly associated with their mother, Helena, in red and gold attire.[113] All the figures are blessed by the Virgin and Christ.[114]

The very luxurious manuscript, now in the Louvre, was sent by Manuel as a gift to the abbot of St-Denis in Paris. The emperor had visited there between 1400 and 1403 on a diplomatic excursion to the west looking for help against the Turks. When Manuel returned from Paris, he apparently wanted to keep up his contact with St-Denis and so sent this manuscript in 1407. It perhaps reflects new optimism in the empire's situation, which had since been reprieved from the Turkish threat by the Mongols.[115]

The ritualistic appearance of the family also represented customary court life, where the children evidently played a somewhat public role.[116] We know this from an account given by Ruy de Clavijo, an ambassador from Castille. He visited Manuel in Constantinople in October of 1403, perhaps at about the same time the portrait was made. And he was received by the emperor in a chamber where the three young princes were present with their mother after attending church.[117] We think of the dynastic portrait as an artificial arrangement set up to display political theories, but the family grouping may be quite close to what a visitor to the court would have viewed.

The apparent formality of Manuel's family portrait is personalized by the presence of the children. They are most likely shown at their real ages: they were aged between four and ten in 1404. However, the children's faces all look similar, with oval chins and narrow features with quite heavy brows. The two younger boys are very alike and, while this may have been true to life, to some extent the portraits may have been generalized.

The children's presence was clearly wrought with political and religious significance. Their serious appearance and regal clothing confirmed their role as inheritors of worldly power and religious faith, but their presence also expanded the viewer's understanding and knowledge of Manuel's own life and situation. Manuel had left his family with his brother while he travelled, so his connections in the west had never seen them. To what extent are they here as official ambassadors to the royal abbey, or as signifiers of Manuel's familial and human context? These images are emblematic, but we also see likenesses of the children, if only generalized ones, and their presence serves to shape the personal identity of the emperor and to provoke personal understanding.

The portrait of Manuel II's family is an example of a diplomatic gift, although the portrait has many similar qualities to the portraits we have seen that appear to have had a private use, those of Basil and his family in Paris, gr. 510, that

---

113 John was born in December 1392, Theodore's birth date is not known, Andronikos was presumably born in 1400 after Manuel had left for the west, Constantine was born in 1404/5 and the birth date of the fifth son, Demetrios, is not known, but the sixth, Thomas was born in 1409. No daughters are mentioned; see Barker (1969) 494–496.

114 For inscriptions, see Spatharakis (1976) 140; Barker (1969) 533.

115 On this history, see Barker (1969) 165–254.

116 R. Cormack points out that diplomatic ceremony centred on the imperial palace by the time of *De Ceremoniis*; see Cormack (1992) 222–223.

117 For text, see Le Strange (1928) 61; see also Barker (1969) 245–246.

of the Empress Eudokia and her sons in Paris, gr. 922 and that of the young emperor John II with his parents in the *Barberini Psalter*. So far, we have not looked at any examples of manuscripts that step beyond a perceived formality of representation. We shall now turn to a series of images accompanying a poem, apparently written and decorated as a souvenir for a young princess on her arrival in Byzantium to marry an imperial heir. These pages contrast with the previous portraits, since the images are not formal representations, but rather form a narrative description.

Vatican, gr. 1851 is a thin volume, composed solely of four bifolia, which contains the partial text of a poem and seven illuminations (pl. 12).[118] The text is addressed to the princess. The poem is written in an informal vernacular, in largely undatable script and is accompanied by brilliantly coloured and expressive images.[119] The poem and the images tell of the arrival of the young newcomer to Constantinople, her reception by the women of the Byzantine court, her visual transformation into a Byzantine *augusta* and a first encounter with her sister-in-law in the splendour of an imperial tent. The manuscript would appear to be the original one given to the princess after her meeting with the groom's sister, and the poem is addressed to the princess. It tells of her father's pain over losing her, the message she sends announcing her arrival and her reception by 70 female relatives, who dress her in appropriate Byzantine costume. The next day she undergoes the even more 'indescribable and dread' meeting with the daughter of the emperor, who comes to meet her where she is encamped in a tent outside Constantinople. The manuscript appears to be a memento of this huge change in her life. The text is clearly for her eyes, as it compares her favourably with the Byzantine princess, who is 'unable to bear comparison with your beauty'. This obviously has political rather than personal significance, but would not probably be primarily for a Byzantine viewer.

Studies have focused on the dating of the manuscript, derived largely from identifying the individuals described in the poem and pictured in the illuminations. In the early twentieth century, S. Papadimitriou argued that the poem concerns the marriage of Agnes, renamed Anna, the daughter of Louis VII of France, and Alexios, later Alexios II, the son of Manuel I, which took place in 1179, when the children were probably aged about ten and eight.[120] It is this view that is currently largely accepted.[121]

Without presenting here a full study of the style and iconography of the manuscript; comparisons with other examples of imperial dress suggest that the illustrations in the manuscript are Palaiologan (thirteenth to fifteenth centuries) and not Komnenian (late eleventh to twelfth centuries), and

---

118 Jeffreys (1981) 101–115; Spatharakis (1976) 210–230, figs 158–173; Canart (1973) XLVI; Canart (1970a) 324; Canart (1970b) 650; Belting (1970) 26–29; Papadimitriou (1902) 452–460; Strzygowski 1901, 546–567; and, although problematic, Iacobini (1995) 361–409. The manuscript measures 230 mm x 175 mm.

119 On the vernacular, see Jeffreys (1981) 104–105.

120 Papadimitriou (1902) 452–460.

121 For instance, Maguire, in Evans and Wixom (1997) 191.

probably fourteenth century.[122] Furthermore, the arguments for the text of the poem being twelfth century are debatable. Certain details given in the poem restrict the field of identification. We know from the text that the emperor's son was a *porphyrogennetos* and that the boy was already made co-emperor, since the foreign princess is referred to as *augusta*.[123] We also know that his father was still living, and he had more than one sister, since the Byzantine *basilissa* is described as the first or 'eldest' daughter and she was a *porphyrogennete*, that is a female born to the emperor.[124] We also know that the groom's bride came from abroad and that her father was also living. If one explores all the possibilities from the thirteenth to the fifteenth centuries, there is only one marriage that seems to fit the necessary criteria: that of Andronikos IV, who was the son of John V. John was born in 1332 and took the throne in 1341, aged nine.[125] He had four sons, Andronikos, Manuel, Theodore and Michael. Andronikos was born in 1348, made co-emperor in 1355 and he married, in 1356, aged eight, Maria, the nine-year-old daughter of the Tsar of Bulgaria, Ivan Alexander.[126] John V was alive at the time, and still young, being only aged 24. John V's wife, Helen, was also living. John and Helen had a disputed number of daughters, one of whom, Irene, was born in 1349, so she was aged seven at her brother's marriage.[127] Irene was therefore a *porphyrogennete* and she had a younger sister. The marriage of Andronikos IV therefore meets all the historical requirements needed for it to be the possible context for the poem.

There is sufficient evidence to suggest that the text, script and the decorated initials are Palaiologan, and more likely fourteenth century. Rather than pursuing these points here, I will leave aside the identification of the figures and the dating of the text and discuss some of the overall meanings of the images.

The text and the images emphasize the role of women, both young and adult, in aspects of court custom. Although we do not have the complete manuscript, and missing pages probably showed the meeting of the bride and groom, the foreign princess's initiation into Byzantine life comes in part through the women of the court. These representations contrast with formal imperial portraits, dominated by sons and dynastic hopes. The narrative of this rite of passage gives women the prominent role, although men retain their formal significance. Men and boys receive messages and make announcements, while women and girls embrace and sit and converse. Yet, the political significance of the women should not be ignored. One goes forward and helps the princess dress in a Byzantine gown before she appears to the court. This is a personal moment and perhaps typical of female behaviour, but it also has diplomatic

---

122   For the full argument, see Hennessy (2006).
123   Fol. 2r, line 11 and fol. 1v, line 17; fols 3r, 18, 5v, line 11, 4r, line 20, and 4v, line 6.
124   Fols 6v, line 19 and 4v, line 4.
125   Papadopoulos (1938) n.73.
126   Papadopoulos (1938) n. 81; on the date of Andronikos's coronation, see Luttrell (1986) 104.
127   Papadopoulos (1938) n. 88.

significance. The transition is political, physical and emotional, and it is metaphorically important and so related in the text and images.

The miniatures certainly depict children, and probably pre-pubescent juveniles, who are placed in official and responsible positions in a diplomatic setting. The images reconstruct the ritual encounter between two young girls, the foreign and the Byzantine princesses. The young bride is welcomed by the sister of the groom, a girl, perhaps of her own age, who was clearly given familial and ambassadorial duties. The manuscript provides a valuable view of the roles played by children at court, particularly girls, and the attention given to affinities between children of the same age. The illuminations depict the princess's liminal experiences, arriving as sylph-like foreigner, shedding her native appearance and becoming transformed into a Byzantine bride, changed from a girl to a woman and from an outsider to an insider. The manuscript appears to be a memento of this turn in her life and to have been made for her.

This is an example of a book apparently made for a young person. One needs to ask if the book's appearance, the choice of imagery and the style of the script may have been adapted especially for young eyes. There are some features of the manuscript that might suggest that it was intended for a child. The text and images are narrative, and together they tell an intriguing story. Foreign princesses were prepared for their new lives in the east before their arrival, and educated in Greek culture.[128] However, it is probable that the newcomer was not yet entirely comfortable with reading Greek. Therefore the images would have held more interest for her than the text and she would have remembered the events through the pictures. The poem is full of drama and excitement, and perhaps the hyperbole in the text is intended to attract the attention of a young listener or reader. Certainly the description of her encounter with her sister-in-law as frightening is understandable: to a child the whole experience would be overwhelming. The illustrations are bright and graphic, with very colourful and visually explicit scenes. Could the unusual language be associated with the age of the intended reader? Byzantine children, especially imperial ones, had books made for them, but we can only speculate in what sense this manuscript has features thought particularly appropriate to a child. The Vatican manuscript is an example of a book apparently created specifically for a child and should be viewed in this way.

We have seen that usually imperial children appear in dynastic, but not in individual portraits. This perhaps is not surprising, since similarly empresses were generally also portrayed with their husbands and were viewed in the context of their association with the supreme ruler. The children were therefore not seen subjectively, but largely contextually and in relation to the structure of power. One could argue that they did not have autonomous value.[129] The portraits tend to be ritualistic and, at a first glance, seem to conform to formal hierarchical patterns in which the figures who take precedence are usually

128 Herrin (1994) 70–71.
129 One exception to this is the *Romanos ivory*, where Romanos is without his parents.

larger and more central. However, this is not the case. Perhaps somewhat surprisingly, Byzantine empresses are shown on very equal terms with their husbands, often of very similar size and comparably attired. Similarly, the children are not relegated to low status. They are depicted as small, but usually at a realistic size for their age, and are often designated by inscriptions stating their names and titles; they also carry signs of office indicating their rank and position. Children did not rule on their own, but shared power, receiving guidance and protection from adults. Adult emperors extended power to their wives, and often their children, principally male ones, while young emperors ruling under a regent also shared it with their mothers and sometimes their siblings. There was strength in numbers and in diversity.

The empresses appear in the dynastic portraits as primarily significant in their roles as mothers of the heirs. For instance, the inscription surrounding Basil's wife, Eudokia Ingerina in Paris, gr. 510 emphasizes that Eudokia was elevated by Basil and that she bore him sons. One could argue that this suggests that females are not important in themselves, but purely as vessels of generation. However, women clearly did have influence at the Byzantine court and, particularly when the men were absent, assumed an instrumental role in politics. The strength and tenacity of the female regents suggests that women had a strong taste for political authority. But, equally, young sons collaborated with their mothers in regencies, as conveyed by the portrait in Paris, gr. 922, to promote an image of male youth united with female maturity.

We have also seen that although the portraits generally conformed to traditional models, they also demonstrated individual situations. The Paris, gr. 510 portrait shows us the emperor, his wife and the young *despotes* and indicates their formal relationships, with the emperor supreme, his wife gaining her power through him and the boys dressed carefully to show hierarchical differentiations between them. Yet personal relations within the family affect the composition of the group. In this portrait the third son is omitted because he was destined for the church and had no political role (though it turns out that he became patriarch aged 16 when appointed by his brother), making it clear that it is specifically a dynastic portrait, unlike the mosaic in the palace, where all Basil's children were portrayed. Within the family, while children could be seen as one of a group, they also each had their own rank and were destined for a particular kind of future, with a position to fulfil. The portraits enforced these roles and expectations.

It is hard to know to what extent the portraits were real likenesses of the children. As noted in the portrait of Manuel II's family, the children were individualized in terms of ceremonial protocol and dress, but it is unclear how specifically the facial features related to their actual appearance. The portraits are not concerned with the children's psychological or inner qualities, although in Vatican, gr. 1851, the images do reveal something of the princess's inward state, which is explored, perhaps in a rather conventional *topos*, in the text.

It is ambiguous whether the images of children in power reveal to us anything about them as children. The children appear very much like the adults, dressed in the same type of costume and sometimes are dressed identically, as with Manuel II and his eldest son. It is incorrect to think that the children are dressed as adults; they are simply dressed in ceremonial costume that has no differentiation according to the size of the wearer. The key is differentiations in status, responsibility, power or future power, and not whether someone is an adult or a child. The children are presented primarily as integral members of the imperial family and in the same way, whatever their age. This is not to say that there is no reference to age: the children do appear, except in rare instances, perhaps tied to an object's public function, to be shown at the age they were. Their dress and regalia received the same detail and elaboration as did that of the parents, and the children are in no way of lesser visual importance than the adults. The depiction of the children tells us that young members of the imperial family were recognized at court as potential rulers and the siblings of rulers and were accorded status and ceremonial roles.

The children's portraits reveal notions about the family and its political importance: the generation of several sons assured direct succession and a united presence promised peace and security for the future. Visual means were an important way of enforcing this in both public and private contexts. Clearly the imperial family liked to see affirmations of its power through its symbols and insignia. But do the images reveal anything about the family as a social unit? Basil's portrait reflected divided family relations, but generally the portraits reveal little. However, again, Vatican, gr. 1851 gives us a graphic depiction of the extended family relations and the ceremonial customs surrounding a betrothal. These images are not dissimilar to the narrative images portraying Ivan Asen's death in Vatican, Slav. 2.

While we know that very young children did not rule independently, the visual material certainly suggests that they were invested with political and religious power from a young age. There is no impression that the children are legally, psychologically or physically unable to rule and clearly the imagery is intended to convey political integrity. The children had religious authority also, anointed by God and filled with spiritual blessing. Just as we saw very young children in S. Demetrios in Thessaloniki endowed with spiritual power, the imperial children were viewed as if wielding that authority at a young age. Sometimes expected to marry as children (even at an age younger than the law permitted) and groomed to rule, they accepted political and religious responsibility.[130]

---

130 Patlagean (1973) 88.

Chapter 6

Jesus and Mary

This chapter looks at the two figures at the acme of religious power, at Christ and the *Theotokos*, the Mother of God, and asks in what ways representations of either of them as children display the features central to the themes discussed so far: elements of childhood, family affiliations, sanctity or power. In what sense are they represented as children with attributes we might associate with childhood? What kind of relationships do they appear to have with their parents? How is their sacred state conveyed to the viewer? And in what sense is potency defined or suggested?

The range of available material is vast and a selection will not give a panoramic or a synthetic view. The aim is to highlight some of the issues and ways of exploring them and to set forward some conclusions. The material concerning Christ's youth can be grouped under three principal types of imagery. First, he is shown in narratives as a baby and as a boy with his mother, his father and the religious authorities; second, he appears in iconic images where he is usually depicted with his mother; and third, he is depicted alone in symbolic representations, as a baby, small child or adolescent, often in the portrait known as Christ Emmanuel. The three categories are not self-contained, and there is a crossover where scenes with narrative content stand for doctrinally symbolic events and ritually complex meanings. The narrative scenes may not have had a strictly narrative role, but the term is used here to refer to the depiction of a series of events that follow one another in sequence and usually reflect the events described in a text, though they may also serve symbolic and representational aims.[1] Iconic images can be highly varied, including icons in any media: the representation of Christ with his mother takes many forms and can be interchangeable with the image of Christ as Emmanuel. Similarly, images of the Virgin as a child have two principal types, narrative and iconic: she is shown as a child with her parents and religious figures in narrative images and also, though not so frequently, appears iconically with her mother, Anna; this last type will not be discussed here. The representation of Christ's and the Virgin's infancy and youth is a crucial part

---

1   On issues of narrative, see, for instance, Bal (1994) esp. 97–101.

of the depiction of each of them and is instrumental in defining their human and doctrinal identities, serving both narrative and theological purposes.

The specific depiction of immaturity, whether portrayed by a child with childlike features or by a small version of a fully grown person, is present in early (in date) depictions of Christ and of the Virgin. Much of the imagery concerning them when young derives from apocryphal texts and is, arguably, developed by popular consent: stories were conceived to account for the Virgin's purity and her son's miraculous birth, but the prevalence of these tales supersedes any doctrinal need. The Virgin's childhood and motherhood are closely interrelated, with the one developed to explain the impossibility of the other. Similarly, the imagery of Christ's childhood, rather than necessarily focusing on him as a child, can serve to explain his birth from a Virgin. While not ignoring this type of significance, this section treats the images primarily as representations of children and asks in what way Jesus and Mary were given status as children and how they may or may not have been differentiated from other children. The representations can be explored to see how they postulate programmatic ritual and verify doctrinal meaning, but also to question how they may have affected viewers who were not necessarily aware of intricate theological metaphysics. It is hard to determine whom the designers of images had in mind when selecting iconography. Particular depictions may have solely perpetrated doctrine, but doctrine also developed as a response to people's spiritual or pragmatic needs. The choices of imagery about the Virgin and Christ as children, if made or influenced by lay patrons, church leaders or theologians, reflect a many-layered tier of interests and respond to larger cultural and human issues current in society. The representations indicate the interests and concerns of church leaders, both secular and monastic, but also those of the followers, whether expert in theological thinking or simply observant of church practice; so, the portrayal of Jesus and Mary as children informs us about society's attitudes to sacred children. And the great number of images of the Virgin and Christ as children suggests a fascination not only with nascent holiness, but also with childhood and its passage to adulthood. Considering that close to half the population of Byzantium at any one time was made up of children or adolescents, as discussed before, many of the worshippers must have been young: one can therefore question how the choice of imagery may have responded to youthful interests, and how in turn children would have reacted to the visual representations. It is impossible to estimate the extent to which the presence of children as recipients of the imagery might have affected the development or success of any iconography, but the influence of children's interests and education on the choice and interpretation of the iconography needs to be kept in mind.

The first part of the chapter looks at textual sources for the infancies of Christ and of the Virgin and discusses their relation to visual representations. The next four topics focus on examples of Christ's and of the Virgin's infancy, treated separately. The discussion starts with Christ's infancy as depicted at S. Maria Maggiore in Rome, which provides an early and unusual portrayal of the Christ child, and at Tokalı kilise in Göreme, Cappadocia, chosen because it gives an early and extensive series of images showing elements of Christ's childhood. The discussion then turns to the Virgin's infancy, as depicted at the church of Joachim and Anna near Çavuşin, Cappadocia, again giving an early but also developed portrayal of Mary's childhood, and in the twelfth-century illustrated homilies of James Kokkinobaphos, which provide detailed illustrations of Mary's life. This brings the discussion to an analysis of the ways in which ties are made between the lives of Christ and of the Virgin, as seen at S. Michael in Cemil, again in Cappadocia, and at the church of St Saviour in the Chora, now the Kariye Camii, in Istanbul. The following sections turn to iconic representations of Christ as a child and focus on images depicting the baby or child Christ with his mother, in icons, ivories and wall paintings, and then move to representations of Christ Emmanuel in monumental decoration and in manuscript illuminations.

In narrative images of the nativity of Christ and its associated events, such as the coming of the magi and the journey to Egypt, the story is, at least in essence, described in the synoptic gospels. Numerous elements, however, were gleaned from the apocryphal writings to develop a colourful and many-levelled story as told in visual imagery. Issues about the formulation and canonization of the gospel texts are well known to be controversial and the selections and emphases given to Christ's infancy can be interpreted in many ways.[2] Certain stories about Christ's childhood, known only in apocryphal texts, are not generally depicted in art. These were first developed in the second century in the *Infancy Gospel of Thomas* and in the *Infancy Gospel of James* and later popularized in the compilation called the *Gospel of Pseudo-Matthew*.[3] On the other hand, the Virgin's childhood is not mentioned in the synoptic gospels, but the apocryphal tales about her childhood became visually represented in a series of scenes. The main events, such as the birth of the Virgin and her presentation in the temple, became incorporated into church festivals and paralleled similar events in Christ's life, whose celebration was also part of the ritual cycle.[4] The textual sources for Christ's and for the Virgin's narrative images of childhood are generally held to predate the visual representations, although visual representations could have affected the formation of the apocryphal narratives. One cannot assume that the texts came first, but we have little evidence by which to refute this common assumption.

The *Infancy Gospel of Thomas* records separate episodes from Christ's childhood, portraying him as a precocious murderer and healer, both rebellious and angelic. These events are rarely used, if ever, in representations of his life, perhaps because they do not appear to serve a direct theological point. On the other hand, the apocryphal stories about the Virgin were constructed

---

2   On the development of the gospel texts, see, for instance, Hopkins (1999) 290–321.

3   On dating of *Thomas* and *James*, see Hock (1997) 8–9, 91–92.

4   The annunciation and dormition were marked as early as the sixth century and, by the eighth, the nativity and dormition became part of the liturgy; see Lafontaine-Dosogne (1964–1965) 24–25.

to establish her purity and status as the bearer of Christ. The *Infancy Gospel of James* presents in narrative form the Virgin's childhood, courtship and early motherhood up until the massacre of the innocents and therefore also elaborates on the early life of Christ.[5] The events of the Virgin's childhood and Christ's birth and early life are entwined with details evolved to reinforce or rationalize the nonrational premise of the virgin birth. The childhood of Jesus and Mary became both sanctioned and favoured: the images of the children were pivotal in defining perceptions of the adult Christ and Virgin and their roles on earth and in relation to God. Equally, the images suggest that society had a clear sense of the centrality of childhood experience, familial bonds and spiritual independence.

The story of the Virgin's early life and the accompanying imagery were developed to reinforce emerging principles concerning her part in Christ's birth and his *hypostasis*. The precise identity of the Virgin and her theological role served the definition of Christ's dual nature, which was determined at the first Nicaean Council in 325 by the recognition of the Son as consubstantial with the Father and therefore sharing in his divinity (*homoousios*). This was reaffirmed at the Council of Ephesus in 431 and again at the Council of Chalcedon in 451, where the hypostatic union was accepted, in Clement of Alexandria's terms, as a mutual interpenetration of the divine and human natures (*perichoresis*). At Ephesus, Mary's title of *Theotokos* was sanctioned, and as the bearer of God, she assumed an elevated role.[6] Images concerning the Virgin's life and motherhood focus on her spiritual and sexual purity, the authenticity of the virgin birth and Christ's divine incarnation. The images present her unsullied childhood and virginity, excuse her relationship with Joseph and explain the nigh unexplainable pregnancy, but also emphasize the physicality of Christ's birth and his incarnate presence as a baby.

Two key apocryphal figures who serve to prove Mary's virginity are the midwife and Salome. Their story is recorded in the *Infancy Gospel of James*: Joseph goes in search of a midwife, whom he finds, and, explaining that Mary is a virgin, he brings her to the cave of the nativity. The midwife responds incredulously, but a cloud withdraws and the infant becomes visible with his mother. Another woman, Salome, then arrives and, expressing her disbelief in the Virgin's virginity, thrusts her hand into the birth canal, only to have it catch fire in punishment. She is healed when she picks up the Christ child (*James* 19:12–20). In early depictions of the nativity, Salome appears alone without the midwife, kneeling by the crib and raising her withered arm to touch the

---

5   For the text and commentary, see Hock (1997) throughout. The earliest known manuscript is dated to the fourth century, *Papyrus Bodmer V*; on the manuscripts, see Hock (1997) 28–29; the original version probably dates to the late-second century; see Hock (1997) 11–12; and also Amann (1910). For *Pseudo-Matthew*, which was possibly as early as the sixth-century, but more probably eighth or ninth, see Hennecke and Schneemelcher (1963) I, 406–407 and for partial text, see 410–413; James (1924) 70–79; for Latin text, see Tischendorf (1853) 50–105.

6   For texts, see Tanner (1990) I, 1–19, 37–74, 75–103; for texts and discussion, see Hefele (1907–1952) I.I, 528–620, II.I, 287–377, II.II, 649–680.

infant Christ. This is found in ivories, such as a plaque in the British Museum, datable to the first half of the sixth century, and another in Manchester, and on pyxes in Berlin and in Vienna.[7] In certain cases, Salome touches the Virgin rather than the Child, as she does in the Chair of Maximian in Ravenna, and in frescoes from Bawit and from S. Maria Antiqua.[8] Similarly, in an ivory from Dumbarton Oaks, Salome sits at Mary's feet, dressed in a *maphorion* with her chin in her hand.[9] Salome beside the crib is also portrayed in conjunction with depictions of both Salome and the midwife washing the Child, a scene that, while borrowed from antiquity, did not develop pictorially in Christ's nativity until the sixth or seventh century.[10] For example, both Salome and the bathing scene are depicted in John VII's oratory at Old St Peter's, Rome, dedicated in 706, in the catacomb of San Valentino in Rome, probably from a similar date, and at Castelseprio.[11]

An early narrative cycle has survived in S. Maria Maggiore in Rome, dated to the pontificate of Sixtus III (432–440), who was the patron.[12] These mosaics predate by about a century the earliest examples of the apocryphal midwife and Salome, the female testifiers at the birth of the Son of God. Although their imagery has been interpreted in many ways, a direct link with the story as told in the *Infancy Gospel of James* has not been made, one that to me seems viable.

The large basilical church is known for two sets of early Christian mosaics. The first is a series of panels that run along both sides of the nave and represent episodes from the Old Testament. Scenes from Christ's infancy are portrayed on the arch, often referred to as the triumphal arch, that divides the chancel from the nave. In the upper left register of the arch the scene shows a seated woman, flanked by two angels on the left and three on the right, while a sixth flies above her head with the white dove of the Holy Spirit (pl. 13). To the right stands a man in a knee-length white toga and a gold cloak over his shoulder. This scene must be read as the annunciation, with the angel in the sky bringing the glad tidings to the Virgin, who must be the seated woman.

---

7   As mentioned in Weitzmann (1951a) 55, n. 57; for the London plaque, see Volbach (1952) n. 131, pl. 41; Vassilaki (2000) n. 3; for the Manchester plaque, see Volbach (1952) n. 127, pl. 39; for the Berlin pyxis, see Volbach (1952) n. 174, pl. 55; for the Vienna pyxis, see Volbach (1952) n. 199, pl. 58.

8   For the Chair, see Volbach (1952) n. 140, pl. 43; on this imagery also see Nordhagen (1961) 333–337, esp. 334 n. 8; for Bawit, see Baldwin Smith, (1918) fig. 21 (reference in Weitzmann (1951a) 55, n. 59); for S. Maria Antiqua, see Grüneisen (1911) fig. 83, pl. IC.XXI; Wilpert (1917) IV.1, pl. 194.

9   Weitzmann (1972) colour plate 3 and XIX, XX, n. 20, from Syro-Palestine and datable to the end of seventh or eighth century.

10   Deshman (1989) 33; Nordhagen (1961) 333–334.

11   For the Oratory, see Nordhagen (1965) 130–134, figs 3–4, pls 7–9; for San Valentino, see Osborne (1981) 86, 88–89, pl. 15a; for Castelseprio, see Weitzmann (1951a) 53–57, pl. 5; Castelseprio has recently been dated between the second half of sixth century and first half seventh century; see de Spiribo (1999).

12   Spain (1979) 518–430; Karpp (1976) figs 6–28, 210; Brenk (1975) 9–52, figs 46–48; Oakeshott (1967) 73–76, pls 55–60; Cecchelli (1956) 197–236, pls XLVII–LX; for further references, see Clarelli (1996) 323–325, fns 1–4; also Vassilaki (2000) pls 4–6.

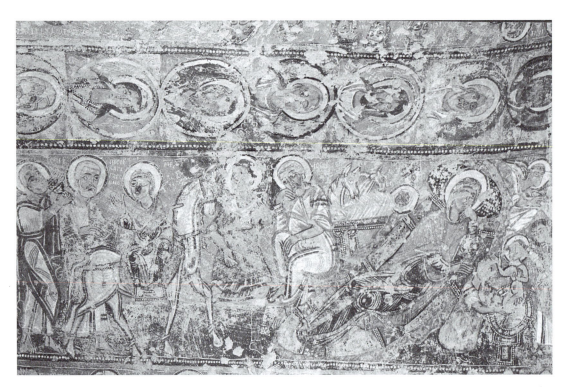

Fig. 6.1   Göreme, Tokalı kilise, old church, first half of the tenth century. In the central register, painted in reds and oranges on a blue ground, are scenes from the journey to Bethlehem and the nativity. Nicole Thierry

However, a striking and anomalous feature of the mosaics' iconography is the portrayal of the Virgin. In this scene and in three others, she does not appear in the blue *maphorion* that later became characteristic of her attire, but rather she is clothed in an elaborate gold dress with white sleeves and a necklace, with her head uncovered and decorated with a jeweled coronet. She resembles an affluent late antique woman. Of the three angels standing to the right of the Virgin, the first turns towards the Virgin, the second faces towards the viewer and the third turns towards the man on the far right, who must be Joseph. In this way the narrative is carried by the angels from the news given to Mary to the assurances given to Joseph, which are developed in the adjacent panel, to the right, portraying Joseph's dream. This scene proves to be next in the chronological narrative, but we shall return to it later.

In the scene directly beneath the annunciation, a child, the Christ child, sits on a very large throne, taking centre stage. He is portrayed not as a baby, but as a small boy, dressed in a white toga with a dark border. Four angels stand behind the throne. A male figure with dark hair and beard, dressed in a white toga, presumably Joseph again, stands on the far left behind one of the magi. The Virgin, recognizable from the annunciation scene, is clothed in the same attire and is seated to the left of the throne with her face turned towards the Christ child. Flanking her, seated to the right of the throne is a woman dressed in the blue *maphorion*, a cloak wrapped over her head and around her body. Suzanne Spain has argued that this figure is the Virgin and that the aristocratic woman, who we see as the Virgin, is Sarah, the wife of Abraham, and the figure normally identified as Joseph is Abraham.[13] There is no justification for this argument, and indeed Sarah and Abraham are depicted differently in panels in the nave, with Abraham having white hair and a long robe and Sarah clothed in a serviceable long dress with her head covered by a white cap. The aristocratic woman must be the Virgin. The three magi are present, indicating that this scene is the adoration of the magi; they are dressed in Persian costume, one standing to the left of the Virgin and the other two to the right of the figure in the *maphorion*.

Yet, who is the figure dressed in the *maphorion*? Among other proposals, C. Cecchelli suggested her to be divine wisdom, H. Karpp suggested a Sybil, L. De Bruyne considered her to be *Ecclesia ex Gentibus* (and indeed she does appear similar to depictions of *Ecclesia*, the Church, as, for instance, in the nave at S. Sabina), and C. Bertelli noted in passing that she was one of the midwives present at the birth.[14] A closer look reveals that she is Salome, the woman whose disbelief led to the proof of the Virgin birth, as told in the *Infancy Gospel of James*. She is recognizable by her distinctive left hand, which is withered, and which she holds on a white cloth or handkerchief, highlighting its malformed shape with burned stubs for fingers. The depiction of her still maimed hand must have served to distinguish her.

Identifying Salome in this scene helps with reading the scenes in the panel in the upper right section of the arch. On the far right a man with dark hair and short beard in a white toga and gold cloak, Joseph, is sleeping while visited by an angel, as recorded in the Gospel of Matthew and in the *Infancy Gospel of James*. The angel assures him of Mary's purity, even though she is with child (*Matthew* 1:20–21, *James* 14:5–7). Behind him is a building that appears to be a temple with two white doves perching at the door, presumably a gift of sacrifice. To the left of the temple a group of mature men, with shoulder-length hair, mostly white, and bearded, walk forward led by a man with shorter white hair and beard, who extends his hands covered by his. In the background is an arcade with seven arches, and framed by the arch to the far left stands a woman, presumably the Virgin, since she is dressed as the Virgin in the annunciation and the adoration. She holds out a child, the Christ child, dressed in the same white toga and holding up his hand. Beneath the second arch stands a man who must be Joseph, since he is dressed as he was before, who gestures towards a woman who stands beneath the third arch. The woman raises her hand in a motion of speaking and is dressed in a *maphorion* similar to that of Salome in the magi scene with a cloak that covers her head and wraps around the body. However, here the dress is brown and red, not blue. Between Joseph and this woman stands an angel.

This scene has been given various interpretations, including Christ's presentation at the temple and the betrothal or marriage of Mary and Joseph

---

13   Spain (1979) 530–539, quote on 536.

14   De Bruyne (1936) 13:239–269, esp. 254; Karpp (1976) fig. 19; Cecchelli (1956) 213–214; for *Ecclesia*, see Oakeshott (1967) pl. 74; Clarelli (1996) 336 and fn 45 for references; for further references, see De Bruyne (1936) 254.

(Grabar, Spain), the prophetess Anna, with Simeon to the right (De Bruyne, Cechelli, Brenk, Karpp); and, again, the woman in the *maphorion* has been described as Ecclesia (Schubert).[15] C. Bertelli mentions that the scene shows Anna accompanying Jesus into the temple with one of the *'levatrici,'* one of the midwives at the birth of Christ.[16] This seems to me to be getting closer to the answer. However, the woman on the far left holding the child must be the Virgin, since she appears with the same dress and overall appearance as in the annunciation and adoration. Following the story in the *Infancy Gospel of James*, Joseph installs Mary in a cave and sets off to find a midwife. When he returns, the midwife is incredulous, but then the mother and child appear (*James* 19:1–17). It seems this is the moment depicted with the midwife being the woman in the *maphorion*. Joseph brings the midwife forward to witness the birth of Christ, and so the scene depicts Christ's first presentation. The setting is not a cave, nor is it in the adoration; the events take place in idealized locations. This scene therefore follows in chronological order after Joseph's dream and before the adoration. Furthermore, there is no figure that appears to have the age of Simeon, and the scene takes place at a distance from the temple, which seems to be more connected with Joseph's dream.

In the scene below, on the second register on the right, Christ is standing towards the centre, depicted at a similar age as in the adoration. Joseph and Mary, dressed as in the previous three scenes, stand behind him with two angels to the left and two to the right. On the far left of the panel is a walled city, in front of which stand a group of men, most of whom are pictured with short dark hair and short or no beards. One figure has blond hair. Two figures stand out, those in the front of the group. One is bare-chested, dressed in white cloth draped over his shoulder, and has a substantial beard; the other appears with short hair and beard and wears a gold tunic and a blue *chlamys* with a gold *tablion*. Both men have their right hands raised, seemingly in a gesture of speech. This episode has traditionally been said to derive from the *Gospel of Pseudo-Matthew* and to refer to an encounter with an Egyptian governor, Aphrodosius.[17] Spain is probably correct in determining that this gospel developed too late to be used and that the iconography does not conform to the text. However, I believe she is mistaken in identifying the man in a *chlamys* as David and his bare-chested companion as Isaiah. It is perhaps more likely that these people are witnesses of the child Jesus speaking with insight or of one of Jesus' many childhood miracles. These are relayed in the *Infancy Gospel of Thomas*. For instance, in one scene, the Jews in his hometown, Nazareth, overhear Jesus speak and marvel at such words from a five-year-old. As Jesus continues talking, he skips forward, taunting them with his wisdom (*Thomas* 6:9–12). The figure wearing a *chlamys* and diadem or headband could be a

---

15   Spain (1979) 536; De Bruyne (1936) 249–251; Cecchelli (1956) 219; Brenk (1975) 19; Karpp (1976) figs 14, 16; Grabar (1936) 217–220; for summary, see Künzle (1961–1962) 172–174; Clarelli (1996) 322–324.

16   Bertelli (1961) 48–49 and n. 32.

17   For extensive references on this, see Spain (1979) 519, n. 7.

community leader rather than a king such as David. This dress is not restricted to kings: for instance, Joshua wears both *chlamys* and headband in a scene in the nave.[18] The man accompanying him, bare-chested with a heavy beard, appears to be a nazarite or prophet. He may well represent a religious figure, so that the men together stand for secular and spiritual authorities. The crowd includes an assortment of other men, presumably the townsfolk of Nazareth.

In the panel below this scene, we see the three magi in front of Herod, being dispatched to find Christ and betray his whereabouts (*James* 21:1–9). And beneath this is a depiction of Jerusalem. In the panel below the adorations is a depiction of the massacre of the innocents, with a group of women holding small children on the right and soldiers advancing towards them on the left (*James* 22:1–2). Below this is a representation of Bethlehem. The scenes therefore are not arranged in chronological order. Rather the four scenes that pertain directly to Christ's birth and revelation to the world are placed in the top two registers, the larger ones, with the two less central scenes below.

In both the scenes where Christ appears as a little boy, he is marked by his independence, standing forward with angels or seated alone; although attended in the adoration on both sides by the magi, Joseph, Mary and Salome, he is not reliant on them. In the centre register on the right, in the scene suggested here to show the townspeople witnessing the boy Christ, he is a central, active participant, unlike the adored child or the babe in the Virgin's arms of more customary adoration and flight to Egypt scenes. The images, as interpreted, together show the first witnesses of Christ's miraculous incarnation. These are the first two people beyond his family to recognize his miraculous birth, that is the midwife in the upper right register, and Salome in the adoration, and subsequent witnesses, the magi, also in the adoration, and, directly across the arch on the right, the people of Nazareth who experienced the lucidly defiant and divinely inspired miracle-working child. The iconography therefore testifies to the recognition of the Son of God, born to a virgin, who is portrayed as a realistic, if idealized, little boy. This seems entirely appropriate in the church that was the Station Church for the First mass of the Nativity celebrating Christ's Incarnation.

The mosaics in S. Maria Maggiore present us with an early portrayal of the birth and first witnesses of Christ's birth. The ambiguity with which they have been interpreted in the past is a mark of their seeming uniqueness. The depictions clearly did not become popularized, for we do not seem to have other examples of their implementation, and we do not easily recognize them. That the mosaics were commissioned by a pope who sanctioned the canon rather than those texts rejected from it, has implications beyond the current remit, although, as we shall see, apocryphal events and details continued to be popular features of representations of the lives of Mary and of Jesus as children.[19]

---

18 See Karpp (1976) fig. 128.
19 On the formation of the canon, see Hennecke and Schneemelcher (1963) 28–59.

We turn now to look at a major church in Cappadocia, which contains examples of infancy representations that, unlike those at S. Maria Maggiore, continued to be employed in many variations throughout Byzantium. The programme of images indicates the importance of Christ's incarnation as a baby and as a small child. The visual message is concerned with the system of belief surrounding Christ's birth from a virgin and is conveyed with specific and demonstrative details of the miraculous birth. The graphic images are prominently placed and the stories greatly elaborated; they serve to show the centrality of imagery about the Christ child, but also his place within Joseph and Mary's 'blended' family, the unconventional relationship between his worldly parents and the participation of various other figures in the infancy. A picture is given, not of a simple nuclear family, mother, father and son, but rather of a more diverse situation with the integration of Joseph and his grown-up sons and of nonfamilial women who take part in the birth. Jesus' birth is surrounded by witnesses who attest to the miracle, but the complexity of details in the story with accompanying elaborations in the imagery do not mask an emphasis on the Christ child as a realistic little baby and boy.

Tokalı kilise comprises three apparently separate churches, generally referred to as the lower, the old and the new churches. It was quite probably the catholicon of a monastery.[20] The lower church has little decoration and will not be discussed here. The old church was decorated in the first half of the tenth century with paintings on the barrel vault, the north and south walls, the west tympanum and on the original east wall (now partially destroyed). The infancy is on the north side of the vault and remnants of the presentation in the temple on the east wall (fig. 6.1).[21] The east wall and the sanctuary were knocked out in order to construct the new church, which has a wide transverse nave extending to the north and south and three apses in the east end. The new church was decorated throughout in two stages, the first perhaps prior to 969, and the infancy scenes are in the north vault and tympanum.[22]

Multiple scenes of the nativity show elements incorporated from the *Infancy Gospel of James*, such as the proof of the Virgin (when she and Joseph are made to prove her virginity by drinking poisoned water), the presence of Joseph's son leading the donkey to Bethlehem (in this apocryphal version, Joseph is a widower) and the two midwives present at the birth (who witness the proof that Mary is still a virgin when she gives birth) (*Infancy Gospel of James* 16:1–8; 17:5; 19:12–20:12). These two are pictured bathing the baby, a scene that as we have seen is not part of the narrative but a later adaptation of the

20   Otherwise known as Göreme 7; summarized by Jolivet-Lévy (1991) 94–96; for earlier analysis, see Jerphanion (1925–1942) I.1, 262–294, I.2, 287–376, pls II, 70–94; Restle (1967) I, 110–116, II, figs 61–123; Rodley (1985) 213–222.

21   The church has been dated by Cormack and Thierry in relation to Ayvali, since the church is decorated by the same artists; see Cormack (1967) 22–23; Thierry (1971) 170–178.

22   Dated in relation to Nikephoros Phokas kilise in Çavuşin: the painting in the dome of this church appears to be based on that of Tokalı; for summary of arguments, with bibliography, see Epstein (1986) 29–31; for the infancy scenes, see Restle (1967) II, figs 62, 64–68; Epstein (1986) figs 14–24.

iconography, first added in the seventh or eighth century. A further addition is the maid observing the visitation, who stands to the right under an archway as a witness; this also does not appear to have a textual source.[23] Another apocryphal scene is the murder of Zechariah, John the Baptist's father, who is killed by Herod (*Infancy Gospel of James* 23:9). The proliferation of the scenes proving the Virgin's virginity add colour to the story while also emphasizing its meaning and the importance of the Child, but Christ never loses his focus as the principal element. In certain cases, the narrative iconography assumed an articulated theological and symbolic significance. For instance, the scene of the presentation in the temple, which in part remains on the south edge of the east wall, had liturgical meaning. Annabel Wharton reasons that this south side would have been used as a *prothesis* (an area generally used for the preparation of the eucharist), which is unusual, but not unprecedented, and that the image is found here since it prefigures the eucharistic sacrifice on the altar.[24] Similarly the presentation of the Virgin and the Virgin fed by an angel, to be discussed below, are foreshadowings of the eucharist.[25]

In the new church, the nativity paintings also depend on the apocrypha and are comparably extensive and well placed. They are similarly in the barrel vault, which runs perpendicular to that in the old church, and in the adjacent tympanum.[26] The infancy cycles in both churches indicate a tendency to depict the baby Christ as the central focus around whom the circumstances of the birth are elaborately detailed in terms of the actions of the other participants. The story of the Virgin's childhood was not included in either programme, but her purity is vouchsafed by other apocryphal details, such as by Joseph's maturity (which appears, debatably, to imply lack of sexual desire), and is indicated by the presence of the son from his first family, by the testing by water and by the presence of the midwives. In both churches, there is emphasis on the maternal relationship between mother and son: the new mother does not hold her son and midwives take over the bathing while she recovers, but in both churches she gazes thoughtfully towards him, raising her hand in protection.[27] The use of the bathing motif may be associated with its precedents in mythological scenes, such as the birth of Dionysos, but it serves here to prove the morality and the miracle of the virgin birth and to establish the female world of childcare and nurture.[28] In the birth scenes in both the old and new churches, Joseph is to the side, his back facing the tableau, caught in contemplation. In the adoration of the magi, the baby is held by his mother and he assumes a new, active role. In the old church he is already quite large,

23   On this iconography, see Deshman (1989) 50–52.

24   Epstein (1986) 6, n. 6. She notes that the presentation appears above the (northeast) *prostheses* in two tenth-century decorations, in Chapel 11 in Göreme and Chapel 1 in Güllü dere: these are el Nazar and Sakli kilise (according to Jolivet-Lévy (1991) 388); on el Nazar, see Jolivet-Lévy (1991) 83.

25   On this, see Teteriatnikov (1996) 90, with further bibliography.

26   Epstein (1986) figs 49–67.

27   Epstein (1986) figs 19, 62.

28   On earlier precedents, see Weitzmann (1951b, 1984 edn) 206.

sitting up on her lap, holding a scroll and raising his hand in a teaching mode, while in the later painting he is small, much more like a baby, but still seated and raising his hand, while the magus leans down in a tender gesture to offer his gift.[29] Still very young, the Child has become educator and source of divine knowledge.

The birth of Christ is a central pictorial image of an importance far greater than its textual place would suggest. The images of the newborn Christ, swaddled in the manger, and the baby or young child receiving the magi were used repeatedly in Byzantium in both narrative and symbolic representations. One could argue that they serve to illustrate doctrinal points, but equally the relevance of the incarnation of Christ, born of a virgin, could have been visually articulated in another form. There is an apparent fascination in the church with this elaborate story centring on the Child's incarnation. The scenes remain essentially narrative, and the amalgamation of events intensifies and enriches the context of each vignette, emphasizing the honouring of the Christ child. He is usually depicted, first, as a tiny swaddled infant lying in his crib, and second, as a young boy, sitting up on his mother's lap. He is not imaged as a symbol, nor as a small but mature figure: he is a child and exemplifies childhood. The image of the favoured, chosen, elevated and pre-eminent child permeated Byzantium's iconography and must have affected the perception and the representation of children in general.

A similar treatment and emphasis, this time directed towards the Virgin, is found in Cappadocia at Kızıl Çukur. Although the pictorial tradition of the apocryphal infancy of the Virgin dates from the sixth century, the church of Joachim and Anna in Kızıl Çukur, to the south of Güllü dere, in Çavuşin may represent the earliest extant extensive cycle of wall paintings representing the childhood and adolescence of the Virgin.[30] The date of the chapel remains controversial. While it was originally assigned to the late ninth or early tenth centuries, more recent studies have suggested the middle of the seventh century as a possibility.[31] The church is unique in being entirely devoted to imagery of Mary and her parents and contains narrative sections illustrating 12 scenes.[32] Although currently known as the church of Joachim and Anna, it was more likely dedicated to the Virgin and not to her parents, since the

---

29   Epstein (1986) figs 20, 64.

30   Joliet-Levy (1991) 47–50; Restle (1967) I, 25–26, 144–145, figs III, 344–354; Lafontaine-Dosogne (1964–1965) 25; Thierry and Thierry (1958) 105–146, esp. 117–146, figs 8–18, 20; Thierry and Thierry (1960) 620–623, pls 82–84, 86; Jerphanion (1925–1942) did not include this church.

31   Thierry and Thierry (1958) 146 (second half of ninth or early tenth century); Thierry and Thierry (1960) 622–623 (likewise); Lafontaine-Dosogne (1964–1965) 37 (ninth to tenth); Lafontaine-Dosogne (1987) 331–332; Restle (1967) I, 25–26 (mid-ninth); Thierry (1994) II, 234–235 (late-sixth or seventh); Jolivet-Lévy (1991) 49–50 (seventh to ninth); on the adjacent chapel with nonfigural decorations, see Thierry (1970) 444–479; Thierry (1976) 81–119; Jolivet-Lévy (1991) 49–50. For related cycles in Cappadocia, see, on Chapel of the *Theotokos*, Lafontaine (1962) 263–284, 270, fig. 11; Jerphanion (1925–1942) I.1, 121–137, esp. 127–129, pl. I, 34. 2; on Sarica kilise, Lafontaine (1962) esp. 270–271, figs 9–11.

32   As observed by Lafontaine-Dosogne (1964–1965) 203.

imagery focuses on the Virgin and the extraordinary events leading up to her conception. The church was not necessarily part of a monastery. The images show an emphasis in depicting family ties as well as a small child's transition from guidance by parental to spiritual authorities. Mary is depicted very much as a little girl, not as a small adult, and the images in general tend to show human and realistic features of the story, conveyed in simple and graphic terms.

The church is entered through a narthex (adjacent to a funerary chamber) at the west end of the southern of two parallel naves with barrel vaults. The wall paintings decorate the northern and larger nave. The narrative begins at the east end of the south vault and largely follows the text in the *Infancy Gospel of James*.[33] The focus of the decoration culminates in the Virgin at the east end at the apex of the triumphal arch, seated with the Child and surrounded by a mandorla.[34] This is rare and focuses the viewer on the Virgin's elevation, her proximity to God and to her son in majesty, who is also encased in a mandorla in the apse behind, as generally found in Cappadocian churches.

The figures are bold, painted in clear fluid brushstrokes. Emphasis is on the principal players in the story, although lesser figures, like shepherds accompanying Joachim, are shown large, suggesting perhaps that the imagery held particular meaning for local people. The figures were originally very easily legible, large and bold with clear interactions between them and distinctive messages conveyed by their actions. For instance, Anna's awareness of the child in her womb is indicated by two women touching her belly, Joachim and Anna embrace warmly to indicate the conception, and Mary is plainly shown taking her first steps, walking away from the arms of her mother. Here, she is depicted with a small body and is dressed in a long blue dress. The focus is on her uncovered head, which turns towards the viewer, as if in movement, to show large, open eyes conveying a sense of innocence. In later depictions, Mary is portrayed walking towards her mother, but here she moves away, as if showing her first separation from the family and towards God. In each of the subsequent scenes she takes a step further from her parents until finally she climbs the altar steps. Mary is clearly a small girl with a childish appearance and movement, as when she pulls up her legs and reaches out her arms towards Zechariah. Unfortunately, the scenes that tell of Mary's growing maturity and her marriage at the age of 12 to Joseph cannot still be read.

Just as the images of Christ's childhood served doctrinal purpose, so with the Virgin's. But these images give a graphic, sensitive impression of a small girl, loved by her parents and dedicated to God. Relationships are

---

33   Lafontaine-Dosogne (1964–1965) 37, n. 4, figs 13–17; Thierry and Thierry (1960) 620–621; the sketches in Thierry and Thierry (1958) figs 9, 12, 14 and 17 are useful; see also Thierry (1994) for sketches and extensive photographs, 203–237, pls 101–120, including comparative material.

34   One other example is in Cyprus at the Panagia Kanakaria, which can perhaps be dated to the early sixth century; mentioned by Thierry (1995) 430; on the Panagia Kanakaria Virgin, see Cormack (2000a) 94–95, fig. 48; Megaw and Hawkins (1977) 49, 61–79, figs 40 and M.

important, particularly the nurturing of the child. Mary is clearly a little girl, not a diminutive but mature figure. She is portrayed in a state of childhood, just as Christ was depicted most clearly as a baby and as a small boy. And, as in Christ's story, the figures are placed in real-life settings, performing daily activities and illustrated with attention to human actions and emotions. The choice of images of the Virgin's childhood throughout the church indicates the respect and devotion accorded to this holy child. Can it also suggest and possibly promote awareness of and respect for children in general? Both Cappadocian narrative cycles discussed, at Tokalı and at Joachim and Anna, illustrate children as children, giving them a finely articulated place within a family structure, but also depicting them as chosen and affiliated with the divine. Closeness to God was not imaged as separate from normal life, nor from a close familial context.

The proliferation of scenes from Mary's life and the appeal of the child Virgin are exemplified in the two illustrated copies of the homilies of James of Kokkinobaphos, Vatican, gr. 1162 and Paris, gr. 1208 (fig. 6.2).[35] Created in the aristocratic milieu of twelfth-century monasticism, they show an interest in imaging elaborate details of Mary's childhood and adolescence and in depicting them in contexts reflecting contemporary life. The manuscripts illustrate six homilies on major events in Mary's life up to the proclamation of her innocence by Zechariah, the priest. Jeffrey Anderson maintains that the Paris manuscript was copied from the Vatican, the first made at the time the sermons were written, in the 1130s, and the second in the 1140s or 1150s.[36] He also suggests that they were probably written by the same hand and illustrated in Constantinople.[37]

The illustrated scenes, in full- or half-page images, follow in detail the Virgin's birth and childhood. The settings evoke real-life situations, transposed into contemporary culture. For instance, the temple scene, in which Mary is fed by an angel, resembles a church interior with a chancel barrier.[38] She is surrounded in most contexts by various people from the community who participate in her life, giving a picture of a child living in a tightly knit society. As at Kızıl Çukur, Mary as an infant in arms leans towards Zechariah with childlike movements and is shown in an affectionate embrace from her mother: emotional and physical attachment is clear.[39] The Virgin does not markedly change her appearance as she grows up: she is dressed from birth in the *maphorion* and simply grows in size. But this consistency is inherent to the story, and beyond it attention to the child's life is implicit:

---

35   *PG* 127:543–700; Omont (1927) throughout; Stornajolo (1910) throughout; Anderson (1991) 69–120; Hutter and Canart (1991) throughout; Maguire (1996) 159–166, figs 141–145; Nelson (1987) 76; on the text, see Jeffreys (1982) 63–71.

36   Anderson (1991) esp. 76–85.

37   Anderson (1991) esp. 85, 90.

38   Omont (1927) fol. 92v, pl. XII; Stornajolo (1910) fol. 68v, pl. 29.

39   Omont (1927) fols 61r, 63v, pl. VIII; Stornajolo (1910) fols 44v, 46v, 67v, pls 17, 18, 28.

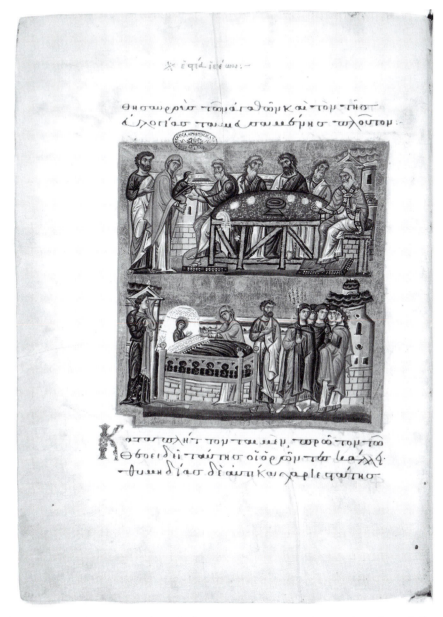

Fig. 6.2   Vatican, gr. 1162, fol. 44v, twelfth century. In the lower register, Anna prepares Mary to get up from her cradle. Above, Anna and Joachim present Mary to Zechariah, the High Priest, and four other priests in the temple. © Biblioteca Apostolica Vaticana (Vatican)

she is captured maturing from baby to young woman in a series of carefully gradated scenes.

Anderson discusses letters written by James, which he considers were written to the Sebastokratorissa Irene, whom he, after Elizabeth Jeffreys, identifies as the wife of Andronikos Komnenos, the second son of John II.[40]

---

40   Paris, gr. 3039; Anderson (1991) 86–87; Jeffreys (1982) 63–71; Jeffreys considers the two authors to be different although she acknowledges the manuscripts are from the same workshop; see 69–70.

He therefore ties the manuscripts with the Contantinopolitan nobility, making this interest in the virginal child a product of courtly monasticism. The images certainly suggest this type of an environment, since all the events take place amidst lavish buildings and comfortable surroundings. Anderson additionally suggests that Jacob commissioned the manuscripts; if this is so, the monk not only chose to dwell verbally on details of the Virgin's youth, but also visually, and to create a complex series of highly developed images about the little girl's passage into adulthood.

In looking at such portrayals of Christ's and the Virgin's lives, in which elaborations are made, it becomes clear that similarities are drawn between their childhoods. Several examples of church decoration, in which Christ's and the Virgin's childhoods are depicted in relation to one another, show that the story of Mary's own birth and childhood was treated in an analogous way to that of her son. The Virgin's life preceded Christ's, but the imagery of her early life developed to reflect his, such as her presentation in the temple. Her life therefore became a sequel to his, and to some extent the representations of her life are dependent on his. The narrative of the Virgin's life is retained, often presented in many scenes, while Christ's early life becomes compressed, sometimes focusing only on the main events in the yearly liturgical cycle.[41] Principal scenes in their lives form visual parallels in terms of iconography and of location: the birth and ritual presentation in the temple of each child visually balance or reinforce the other, so that the lives of mother and son reflect each other.[42]

The pairing of scenes of the Virgin and of Christ as children suggests the narrative and doctrinal parallels, but these are perhaps also an indication of social customs and aspirations directed towards female as well as male children. Of many examples of this mirroring, one is in Agios Athanasios in Geraki, Greece.[43] The church is an inscribed cross plan, dated to the middle of the twelfth century, and the vault is decorated, in the north, with the presentation of the Virgin in the temple and, in the south, with Christ as a boy seated in the temple surrounded by the Jewish doctors. The placing of images of the Virgin's childhood in relation to those of Christ's indicate the significance and prevalence of doctrine concerning the Virgin. But it also suggests an attitude of equality between the lives of Christ and of his mother.

Similarly, the paintings at S. Michael, near Cemil in Cappadocia, show a conjunction of the lives of Christ and of the Virgin.[44] The date of the church, because of the very dark state of the paintings, is not known, but suggestions

---

41   On issues about the feast cycle, see Demus (1948) 22–26, who adopted the idea from Millet (1916) 16–25; more recently, see Kitzinger (1988) 51–73; Mathews (1988) 11–21, esp. 14–15.

42   Henry Maguire has made related observations combined with textual evidence; see Maguire (1996) 156–157.

43   For bibliography on Geraki, see Skawran (1982) under catalogue entries on Evangelistria church and H. Sozon, 168–169; Mouriki (1971).

44   Jerphanion (1925–1942) II.1, 128–145; Jolivet-Lévy (1991) 157–160; Restle (1967) 1, 154–155; Rodley (1985) 157–158.

range from the eleventh to the thirteenth centuries.[45] The extant paintings depict the childhood of the Virgin in only one scene: her presentation in the temple and feeding by an angel. This is placed directly adjacent to Christ's presentation, drawing direct analogies between the two.[46] The Virgin's presentation is an elaborate scene showing Joachim and Anna, accompanied by seven virgins, approaching an enthroned Zechariah. Mary sits on the altar steps, while an angel reaches towards her with bread. This appears on the east vault of the narthex, running from north to south, preceded by the annunciation to Mary, and the visitation. On the west vault, again running from north to south, is an indecipherable scene, then the flight to Egypt, Joseph and the angel, the dormition of the Virgin and another indeterminate scene.[47] The equal size and prominence of the images of both Christ and the Virgin, just as at Geraki, suggest that in these contexts the life of the Virgin was accorded comparable status to the early life of her son.

As the boy Christ was viewed as a paradigm of sanctity and devotion to God, so Mary represented the female equivalent. In another twist of narratological and theological iconography, mother and son slip out of their generative relationship and instead they appear to become the exemplary boy and girl. In the scene when Mary approaches Zechariah, she draws other young girls into her circle, for she is shown with the seven maidens who accompany her to the temple. Yet, they remain in the background, and it is Mary's parents who take pre-eminence as her protectors and dedicators. Similarly Christ's parents first nurture and then present him to God, ideal illustrations of obedient selflessness. Both sets of parents are unblemished and both children modelled in perfection. The images present idealized family values and the ultimate sacrifice of those mores for a higher ideal of service to God.

The detailed representation of the Virgin's early life and its reflection in Christ's own experiences cannot be entirely attributed to theological ends. The choice of placing the young Virgin in a prominent place and in parallel relation to her son de-emphasizes the relation of mother to son and presents each as a child in God's temple. The imagery must have influenced the aspirations and imagination of young believers and their parents. In both cases the children are separating themselves from their families and moving towards an independent relationship with God. The depictions suggest equivalency in their early lives, which perhaps not only served theological ends but also reflected the interests of parents and children who worshipped in the church. Parents were concerned with raising children worthy of God, while children aspired to devotion, or at least were intended to. The image of Mary presents to girls and to women an ascetic ideal, the pinnacle of chastity, obedience and self-sacrifice. As Christ is the supreme male child, so Mary is the female.

---

45   Jolivet-Lévy (1991) 160.

46   This does not photograph well; see line drawing by M.E. Mamboury in Jerphanion (1925–1942) pl. III, 156.2.

47   Jerphanion tentatively suggests it is Joshua stopping the sun, but this seems unlikely (1925–1942) II.1, 130, 134.

At the monastic church of St Saviour in Chora, now known as Kariye Camii, in Istanbul, the mosaic cycles in the narthexes depict the birth and youth of both Christ and the Virgin.[48] In each cycle, the narrative is extended, giving numerous scenes of their childhoods. After the scenes of Christ's nativity, he is depicted being carried as a toddler on Joseph's shoulders when returning from Egypt and going at the age of 12 with his parents to Jerusalem.[49] The Virgin's childhood is traced in an elaborate series of images. The structure of the vaults allows for a complex unfolding of the story with many components, simultaneously elaborating on the narrative and providing didactic motifs. Although a monastic church, the space was used for worship by Theodore Metochites (a prominent politician and intellectual), who restored the building (1316–1321), by his family and probably also by the inhabitants of the adjacent district.[50] Since the narthex was the periphery of the church and had in earlier times traditionally been used for catechumens and doctrinal education, the images may have been of specific relevance in teaching children.[51] The choice of iconography made by Metochites, with its emphasis on the childhood of Christ and of the Virgin, must reflect his own interests.[52]

Christ is realistically depicted as a 12-year-old, with shortish hair swept away from his face, and a round, hairless face. He is dressed in billowing gold robes and strides forwards to Jerusalem, following Joseph and followed by his older half-brothers.[53] The resplendent gold of his clothes appears in many icons where Christ is depicted as a child. As an adult in narrative images he is not generally richly dressed. The garment's opulence could imply wealth and luxury, but probably not, since Christ's family are not usually portrayed in this way but are consistently dressed in plain clothes, with Mary usually dressed in the sombre blue *maphorion* and Joseph in a simple cloak. The gold connotes Christ's celestial parentage, and this reference is maintained in the scene in the temple among the doctors where, although largely lost, the bottom of his gold robe is visible. This event is seen as Christ's move into adulthood and ministry, for it is placed in one of the domical vaults with other events from his public life, separate from the scenes of his infancy in the lunettes around the walls of the narthex.

Conversely, the Virgin is dressed in the same way as she generally appears in portrayals as an adult (fig. 6.3). As already seen in the Kokkinobaphos manuscripts, Mary's transition to an adult role is imaged through actions and events and through her change from a small person to a fully grown one.

---

48   Underwood (1966–1975) II, nos. 102 –112, pls 166–210.

49   Underwood (1966–1975) II, nos. 111, 112, 113, pls 200–214.

50   On this, see Nelson (1999a) 70.

51   However, Taft suggests catechumens were not dismissed during the liturgy from some time around the seventh century; see Taft (1998) 60–61.

52   For more on this, but not directly related to images of children, see Nelson (1999a) 56–82; and less directly, Nelson (1999b) esp. 74–81.

53   The inclusion of Joseph's apocryphal first family is an interesting spin, necessary to explain a gospel reference to Jesus' brothers, but they also become further attestors to the Virgin birth and make themselves useful by leading their stepmother-to-be on the donkey.

She is dressed the same way throughout, with full-length blue gown with long, tight sleeves and with her head and shoulders covered with the gold-edged blue *maphorion*. Even as a tiny baby caressed by her parents, she is swathed in her virginal robes.[54] The imagery suggests that she is unchanging, born in virtue and perpetuating it, unadulterated by the world. It leads us to believe that her early years only served to prepare her for adulthood, but at the same time it emphasizes her youth: she appears very small and petite in relation to the adults surrounding her. She seems vulnerable and precious, a diminutive form sheltered and preserved for a supreme responsibility. This is important theologically, since she keeps her virginity and her childhood innocence into adulthood by maintaining a purity and asceticism. She is also the ultimate conformist, totally obedient to the will of her parents and of God. The consistency in her appearance and her actions contributes to this sense of compliance and submission, a quality essential to the significance she was accorded from early times as the redeemer of Eve.[55] In this way she comes to stand for all female children and for all women who are retrieved from sin by Christ's sacrifice. But, at the same time, the Virgin is seen to experience childhood. When entrusted to Joseph, she has the face of a little girl, with rounded chin and small eyes, but when she is taken by Joseph to his house, she

Fig. 6.3 Istanbul, Kariye Camii, Church of St Saviour in the Chora, narthex, 1316-21. The infant Virgin, dressed in her blue *maphorion*, is embraced by her parents, Joachim and Anna

---

54   Underwood (1966–1975) II, n. 90, pls 114–115.

55   Justin, *Dialogue with Trypho*, *PG* 6:709–712; Irenaeus, *Contra Haereses* bk 3. Ch. 22, *PG* 7:959–960, bk 5, ch. 19, *PG* 7:1175–1176; references in Cameron (2000) n. 7.

has the fine features of a young woman, and by the time of the annunciation at the well, she has become fully grown.[56]

The mosaics at Kariye Camii show the significance tied to the childhood of both Christ and his mother. Each cycle shows the nurturing by the parents followed by their separation from them. Each is singled out by his or her clothes: the Christ child as resplendent Son of God, the *Theotokos* as dutiful mother-to-be of God. Each child is clearly sacred, imaged as chosen, closely tended by the biological family, but standing independent from worldly ties and bound to his or her divine mission on earth.

In narrative images of the Virgin and of Christ, they are pictured very much as children. The Virgin experiences various stages in her growth and maturing; Christ appears as a boy and as an adolescent. The frequency of the images and the pairing of their lives suggest an identification with the children as an individual boy and girl. But also the images define their identities, emphasizing Christ's power and authority, the Virgin's purity and, in both cases, their destiny from childhood.

We have looked so far at narrative images, which tell stories and help to enunciate theological belief. Non-narrative images are primarily linked with ideology. An issue for this discussion rests on the extent to which such representations centre on Christ or the Virgin as a child, as opposed to an adult, and in what ways Jesus and Mary are given status as children. The focus in this discussion will be on Christ. Visual definitions of the Christ child occur in iconic images of Christ with his mother. Both portable paintings on a wooden back and monumental images of the Virgin and Christ depicted in apses represent a universal rapport of mother with child, but also articulate subtleties of the relationship between *Theotokos* and son. Images of the Virgin and Child stress Mary's role as mother and correspond to ubiquitous representations of children held by their mothers. This reinforces the orthodox recognition, as defined by John of Damascus, that Christ was born *of* his mother and not *through* her.[57] Although she bore God, she is imaged as biological mother in unstated apposition to God as spiritual father. The iconographic formulations of Mother and Child substantiate this notion of physical propagation. However, there is no perception that Christ receives his nonhuman or divine qualities from her; rather she is the emblem of human generation, but one that is unblemished by the physical act of creating children.

The Christ child additionally appears independently in iconic images, most often in a pictorial type known as the Emmanuel. This graphically separates him from the physically dominating presence of the mother and announces the baby, child or adolescent as an independent authority.

Christ, in symbolic portraits both as an adult and as a child, was concurrently depicted in several differing representations in Byzantium, suggesting that each conveyed its own meaning. The line between adult, adolescent and juvenile portraits can be fluid and variances indicate the complexity of

---

56   Underwood (1966–1975) II, nos. 96–98, pls 138–147.

57   John of Damascus, *De fide orthodoxa*, bk III, ch. XII, *PG* 94:1030.

perceptions about him and the ambivalence about his maturity. From the eleventh century the image of Christ Emmanuel, as boy and as adolescent, became prevalent, along with more frequently employed distinctions between certain representations of the godhead differentiated by age. As discussed in relation to young saints, adolescence, for whatever reason, was apparently appealing to a Byzantine audience. But Christ as a baby and child was also widely popular.

Early images of Christ with his mother show the Child, not as a babe in arms, but as a young boy. He has an attitude of independence, although clearly a child. One example from St Catherine's monastery in the Sinai from the sixth century shows the Virgin flanked by Saints Theodore and (probably) George, with angels behind her throne.[58] The Child sits on his mother's lap with an air of autonomy; he holds up his face, pictured under a good head of curls, and reaches his arms forwards, with the left one clasping a scroll. The Child's eyes are attracted to his left, as are his mother's; while much has been written on the different gazes of the subjects, this has not been satisfactorily explained.[59] Weitzmann points to the Child's high forehead, defining him as a *paidariogeron* or *puer senex* and making a distinction between the human, with a childlike body, and the divine, with a spiritual head.[60] An ivory of the adoration of the magi in the British Museum, from the first half of the sixth century and thought to come from the eastern Mediterranean, shows a similar image of the Child, although here he is somewhat larger, with longer, leaner limbs (fig. 6.4).[61] Again, he has short curly hair and sits upright, with the scroll in his left hand and his right hand raised and dressed again in a simple robe. These are just two examples that show images, one derived from narrative, where the Christ child maintains his autonomy from his mother and has a participatory role. Unlike images of the nativity, where the Child is a baby, swaddled and unmoving, these representations define the Child as active and old enough to observe and to respond, to play a part.

But what is this role? The exact meaning of the scroll and the raised hand remains elusive, although they must have had clear, if various, implications in the sixth century. While not specifically referring to child images, Paul Zanker has interpreted the scroll in representations of Christ as a reference to the pagan cult of learning and to Christ's role as a teacher. Representations of the older bearded and younger beardless figures can be explained by the imagery of adult teachers, but also the Christ child with a scroll is derived from images of clever Roman children, the *wunderkinder*.[62] The scroll is clearly different from the gospel book held, for instance, by Christ in the guise of Pantokrator, and while Zanker interprets it as an allusion to the act of teaching, it refers specifically to the teaching of Christ, the logos. Thus the child Christ

---

58   Soteriou and Soteriou (1956–1958) II, 21–22, I, figs 4–7 and colour plate; Weitzmann (1976) B3, 18–21, pls 4–6, 43–46; Vassilaki (2000) n. 1.

59   Most recently by Barber (2000) 253–261.

60   Weitzmann (1976) 20; on the *puer senex*, see Antonopoulos (1998) 215–231.

61   Vassilaki (2000) n. 3.

62   Zanker (1995) 290–293.

Fig. 6.4
London, British
Museum, first
half of the sixth
century, MME
1904. 7-2.1. In the
main image, the
Virgin is seated
with the Child
on her lap as
she receives the
magi. Beneath,
the Virgin rests
on the left, while
on the right,
Salome holds
her withered
hand to the
manger in order
to be healed. ©
Copyright The
Trustees of The
British Museum

becomes the teacher of mankind, a reference emphasized by his raised hand which, while it may be interpreted as a blessing, seems to refer to speaking or specifically to teaching. Karen Boston discusses this in relation to a sixth-century icon of Christ in Sinai and argues that Christ is in the act of speaking; the same gesture is said to change later in the ninth century and to refer to blessing, but it also kept its meaning of speech.[63] But speaking, teaching and blessing all imply the gift of knowledge and salvation, the ultimate blessing, so differentiations between these acts may be deceptive. Christ has universal knowledge and blesses the viewer with his knowledge and his incarnate life.

The seated Virgin, then, is essentially a support for the incarnate Christ, who as a child teaches mankind. She takes this role also in early monumental images of the Virgin and child, principally found in apses.[64] These depictions do not emphasize the Virgin's role as nurturing mother, but rather as the mother who bears Christ and presents him to the world.[65] The Virgin provides Christ with a physical context, both literally, in the shape of the lap on which he sits, and symbolically, in that she bore his incarnate form.

In the ninth-century mosaic of the Virgin and Child in the apse at Hagia Sophia in Istanbul, the Child is clad again in gold, as in the Sinai icon, and sits on his mother's lap (fig. 6.5). Both figures face frontally, but their eyes are directed to their right, the opposite direction from that in the Sinai version. The Virgin, dressed entirely in dark blue and seated on a cushioned bench with her feet on a footstool, rests one hand on her son's shoulder and one on his knee. It is generally thought that the patriarch Photios's seventeenth homily, dated to 867, concerning an image of the Virgin and Child, described this mosaic.[66] Photios's *ekphrasis* is said to be both traditional and imaginative in adhering to accepted modes of speech and in embroidering the visual effect. His comments on the relationship of mother to child, emphasizing their visually close rapport, may be nonspecific in that mother and child do not look at each other, but specific in conveying the sense of the relationship: she 'fondly turns her eyes on her begotten child in the affection of her heart, yet assumes the expression of a detached and imperturbable mood at the passionless and wondrous nature of her offspring, and composes her gaze accordingly'.[67] Photios seems to be speaking about the kind of imagery found in later icons. The earliest image that appears to convey the emotional tenderness he describes is a painting in a niche between the central and northern apse in the

---

63   On this, see Boston (1999) 142–144, esp. 142, fn. 14 for bibliography on gesture; for a discussion of the relative use of books and codices by early Christians and the meaning of the book in general, see Boston (1999) esp. 93–106.

64   On this, see Cormack (2000a) 91–105.

65   On images of the mother, see Kalavrezou (2000) 41–46; Kalavrezou (1990) 165–172.

66   For text in Greek, see Laourdas (1959) 164–172; in English, see Mango (1958) 286–296; Mango (1972) 187–190; for a discussion of the apse as well as rhetoric and images, see James and Webb (1991) 1–17; Mango and Hawkins (1965) 113–149, plus illustrations; Oikonomidès (1965) 113–152; also on the apse, see Nelson (2000) esp. 143–150, who discusses optical theory.

67   Laourdas (1959) 167; Mango (1958) 290; Mango (1972) 187; also in Cormack (2000b) 112.

Fig. 6.5 Istanbul, S. Sophia, apse, ca. 867. The Virgin and Child in mosaic preside over the apse. © Liz James

new church at Tokalı, dated to the tenth century. It emphasizes close physical love and contact.[68] Photios perhaps articulated an idea, which was, as yet, from our point of view, not found in visual representations. But if this is so, it may point to a need to temper present-day perceptions of Byzantine portrayals of emotional or maternal bonding.

In images of the *Hodegetria*, the viewer is aware primarily of the relationship between mother and son, for even though she rarely looks at him, she points towards him, as in the miniature of the veneration of the icon in the *Hamilton Psalter*.[69] In other representations the emotional relationship between them, becomes, at least to us, more evident. In depictions such as the *Eleousa* and the *Brephokratousa*, the Virgin appears to be drawing the attention of Christ, the baby, towards her, so the two are cocooned in a reciprocal and intimate bonding of love, which in some sense excludes the viewer.[70] In certain cases, the *Eleousa* and *Hodegetria* images allude not only to birth but also to the suffering of the passion; some representations make this explicit by showing the instruments of Christ's death.[71] In these cases, the childhood of Christ is linked with his death and the image appears to centre on a mother's grief rather than joy. One could justifiably argue that this is theologically slanted, to remind the believer of Christ's sacrifice to mankind, but its poignancy is perhaps effective in alluding to any mother's suffering in bearing and losing children, or simply to the pain of bringing them up.

A further form of the Christ child also appears in icons of the *Blachernitissa* type where the Virgin holds a medallion image of the Child on her belly, suggesting his incarnate state. The placement of the image of the Child refers to the Virgin's pregnancy, yet the connection is not emphatically made, since

---

68   Pointed out by Kalavrezou (1990) 172, fig. 16, and (2000) 43, fig. 18.

69   Berlin, Staatliche Museen, Hamilton 119, fol. 39v; see Vassilaki (2000) n. 54.

70   For instance, the icon of the Virgin of Vladimir, Tretyakov Gallery, Moscow; see Vassilaki (2000) fig. 24.

71   Baltoyanni (2000) 149–151, with further bibliography; Vassilaki and Tsironis (2000) 453; see also the double-sided twelfth-century mosaic in Kastoria, showing the Virgin Hodegetria and the Man of Sorrows in Vassilaki (2000) n. 83.

Christ is depicted as a child not as a baby.[72] Two examples from St Catherine's monastery in the Sinai show the range of depictions within types. In one, dated to the twelfth century, Christ is small and childlike with a round head (fig. 6.6). He has a cheerful wide-eyed face, similar to the expression in a comparable image of Mother and Child in the *Khludov Psalter*, where Christ and his mother appear atop a phallic Cappadocian-style mountain: Christ is imaged as a small boy in front of his mother, who places a hand on his shoulder.[73] In the second Sinai example, possibly dated to the thirteenth century, Christ appears older, but still a boy with defined features and serious expression.[74] This latter has a high forehead and a characteristic hairstyle that appears to recede at the temples. This may suggest wisdom, associated with age, but here marked on a youthful face, as seen in certain representations of Saint Nicholas, which were discussed in Chapter 4. In most images, as here, the boys have accentuated features: large expressive eyes and clearly articulated ears, which sometimes protrude. The boy in the twelfth-century image wears a gold robe and bright halo. The other is nimbed by the entire mandorla and wears a rich embroidered tunic and stole.

The many variations in images of the Emmanuel indicate that the specific representation of the Child was open to interpretation and could follow regional, stylistic or individual trends. But, in what sense is he represented as a child? Emblematized on the Virgin's belly, he is boyishly incarnate, clearly young, though sometimes with allusions to age, dressed richly but not imperially, apparently born to rule. He actively addresses the worshipper. He could have appeared as an inanimate symbol or as a mature figure; instead he looks forth as a realizable child. He is imaged with his mother, and a clear message is the relation of the two, but also his relation with the worshipper to whom she presents him.

This same form of Christ, often in a mandorla or medallion, facing frontally, as a small boy or adolescent, is used in depictions of Christ alone. The image is usually termed Christ Emmanuel, although Jesus with his mother can also bear this name. He is seen as immature, although of variable age, ranging from a small child to a young adolescent. He is generally shown alone, although he may be grouped with other figures, sometimes with alternate ways of representing the godhead, such as the Ancient of Days, the *Hetoimasia* (the throne prepared for Christ's second coming), or the Pantokrator.[75]

Representations of the Ancient of Days and the Emmanuel became popular in the eleventh and twelfth centuries, but they were understood and used

---

72   On the relation of this image to the Akathistos hymn, see Baltoyanni (2000) 140–141.

73   See Ščepkina (1977) fol. 64r; Corrigan (1992) fig. 50, 37–40; Ševčenko (2000) 155–166, esp. 156, fig. 100.

74   Vassilaki (2000) figs 84–85.

75   On Emmanuel, see Galavaris (1979) 100–109, 125–127; Galavaris (1969) 173–174; Millet (1945) 63–81; Grabar (1948a) 132–135; *RBK* I, 1008–1010; on Ancient of Days, see Galavaris (1979) 93–100; Grabar (1948a) 131; Millet (1945) 42–44; on Pantokrator, see Mathews (1990) esp. 201.

Fig. 6.6 The Monastery of Saint Catherine at Sinai. twelfth century. An icon of the Virgin Blachernitissa which took its name from the famous image housed at Blachernai in Constantinople. Published through the courtesy of the Michigan-Princeton-Alexandria Expeditions to Mount Sinai

to some extent much earlier. A literary metaphor of Christ's two extremes in age was used at least from the fourth century, for Ephraem the Syrian gives to Simeon the words, 'the infant truly was the Ancient of Days'. [76] It was adopted in the fifth or sixth century by Pseudo-Dionysius, who had visions of Christ as an old man and as a youth, the one indicating that he exists

---

76 Ephraem, *Hymnus de Simeone sene*, ed. Lamy, II, 628–638, esp. §28, 638, in Kantorowicz (1963) 123, in (1965 edn) 29 (with further references).

from the beginning and the other that he escapes all ageing, so his power is eternal.[77] Other associations between God's youth and age are made in the office of the *Hypapante* (presentation of Christ in the temple), where the aged Simeon greets the young Christ. For instance, a phrase perhaps attributed to the patriarch Germanos (715–730) reads, 'The Ancient of Days has become a babe in the flesh, and has been brought by his Virgin Mother to the temple'.[78] Later ecclesiastics developed the association of the white beard with eternity, with the one who exists from the origin but who is incarnated as a child.[79] An early and unusual example showing the amalgamation of concepts of age and youth is an icon from the Sinai, thought to be from the seventh century, which shows a white-haired figure seated in a mandorla and holding an open book, with an inscription reading 'Emmanuel' (fig. 6.7).[80] This suggests a conflation between the identities of Christ, whereby youth and age become interrelated, although the Ancient of Days may possibly be representing God and the image referring to part of the Trinity. Alternatively, it may not have been until later that the label Emmanuel was associated with youth, although the biblical references both speak of the naming of the Child after his birth. It seems likely that the icon refers to Christ's eternal life.

Theologians identified the infant embodied in the Ancient of Days and saw the image of the young Christ associated with eternal life: the one who has eternal life was incarnated as a child.[81] An example in the Vatican edition of John Klimakos's *Heavenly Ladder*, Vatican, gr. 394, shows the young Christ on the lap of the Ancient of Days, suggesting a further extension of the parent and child, youth and age relationship.[82] An apocryphal story about the magi gives rise to intriguing imagery concerning the young Christ. This appears in an eleventh-century copy of the *Homilies of Gregory of Nazianzos*, Taphou 14, now in Jerusalem.[83] As each of the three magi hold the baby, Christ takes on a different form, according to the age of the sage. Therefore the youngest magus holds the Ancient of Days and the eldest the Christ child.

In the eleventh and twelfth centuries, the Emmanuel image became prevalent and was used in various contexts, in monumental decoration and in manuscripts. Annemarie Weyl Carr has associated the popularity of the

---

77 The idea was used in the sixth-century by Andrew of Caesarea, *Commentary on the Apocalypse*, PG 106:228, in Millet (1945) 42–43; in Grabar (1948a, 1968 edn) I, 55; also in Tsuji (1975) 165–203, fn. 1; Pseudo-Dionysius, *De divinis nominibus* 10, §2, PG 3, 937; in Grabar (1948, 1968 edn) I, 55–56; also in Kantorowicz (1963) 132, in (1965) 35.

78 *Menaia* III, 479; in Kantorowicz (1963/1965) 122/28.

79 Such as the twelfth-century Michael Acominatus; in Millet (1945) 43; similar reference in Kantorowicz to *Anthologia Palatina*, I, 21: 'Child, old man, born before the ages, coeval with the Father'.

80 Soteriou and Soteriou (1956–58) II, 23–25, I, figs 8–9; Weitzmann (1976) B. 16, 41–42, pls 62–63.

81 For further references, see Kantorowicz (1963) 122–123, 132, or (1965) 28–29, 35; Grabar (1948a) 131–135; Millet (1945) 42–43; Tsuji (1975) 165, fn. 1.

82 See Martin (1954) fol. 7r, fig. 70; Roussanova (1999) 22; reference in Carr (1982) n. 49.

83 Fol. 106 (107) v; see Vassilaki (2000) n. 56.

Fig. 6.7   The Monastery of Saint Catherine at Sinai. An icon with the inscription of Christ Emmanuel, but showing the Ancient of Days in a starry mandorla of light held up by angels. He holds a gospel and rests on a rainbow. Published through the courtesy of the Michigan-Princeton-Alexandria Expeditions to Mount Sinai

image at this time with a play on the name of Manuel I (1143–80), who put the Emmanuel on his coins; the adult, though young, emperor was keen to associate himself with the ultimate child ruler. On the reverse of certain coins, Manuel is also beardless and clearly identifying with the Emmanuel.[84] At the same time, the various interpretations of the Ancient of Days and the Pantokrator combined with the Emmanuel suggest an interest in exploring the

---

84   Hendy (1969) 111–112, 114, pls 12:1–12; 13:1–2, 10–12; in part in Carr (1982) 9. Hendy does not reference the coins on pl. 12 as Emmanuel, but they appear to be so; for beardless Manuel, see pl. 13.1–2.

various facets of Christ's identity and finding complex analogies and visual references. His childhood formed a central aspect of this iconographic play.

Examples of the Emmanuel are at Hagioi Anargyroi in Kastoria, which has a complex and unusual combination of late eleventh or early twelfth century iconography in the bema emphasizing Christ's eternal nature and sacrifice.[85] The Emmanuel appears twice. The first representation is on the tympanum over the apse with the *Hetoimasia* below on the soffit. A view towards the altar includes the entire series of identities, culminating with Christ's sacrifice. The second is the portrayal of Emmanuel standing in the apse of the *prothesis*, the site of the preparation of the eucharistic sacrifice, with John the Baptist and the Virgin flanking him on the adjacent walls. He is standing on a decorated footstool, wearing rich robes.[86] He is quite tall, perhaps a boy in his teenage years, and has a rounded face, with strong features including the high forehead and small protruding ears familiar from Virgin and Child representations. It is a striking image of a child, graceful but powerful. In the explorations of Christ's identity, his presence as a child and adolescent offered both doctrinal and visually favoured images.[87] The child Christ again appears with the enthroned Virgin in the apse, below which is a representation of Christ *Melismos*, a sacrificial image of the child Christ.[88] This is another conceptualization of the form of Christ centred on the youthful Christ, who lies on a paten or altar.[89] Christ's body literally represents the eucharistic offering, sacrificed from the moment of his birth.[90] The image extends the ideology behind the presentation of the child in the temple, but also reiterates the idea of Christ's body and blood in the eucharist. This idea of the sacrificial child is graphically imaged in a copy of the *Homilies of Gregory of Nazianzos*, where the child Christ is seen diving into the chalice.[91]

The Ancient of Days, Pantokrator and Emmanuel are also depicted in two eleventh-century manuscripts, in Paris, gr. 74 and in the *Theodore Psalter*,

---

85   Pelekanidis and Chatzidakis (1985) 22–49; Stylianos Pelekanides dates this to the late eleventh or early twelfth centuries, but Manolis Chatzidakis to 1170–1180; see 28, 44.

86   Pelekanidis and Chatzidakis (1985) fig. 13.

87   For the more common appearance of a bust in a medallion, see Hagios Stephanos, also in Kastoria, with the Emmanuel in centre stage near the altar; Pelekanidis and Chatzidakis (1985) 6–21, plan on 8–9, dating on 11, 19 (Pelekanidis and Chatzidakis differ).

88   For plan of the decorative programme, see Pelekanidis and Chatzidakis (1985) 24–25.

89   'Christusbild', *RBK* I, 1010–1011; Gerstel (1999) 444; Christ is sometimes shown as an adult, as in St George at Kurbinovo, but more often as a child, as in St Nicholas in Manastir, from 1271; see Gerstel (1999) figs 25–26 and 40. On child Christ as eucharistic offering, see Gerstel (1999) 42, with references; also Walter (2000) 229–242.

90   Stated by Nicholas Cabasilas, fourteenth century; Cabasilas (1967 edn) ch. VI.1; see Gerstel (1999) 41–42, with alternate reference.

91   Turin Univ. Lib. C.I.6, fol. 88v; see Galavaris (1969) 172–173, fig. 58. For a related image, the Christ *Anapeson*, depicted as a youth lying down and waiting for the resurrection with a scroll in his left hand, see *RBK* I, 1011–1012. For an example at the Peribleptos, Mystra, accompanied by two angels and symbols of the passion, see Dufrenne (1970) 33, 54.

B. M., Add. 19352.[92] Tsuji finds liturgical meaning in the placement of these representations of Christ in both the manuscripts, but the presence of the adolescent child is still indicative of an attitude towards youth that cannot be entirely attributed to doctrine. Additionally, the Emmanuel appears in several gospel frontispieces in the eleventh and twelfth centuries, often in a mandorla and surrounded by angels, prophets or the evangelist symbols.[93] Carr emphasizes that the Emmanuel is present, first, as the Word Incarnate and as a symbol of the eucharist; second, as the Messianic Christ in the glory of the second coming, and third, in the typological form, which was prophesied by Moses (*Deuteronomy* 18:15).[94] So, the child Christ has three contexts, 'the Christological, the soteriological, and the typological'.[95] The representations of the young Christ held many elaborate meanings, but behind the theological reasoning is their apparently widespread appeal: another image would have served to represent the incarnate word, the second coming and the Old Testament prophecies, but the youthful boy became prevalent.

A rather different version of the Emmanuel appears at Karanlık in Göreme, but one that emphasizes Christ's youthful attraction. This church was discussed in relation to the depiction of young and mature saints in Chapter 4, and evidently the designers of the iconography were highly aware of issues about age.[96] Its dating is controversial, varying from the mid-eleventh to the late twelfth century, though the earlier date seems more likely.[97] It was not a monastic church.[98] The church is an inscribed cross plan with a central dome and a dome adjacent to it in the eastern arm of the cross. Christ Pantokrator appears in the centre of both these domes, in an image of maturity. He has dark hair falling to his shoulders, a broad face with a cleft beard and wide shoulders. In the eastern dome, the smaller of the two, he holds an open gospel book. The Pantokrator in the adjacent, central dome, looks nearly identical, but holds a closed book in his left hand. In the drum of this dome and on the axis, and therefore visible as the viewer faces the altar, is the contrasting youthful image of Christ Emmanuel surrounded by six angels, each in medallions

---

92 Tsuji (1975) figs 1–4; for the *Theodore Psalter*, fols 1r, 100r, 189v, see Der Nersessian (1970) figs 1, 163, and 296.

93 For analysis of these, see Carr (1982) 3–20, esp. 6–10; Galavaris (1979) 100–109, figs 79–101; examples are Venice, Marciana Z 540, fol. 11v and Laurenziana Plut. VI 32, fol. 8r; see Carr (1982) figs 2, 7; see also Galavaris (1979) figs 79, 99.

94 The Emmanuel appears in the Burning Bush in Sinai icons, and in depictions of the Sermon on the Mount; see Paris, gr. 74, fol. 8v, in Omont (1908) I, pl. 12; Vatican gr. 1927, fol. 289v, in De Wald (1941) fig. LXXIII; both in Carr (1982) n. 68.

95 Carr (1982) 9.

96 Also known as chapel 23; Jerphanion (1925–1942) I.2, 393–430; pls II, 96–110; Restle (1967) I, 128–129, II, figs 218–244; Rodley (1985) 48–56; Jolivet-Lévy (1991) 132–135. It is thought to have been decorated by the same workshop as the other so-called column churches, Elmali and Çarikli; on Elmali, see Jerphanion (1925–1942) I.2, 431–454, pls II, 113–124; on Çarikli, see Jerphanion (1925–1942) I.2, 455–473, pls II, 125–132; on dating and style, see Epstein (1980–1981) 27–45; Wharton (1988) 45–51.

97 For a summary of the opinions, and bibliography, see Epstein (1980–1981) 27, n. 1.

98 On this, see Wharton (1988) 45–46.

(pl. 14).[99] The angels, young and curly-haired, all look towards Christ, who is named IC XC within the medallion and O EMANYHL beneath it; the angels are each also named. Around the dome is an inscription from Psalm 53:2, which is very similar to Psalm 14.2 and reads, 'God looks down from heaven on the sons of men, to see if there are any who understand, any who seek God'.[100] As noted above, in the pendentives of the dome are four youthful disciples, all beardless: Philip, Judas Thaddeos, Prochoros and Thomas.[101] Jerphanion explains the inclusion of Prochoros with the apostles as confusion on the part of the artist, since Prochoros is mentioned with Philip as one of the first seven deacons, but he may well be included because of his youth.[102] The prevalence of young figures, discussed before, cannot be unrelated to the unusual and central image of Christ Emmanuel.[103]

Christ Emmanuel appears, not as the rather odd child with large forehead and protruding ears, often typical of Emmanuel imagery, but rather as a well-proportioned, attractive-looking boy.[104] He has short, curly, brown hair and an oval face, and he wears a simple robe with a cloak over one shoulder. He gestures with his right hand in the same fashion as the Pantokrator, that is with two fingers of his right hand raised and the other two touching the thumb, while the left hand holds a scroll. He looks to his right and slightly downwards towards the 'sons of men'. His face has similar shape, features and expression to those of the angels, who are equally youthful and have large almond-shaped eyes and small mouths. Rossitza Roussanova suggests that rather than symbolizing the feast of the *Synaxis* of the archangels, the dome shows Christ and the angels as an intermediary between heaven and humankind.[105] This interpretation (although she, perhaps mistakenly in this case, gives Christ the identity of an awesome saviour), fits with the image of the youthful Christ, the incarnate godhead, whose reality as a child emphasizes his incarnation but also suggests his divine eternity. The image of an appealing, normal and well-formed adolescent boy was appropriate as an intermediary between human and God.

The widespread use of these images, in their various and rather complex types, indicates a fascination with the image of the Christ child as an aspect of the Saviour's incarnation. While the representations of the Ancient of Days and of the Pantokrator are used in exploratory ways, images of Christ as a child and youth are particularly varied and avant-garde. His youth makes

---

99   Restle (1967) II, fig. 220.

100 For inscriptions, see Jerphanion (1925–1942) I.2, 406. Roussanova implies that this quotation is not used elsewhere in a dome; see Roussanova (1999) 17–18.

101 Restle (1967) II, fig. 220.

102 Jerphanion (1925–1942) I.2, 407, n. 1.

103 Emmanuel also appears at Çarikli kilise in a similar position in the central dome where the Pantocrator is surrounded by five busts of angels and the Emmanuel; the decoration of the church closely follows that of Karanlık; see Jerphanion (1925–1942) I.2, 459; Jolivet-Lévy (1991) 129.

104 See the watercolour by M. T. Ridolfi in Jerphanion (1925–1942) pl. II, 107.

105 Roussanova (2000) 18–19; for more on Emmanuel in Karanlık, see Roussanova (1999) 13–39.

him especially appropriate as a symbol of Christ's incarnate state, his existence from the origin, and the promise of eternal life. Youth is fit for images of the maiestas, surrounded in glory by a mandorla, and for the *Melismos* and *Anapeson*, where Christ is sacrificed in the eucharist. Manuel I's choice of Emmanuel on his coins increased the popularity of the Christ type, but was also a reflection of society's interest in the Christ child, which began prior to his reign. But placing an image on public coinage is a sure way of making it well known. The Christ child's popularity reflects doctrinal and liturgical meanings, but also a societal acceptance of and an enthusiasm for the power and significance of the young Christ. These references give youth a special place as container and purveyor of power and sanctity as well as selflessness and suffering. Such associations cannot but have affected the Byzantine young who experienced these images, and their parents too.

From a nondoctrinal point of view, one could look at the repeated images of the Christ child in narrative and iconic representations and at the extensive cycles of the Virgin's life and infer that the Byzantines were captivated by both male and female children, by their growth, by their power and authority and by their influence over adults. One sees children who attract a swarm of adults intent on nurturing them and learning from them; children who go through the process of growing up, with clearly defined rites of passage and maturation; and children, like the Emmanuel, who take pride of place near altars, in gospel headpieces and in frontispieces, emanating fine features, power and grace. Doctrinal and theological approaches to the Christ and the Virgin as young cannot be ignored, but still, the attraction to imagery about children and the ways in which it was articulated are significant both for what they tell about how children were viewed and the place that imagery about children held in Byzantine society.

It is true that apocryphal details associated with the activities of children are not represented unless they are closely connected with orthodox meaning. For instance, when Mary is depicted learning how to walk, the viewer is aware of the spiritual corollary that from this point on her feet will not be sullied by the ground, by earthly life. The will of theologians, patrons, artists and popular consent contributed to an iconographic tradition that included various aspects of early childhood and adolescence. These could have been omitted and the meaning conveyed in other ways through adult representations. But it was deemed relevant to include scenes from daily life: details in the children's upbringings, like their first baths and their presentations in the temple are events experienced by all Hebraic children and have Byzantine parallels. These are significant moments showing their dedication to God. Christ and the Virgin are clearly depicted as children, growing up in stages and generally shown at the appropriate age for the event in which they participate. And from the visual evidence, these formative years were seen as crucial times of spiritual development and the children were perceived to need careful nurturing and guidance by their parents.

Joachim and Anna present the image of a devoted couple, assiduous and worthy parents, blessed with a despaired-of child in the Old Testament tradition. They jointly take responsibility for Mary and seem equally involved in her upbringing, although Mary's first steps are usually taken near her mother, suggesting that in this first move away from the family bonds towards a life dedicated to God, the crucial link is with the mother. However, Joachim, as well, is shown doting over his child. Many of the images convey a sense of nurturing and care for the little girl which, while it reflects a need to portray Mary's purity, also gives a sense of familial love and affection. The figures touch one another, embrace and exchange direct looks, giving the viewer a poignant, if moralistic, impression of what present-day society terms family values.

Regarding family, Christ is in an odd situation, for his worldly father has only a secondary role to his mother who conceived by the Spirit. Christ's family is unconventional: a young mother, Mary, an aged father, Joseph, and a set of mature half-brothers. Joseph has an ambiguous role, since he is not the generator of the Christ child. He takes a reticent part in the synoptic gospels, in church doctrine and in the visual representations. Women and the world of women take precedence, although Joseph's often-present sons, witnesses to the miracle, somewhat redress the balance. But Joseph is included in Christ's upbringing and attendant, if often in a secondary position, at the presentation in the temple and on the road to Jerusalem when Christ is 12.

In the icons of the Virgin and Christ child together, family values do not always count. In many Middle and Late Byzantine images, the fond embrace of a single mother and her son is imaged, but in many others throughout the period, including the monumental apse decorations, the bonding between mother and child is subsumed by the independent presence of the child. He sits up, clasping his scroll, raising his hand as if teaching, and taking on an authoritative air. The image of mother and child is universal, and Byzantine society was clearly receptive to the image of a lone mother with her child. It is intriguing that there are few attempts in these images to insert a father or a second generative figure, whether Joseph, God the father or the Holy Spirit, but rather the emphasis is on Mary's role as bearer of God. A well-known exception to this is the sixth-century Sinai icon of the Virgin and Child, discussed above, where the hand of God is present in the sky and the young mother is accompanied by the spiritual family of saints and angels. [106]

The sanctity and consequence of the children are often marked by haloes, but aspects of their dress are also signifiers of their roles: Mary wears her shrouding blue *maphorion* and Christ is clad in voluminous gold robes, the one suggesting modesty, the other spiritual splendour. Often, as at Kariye Camii, the gold robes of Christ's youth are contrasted with the muted browns and blues of the clothes of Christ the working adult, no longer the splendid glory of the chosen child. The import of the children is often conveyed by the

---

106 Soteriou and Soteriou (1956–58) II, 21–22, I, figs 4–7 and colour plate; Weitzmann (1976) B3, 18–21, pls 4–6, 43–46; Vassilaki (2000) n. 1.

actions of the adults around them, such as the obeisance of the magi or the nurturing by Joachim and Anna. In the nativity and often in the presentation scenes, he is very much a baby, singled out by God, frequently bathed in celestial light, but not yet displaying his power. However, later, both boy and girl are depicted asserting their religious maturity and closeness to the divine; Mary climbs the steps of the altar, and Christ sits upright and teaches.

This assertiveness gives both of them power. The Christ child is not depicted as a young imperial prince and equally the Virgin has no vestiges of earthly power, excepting the thrones on which they sometimes sit, yet this does not necessarily associate them with secular rule.[107] Images of Christ seated on his mother's lap, whether receiving the magi or in icons, demonstrate the dominance of the young leader, who is given the attributes of a teacher – the scroll and raised hand. He is the omniscient child. This image is explored in the scenes of Christ with the doctors, where he is surrounded by adults listening to his words. The Virgin as a child is portrayed very consistently, with emphasis on her humility, purity and preciousness, and the careful preparation needed for her role. This gives her the power of devotion and spiritual independence. But she also gains status through the reflected power of the Son and the mimicking in her life of events that will happen in his. This visualization gives her life a related value.

This prevalence of imagery of Jesus and Mary as children, present in some form in virtually every decorated Byzantine religious building and illustrated religious text, must, if nothing more, show a sensitivity to, and acceptance of, the centrality of children in concepts of belief and in society. The proclivity for images of the children, evidenced by the various repetitions, permutations and elaborations on the themes, indicates both a respect for the power, sanctity and intelligence possible in children and their influence, specifically in religious life, and, by extension, in Byzantium's closely related secular life.

---

107 On this, in relation to Christ, see Mathews (1993) 103–109.

Chapter 7

Conclusions

This book has a simple thesis: children form a significant and important part of Byzantine visual representation. But, however elementary, this assertion deserves a full treatment, for children are not usually associated with Byzantine art history. It is an open question as to why their primary place in imagery has not previously been signalled. Perhaps it has more to do with our own orientations in looking at art and in perceiving children than with the images themselves. The various depictions that have been discussed are, mostly, well known and accessible. Certain fresh interpretations have been offered for a few objects or programmes, but generally the book has not attempted to solve iconographical complexities or to find new attributions. The aim has been to explore a series of issues, probing the contexts and manner in which children were portrayed and assessing to what ends the images were intended. And I have argued that children were depicted often and with considerable attention, and that they were frequently pivotal to the appearance and meaning of representations.

If children appear so often and so significantly in visual imagery, this suggests that children held a visible role in familial and societal life. We know that they were politically important, with imperial sons holding titles of co-emperor from a young age, and with imperial sons and daughters being affianced in their youth to secure diplomatic détente. Valuable as political heirs, children also appear to have been valued as individuals, imaged in familial portraits in central and assertive ways. Whether illustrating biblical scenes or ornamenting diverting margins, children's presence in various settings suggests that they, and childhood, had significant associations. For the most part these were positive and pleasurable. The only recurring images of children that are evil or disconcerting are those of young victims, such as the babies in the massacre of the innocents, or young martyrs such as Quiricus or the potential martyr, Isaac, in scenes of Abraham's sacrifice. We have seen no examples of children behaving wickedly, which might indicate that no such view was largely held about them.

Children were, both legally and in practice, seen as living through a distinct and recognizable phase in life. We have to remember that they were close the majority of the population. Power and influence may have been mostly held by the mature, but children and adolescents equally numbered the adults in most given situations both in the home, in the marketplace, in the workshop and even perhaps on the battle field. We should recall that it was not until 1830 in Britain that children under the age of 14 were limited to working eight hours a day and, even more significantly, children under nine were only then prevented from working in the factories. But they could work anywhere else. The little children were the ones spending their hours in the fields, in the smithies, the bakery, the cobblers, the wash house and doing the chores at home. Our ideal that children should not work for mammon but just to improve their minds and skills is a very modern one. Undoubtedly in Byzantium much of the daily toil was undertaken by young people, both girls and boys, though it could be argued that much of the girls' duties were undertaken within the home. We also tend to see the making of art as the work of the artist, an often elevated, isolated and cerebral creative activity. Much of the art we have been examining does not fit into this category; it is either church or domestic decoration, always created by groups of people; metalwork or enamelling, also made in some kind of a workshop; manuscript illuminations, produced in a scriptorium, whether monastic or secular with a group of artisans working together on a project; and ivories, which again would be made in a workshop environment. The making of art in Byzantium was not the work of an isolated master, but the product of groups of artisans. Many of those artisans would have been young, even if the novices started by sweeping the floors and dusting the shelves and then progressed to mixing the paints and filling in the backgrounds. If a child started work at perhaps seven years of age, even if it that was how they only filled up the afternoon hours, by the age of 14 or so the young person would be well advanced in the skills of the profession and earning some kind of income.

With children marrying as young teenagers, many objects must have been given to those we would consider to be children as wedding gifts. Certainly, many of the rings and bracelets that have survived from Byzantium are very small and were made for children. We do not know to what extent the children were themselves commissioners of purchasers of the objects, but it stands to reason that, just as children today who have access to money buy and sell, children in Byzantium did likewise. While Byzantine artefacts were mass produced to some extent, far more of the market was created on a commissioned basis, by people deciding on a particular style or size or decoration and asking for it to be made, as is still the case in most places unaffected by the industrial revolution. Many of those things commissioned must have been commissioned by the young. This suggests that children had taste and discrimination and made artistic choices. In turn, the artefacts were being made at some level by children themselves.

Discussion of the floor at Piazza Armerina in Sicily showed the frequent portrayal of children from various walks of life in a luxury villa setting, and it was suggested that the suites with floors depicting children may well have been intended for the use of the family, implying that the imagery was intentionally suited to children. Similarly, the *Barberini Psalter*, a manuscript with a portrait of a child receiving a book as its frontispiece, was very likely given as a gift to the boy in the image. The codex, Vatican, gr. 1851, containing an illustrated poem dedicated to a young royal bride, was probably intended for the princess and, it was proposed here, illustrated in ways intended to appeal to her as a child. Similarly, it was suggested that the *David plates* were intended for a young prince. These latter examples all have imperial recipients and were probably for private use. However, if the concept of art for children existed in Byzantine imperial circles, it quite probably was current down the social scale. The attention of not only the imperial children, but children in general must have been sought by purveyors of visual images. While much of what survives is of high quality, as is characteristic, we do have considerable evidence in other contexts. The most pervasive example is decorations on the interior of churches. While some of these are imperial, with limited access, others are monastic (and we recognized the presence of children in monasteries, where presumably they would have had access also to books, some of them illustrated), and others are ecclesiastic, intended to be seen by the clergy and by the people. The representations in these public places of worship would have been viewed to a large extent by children. It seems only logical that in some contexts those designing them would have had children's interests, concerns and education in mind. Adults chose to have their own children depicted for their personal satisfaction, but also for the benefit of the children. The presence of children in donor portraits was intended to be seen by the parents, by their children and by others, both adults and children. For instance, worshippers standing close to the Theodotus chapel at S. Maria Antiqua were able to view the elevated placement of the boy and girl flanking the Virgin. Similarly, images such as the Christ child and the Virgin and the lives of young saints must have often been intended to entertain, to educate and to influence children. From the hagiographical texts we know that a central tenet of Byzantine life was to bring up children close to God and well versed in the scriptures. What better way to educate them than through visual imagery?

The gold-glass portraits from the catacombs give a view, if narrow, of early Christian ideal family groups, with favoured sons and daughters at the centre, not unlike other family portraits that occur throughout western history. Representations such as Joseph's family in the *Vienna Genesis* show human affection, particularly, in this context, between males. Similarly, close physical proximity and communication was identified in the depiction of the Maccabee family at S. Maria Antiqua, which indicates the significance of the sons as individualized martyrs. Donor portraits, on the other hand, may suggest corporal intimacy, but not necessarily affection, for they tend to be formal and frontal, with the figures often standing in relation to a saint or to the Virgin, as in the Theodotus chapel. In the mosaic on the north pier at S. Demetrios in Thessaloniki, two small children appear in a highly visible place, embraced and protected by a youthful male saint, but imaged without parental support, making a statement about the direct protection given to children by saints. The *Lincoln College Typikon* illuminations demonstrate two distinct spheres of familial orientation, the humble and spiritual and the affluent and worldly. This manuscript was discussed in relation to the centrality of the child, Euphrosyne, who, it was suggested, was the focus of the original group of four illuminations. It was also proposed that Euphrosyne, for whom the monastery was founded, was the original recipient of a manuscript of the typikon, which was later copied with the addition of the secular portraits.

The central place of the portrayals of Maria in S. Demetrios, Thessaloniki, and their preservation over nine centuries until masked in the Islamic period, indicates the concept of a chosen child destined for a life close to God. The domestication and elevation of the boy saint in depictions of Saint Nicholas suggest an inclination to identify and single out young spiritual prodigies by portraying them in normal situations of daily life in which they can excel. The idealization of the young biblical hero in the *David plates*, with the portrayal of his youth and his growth from chosen shepherd to anointed and married leader, illustrate the glorification of boyhood and adolescence and focus on the steps taken towards maturity. The discussion suggested that the plates were made for Herakleios's son David and intended to exemplify the goals of a young leader. From the earliest manuscripts, child heroes in biblical illustrations, such as David and Joseph, are depicted as idealized boys and young men. Moses, for instance, is imaged as a glorious youth.

An examination of Paris, gr. 510 led to the suggestion that the young rulers depicted in the opening portraits, Leo and Alexander, were the recipients of the manuscript. The portraits exemplify dynastic succession as well as subtle and personal distinctions in their father's approach to his children. At the same time, perhaps, the choice of images in the book highlighted and promoted youthful heroes with whom the boys might identify. On a different note, the manuscript, Vatican, gr. 1851, depicting the arrival and welcome of the princess bride mentioned above, demonstrates the respect accorded to young females at court and the ceremonial but also intimate aspects of imperial rituals.

The mosaics on the triumphal arch at S. Maria Maggiore show the Christ child as a realistic, curly-haired boy, dressed in a simple white tunic but marked in glory by his halo and surrounded by attestors to his birth, marvelling at his incarnation. It was suggested that the images portray scenes from the *Infancy Gospel of James* and of *Thomas*, and that the figures dressed in *maphoria* are the midwife and Salome, the two first witnesses to Christ's birth. Additionally, the scene often said to portray a miracle attributed to the Virgin in Egypt is more likely to depict leaders and townspeople recognizing the child Christ's miraculous deeds or divinely inspired speech. This interpretation again places the child at the centre of the representations.

Imagery from three Cappadocian churches, probably datable to the ninth to twelfth centuries, Joachim and Anna, Tokalı kilise and S. Michael in Cemil, indicates a definite focus on Christ and the Virgin as children. Images in S. Michael point to the perceived relationship of their lives, whereby Jesus and Mary stand for the idealized boy and girl. Constantinopolitan examples, from the twelfth and fourteenth centuries, the manuscripts illustrating the homilies of James of Kokkinobaphos and the mosaics at the church of the monastery at Chora, suggest both aristocratic and monastic enthusiasm for the apocryphal tales of Mary's life and, at Chora, an interest in the relationship between the experiences of Jesus and of Mary. The portrayal of a radiant and attractive boy as Christ Emmanuel in Karanlık kilise highlights the allure and the spiritual significance of the young. The conscious depiction of paired mature and youthful saints in this same church shows an overall awareness of physical immaturity as an aspect of sanctity.

Through this study it has become apparent that, first, there are many representations of children in Byzantium, second, the children are often central to the depictions, and third, children retain their qualities as children and are portrayed as such, not as small adults. These observations imply that children were perceived to have childlike attributes, that they could be seen to be significant members of familial and community life, that they could have religious and secular integrity and authority, and that their youth held emotional, physical or spiritual appeal. Byzantine society was heavily populated with children who did not form an invisible plurality. The patrons, designers and creators of sculptures, manuscripts, icons and monumental programmes, in fact of all forms of visual representations, employed images of children. The impetus for portrayals of children seems to have come from a variety of generators of art: the secular and the monastic church, the imperial court, the wealthy elite and also, on occasion, the less affluent. They all frequently found children to be a relevant and engaging subject for visual representations. And in turn the imagery was viewed by children.

The demographic dominance of youth in Byzantium may have a relevant extension. The same statistics can be applied to other pre-modern societies, where equally, for the most part, half the population was under the age of 20. A significant quantity of visual representations in other pre-modern societies were arguably intended for and made by young people. I would suggest that the creation and reception of art in ancient, medieval and late-medieval societies has been generally viewed from the perspective of adults, not of children, and this may distort our understanding of it.

Bibliography

Primary Sources

For the sake of clarity, the sources are arranged in the following order:

Apocrypha
Ecclesiastical Councils And Theological Texts
Historical, Ceremonial And Instructional Texts
Laws
Lives Of Saints, Popes And Clergy
Typika

APOCRYPHA

Amann, E. (1910). *Le protévangile de Jacques le Mineur et ses remaniements latins. Introduction, textes, traduction et commentaires*. Paris.

Charles, R. (1913). *The Apocrypha and Pseudepigrapha of the Old Testament in English*. 2 vols. Oxford.

Hennecke, E. and W. Schneemelcher (1963). *New Testament Apocrypha*. London.

Hock, R. (1997). *The Infancy Gospels of James and Thomas*. Santa Rosa, CA.

James, M.R. (1924). *The Apocryphal New Testament*. Oxford.

Tischendorf, C. (1853). *Evangelia apocrypha*. In Greek and Latin. Lipsiae.

ECCLESIASTICAL COUNCILS AND THEOLOGICAL TEXTS

Ambrosius. *De excessu fratris sui satyri*. PL 16:1345–1414.

Ambrosius. *De Jacob et vita beata*. PL 14:626–670.

Augustine, S., Bishop of Hippo (1981 edn). *Sancti Augustini Confessionum libri XIII*. Edited by M. Skutella and L. Verheijen, *Corpus christanorum series Latina 27*. Turnholti.

Basilii Ancyrani; attributed to Basilius Magnus Caesareae (Basil the Great). *De vera virginitate*. PG 30:669–810.

Cabasilas, N. (1967 edn). *Explication de la divine liturgie, traduction et notes*. Edited and translated by S. Salaville. *SC*, no. 4 bis. Paris.

Cyrillus Alexandrinus. *Homilia in sanctum festum Palmarum* (13). *PG* 77:1049–1072.

Eustathius Thessalonicensis. *Invocationes S. Demetrii*. *PG* 136:161–168.

Eustathius Thessalonicensis. *Laudatio S. Demetrii*. *PG* 136:169–216.

Gregorius Nazianzenus. *Oratio ad eos qui acciverant nec occurrerant* (3). *PG* 35:517–526.

Gregorius Nazianzenus. *Oratio de pauperum amore* (14). *PG* 35: 858–909.

Gregorius Nazianzenus. *Oratio in laudem Basilii magni* (43). *PG* 36:493–606.

Gregorius Nazianzenus. *Oratio in Macchabaeorum laudem* (15). *PG* 35:911–934.

Gregorius Nazianzenus. *Oratio in novam dominicam* (44). *PG* 36:608–621.

Gregory of Nazianzos (1978 edn). *Grégoire de Nazianze. Discours 1–3, introduction, texte critique, traduction et notes*. Edited and translated by J. Bernardi. *SC*, no. 247. Paris.

Gregory of Nazianzos (1992 edn). *Grégoire de Nazianze. Discours 42–43, introduction, texte critique, traduction et notes*. Edited and translated by J. Bernardi, *SC*, no. 384. Paris.

Gregory of Nazianzos (1995 edn). *Grégoire de Nazianze, Discours 6–12, introduction, texte critique, traduction et notes*. Edited and translated by M.-A. Calvet-Sebaste. *SC*, no. 405. Paris.

Gregorius Turonensis. *Liber in gloria martyrum*. *PL* 71:705–800.

Gregory of Tours (1885 edn). *Liber in gloria martyrum*. Edited by B. Krusch, *Scriptores rerum merovingiarum*. Hannover.

Gregory of Tours (1988 edn). *Glory of the Marytrs*. Translated by R. Van Dam. Liverpool.

Grumel, V. (1947). *Régestes des actes du patriarcat de Constantinople. Vol. 1, part 3, Les régestes de 1043 à 1206*. Istanbul.

Hefele, C.J. (1907–1952). *Histoire des conciles*. Translated by J. Leclercq. 11 vols.

Irenaeus. *Contra haereses*. *PG* 7:437–1224.

Jacobi Monachi Kokkinobaphos. *Oratio in conceptionem SS. Deiparae*. *PG* 127:543–700.

Jerome (1912 edn). *Sancti Eusebii Hieronymi epistulae*. Edited by I. Hilberg. *Corpus scriptorum ecclesiasticorum latinorum*. Vol. 55, part II. Vindobonae.

Joannes Chrysostomus. *XI Homilia, de Eleazaro et septem pueris*. *PG* 63:523–530.

Joannes Damascenus. *De fide orthodoxa*. *PG* 94:789–1228.

John Chrysostom (1951 edn). *Christianity and Pagan Culture in the Later Roman Empire; Together with an English Translation of John Chrysostom's Address on Vainglory and the Right Way for Parents to Bring up Their Children*. Edited by M. Laistner. Ithaca, NY.

Joannes Diaconus. *S. Gregorii Magni vita*. *PL* 75:59–242.

Justinus Philosophus. *Dialogus cum Tryphone*. *PG* 6:471–800.

Klosterman (1935). See Origen (1935 edn).

Laurent (1964). See Leo the Philosopher (1964 edn).

Leo the Philosopher (1964 edn). *Une homélie inédite de l'archevêque de Thessalonique, Léon le Philosophe, sur l'Annonciation (25 mars 842)*. Edited by V. Laurent. In *Mélanges Tisserant*. Vol. 2, 281–302. Vatican.

Origen (1935 edn). *Origenes Matthäuserklärung*. Edited by E. Klosterman, *Die griechischen christlichen Schrifsteller der ersten drei Jahrhunderte, Origenes zehnter Band*. Vol. 1. Leipzig.

Origenes. *Commentariorum in evangelium secundum Matthaeum*. PG 13:829–1600.

Symeon Logotheta Metaphrastes. *Panteleemon*. PG 115:447–478.

Tanner, N., ed. (1990). *Decrees of the Ecumenical Councils*. 2 vols. London and Washington, DC.

Theodorus Studita. *Testamentum*. PG 99:1813–1824.

Theodorus Studita. *Epistolarum lib*. 1, XVII. PG 99:961–964.

Van Dam (1988). See Gregory of Tours (1988 edn).

Historical, Ceremonial and Instructional Texts

Aegineta, Paulus (1844–1887 edn). *The Seven Books of Paulus Aegineta*. Edited and translated by F. Adams. 3 vols. London.

Basilius I. *Paraenesis ad leonem Filium*. PG 107:XXI–LVI.

Choniates, Nicetas (1975 edn). *Nicetae Choniatae historia*. Edited by I.A. Van Dieten, *CFHB*. Vol. 11, 1–2. Berlin.

Choniates, Niketas (1984 edn). *O City of Byzantium: Annals of Niketas Choniates*. Translated by H. Magoulias. Detroit.

Clavijo, Gonzales Ruy de (1928 edn). *Embassy to Tamerlane, 1403–1306*. Edited and translated by G. Le Strange. London.

Comnena, Anna. *Alexiadis*. PG 131:79–1212.

Comnene, Anna (1937 edn). *Anna Comnène. Alexiade*. Edited and translated by B. Leib. 3 vols. Paris.

Comnene, Anna (1969 edn). *The Alexiad of Anna Comnena*. Edited and translated by E.R.A. Sewter. London.

Constantinus VII Porphyrogenitus. *De administrando imperio*. PG 113:157–422.

Constantine Porphyrogenitus (1967 edn). *De administrando imperio*. Edited by Gy. Moravcsik. Translated by R. Jenkins. *CFHB*. Vol. 1. Washington, DC.

Constantine VII (1829–1830 edn). *De ceremoniis aulae byzantinae*. Edited by J.-J. Reiske. 2 vols. Bonn.

Constantine VII Porphyrogénète (1935–1939 edn). *Le livre des cérémonies*. Edited and translated by A. Vogt. 2 vols. Paris.

Constantinus VII Porphyrogenitus. *Vita Basilii*. PG 109:225–370.

Constantine VII Porphyrogennetos (1838 edn). *Theophanes Continuati*. Bk 5. *De Basilio Macedone*. *CSHB*. Vol. 48. Bonn.

Cross, S., ed. (1953 edn). *The Russian Primary Chronicle. Laurentian Text*. Cambridge, MA.

Kekaumenos (1896 edn). *Cecaumeni stratigioni.* Edited by B. Wassiliewsky and W. Jernstedt. In Greek. Petropoli.

Kekaumenos (1964 edn). *Vademecum des byzantinischen Aristokraten (Kekaumenos).* Edited and translated by H.-G. Beck. In German. Graz, Vienna, Cologne.

Kinnamos, John (1976 edn). *Deeds of John and Manuel Comnenus by John Kinnamos.* Translated by C. Brand. In English. New York.

Leib (1937). See Comnene (1937 edn)

Le Strange (1928). See Clavijo (1928 edn).

Liudprand of Cremona (1930 edn). *The Works of Liudprand of Cremona.* Edited by F. Wright. London.

Liudprand of Cremona (1998 edn). *Liudprandi Cremonensis Antapodosis.* Edited by P. Chiesa. Turnhout.

Mango (1958). See Photios (1958 edn).

Moravcsik (1967). See Constantine Porphyrogenitus (1967 edn)

Pachymérès, George (1984 edn). *Relations historiques.* Edited by A. Failler. Translated by V. Laurent. *CFHB.* Vol. 24, in 4 parts. In Greek and French. Paris.

Photius (1958 edn). *The Homilies of Photius, Patriarch of Constantinople,* English Translation, Introduction and Commentary by C. Mango. *Dumbarton Oaks Studies,* No. 3. Cambridge, MA.

Photius (1959 edn). *Homiliae.* Edited by B. Laourdas. Thessaloniki.

Procopios (1914–1940 edn). *Procopius with an English Translation.* Vol. 7. *Buildings.* Edited and translated by H.B. Dewing. Loeb Classical Library. Cambridge, MA.

Psellus, Michael (1928 edn). *Chronographie ou histoire d'un siècle de Byzance (967–1077).* Text and translation by E. Renaud. 2 vols. Paris.

Psellus, Michael (1953, 1966 edn). *Fourteen Byzantine Rulers.* Edited and translated by E.R.A. Sewter. London.

Psellus, Michael (1876). Epitafioi logoi eis tin thugatera stulianin. *Michail Psellou: Istrikoi logoi, Epistolai, kai alla anekdota. Mesaioniki bibliothiki.* Vol 5, 62–87. Editedby K.N. Sathas. Paris.

Pseudo Kodinos (1966 edn). *Traité des offices: Pseudo-Kodinos: Introduction, texte et traduction.* Edited and translated by J. Verpeaux.

Renaud (1928). See Psellus (1928 edn).

Sewter (1953, 1966 edn). See Psellus (1953, 1966 edn).

Sewter (1969). See Comnene, Anna (1969 edn)

Theophylact (1980–1986 edn). *Theophylacte d'Achrida, introduction, texte, traduction et notes.* Edited and translated by P. Gautier. Thessaloniki.

Theophylactus. *Paideia basiliki. PG* 126:253–286.

Verpeaux (1966). See Pseudo Kodinos (1966 edn).

Vogt (1935–1939). See Constantine VII Porphyrogénète (1935–1939 edn).

LAWS

Freshfield, E.H., ed. (1926). *A Manual of Roman Law: The Ecloga Published by the Emperors Leo III and Constantine V of Isauria at Constantinople AD 726.* In English. Cambridge.

Freshfield, E.H., ed. (1927). *A Revised Manual of Roman Law: Founded upon the Ecloga of Leo III and Constantine V, of Isauria, Ecloga privata aucta.* In English.Cambridge.

Freshfield, E.H., ed. (1928). *A Manual of Eastern Roman Law: The Procheiros Nomos, Published by the Emperor Basil I at Constantinople, between 867 and 879 AD.* In English. Cambridge.

Krueger, P. and T. Mommsen, eds (1928). *Corpus iuris civilis: Institutiones, Digesta, Codex Justinianus, Novellae.* In Latin. 3 vols. Berlin.

Mommsen, T. and P. Kreuger (1985). *The Digest of Justinian.* Translated by A. Watson. In English. 4 vols. Philadelphia.

Noailles, P. and A. Dain, eds (1944). *Les novelles de Léon VI, le Sage, texte et traduction.* In Greek and French. Paris.

Pharr, Clyde, ed. (1952). *The Theodosian Code and Novels and the Sirmondian Constitutions. Corpus of Roman Law.* Vol. 1. Princeton.

Scott, S.P., ed. (1932, 1973 edn). *Corpus iuris civilis, the Civil Law.* In English. 7 vols. New York.

LIVES OF SAINTS, POPES AND CLERGY

Anrich, G. (1913, 1917). *Hagios Nikolaos: der heilige Nikolaus in der griechischen Kirche: Texte und Untersuchungen.* 2 vols. Leipzig, Berlin.

Auzépy, M.-F. (1997). *La vie d'Etienne le Jeune par Etienne le Diacre.* Aldershot.

Connor, C. and W. Connor (1994). *Life and Miracles of Saint Luke of Steiris: Text, Translation and Commentary.* Brookline, MA.

Davis, R. (1989). *The Book of Pontiffs: The Ancient Biographies of the First 90 Roman Bishops to AD 715.* Liverpool.

Davis, R. (1992). *Lives of the Eighth Century Popes (Liber pontificalis): The Ancient Lives of Nine Popes from AD 715 to AD 817.* Liverpool.

Davis, R. (1995). *The Lives of the Ninth-Century Popes (Liber pontificalis): The Ancient Lives of Ten Popes from AD 817–891.* Liverpool.

Dawes, E. and N. Baynes (1948). *Three Byzantine Saints: Contemporary Biographies.* Oxford.

Delehaye, H., ed. (1902). *Synaxarium ecclesiae Constantinopolitanae e codice Sirmondiano nunc Berolinensi. Propylaeum ad acta sanctorum novembris.* Brussels.

Delehaye, H., ed. (1910). *Vita S. Lazari auctore Gregorio monacho.* In *Acta Sanctorum novembris.* Vol. 3, 508–606. Brussels.

Delehaye, H., ed. (1925). *Vita S. Thomaïdis.* In *Acta sanctorum novembris.* Vol. 4, 234–242. Brussels.

Delehaye, H., ed. (1925). *Vita S. Mariae Iunoris.* In *Acta sanctorum novembris.* Vol. 4, 692–705. Brussels.

Duchesne, L., ed. (1886–1892, 1955–1957 edn). *Le liber pontificalis, texte, introduction et commentaire*. 3 vols.

Festugière, A-J., ed. (1970). *Vie de Théodore de Sykeon*. Brussels.

George of Cyprus (1993 edn). *The Autobiography of George of Cyprus (Ecumenical Patriarch Gregory II)*. Edited and translated by A. Pelendrides. London.

Gill, J. (1950). Life of Euthymios the Great by Cyril of Skythopolis. *Orientalia christiana periodica* 6:114–20.

Halkin, F. (1973). Sainte Elisabeth d'Héraclée, Abesse à Constantinople. *Analecta Bollandiana* 91:249–264.

Lemerle, P. (1979–1981). *Les plus anciens receuils des miracles de saint Démétrios. I, Texte. II, Commentaire*. Paris.

SS. Sergii et Bacchi. Passio Antiquior (1895 edn). *Analecta Bollandiana* 14:375–395.

Ševčenko, I. and N.P. Ševčenko, eds (1984). *The Life of Saint Nicholas of Sion*. Brookline, MA.

Stephanus Diaconus. *Vita S. Stephani Junioris*. PG 100:1069–1186.

Talbot, A.M., ed. (1996). *Holy Women of Byzantium: Ten Saints' Lives in English Translation*. Washington, DC.

Usener, H. (1913). Eine Spur des Petrusevangeliums. In *Kleine Schriften*, 417–421. Leipzig and Berlin.

Typika

Delehaye, H. (1921). *Deux typica byzantins de l'époque des Paléologues*. Paris.

Dmitrievskij, A. (1895–1901). *Opisanie liturgitseskich rukopisej*. 2 vols. Kiev.

Gautier, P. (1974). Le typikon du Christ Sauveur Pantocrator. *REB* 32:1–145.

Gautier, P. (1985). Le typikon de la Théotokos Kecharitöméné. *REB* 43:5–155.

Meyer, P. (1894). *Die Haupturkunden für die Geschichte der Athosklöster*. Leipzig.

Miklosich, F. and J. Müller (1860–1890, reprinted Aalen 1968). *Acta et diplomata graeca medii aevi*. Vol 6. *Patmos*. Vienna.

Petit, L. (1900). Le monastère de Notre-Dame de Pitié en Macédonie. *Izvestiia Russkago Archeologicheskago Instituta v Konstantinople* 6:1–153.

Thomas, J. and A.C. Hero, eds. (2000). *Byzantine Monastic Foundation Documents: A Complete Translation of the Surviving Founder's Typika and Testaments*. 5 vols. Washington, DC.

Secondary Sources

The bibliography is restricted to cited works

Adontz, N. (1933). La portée historique de l'oraison funèbre de Basile I par son fils Léon VI le Sage. *Byzantion* 8:501–513.

Alexiou, M. (1977). A Critical Reappraisal of Eustathios Makrembolites' *Hysmine and Hysminias*. BMGS 3:23–43.

Amedick, R., ed. (1991). *Die antiken Sarkophagreliefs*. Vol. 1, *Die Sarkophage mit Darstellungen aus dem Menschenleben*. Teil 4, *Vita Privata*, Berlin.

Anderson, J. (1979). The Illustration of Cod. Sinai. Gr. 339. *Art Bulletin* 61:167–185.

Anderson, J. (1983). The Date and Purpose of the Barberini Psalter. *CahArch* 31:35–67.

Anderson, J. (1988). On the Nature of the Theodore Psalter. *ArtB* 70:550–568.

Anderson, J. (1991). The Illustrated Sermons of James the Monk: Their Dates, Order, and Place in the History of Byzantine Art. *Viator* 22:69–120.

Anderson, J. (2000). A Note of the Sanctuary Mosaics of St. Demetrius, Thessalonike. *CahArch* 47:55–65.

Anderson, M. (1980). *Approaches to the History of the Western Family, 1500–1914*. London.

Angold, M. (1984). *The Byzantine Empire 1025–1204*. London and New York.

Antoniadis-Bibicou, H. (1972). Démographie, salaires et prix à Byzance, au XIe siècle. *Annales: Économies–sociétés–civilisations* 27:215–246.

Antoniadis-Bibicou, H. (1973). Quelques notes sur l'enfant de la moyenne époque byzantine (du VIe au XIIe siècle). *Annales de démographie historique (enfant et société)* 77–83.

Antonopoulos, E. (1986). Prolégomènes à une typologie de l'enfance et da la jeunesse. In *Historicité de l'enfance et de la jeunesse* 271–287. Athens.

Antonopoulos, E. (1998). Paidariogeron: i apeikonisi tis proimis sofias. *Les temps de l'histoire en vue d'une histoire de l'enfance et de la jeunesse* 33:215–231.

Ariès, P. (1962, 1996 edn). *Centuries of Childhood*. Translated by R. Baldick. London. Originally published as *L'enfant et la vie familiale sous l'Ancien Regime* (Paris, 1960).

Athos (1974). *The Treasures of Mount Athos: Illuminated Manuscripts*. Vol 1, *The Protaton and Monasteries of Dionysiou, Koutloumousiou, Xeropotamou and Gregoriou*. Athens.

Athos (1975). *The Treasures of Mount Athos: Illuminated Manuscripts*. Vol 2, *The Monasteries of Iveron, St. Panteleimon, Esphigmenou, and Chilandari*. Athens.

Bakalova, E. (1986). Society and Art in Bulgaria in the Fourteenth Century. *Byzantinobulgarica* 8:17–72.

Bakirtzis, C. (2002). Pilgrimage to Thessalonike: The Tomb of St. Demetrios. *DOP*:56:175–192.

Bal, M. (1994). Telling Objects: A Narrative Perspective on Collecting. In *The Cultures of Collecting*, edited by J. Elsner and R. Cardinal, 97–115. London.

Baldwin, B. (1981). Physical Descriptions of Byzantine Emperors. *Byzantion* 51:8–21.

Baldwin Smith, E. (1918). *Early Christian Iconography and A School of Ivory Carvers in Provence, Princeton Monographs in Art and Archeology*. Princeton.

Baltoyanni, C. (2000). The Mother of God in Portable Icons. In Vassilaki (2000),139–154. Athens.

Bank, A. (1977). *Byzantine Art in the Collections in the USSR*. Leningrad.

Bárány von, M. (1961). *Die Sankt Stephans-Krone und die Insignien des Königreiches Ungarn*. Vienna and Munich.

Barber, C. (2000). Early Representations of the Mother of God. In Vassilaki (2000), 253–261. Athens.

Barker, E. (1957). *Social and Political Thought in Byzantium*. Oxford.

Barker, J. (1969). *Manuel II Palaeologus (1391–1425): A Study in Late Byzantine Statesmanship*. New Brunswick, NJ.

Barzos, K. (1984). *H genealogia ton Komnenon*. 2 vols. Thessalonike.

Baun, J. (1994). The Fate of Babies Dying before Baptism in Byzantium. In *The Church and Childhood. Studies in Church History* 31, edited by D. Wood, 115–125. Oxford.

Beaton, R. (1989, 1996 edn). *The Medieval Greek Romance*. London and New York.

Beaucamp, J. (1977). La situation juridique de la femme à Byzance. *Cahiers de civilisation médiévale* 20:145–176.

Beaucamp, J. (1990). *Le statut de la femme à Byzance (4e–7e siècle)*. Vol. 1, *Le droit impérial*. Paris.

Beck, H.-G. (1976). Review of Wessel (1975). *BZ* 69:184.

Beckwith, J. (1962). *The Veroli Casket*. London.

Belting, H. (1970). *Das illuminerte Buch in der spätbyzantinischen Gesellschaft*. Heidelberg.

Belting, H. (1987). Eine Privatkapelle im frühmittelalterlichen Rom. *DOP* 41:55–69.

Belting, H. (1994). *Likeness and Presence*. Translated by E. Jephcott. Chicago and London. First published as *Bild und Kult – Eine Geschichte des Bildes vor dem Zeitalter der Kunst* (Munich, 1990).

Bensammar, E. (1976). La titulature de l'impératrice et sa signification. *Byzantion* 46:243–91.

Bergmann, B. (1991). Painted Perspectives of a Villa Visit: Landscape as Status and Metaphor. In *Roman Art in the Private Sphere*, edited by E. Gazda, 48–70. Ann Arbor, MI.

Bertelli, C. (1961). *La Madonna di Santa Maria in Trastevere*, Rome.

Bielefeld, D., ed. (1997). *Die antiken Sarkophagreliefs*. Vol. 5, part 2, *Stadtrömische Eroten-Sarkophage*. Faszikel 2, *Weinlese und Ernteszenen*. Berlin.

Blum, W. (1981). *Byzantinische Fürstenspiegel: Agapetos, Theophylact von Ochrid, Thomas Magister*. Stuttgart.

Boas, G. (1966). *The Cult of Childhood*. London.

Bonicatti, M. (1960). Per l'origine del Salterio Barberiniano greco 372 e la cronologia del Tetraevangelo Urbinate greco 2. *Rivista di cultura classica e medioevale* 2:41–61.

Bordier, H. (1883). *Description des peintures et autres ornements contenus dans les manuscrits grecs de la Bibliothèque nationale*. Paris.

Boston, K. (1999). Imaging the Logos: Display and Discourse in Justinian's Hagia Sophia. Ph.D. Thesis, Courtauld Institute of Art, University of London.

Boswell, J. (1988). *The Kindness of Strangers: The Abandonment of Children in Western Europe from Antiquity to the Renaissance*. New York.

Boswell, J. (1995, 1996 edn). *The Marriage of Likeness: Same-Sex Unions in Pre-Modern Europe*. London.

Braun, A. (1925, 2nd edn). *The Child in Art and Nature*. London.

Bréhier, L. (1947–1950). *Le monde byzantin*. 3 vols. Paris.

Brenk, B. (1975). *Die frühchristlichen Mosaiken in S. Maria Maggiore zu Rom*. Wiesbaden.

Brett, G. (1942). The Mosaic of the Great Palace in Constantinople. *JWarb* 5:34–43.

Brett, G., W. Macaulay and R. Stevenson, eds. (1947). *The Great Palace of the Byzantine Emperors. Being a First Report on Excavations Carried Out in Istanbul on Behalf of the Walker Trust (the University of St. Andrews) 1935–1938*. Oxford.

British Archaeological Discoveries. (1936). *British Archaeological Discoveries in Greece and Crete 1886–1936, Catalogue of the Exhibition*. London.

Brown, P. (1981). *The Cult of the Saints*. Chicago.

Brown, P. (1988). *The Body and Society: Men, Women and Sexual Renunciation in Early Christianity*. New York.

Browning, R. (1978). Literacy in the Byzantine World. *BMGS* 4:39–54.

Brubaker, L. (1983). The Illustrated Copy of the Homilies of Gregory of Nazianzus in Paris (Bibliothèque Nationale, cod. gr. 510). Ph.D. Dissertation, Johns Hopkins University.

Brubaker, L. (1985). Politics, Patronage, and Art in Ninth-Century Byzantium: The *Homilies* of Gregory of Nazianzus in Paris (B.N.gr.510). *DOP* 39:1–13.

Brubaker, L. (1999). *Vision and Meaning in Ninth-Century Byzantium: Image as Exegesis in the Homilies of Gregory of Nazianzus*. Cambridge.

Buberl, P. (1937–1938). *Die byzantinischen Handschriften*. Vol. 8, pt 4. *Die Wiener Genesis*. Leipzig.

Buchthal, H. (1938, 1968 edn). *The Miniatures of the Paris Psalter*. London and Lichtenstein.

Buchthal, H. (1974). The Exaltation of David. *JWarb* 37:330–333.

Buchthal, H. (1975). Toward a History of Palaeologan Illumination. In *The Place of Book Illumination in Byzantine Art*, edited by K. Weitzmann, 143–177. Princeton.

Buckler, G. (1948). Byzantine Education: An Introduction to East Roman Civilization. In *Byzantium*, edited by N. Baynes and H. Moss, 200–220. Oxford.

Buckton, D. (1994). *Byzantium: Treasures of Byzantine Art and Culture*. Exhibition Catalogue. London.

Burguière, A., ed. (1996). *History of the Family*. Oxford.

Byzance. (1958). *Byzance et la France médiévale. Manuscrits à peintures du IIe au XVIe siècle*. Exhibition Catalogue. Paris.

Cameron, A. (1973). *Porphyrius the Charioteer*. Oxford.

Cameron, A. (1976). *Circus Factions: Blues and Greens at Rome and Byzantium*. Oxford.

Cameron, A.M. (1978). The Theotokos in Sixth-Century Constantinople: A City Finds Its Symbol. *Journal of Theological Studies* 29:79–108.

Cameron, A.M. (1999). Desire in Byzantium: The Ought and the Is. In James (1999), 205–213. Aldershot.

Cameron, A.M. (2000). The Early Cult of the Virgin. In Vassilaki (2000), 3–15. Athens.

Camille, M. (1992). *Image on the Edge: The Margins of Medieval Art.* Cambridge, MA.

Canart, P. (1970a). *Codices vaticani graeci. Codices 1745–1962.* Vatican.

Canart, P. (1970b). *Sussidi bibliografici per i manoscritti greci della Biblioteca vaticana (studi e testi).* Vatican.

Canart, P. (1973). *Codices vaticani graeci. Codices 1745–1962, II, introductio, addenda, indices.* Vatican.

Carandini, A., A. Ricci and M. De Vos. (1982). *The Villa of Piazza Armerina: The Image of a Roman Aristocrat in the Time of Constantine.* Palermo.

Carr, A.W. (1982). Gospel Frontispieces from the Comnenian Period. *Gesta* 21:3–20.

Carr, A.W. (1985). Women and Monasticism in Byzantium: Introduction from an Art Historian. *Byzantinische Forschungen* 9:1–15.

Carr, A.W. (1997a). Women as Artists in the Middle Ages: The Dark is Light Enough. In *Dictionary of Women Artists.* Vol. 1.

Carr, A.W. (1997b). Court Culture and Cult Icons in Middle Byzantine Constantinople. In *Byzantine Court Culture from 829–1204,* edited by H. Maguire. Washington, DC.

Carr, A.W. (2000). The Mother of God in Public. In Vassilaki (2000), 325–337. Athens.

Cecchelli, C. (1956). *I mosaici della basilica di S. Maria Maggiore.* Turin.

Cecchelli, C., G. Furlani and M. Salmi, eds. (1959). *The Rabbula Gospels: Facsimile Edition of the Miniatures of the Syriac Manuscript Plut. 1, 56 in the Medicaean–Laurentian Library.* Olten and Lausanne.

Chaisemartin de, N. (1993). Agonistic Images on Aphrodisian Sarcophagi. In *Performers and Partisans at Aphrodisias in the Roman and Late Roman Periods,* by C.Roueché, 241–248. London.

Chalandon, F. (1912). *Les Comnène.* Vol. 2, parts 1 and 2, *Jean II Comnène (1118–1143) et Manuel Comnène (1143–1180).* Paris.

Chatzidakis, M. (1992). *Mystras, the Medieval City and the Castle.* Athens.

Ciurca, S. (n.d.). *Mosaics of Villa 'Erculia' in Piazza Armerinai–Morgantina.* Piazza Armerina.

Clarelli, M.V.M. (1996). La cotroversia nestoriana e i mosaici dell'arco trinofale di S. Maria Maggiore. *Bisànzio e l'Occidente: Arte, Archaeologia, Storia.* Rome.

Clarke, J. (1991). *The Houses of Roman Italy, 100 BC–AD 250: Ritual, Space and Decoration.* Berkeley.

Coale, A. and P. Demeny (1966). *Regional Model Life Tables and Stable Populations.* Princeton.

Coleman, S. and J. Elsner (1994). The Pilgrim's Progress: Art, Architecture and Ritual Movement at Sinai. *World Archaeology* 26:73–89.

Connor, C. (1991). New Perspectives on Byzantine Ivories. *Gesta* 30:100–111.

Connor, C. (1998). *The Color of Ivory: Polychromy on Byzantine Ivories*. Princeton.

Connor, C. (2000). A Sense of Family: Monastic Portraits in the Lincoln College Typikon. In *Twenty-Sixth Byzantine Studies Conference, Abstracts of Papers*, 107–108. Cambridge, MA.

Constantelos, D. (1968). *Byzantine Philanthropy and Social Welfare*. New Brunswick, NJ.

Cooper, K. (1996). *The Virgin and the Bride: Idealized Womanhood in Late Antiquity*. Cambridge, MA. and London.

Cormack, R. (1967). Byzantine Cappadocia: The Archaic Group of Wall Paintings. *Journal of the British Archaeological Association* 30:19–36. In Cormack (1989) Study VI.

Cormack, R. (1969). The Mosaic Decoration of S. Demetrios, Thessaloniki; a Re-Examination in the Light of the Drawings of W.S. George. *Annual of the British School of Archaeology at Athens* 64:17–52. In Cormack (1989) Study VI.

Cormack, R. (1984). Aristocratic Patronage of the Arts in 11th- and 12th-Century Byzantium. In *The Byzantine Aristocracy IX to XIII centuries*, edited by M. Angold, 158–172. Oxford. In Cormack (1989) Study IX.

Cormack, R. (1985a). *Writing in Gold. Byzantine Society and Its Icons*. London.

Cormack, R. (1985b). *The Church of Saint Demetrios: The Watercolours and Drawings of W S. George*. Thessaloniki.

Cormack, R. (1986). Patronage and New Programs of Byzantine Iconography. In *The Seventeenth International Byzantine Congress, Major Papers*, 609–638. New York. In Cormack (1989) essay X.

Cormack, R. (1989). *The Byzantine Eye: Studies in Art and Patronage*. London.

Cormack, R. (1992). But Is It Art? In *Byzantine Diplomacy*, edited by J. Shepard and S. Franklin, 219–236. Aldershot.

Cormack, R. (1994). The Emperor at St. Sophia: Viewer and Viewed. In *Byzance et les images*, 223–253. Paris.

Cormack, R. (1997). *Painting the Soul: Icons, Death Masks and Shrouds*. London.

Cormack, R. (1998a). Away from the Centre: 'Provincial' Art in the Ninth Century. In *Byzantium in the Ninth Century: Dead or Alive?*, edited by L. Brubaker, 151–163. Aldershot.

Cormack, R. (1998b). Lessons from 'The Glory of Byzantium'. *Dialogos* 5:27–39.

Cormack, R. (2000a). The Mother of God in Apse Mosaics. In Vassilaki (2000), 91–105. Athens.

Cormack, R. (2000b). The Mother of God in the Mosaics of Hagia Sophia at Constantinople. In Vassilaki (2000), 107–124. Athens.

Corrigan, K. (1992). *Visual Polemics in the Ninth-Century Byzantine Psalters*. Cambridge.

Crawford, S. (2000). *Childhood in Anglo-Saxon England*. Stroud.

Cross, S. and K. Conant. (1936). The Earliest Mediaeval Churches of Kiev. *Speculum* 11:477–499.

Cunningham, H. (1995). *Children and Childhood in Western Society since 1500*. London and New York.

Currie, S. (1993). Childhood and Christianity from Paul to the Council of Chalcedon. Ph.D. Thesis, University of Cambridge.

Currie, S. (1996). The Empire of Adults: The Representation of Children on Trajan's Arch at Beneventum. In *Art and Text in Roman Culture*, edited by J. Elsner. Cambridge.

Cutler, A. (1984). *The Aristocratic Psalters in Byzantium*. Paris.

Cutler, A. (1984–1985). On Byzantine Boxes. *Journal of the Walters Art Gallery* 42–43:32–47.

Cutler, A. (1985). *The Craft of Ivory*. Washington, DC.

Cutler, A. (1987). The Cult of the Galaktotrophousa in Byzantium and Italy. *JÖB* 37:335–350.

Cutler, A. (1988). Un triptyque byzantin en ivoire: la nativité du Louvre. *Revue du Louvre* 38:21–28.

Cutler, A. (1994). *The Hand of the Master: Craftsmanship, Ivory, and Society in Byzantium*. Princeton.

Cutler, A. (1995). The Date and Significance of the Romanos Ivory. In *Byzantine East, Latin West: Art Historical Studies in Honor of Kurt Weitzmann*, edited by D. Mouriki, 605–610. Princeton.

Cutler, A. (1998). A Byzantine Triptych in Medieval Germany and Its Modern Recovery.*Gesta* 37:3–12.

Cutler, A. and P. Magdalino (1978). Some Precisions on the Lincoln College Typikon. *CahArch* 27:179–198.

Cutler, A., and J.-M. Spieser (1996). *Byzance médiévale*. Paris.

Dagron, G. (1994). Nés dans la pourpre. *Travaux et mémoires* 12:105–142.

Dalton, O.M. (1901). *Catalogue of Early Christian Antiquities and Objects from the Christian East in the Department of British and Mediaeval Antiquities and Ethnography of the British Museum*. London.

Davidson, J. (1997). *Courtesans and Fishcakes: The Consuming Passions of Classical Athens*. London.

De Benedictis, E. (1981). The Senatorium and Matroneum in the Early Roman Church. *Rivista di archeologia cristiana* 57:69–85.

De Bruyne, L. (1936). Nuove ricerche iconografiche sui mosaici dell'arco trionfale di S. Maria Maggiore. *RivAC* 13

De Wald, E. (1941). *The Illustrations of the Manuscripts of the Septuagint*. Vol. 3, *Psalms and Odes*. Part 1, *Vaticanus Graecus 1927*. Princeton.

De Wald, E. (1942). *The Illustrations of the Manuscripts of the Septuagint*. Vol. 3, *Psalms and Odes*. Part 2, *Vaticanus Graecus 752*. Princeton.

De Wald, E. (1944). The Comnenian Portraits in the Barberini Psalter. *Hesperia* 13:78–86.

Demus, O. (1948). *Byzantine Mosaic Decoration: Aspects of Monumental Art in Byzantium*. London.

Dennis, G.T. (1967) An Unknown Byzantine Emperor, Andronicus V Palaeologus (1400–1407?).*JÖB* 16:175–187.

Der Nersessian, S. (1927). Two Slavonic Parallels of the Greek Tetraevangelia: Paris 74. *ArtB* 9:1–52.

Der Nersessian, S. (1962). The Homilies of Gregory of Nazianzus. *DOP* 16:197–228.

Der Nersessian, S. (1970). *L'illustration des psautiers grecs du moyen-âge.* Vol. 2,*Londres Add. 19352*. Paris.

Deshman, R. (1989). Servants of the Mother of God in Byzantine and Medieval Art. *Word and Image* 5:33–70.

Diehl, C. (1925–1926, 2nd edn). *Manuel d'art byzantin*. Paris.

Diehl, C. and M. Le Tourneau (1910). Les mosaïques de Saint-Démétrius de Salonique. *Monuments et mémoires (Fondation Piot)* 18:225–247.

Diehl, C., M. Le Tourneau and H. Saladin (1918). *Les monuments chrétiens de Salonique*. 2 vols. Paris.

Dimitrova, E. (1994). *The Gospels of Tsar Ivan Alexander*. London.

Dixon, S. (1988). *The Roman Mother*. London.

Dixon, S. (1997). Continuity and Change in Roman Social History: Retrieving 'Family Feeling(s)' from Roman Law and Literature. In *Inventing Ancient Culture: Historicism, Periodization, and the Ancient World*, edited by P. Toohey and M. Golden, 79–90. London.

Dodd, E.C. (1961). *Byzantine Silver Stamps, with an Excursus on the Comes Sacrarum Largitionem by J.P.C. Kent*. Washington, DC.

Dorigo, W. (1971). Late Tetrarchic Painting and the Constantinian 'Fine Style' at Piazza Armerina villa. In *Late Roman Painting: A Study of Pictorial Records 30 BC–AD 500*, 127–168. London.

Dover, K. (1978). *Greek Homosexuality*. London.

Du Cange, C. (1680). *Historia Byzantina. I, Familiae Byzantinae. II, Constantinopolis Christiana*. Paris.

Duchesne, M. (1903, 1923 edn). *Christian Worship: Its Origin and Evolution*. London.

Dufrenne, S. (1970). *Les programmes iconographiques des églises byzantines de Mystra*. Paris.

Dujčev, I. (1963). *Les miniatures de la chronique de Manasses*. Sofia.

Dunbabin, K. (1978). *The Mosaics of Roman North Africa*. Oxford.

Dunbabin, K. (1999). *Mosaics of the Greek and Roman World*. Cambridge.

Durand, J., ed. (1992). *Byzance: L'art byzantin dans les collections publiques françaises*. Exhibition Catalogue. Paris.

Durantini, M. (1983). *The Child in Seventeenth-Century Dutch Painting*. Epping.

Eade, J. and S. Sallnow, eds (1991). *Contesting the Sacred: The Anthropology of Christian Pilgrimage*. London.

Eastmond, A. (1998). *Royal Imagery in Medieval Georgia*. University Park, PA.

Ebersolt, J. (1926). *La miniature byzantine*. Paris.

Elsner, J. (1994). The Viewer and the Vision: The Case of the Sinai Apse. *Art History* 7:81–102.

Elsner, J., ed. (1996). *Art and Text in Roman Culture*. Cambridge.

Elsner, J. (1998). *Imperial Rome and Christian Triumph*. Oxford.

Epstein, A.W. (1980–1981). The Fresco Decoration of the Column Churches, Göreme Valley, Cappadocia: A Consideration of Their Chronology and Their Models. *CahArch* 29:27–45.

Epstein, A.W. (1986). *Tokali Kilise: Tenth-Century Metropolitan Art in Byzantine Cappadocia*. Washington, DC.

Evans, H. and W. Wixom, eds (1997). *The Glory of Byzantium: Art and Culture of the Middle Byzantine Era, AD 843–1261*. Exhibition Catalogue. New York.

Eyben, E. (1993). *Restless Youth in Ancient Rome*. Translated by P. Daly. London and New York.

Ferguson, E. (1979). Inscriptions and the Origins of Infant Baptism. *Journal of Theological Studies* 30:37–46.

Ferrua, A. (1960). *Le pitture della nuova catacomba di Via Latina*. Vatican.

Ferrua, A. (1990). *The Unknown Catacomb: A Unique Discovery of Early Christian Art*. Florence.

Fildes, V. (1988). *Wet Nursing: A History from Antiquity to the Present*. Oxford.

Filov, B. (1927). *Les miniatures de la chronique de Manasses à la Bibliothèque du Vatican (Cod. Vat. Slav. II)*. Sofia.

Filov, B. (1934). *Les miniatures de l'évangile du roi Jean Alexandre à Londres*. Sofia.

Finaldi, G. (2000). *The Image of Christ: The Catalogue of the Exhibition Seeing Salvation*. London.

Franses, H. (1992). Symbols, Meaning, Belief: Donor Portraits in Byzantine Art. Ph.D. Thesis, Courtauld Institute of Art, University of London.

Galavaris, G. (1969). *The Illustrations of the Liturgical Homilies of Gregory of Nazianzenus*. Princeton.

Galavaris, G. (1979). *The Illustrations of the Prefaces in Byzantine Gospels*. Vienna.

Garland, R. (1990). *The Greek Way of Life*. Ithaca, NY.

Garrucci, R. (1857). *Vetri ornati di figure in oro trovati nei cimiteri dei cristiani primitivi di Roma*. Rome.

Garrucci, R. (1873–1880). *Storia dell'arte cristiana nei primi otto secoli della chiesa*. 6 vols. Prato.

Gautier, P. (1966). Monodie inédite de Michel Psellos sur le basileus Andronic Doucas. *REB* 24:153–170.

Geertz, C. (1966). Religion as a Cultural System. In *Anthropological Approaches to the Study of Religion: Conference on New Approaches in Social Anthropology, 1963*, edited by M. Banton, 1–46. London.

Gentili, G. (1954). *La villa imperiale di Piazza Armerina*. Rome.

Gentili, G. (1959). *La villa Erculia di Piazza Armerina. I mosaici figurati*. Rome.

Gentili, G. (1966). *The Imperial Villa of Piazza Armerina*. Rome.

Gerstel, S. (1998). Painted Sources for Female Piety in Medieval Byzantium. *DOP* 2:89–111.

Gerstel, S. (1999). *Beholding the Sacred Mysteries: Programs of the Byzantine Sanctuary*. Seattle, WA and London.

Gerstinger, H. (1931). *Die Wiener Genesis: Farbenlichtdruckfaksimile der griechischen Bilderbibel aus dem 6. Jahrhundert n. Chr. Cod. purpur. vindob. graec. 31*. Vienna.

Golden, M. (1990). *Children and Childhood in Classical Athens*. Baltimore and London.

Goldschmidt, A. and K. Weitzmann (1930, 1979 edn). *Die byzantinischen Elfenbeinskulpturen des X.–XIII. Jahrhunderts*. Vol. 1, *Kästen*. Berlin.

Gombrich, E. (1957). *Art and Scholarship*. London.

Goody, J. (1983). *The Development of the Family and Marriage in Europe*. Cambridge.

Grabar, A. (1935). Les fresques des escaliers à Sainte-Sophie de Kiev et l'iconographie impériale byzantine. *Seminarium Kondakovianum* 7:103–117.

Grabar, A. (1936). *L'empereur dans l'art byzantin: Recherches sur l'art officiel de l'empire d'Orient*. Paris.

Grabar, A. (1946). *Martyrium: Recherches sur le culte des reliques et l'art chrétien*. 3 vols. Paris.

Grabar, A. (1948a). La représentation de l'intelligible dans l'art byzantin du moyen âge. In *Actes du VIe congrès international des études byzantines*. Paris.

Grabar, A. (1948b). *Les peintures de l'évangéliaire de Sinope (Bibliothèque nationale, suppl. gr. 1286)*. Paris.

Grabar, A. (1953). *Byzantine Painting: Historical and Critical Study*. Geneva.

Grabar, A. (1954). Un rouleau liturgique constantinopolitain et ses peintures. *DOP* 8:161–199.

Grabar, A. (1957). *L'iconoclasme byzantin: dossier archéologique*. Paris.

Grabar, A. (1960). Une pyxide en ivoire à Dumbarton Oaks. *DOP* 14:123–146.

Grabar, A. (1978). Notes sur les mosaïques de Saint-Démétrios à Salonique. *Byzantion* 48:64–77.

Grimal, P. (1991). *A Concise Dictionary of Classical Mythology*. Translated by A. Maxwell-Hyslop. London.

Grüneisen, W. (1911). *Sainte Marie Antique*. Rome.

Guilland, R. (1943). Les eunuques dans l'empire byzantin. *Etudes byzantines* 1:197–238.

Guilland, R. (1953). La vie scolaire à Byzance. *Bulletin de l'Association Guillaume Budé* 1:63–83.

Gutmann, J. (1966). The Illustrated Jewish Manuscript in Antiquity: The Present State of the Question. *Gesta* 5:39–41.

Gutmann, J. (1973). Joseph Legends in the Vienna Genesis. In *The Fifth World Congress of Jewish Studies*, 181–185.

Guzzo, P. and A. d'Ambrosio (1998). *Pompeii*. Translated by M. Weir. Naples.

Hadjinicolaou-Marava, A. (1950). *Recherches sur la vie des esclaves dans le monde byzantin*. Athens.

Hallett, J. (1984). *Fathers and Daughters in Roman Society: Women and the Elite Family*. Princeton.

Halperin, D. (1990). *One Hundred Years of Homosexuality: And Other Essays on Greek Love*. London and New York.

Hamann-MacLean, R. and H. Hallensleben (1963–1976). *Die Monumentalmalerei in Serbien und Makedonien: Von 11. bis zum frühen 14. Jahrhundert*. Giessen.

Hamburger, J. (1993). Review of Camille (1992). *ArtB* 75:319–326.

Hanawalt, B. (1986). *The Ties that Bound: Peasant Families in Medieval England*. New York.

Hanawalt, B. (1993). *Growing Up in Medieval London: The Experience of Childhood in History*. Oxford.

Hanfmann, G. (1951). *The Season Sarcophagus in Dumbarton Oaks*. 2 vols. Cambridge, MA.

Hannick, C., and G. Schmalzbauer. (1976). Die Synadenoi: Prosopographische Untersuchung zu einer byzantinischen Familie. *JÖB* 25:125–161.

Hanson, J. (1996). The Ivory Casket in Sens Known as La Sainte Châsse. Ph.D. Thesis, Courtauld Institute of Art, University of London.

Hanson, J. (1999). Erotic Imagery on Byzantine Ivory Caskets. In James (1999), 173–184. Aldershot.

Harden, D. (1987). *Glass of the Caesars*. Milan.

Hardyment, C. (1998). *The Future of the Family*. London.

Harris, W. (1989). *Ancient Literacy*. Cambridge, MA.

Hartel, W. von and F. Wickhoff (1895). *Die Wiener Genesis*. Vienna.

Head, C. (1980). Physical Descriptions of the Emperors in Byzantine Historical Writing. *Byzantion* 50:226–240.

Hendy, M. (1969). *Coinage and Money in the Byzantine Empire 1081–1261*. Washington, DC.

Hennessy, C. (1996). Representations of Byzantine Imperial Children: Late-Ninth to Early-Twelfth centuries. MA Thesis, University of Washington, Seattle, WA.

Hennessy, C. (2003). Children as Iconic Images in S. Demetrios, Thessaloniki. In *Icon andWord: The Power of Images in Byzantium*, edited by A. Eastmond and L. James, 157–172. Aldershot.

Hennessy, C. (2006). A Child Bride and her Representation in the Vatican *Epithalamion*, cod. Gr. 1851. *BMGS* 30:115–150.

Hennessy, C. (2008) The *Lincoln College Typikon*: The Influences of Church and Family. *Under the Influence: The Concept of Influence and the Study of Illuminated Manuscripts*, edited by A. Bovey. Brepols.

Herrin, J. (1987, 1989 edn). *The Formation of Christendom*. London.

Herrin, J. (1994). Theophano: Considerations on the Education of a Byzantine Princess. In *Empress Theophano*, edited by A. Davids, 70–71. Cambridge.

Hesseling, D. (1909). *Miniatures de l'Octateuque grec de Smyrne*. Leiden.

Higgonet, A. (1998). *Pictures of Innocence: The History of the Crisis of Ideal Childhood*. London.

Hiller, S. (1969). Divino sensu agnoscere: zur Deutung des Mosaikbodens im Peristyl des grossen Palästes zu Konstantinopel. *Kairos* 11:275–305.

Hopkins, K. (1966). On the Probable Age Structure of the Roman Population. *Population Studies* 20:245–264.

Hopkins, K. (1999). *A World Full of Gods, Pagans, Jews and Christians in the Roman Empire*. London.

Hüber, P. (1986). *Hiob, Dulder oder Rebel?* Dusseldorf.

Hunger, H. (1978). *Die hochsprachliche profane Literatur der Byzantiner*. Vol. 1. Munich.

Huskinson, J. (1974). Some Pagan Mythological Figures and Their Significance in Early Christian Art. *Papers of British School at Rome* 42:68–97.

Huskinson, J. (1996). *Roman Children's Sarcophagi: Their Decoration and Its Social Significance*. Oxford.

Hutter, I. (1995). Die Geschichte des Lincoln College Typikons. *JÖB* 45:79–114.

Hutter, I. and P. Canart (1991). *Das Marienhomilar des Monchs Jakobos von Kokkinobaphos: Codex Vaticanus graecus 1162*, facsimile and commentary, 2 vols. Zurich.

Iacobini, A. (1995). L'epitalamio di Andronico II. Una cronaca de nozze dalla Constantinopoli Paleologa. In *Arte profana e arte sacra a Bisano*, edited by A. Iacobini and E. Zanini, 361–409. Rome.

Itnyre, C., ed. (1996). *Medieval Family Roles*. New York and London.

Ivison, E. (1996). Burial and Urbanism at Late Antique and Early Byzantine Corinth (c. AD 400–700). *Towns in Transition*, edited by N. Christie and S.T. Loseby, 99–125. Aldershot.

Jacob, X. (1971–1973). La vie de Marie interpretée par les artistes des églises rupestres de Cappadoce. *Cahiers de l'art médiéval* 6:15–30.

Jaeger, W. (1961). *Early Christianity and Greek Paideia*. Cambridge, MA.

James, L., ed. (1997). *Women, Men and Eunuchs*. London and New York.

James, L., ed. (1999). *Desire and Denial in Byzantium*. Aldershot.

James, L. and R. Webb (1991). 'To Understand Ultimate Things and Enter Secret Places': Ekphrasis and Art in Byzantium. *Art History* 14:1–17.

Jeffreys, E. (1982). The Sevastokratorissa Eirene as Literary Patroness: The Monk Iakovos. *JÖB* 32/3:63–71.

Jeffreys, M. (1974). The Nature and Origins of the Politcal Verse. *DOP* 28:157–181.

Jeffreys, M. (1981). The Vernacular for Agnes of France. In *Byzantine Papers: Australian Byzantine Studies Conference*, 101–115. Canberra.

Jerphanion de, G. (1925–1942). *Les églises rupestres de Cappadoce*. 2 vols in 4 parts, 3 vols of plates. Paris.

Jerphanion de, G. (1930). Le 'thorakion' caractéristique iconographique du XIe siècle. In *Mélanges Charles Diehl*, 71–79. Paris.

Jevtic, I. (2000). Sur le symbolisme du *spinario* dans l'iconographie de l'entrée à Jérusalem: Deux representations inédites dans les églises Serbes. *CahArch* 47:119–126.

Jobst, W., R. Kastler, V. Scheibelreiter and E. Bolognesi Rechi-Franceschini (1999). *Neue Forschungen und Restaurierungen im byzantinischen Kaiserpalast von Istanbul.*Vienna.

Jolivet-Lévy, C. (1991). *Les églises byzantines de Cappadoce, le programme iconographique de l'abside et de ses abords.* Paris.

Kähler, H. (1973). *Die Villa des Maxentius bei Piazza Armerina.* Berlin.

Kalavrezou, I. (1990). Images of the Mother: When the Virgin Mary Became Meter Theou. *DOP* 44:165–172.

Kalavrezou, I. (2000). The Maternal Side of the Virgin. In Vassilaki (2000), 41–46. Athens.

Kalavrezou, I., ed. (2003). *Byzantine Women and their World.* Cambridge, MA. and New Haven.

Kalavrezou-Maxeiner, I. (1977). Eudokia Makrembolitissa and the Romanos Ivory. *DOP* 31:307–325.

Kalavrezou-Maxeiner, I. (1978). The Portraits of Basil I in Paris gr. 510. *JÖB* 27:19–24.

Kalogeras, N. (2000). Byzantine Childhood Education and Its Social Role from the Sixth Century until the End of Iconoclasm. Ph.D. Thesis, University of Chicago.

Kalogeras, N. (2001). What Do They Think about Children Perceptions of Childhood in Early Byzantine Literature? *BMGS* 25:2–19.

Kämpfer, F. (1978). *Das russische Herrscherbild von den Anfängen bis zu Peter dem Grossen: Studien zur Entwicklung politischer Ikonographie im byzantinischen Kulturkreis.* Recklinghausen.

Kämpfer, F. (1992). Neue Ergebnisse und neue Problem bei der Eforschung der profanen Fresken in der Kiever Sophienkirche. *Jahrbücher für Geschichte Osteuropas* 40:76–95.

Kantorowicz, E. (1963). Puer Exoriens. On the Hypapante in the Mosaics of S. Maria Maggiore. In *Perennilas. P. Thomas Michels OSB zum 70. Geburtstag,* 25–36. Münster. In Kantorowicz (1965).

Kantorowicz, E. (1965). *Selected Studies.* New York.

Karpp, H. (1976). *Die frühchristlichen und mittelalterlichen Mosaiken in Santa Maria Maggiore zu Rom.* Baden-Baden.

Kartsonis, A. (1967). David and the Choirs (Vat. gr. 699). MA Thesis, New York University.

Kartsonis, A. (1982). *Anastasis: The Making of an Image.* Princeton.

Kazhdan, A. (1984). The Aristocracy and the Imperial Ideal. In *The Byzantine Aristocracy, IX to XIII centuries,* edited by M. Angold. Oxford.

Kazhdan, A. (1998). Women at Home. *DOP* 52:1–17.

Kazhdan, A. and H. Maguire (1991). Byzantine Hagiographical Texts as Sources on Art. *DOP* 45:1–22.

Kazhdan, A. and A. Wharton Epstein (1985, 1990 edn). *Change in Byzantine Culture in the Eleventh and Twelfth Centuries.* Berkeley and London.

Kelleher, P. (1951). *The Holy Crown of Hungary*. Rome.

Kirschbaum, E. (1968–1976). *Lexikon der christlichen Iconographie*. 8 vols. Freiburg.

Kislinger, E. (1983). Eudokia Ingerina, Basileios I, und Michael III. *JÖB* 33:119–136.

Kitzinger, E. (1955). On some Icons of the Seventh Century. In *Late Classical and Medieval Studies in Honor of A. M. Friend*. Princeton.

Kitzinger, E. (1958). Byzantine Art in the Period between Justinian and Iconoclasm. In *Berichte zum XI. internationalen Byzantinisten-Kongresses, München 1958*. Vol. 4/1, 1–50. Munich. In Kitzinger (1976), Study VI.

Kitzinger, E. (1963). The Hellenistic Heritage in Byzantine Art. *DOP* 17:95–115.

Kitzinger, E. (1976). *The Art of Byzantium and the Medieval West: Selected Studies by E. Kitzinger*, edited by E. Kleinbauer.

Kitzinger, E. (1977). *Byzantine Art in the Making: Main Lines of Stylistic Development in Mediterranean Art, 3rd–7th Century*. Cambridge, MA.

Kitzinger, E. (1988). Reflections on the Feast Cycle in Byzantine Art. *CahArch* 36:51–73.

Kleijwegt, M. (1991). *Ancient Youth: The Ambiguity of Youth and the Absence of Adolescence in Greco-Roman Society*. Amsterdam.

Kollwitz, J. (1933). *Die Lipsanothek von Brescia*. Berlin, Leipzig.

Kominis, A., ed. (1988). *Patmos, Treasures of the Monastery*. Athens.

Kraeling, C. (1956). *The Excavations at Dura Europos, Final Report*. Vol. 8, part 1, *The Synagogue*. New Haven.

Kraemer, D. (1989). Images of Childhood and Adolescence in Talmudic Literature. In *The Jewish Family: Metaphor and Memory*, edited by D. Kraemer, 65–80. Oxford and New York.

Krautheimer, R. (1937–). *Corpus basilicarium christianarum Romae: The Early Christian Basilicas in Rome (IV–IX cent)*. Vatican.

Krautheimer, R. (1960). Mensa-coemeterium-martyrium. *CahArch* 11:15–40.

Krautheimer, R. (1965, 1975 edn). *Early Christian and Byzantine Architecture*. Harmondsworth.

Krautheimer, R. (1969). *Studies in Early Christian, Medieval, and Renaissance Art*. London.

Krautheimer, R. (1980). *Rome, Profile of a City, 312–1308*. Princeton.

Kronberger-Frentzen, H. (1940). *Das deutsche Familienbildnis*. Leipzig.

Künzle, P. (1961–1962). Per una visione organica dei mosaici antichi di S. Maria Maggiore. *Atti della Pontificia Accademia Romana di Archeologia. Rendiconti* ser. III, 34:172–174.

Ladner, G. (1941). The So-Called Square Nimbus. *Mediaeval Studies* 3:15–45.

Lafontaine, J. (1962). Sarica kilise en Cappadoce. *CahArch* 12:263–284.

Lafontaine-Dosogne, J. (1964–1965). *Iconographie de l'enfance de la Vierge dans l'empire byzantin et en occident*. 2 vols. Bruges.

Lafontaine-Dosogne, J. (1975a). Iconography of the Cycle of the Infancy of the Virgin. In Underwood (1966–1975) vol. 4, 161–194.

Lafontaine-Dosogne, J. (1975b). Iconography of the Cycle of the Infancy of Christ. In Underwood (1966–1975) vol. 4, 195–241.

Lafontaine-Dosogne, J. (1987). La peinture d'église byzantine a l'époque iconoclaste. *DOP* 41:321–337.

Laiou, A. (1977). *Peasant Society in the Late Byzantine Empire: A Social and Demographic Study*. Princeton.

Laiou, A. (1981). The Role of Women in Byzantine Society. *JÖB* 31/1:249–60.

Laiou, A. and D. Simon, eds (1994). *Law and Society in Byzantium: Ninth–Twelfth Centuries*. Washington, DC.

Laiou, A. (1992). *Mariage, amour et parenté à Byzance aux XIe–XIIIe siècles*. Paris.

Laiou, A. (2003). Women in the History of Byzantium. In *Byzantine Women and their World*, edited by I. Kalavrezou, 23–32. Cambridge, MA. and New Haven.

Laslett, T. (1972). The History of the Family. In *Household and Family in Past Time*, edited by T. Laslett, 1–90. Cambridge.

Lazarev, V. (1966). *Old Russian Murals and Mosaics from the XI to the XVI centuries*. London.

Lazarev, V. (1967). *Storia della pittura bizantina*. Turin.

Lazarev, V. (1971). Regard sur l'art de la Russie prémongole. II, Le système de la décoration de Sainte-Sophie de Kiev. *Cahiers de civilisation médiévale* 14:221–238.

Leader, R. (2000). The David Plates Revisited: Transforming the Secular in Early Byzantium. *ArtB* 82:407–427.

Leader-Newby, R. (2004). *Silver and Society in Late Antiquity: Functions and Meanings of Silver Plate in the Fourth to Seventh Centuries*. Aldershot.

Lehmann, K. (1955). Santa Costanza. *ArtB* 37:193–6, 291.

Leloir, L. (1980). Attitude des pères du désert vis-à-vis des jeunes. In *L'enfant dans les civilisations orientales*, edited by A. Théodoridès, P. Naster and J. Ries, 145–152. Leuven.

Lemerle, P. (1986). *Byzantine Humanism: The First Phase*. Canberra. Originally published as *Premier humanisme byzantin: notes et remarques sur l'enseignement et culture à Byzance des origines au Xe siècle* (Paris, 1971).

Levin, E. (1989). *Sex and Society in the World of the Orthodox Slavs, 900–1700*. Ithaca and London.

Levin, M. (1972). Some Jewish Sources for the Vienna Genesis. *ArtB* 54:241–244.

Lloyd, J.B. (1986). The Building History of the Medieval Church of S. Clemente in Rome. *Journal of the Society of Architectural Historians* 45:197–223.

Logvin, H. (1971). *Kiev's Hagia Sophia*. Kiev.

Lowden, J. (1988). *Illuminated Prophet Books*. University Park, PA. and London.

Lowden, J. (1992a). The Luxury Book as Diplomatic Gift. In *Byzantine Diplomacy*, edited by J. Shepard and S. Franklin, 249–260. Aldershot.

Lowden, J. (1992b). *The Octateuchs: A Study in Byzantine Manuscript Illumination*. University Park, PA.

Lowden, J. (1997). *Early Christian and Byzantine Art*. London.

Luttrell, A. (1986). John V's daughters: A Palaiologan Puzzle. *DOP* 40:103–112.

Mackie, G. (1998). A New Look at the Patronage of Santa Costanza, Rome. *Byzantion* 67:383–406.

Macrides, R. (1987). The Byzantine Godfather. *BMGS* 11:139–162.

Macrides, R. (1992). Dynastic Marriages and Political Kinship. In *Byzantine Diplomacy*, edited by J. Shepard and S. Franklin, 263–280. Aldershot.

Magdalino, P. (1996). Innovations in Government. In *Alexios I Komnenos*, edited by M. Mullett and D. Smythe. Belfast.

Maguire, H. (1981). *Art and Eloquence in Byzantium*. Princeton.

Maguire, H. (1995). A Murderer Among the Angels: The Frontispiece Miniatures of Paris. Gr. 510 and the Iconography of Archangels in Byzantine Art. In *The Sacred Image East and West*, edited by R. Ousterhout and L. Brubaker, 63–71. Urbana, IL.

Maguire, H. (1996). *The Icons of Their Bodies: Saints and Their Images in Byzantium*. Princeton.

Maguire, H. (1997). Images of the Court. In *Glory of Byzantium*, edited by H. Evans and W. Wixom. New York.

Maguire, H. (1999). The Profane Aesthetic in Byzantine Art and Literature. *DOP* 53:189–205.

Malbon, E.S. (1990). *The Iconography of the Sarcophagus of Junius Bassus*. Princeton.

Mango, C. (1951). Autour du grand palais de Constantinople. *CahArch* 5:179–186.

Mango, C. (1962). *The Mosaics of St. Sophia at Istanbul*. Washington, DC.

Mango, C. (1963). Antique Statuary and the Byzantine Beholder. *DOP* 17:55–75.

Mango, C. (1972, 1986 edn). *The Art of the Byzantine Empire, 312–1453*. Toronto.

Mango, C. (1973). Eudocia Ingerina, the Normans, and the Macedonian Dynasty. *Zbornik radova Vizantološkog Instituta* 14–15:17–27.

Mango, C. (2000). Review of Brubaker (1999). *BMGS* 24:278–281.

Mango, C., and E.J.W. Hawkins (1965). The Apse Mosaics of St. Sophia at Istanbul. *Dumbarton Oaks Papers* 19:113–149.

Mango, C. and I. Lavin (1960). Review of Talbot Rice (1958), *The Great Palace of the Byzantine Emperors, Second Report* (Edinburgh). *ArtB* 42:67–73.

Martin, J. (1954). *Studies in Manuscript Illumination. No. 5, The Illustration of the Heavenly Ladder of John Climacus*. Princeton.

Maslev, S. (1966). Die staatsrechtliche Stellung der byzantinischen Kaiserinnen. *Byzantinoslavica* 27:308–343.

Mathews, T.F. (1971). *The Early Churches of Constantinople: Architecture and Liturgy*. University Park, PA and London.

Mathews, T.F. (1988). The Sequel to Nicaea II in Byzantine Church Decoration. *Perkins Journal*: 11–21.

Mathews, T.F. (1990). The Transformation Symbolism in Byzantine Architecture and the Meaning of the Pantocrator in the Dome. In *Church and People in Byzantium*, edited by R. Morris, 191–214. Birmingham.

Mathews, T.F. (1993). *The Clash of Gods: A Reinterpretation of Early Christian Art*. Princeton.

McGrath, R. (1965). The Martyrdom of the Maccabees on the Brescia Casket. *ArtB* 47:257–261.

Mead, M. (1928, 1977 edn). *Coming of Age in Samoa: A Study of Adolescence and Sex in Primitive Societies*. London.

Megaw, A.H.S. and E.J.W. Hawkins (1977). *The Church of the Panagia Kanakaria at Lythrankomi in Cyprus*. Washington, DC.

Meyendorff, J. (1981). *Byzantium and the Rise of Russia*. Cambridge.

Miller, T. (1996). The Care of Orphans in the Byzantine Empire. In *Medieval Family Roles*, edited by C. Itnyre, 121–136. New York, London.

Miller, T. (2003). *The Orphans of Byzantium*. Washington, DC.

Millet, G. (1916). *Recherches sur l'iconographie de l'évangile*. Paris.

Millet, G. (1945). *La dalmatique du Vatican*. Paris.

Miniature. (1905). *Miniature della Bibbia, cod. vat. regin. greco 1 e del Salterio cod. vat. palat. greco 381, Collezione paleografica vaticana, facs. 1*. Milan.

Moffatt, A. (1977). Schooling in the Iconoclast centuries. In *Iconoclasm*, edited by A. Bryer and J. Herrin, 85–92. Birmingham.

Moffatt, A. (1986). The Byzantine Child. *Social Research* 53:705–723.

Molajoli, B. (1943, 2nd edn). *La basilica Eufrasiana di Parenzo*. Padua.

Molno, S., ed. (1962, 2nd edn). *Monuments of Thessalonike*. Thessalonike.

Montfaucon de, B. (1708). *Palaeographia graeca*. Paris.

Moravcsik, G. (1961). Sagen und Legenden über Kaiser Basileios I. *DOP* 15:61–126.

Morey, C.R. (1959). *The Gold-Glass Collection of the Vatican Library*. Edited by G. Ferrari. Vatican.

Morris, R. (1995). *Monks and Laymen in Byzantium, 843–1118*. Cambridge.

Mouriki, D. (1970–1972). The Theme of the 'Spinario' in Byzantine Art. *Deltion tes Christianikes Archaiologikes Hetaireias* 6:53–66.

Mouriki, D. (1971). Communications on the Domes of the Evangelistria and H. Sozon, Geraki. *Archaiologike Ephemeris*: 1–7.

Mouriki, D. (1983) Revival Themes in Two Palaeologan Frescoes. In *Okeanos: Essays presented to Ihor Ševčenko on his Sixtieth Birthday*, edited by C. Mango and O. Pritsak, 458–488. Cambridge, MA.

Mouriki, D. (1985). *The Mosaics of Nea Moni on Chios*. Translated by R. Burgi. 2 vols. Athens.

Moxnes, H., ed. (1997). *Constructing Early Christian Families: Family as Social Reality and Metaphor*. London.

Muir, E. (1997). *Ritual in Early Modern Europe*. Cambridge.

Mullett, M. (1990). Writing in Early Mediaeval Byzantium. In *The Uses of Literacy in Early Mediaeval Europe*, edited by R. Mc.Kitterick, 156–185. Cambridge.

Mullett, M. (1996) The Imperial Vocabulary of Alexios I Komnenos. In *Alexios I Komnenos: Papers of the Second Belfast Byzantine Colloquium, 14–16 April 1989*, edited by M. Mullett and D. Smythe, 359–397. Belfast.

Mullett, M. (1997). *Theophylact of Ochrid: Reading the Letters of a Byzantine Archbishop*. Aldershot.

Mundell Mango, M. (1994). Imperial Art in the Seventh Century. In *New Constantines: The Rhythm of Imperial Renewal in Byzantium, 4th–13th Centuries*, edited by P. Magdalino, 109–138. London.

Murray, Sister C. (1981). *Rebirth and Afterlife: A Study in the Transmutation of Some Pagan Imagery in Early Christian Funerary Art*. Oxford.

Nathan, G. (2000). *The Family in Late Antiquity*. London.

Nelson, R. (1980). *The Iconography of Preface and Miniature in the Byzantine Gospel Book*. New York.

Nelson, R. (1987). Theoktistos and Associates in Twelfth-Century Constantinople: An Illustrated New Testament of AD 1133. *The J. Paul Getty Museum Journal* 15:53–78.

Nelson, R. (1999a). Taxation with Representation: Visual Narrative and the Political Field of the Kariye Camii. *Art History* 22:56–82.

Nelson, R. (1999b). The Chora and the Great Church. *Byzantine and Modern Greek Studies* 23:67–101.

Nelson, R. (2000). To Say and to See: Ekphrasis and Vision in Byzantium. In *Visuality Before and Beyond the Renaissance: Seeing as Others Saw*, edited by R. Nelson. Cambridge.

Néraudau, J.-P. (1984). *Etre enfant à Rome*. Paris.

Nicol, D. (1968). *The Byzantine Family of Kantakouzenos (Cantacuzenus) ca. 1100–1460, Dumbarton Oaks Studies, XI*. Washington DC.

Nicol, D. (1988). Byzantine Political Thought c. 350–1450. In *Cambridge History of Medieval Political Thought*, edited by J.H. Burns, 51–79. Cambridge.

Nordhagen, P.J. (1960). New Research in S. Maria Antiqua. In *Akten des XI. internationalen Byzantinisten-Kongresses, München 1958*.

Nordhagen, P.J. (1961). The Origin of the Washing of the Child in the Nativity Scene. *BZ* 54:333–337.

Nordhagen, P.J. (1962). The Earliest Decorations in Santa Maria Antiqua and Their Date. *ActaNorv* 1:53–72.

Nordhagen, P.J. (1963). The Mosaics of the Great Palace of the Byzantine Emperors. *BZ* 56:53–68.

Nordhagen, P.J. (1965). The Mosaics of John VII (AD 705–707): The Mosaic Fragments and Their Technique. *Acta ad archaeologiam et artium historiam pertinentia* 2.

Nordhagen, P.J. (1968). The Frescoes of John VII (AD 705–707). *ActaNorv* 3.

Nordhagen, P.J. (1972). 'Hellenism' and the Frescoes in S. Maria Antiqua: Notes on the Evolution of an Art Historical Theory. *Konsthistorisk tidskrift* 41.

Nordhagen, P.J. (1978). S. Maria Antiqua: The Frescoes of the Seventh Century. *ActaNorv* 8.

Nordhagen, P.J. (1985). Working with Wilpert: The Illustrations in 'Die römischen Mosaiken und Malereien' and Their Source Value. *ActaNorv* 8.5.

Nordhagen, P.J. (1987). Icons Designed for the Display of Sumptuous Votive Gifts. *DOP* 41:453–460.

Nordström, C. (1955–1957). Some Jewish Legends in Byzantine Art. *Byzantion* 25–27:489.

Oakeshott, W. (1967). *The Mosaics of Rome*. London.

Obolensky, D. (1957). Byzantium, Kiev and Moscow: A Study in Ecclesiastical Relations. *DOP* 23–78. In Obolensky (1971a) Study VI.

Obolensky, D. (1971a). *Byzantium and the Slavs: Collected Studies*. London.

Obolensky, D. (1971b, 1974 edn). *The Byzantine Commonwealth: Eastern Europe, 500–1453*. London.

O'Brien, M. (2000). The Gynaeceum, the Kindergarten, and the Vienna Genesis: Biblical and Extra-Biblical Imagery in Folio 16r. In *Twenty-Sixth Byzantine Studies Conference, Abstracts of Papers*, 109–110. Harvard University.

Odorico, P. (1987). Il calamo d'argento. *JÖB* 37:65–93.

Oikonomides, N. (1963). Le serment de l'impératrice Eudocie (1067). *REB* 21:101–128.

Oikonomides, N. (1965). Some Remarks on the Apse Mosaics of St Sophia. *DOP* 19:113–152.

Oikonomides, N. (1977). John VII Palaeologus and the Ivory Pyxis at Dumbarton Oaks. *DOP* 31:329–339.

Oikonomides, N. (1979). *Hommes d'affaires grecs et latins à Constantinople (XIIIe–XVe siècles)*. Montreal.

Omont, H. (1886–1898). *Inventaire sommaire de manuscrits grecs de la Bibliothèque nationale du VIe au XIe siècle*. Paris.

Omont, H. (1892). *Fac-similés des miniatures des plus anciens manuscrits en onciale et en minuscule de la Bibliothèque nationale du IVe au XIIe siècle*. Paris.

Omont, H. (1902). *Fac-similés des miniatures des plus anciens manuscrits grecs de la Bibliothèque nationale du VIe au XIVe siècle*. Paris.

Omont, H. (1904). Portraits de différents membres de la famille des Comnène peints dans le typicon du monastère de Notre-Dame-de-Bonne-Espérance à Constantinople.*Revue des etudes grecques* 17:361–373.

Omont, H. (1908). *Evangiles avec peintures byzantines du XIe siècle. Reproduction des 361 miniatures du manuscrit grec 74 de la Bibliothèque nationale*. 2 vols. Paris.

Omont, H. (1927). *Miniatures des homélies sur la Vierge du moine Jacques: manuscrit grec 1208 de la Bibliothèque nationale de Paris*. Paris.

Omont, H. (1929). *Miniatures des plus anciens manuscrits grecs de la Bibliothèque nationale du VIe au XIVe siècle*. Paris.

Orme, N. (2001) *Medieval Children*. New Haven and London.

Osborne, J. (1979). The Portrait of Pope Leo IV in San Clemente, Rome: A Re-Examination of the So-Called 'Square' Nimbus in Medieval Art. *Papers of the British School atRome* 57:57–65.

Osborne, J. (1981). Early Medieval Wall-paintings in the Catacomb of San Valentino, Rome. *PSBR* 49.

Osborne, J. (1984). *Early Mediaeval Wall-Paintings in the Lower Church of San Clemente, Rome*. New York.

Osborne, J. (1997). Proclamations of Power and Presence: The Setting and Function of Two Eleventh-Century Murals in the Lower Church of San Clemente, Rome. *Mediaeval Studies* 59:155–172.

Ostrogorsky, G. (1956, 1980 edn). *History of the Byzantine State*. Oxford and Cambridge, MA.

Papadimitriou, S. (1902). Ho epithalamios Andronikou B tou Palaiologou. *BZ* 11:452–60.

Papadopoulos, A. (1938). *Versuch einer Genealogie der Palaiologen, 1259–1453*. Munich.

Papadopoulos-Kerameus, A. (1907). Sylloge Palaistines kai Syriakes Hagiologias 19.3 in *Pravo-slavnyi Palestiniskii Sbornik* 57:42–59.

Papageorgiou, P. (1908). Mnemeia tis en Thessaloniki latreias tou megalomarturos hagiou Dimitriou. *BZ* 17:321–81.

Parani, M. (2001).The *Romanos Ivory* and the New Tokali Kilise. Imperial Costume as a Tool for Dating Byzantine Art. *CA* 49:15–28.

Patlagean, E. (1966) Une représentation Byzantine de la parenté et ses origins ocidentales. *L'Homme* 6:59–83. In Patlagean (1981). Study VII.

Patlagean, E. (1968, 1983 edn) (first published in *Annales: Économies—sociétés—civilizations* 23:106–26). Ancient ByzantineHagiography and Social History. In *Saints and Their Cults*, edited by S. Wilson. Cambridge.

Patlagean, E. (1973). L'enfant et son avenir dans la famille byzantine (IVe–XIIe siècles). *Annales démographie historique*: *Enfant et Sociétés* 85–93. In Patlagean (1981). Study X.

Patlagean, E. (1977). *Pauvreté économique et pauvreté sociale à Byzance, 4e–7e siècles*. Paris.

Patlagean, E. (1978a). Christianisation et parentés rituelles: Le domaine de Byzance. *Annales:Economies—sociétés—civilisations* 33:652–636. In Patlagean (1981). Study XII.

Patlagean, E. (1978b). Familles chrétiennes d'Asie Mineure et histoire démographique du IVème siècle. In Patlagean (1981). Study IX.

Patlagean, E. (1981). *Structure sociale, famille, Chrétienté à Byzance (IVe–Xie siècle)*. London.

Patlagean, E. (1986). L'entrée dans l'âge adulte à Byzance au XIIIe–XIVe siècles. In *L'Historicité de l'enfance et de la jeunesse*. Athens.

Patlagean, E. (1987). Byzantium in the Tenth and Eleventh Centuries. In *History of Private Life*. Vol. 1, *From Pagan Rome to Byzantium*, edited by P. Veyne, 567–590. Cambridge, MA and London.

Patlagean, E. (1996). Families and Kinship in Byzantium. In *History of the Family*, edited by A. Burguière, 467–488. Oxford.

Patterson, C. (1998). *The Family in Greek History*. Cambridge, MA.

Peirce, H. and R. Tyler (1927). Deux mouvements dans l'art byzantin du Xe siècle. *Arethuse* 16:129–136.

Peirce, H. and R. Tyler (1941). Three Byzantine Works of Art. A Byzantine Ivory of the Xth Century. *DOP* 2:13–18.

Pelekanidis, S. and M. Chatzidakis (1985). *Kastoria*. Edited by M. Chatzidakis. Athens.

Percival, J. (1970, 1981 edn). *The Roman Villa: An Historical Introduction*. London.

Piatnitsky, Y., O. Baddeley, E. Brunner and M. Mundell Mango, eds (2000). *Sinai Byzantium Russia: Orthodox Art from the Sixth to the Twentieth Century*. Exhibition Catalogue. London.

Piltz, E. (1994). *Le costume officiel des dignitaires byzantins à l'époque Paléologue*. Uppsala.

Piltz, E. (1997). Middle Byzantine Court Costume. In *Byzantine Court Culture from 829 to 1204*, edited by H. Maguire, 39–51. Washington, DC.

Polemis, D. (1968). *The Doukai: A Contribution to Byzantine Prosopography*. London.

Pollock, L. (1983). *Forgotten Children: Parent–Child Relations from 1500–1900*. Cambridge.

Poppe, A. (1968). Komposycja fundacyjna Sofii Kijowskiej w poszukiwaniu uklady pierwotnego. *Biuletyn historii sztuki i kultury* 30:3–29.

Poppe, A. (1981). The Building of the Church of St Sophia in Kiev. *Journal of Medieval History* 7:15–66.

Powstenko, O. (1954). *The Cathedral of St. Sophia in Kiev*. New York.

Rawson, B. (1986, 1992 edn). *The Family in Ancient Rome: New Perspectives*. London.

Rawson, B., ed. (1991). *Marriage, Divorce, and Children in Ancient Rome*. Oxford.

Reinhold, M. (1970). *History of Purple as a Status Symbol in Antiquity*. Brussels.

Restle, M. (1967). *Die byzantinische Wandmalerei in Kleinasien*. 3 vols. Recklinghausen.

Riché, P. and D. Alexandre-Bidou, eds (1994). *L'enfance au moyen âge*. Paris.

Rodley, L. (1985). *Cave Monasteries of Cappadocia*. Cambridge.

Rose, J. (1984). *The Case of Peter Pan: Or the Impossibility of Children's Literature*. Basingstoke and London.

Roueché, C. (1993). *Performers and Partisans at Aphrodisias in the Roman and Late Roman Periods*. London.

Roussanova, R. (1999). Images of Christ in Karanlik Kilise. MA Thesis, Southern Methodist University.

Roussanova, R. (2000). The Image of Christ Emmanuel in the Dome of Karanlik Kilise. In *Twenty-Sixth Byzantine Studies Conference, Abstracts of Papers*. Cambridge, MA.

Rousselle, A. (1988). *Porneia. On Desire and the Body in Antiquity*. Translated by F. Pheasant. Oxford and New York.

Rowling, J.K. (1997). *Harry Potter and the Philosopher's Stone*. London.

Rushforth, G. (1902). The Church of S. Maria Antiqua. *Papers of the British School at Rome* 1:1–123.

Sacopoulo, M. (1966). *Asinou en 1106 et sa contribution à l'iconographie*. Brussels.

Salomonson, J. (1965). *La mosaïque aux chevaux de l'antiquarium de Carthage*. The Hague.

Sandnes, K. (1997). Equality within Patriarchal Structures: Some New Testament Perspectives on the Christian Fellowship as a Brother- or Sisterhood and a Family. In Moxnes (1997) 150–165.

Sansterre, J.-M. (1991). A propos des titres d'empereur et de roi dans le haut moyen âge. *Byzantion* 61:15–46.

Ščepkina, M. (1977). *Miniatjury Chludovskoj psaltyri: Grečeskij illjustrirovannyj kodeks IX veka*. Moscow.

Schauenburg, K., ed. (1995). *Die antiken Sarkophagreliefs. 5, part 2. Stadtrömische Eroten-Sarkophage. Faszikel 3. Zirkusrennen und verwandte Darstellungen*. Berlin.

Schreiner, P. (1985). Eine Obituarnotiz über eine Frühgeburt. *Studi di Filologia Bizantina* 3:209–216.

Schubert, U. (1971). Der politische Primatanspruch des Papstes Dargestellt am Triumphbogen von Santa Maria Maggiore in Rom. *Kairos* 13:201–236.

Settis, S. (1975). Per l'interpretazione di Piazza Armerina. *Mélanges de l'école française de Rome: Antiquité* 87:873–994.

Ševčenko, N. (1983). *The Life of Saint Nicholas in Byzantine Art*. Turin.

Ševčenko, N. (2000). The Mother of God in Illuminated Manuscripts. In Vassilaki (2000), 155–166. Athens.

Shahar, S. (1990, 1992 edn). *Childhood in the Middle Ages*. Translated by C. Galai. London and New York.

Simon, E. (1964). Nonnos und das Elfenbeinkästchen aus Veroli. *Jahrbuch des deutschen archäologischen Instituts* 79:279–336.

Sinkević I. (2000). *The Church of St. Panteleimon at Nerezi: Architecture, Programme, Patronage*. Wiesbaden.

Skawran, K. (1982). *The Development of Middle Byzantine Fresco Painting in Greece*. Pretoria.

Smith, C. (1913). *Collection of J. Pierpont Morgan. Bronzes: Antique Greek, Roman, etc. Including Some Antique Objects in Gold and Silver*. Paris.

Smythe, D. (1999). In Denial: Same-Sex Desire in Byzantium. In *Desire and Denial in Byzantium*, edited by L. James, 139–148. Aldershot.

Solkin, D. (1992). *Painting for Money: The Visual Arts and the Public Sphere in Eighteenth-Century England*. New Haven.

Sörries, R. (1991). *Die syrische Bibel von Paris: Paris, Bibliothèque nationale, syr. 341, einer frühchristliche Bilderhandschrift aus dem 6. Jahrhundert*. Wiesbaden.

Soteriou, G. and M. Soteriou (1952). *He basilike tou Hagiou Demetriou Thessalonikes*. 2 vols. Athens.

Soteriou, G. and M. Soteriou (1956–1958). *Icônes du Mont Sinai*. Athens.

Spain, S. (1977). Heraclius, Byzantine Imperial Ideology, and the David Plates. *Speculum* 52:217–237.

Spain, S. (1979). 'The Promised Blessing': The Iconography of the Mosaics of S. Maria Maggiore. *ArtB* 61:518–540.

Spatharakis, I. (1976). *The Portrait in Byzantine Illuminated Manuscripts*. Leiden.

Spatharakis, I. (1981). *Corpus of Dated Greek Manuscripts to the Year 1453*. 2 vols. Leiden.

Spatharakis, I. (1989). A Note on Imperial Portraits and the Date of Par. gr. 510. *JÖB* 38:89–93.

Speck, P. (1974). *Die kaiserliche Universität von Konstantinopel: Präzisierungen zur Frage des höheren Schulwesens in Byzanz im 9. und 10. Jahrhundert*. Munich.

Speck, P. (1993–1994). Die Rosettenkästchen: Originalarbeiten oder Versuche einer Verwendung von vorhandenem Material? *BZ* 86–87:79–85.

Spiribo, G. de. (1999). A Propos des Peintures Murales de l'Eglise Santa Maria Foris Portas de Castelseprio. *CahArch* 46:23–64.

Stanley, D. (1994). New Discoveries at Santa Costanza. *DOP* 48:257–261.

Stern, H. (1958). Les mosaïques de l'église de Sainte-Costance à Rome. *DOP* 12:157–218.

Stern, H. (1974). Orphée dans l'art paléochrétien. *CahArch* 33:1–16.

Stone, L. (1977). *The Family, Sex and Marriage in England 1500–1800*. London.

Stornajolo, C. (1908). *Le miniature della Topografia Cristiana di Cosma Indicopleuste: Codice vaticano greco 699*. Milan.

Stornajolo, C. (1910). *Miniature delle Omilie di Giacomo Monaco (cod. Vatic. gr. 1162) e dell'evangeliario greco urbinate (cod. Vatic. Urbin. gr. 2)*. Rome.

Strzygowski, J. (1899). *BZ* 8:262.

Strzygowski, J. (1900). Die byzantinische Kunst auf dem Orientalistenkongress in Rom. *BZ* 9:320–321.

Strzygowski, J. (1901). Das Epithalamion des Paläologen Andronikos II. *BZ* 10:546–567.

Stuveras, R. (1969). *Le putto dans l'art romain*. Brussels.

Svoronos, N. (1951). Le serment de fidelité à l'empereur byzantin et sa signification constitutionelle. *REB* 9:106–142.

Taft, R. (1980). The Pontifical Liturgy of the Great Church According to a Twelfth-Century Diataxis in Codex *British Museum Add. 34060*. *Orientalia christiana periodica* 46:89–124.

Taft, R. (1998). Women at Church in Byzantium. *DOP* 52:27–87.

Talbot, A.M. (1984). Old Age in Byzantium. *BZ* 77:267–278.

Talbot, A.M. (1985). Late Byzantine Nuns: By Choice or Necessity? *Byzantinische Forschungen* 9:103–117.

Talbot Rice, D. (1958). *The Great Palace of the Byzantine Emperors, Second Report*. Edinburgh.

Talbot Rice, D. (1959). *The Art of Byzantium*. London.

Tea, E. (1937). *La basilica di Santa Maria Antiqua*. Milan.

Teteriatnikov, N. (1993). For Whom is Theodotus Praying? An Interpretation of the Program of the Private Chapel in S. Maria Antiqua. *CahArch* 41:37–46.

Teteriatnikov, N. (1996). *The Liturgical Planning of Byzantine Churches in Cappadocia.* Rome.

Thierry, N. (1970). Les peintures murales de six églises du haut moyen âge en Cappadoce. *Comptes rendus des séances de l'Académie des inscriptions et belles-lettres*: 444–479.

Thierry, N. (1971). Un atelier de peinture du début du Xe siècle en Cappadoce: L'atelier de l'ancienne église de Tokali. *Bulletin de la Société nationale des antiquaires de France, séance du 12 Mai 1971*: 170–178.

Thierry, N. (1976). Mentalité et formulation iconoclastes en Anatolie. *Journal des savants*: 81–119.

Thierry, N. (1983 (I) 1994 (II)). *Haut moyen-âge en Cappadoce: Les églises de la région de Çavuşin*. 2 vols. Paris.

Thierry, N. (1995). De la datation des églises de Cappadoce. *BZ* 88:419–455.

Thierry, N. and M. Thierry (1958). Eglise de Kizil-Tchoukour, chapelle iconoclaste, chapelle de Joachim et d'Anne. *Monuments Piot* 50:105–146.

Thierry, N. and M. Thierry (1960). Iconographie inédite en Cappadoce. Le cycle de la conception et de l'enfance de la Vierge à Kizil-Tchoukour. In *Akten des XI. internationalen Byzantinisten-Kongresses, München 1958*, edited by F. Dölger and H.-G. Beck. Munich.

Thierry, N. and M. Thierry (1965). Ayvali kilise ou pigeonnier de Gülli dere, église inedite de Cappadoce. *CahArch* 15:97–154.

Thornton, B.S. (1997). *Eros: The Myth of Ancient Greek Sexuality*. Boulder, CO and Oxford.

Toohey, P. and M. Golden (1997). *Inventing Ancient Culture: Historicism, Periodization, and the Ancient World*. London.

Toubert, H. (1976). 'Rome et le Mont-Cassin': Nouvelles remarques sur les fresques de l'église inférieure de Saint-Clément de Rome. *DOP* 30:1–33.

Tougher, S. (1997a). Byzantine Eunuchs: An overview, with Special Reference to Their Creation and Origin. In James (1997) 168–184. London.

Tougher, S. (1997b). *The Reign of Leo VI (886–912): Politics and People*. Leiden.

Treasures. (1997). *Treasures of Mount Athos*. Exhibition Catalogue. Thessaloniki.

Trilling, J. (1978). Myth and Metaphor at the Byzantine Court: A Literary Approach to the David Plates. *Byzantion* 48:249–263.

Trilling, J. (1989). The Soul of the Empire: Style and Meaning in the Mosaic Pavement of the Byzantine Imperial Palace in Constantinople. *DOP* 43:27–72.

Tsuji, S. (1975). The Headpiece Miniatures and Genealogy Pictures in Paris. gr. 74. *DOP* 29:165–203.

Turner, V. and E. Turner (1978). *Image and Pilgrimage in Christian Culture*. New York.

Twining, E. (1960). *A History of the Crown Jewels of Europe*. London.

Underwood, P. (1966–1975). *The Kariye Djami*. 4 vols. New York.

Uspenskij, T. (1909). On the Newly Discovered Mosaics in the Church of St. Demetrios at Thessaloniki. *Izvestiia Russkago arkheologicheskago Instituta vKonstantinopole* 14:1–61.

Uspenskij, T. and N. Kluge (1909). The Technique of the Mosaic Work in the Church of St. Demetrios at Thessaloniki. *Izvestiia Russkago arkheologicheskago Instituta v Konstantinopole* 14:62–67.

Van Gennep, A. (1909). *Les rites de passage*. Paris.

Vasiliev, A. (1948). The Monument of Porphyrius in the Hippodrome at Constantinople. *DOP* 4:29–49.

Vassilaki, M., ed. (2000). *Mother of God: Representations of the Virgin in Byzantine Art*. Exhibition Catalogue. Athens.

Vassilaki, M., and N. Tsironis (2000). Representations of the Virgin and Their Association with the Passion of Christ. In Vassilaki (2000). Athens.

Velmans, T. (1977). *La peinture murale byzantine à la fin du moyen âge*. Paris.

Vergari, G. (1989). Sull'*Epitafio* Pselliano per la figlia Stiliana. *JÖB* 39:69–76.

Veyne, P. (1978). La famille et l'amour sous le haut-empire romain. *Annales: Économies—sociétés–civilisations* 33:36–63.

Vikan, G. and J. Nesbitt (1980). *Security in Byzantium: Locking, Sealing and Weighing*. Washington, DC.

Vogt, A. (1908). *Basile Ier, empereur de Byzance (867–886)*. Paris.

Volbach, F. (1952) *Elfenbeinarbeiten der Spätantike und des frühen Mittelalters*. Mainz, 2nd edition.

Vryonis, S. (1992). The Vita Basilii of Constantine Porphyrogennetos and the Absorption of Armenians in Byzantine Society, 673–693. Athens.

Wallace-Hadrill, A. (1994). *Houses and Society in Pompeii and Herculaneum*. Princeton.

Walter, C. (1971). Liturgy and the Illustration of Gregory of Nazianzen's Homilies. *REB* 29:183–212.

Walter, C. (1982). *Art and Ritual of the Byzantine Church*. London.

Walter, C. (2000). The Christ Child on the Altar in the Radoslav Narthex: A Learned or a Popular Theme? in *Pictures as Language: How the Byzantines Explored Them*. Study XIII. London. First published in *Studenica et l'art byzantin autour de l'année 1200* (Belgrade, 1988).

Wander, S. (1973). The Cyprus Plates: The Story of David and Goliath. *Metropolitan Museum Journal* 8:89–104.

Wander, S. (1975). The Cyprus Plates and the Chronicle of Fredegar. *DOP* 29:345–6.

Warland, W. (1986). *Das Brustbild Christi. Studien zur spätantiken und frühbyzantinischen Bildgeschichte*. Rome, Freiburg and Vienna.

Webb, R. (1997). Salome's Sisters: The Rhetoric and Realities of Dance in Late Antiquity and Byzantium. In *Women, Men and Eunuchs*, edited by L. James, 119–148. London and New York.

Weitzmann, K. (1951a). *The Fresco Cycle of S. Maria di Castelseprio*. Princeton.

Weitzmann, K. (1951b, 1984 edn). *Greek Mythology in Byzantine Art*. Princeton.

Weitzmann, K. (1966). The Classical in Byzantine Art as a Mode of Individual Expression. In *Byzantine Art—an European Art, Ninth Exhibition Held under the Auspices of the Council of Europe. Lectures*. Athens. In Weitzmann (1971a), 151–175.

Weitzmann, K. (1970). Prolegomena to a Study of the Cyprus Plates. *Metropolitan Museum Journal* 3:97–111.

Weitzmann, K. (1971a). *Studies in Classical and Byzantine Manuscript Illumination*. Edited by H. Kessler. Chicago and London.

Weitzmann, K. (1971b). The Classical Heritage in the Art of Constantinople. In Weitzmann (1971a), 126–150.

Weitzmann, K. (1971c). The Character and Intellectual Origins of the Macedonian Renaissance. In Weitzmann (1971a), 176–223.

Weitzmann, K. (1972). *Catalogue of the Byzantine and Early Mediaeval Antiquities in the Dumbarton Oaks Collection*. Vol. 3, *Ivories and Steatites*. Washington, DC.

Weitzmann, K. (1976). *The Monastery of Saint Catherine at Mount Sinai. The Icons*. Vol. 1, *From the Sixth to the Tenth Century*. Princeton.

Weitzmann, K. (1977). *Late Antique and Early Christian Book Illumination*. New York.

Weitzmann, K. (1979a). *The Miniatures of the Sacra Parallela Parisinus Graecus 923*. Princeton.

Weitzmann, K., ed. (1979b). *Age of Spirituality: Late Antique and Early Christian Art, Third to Seventh Century*. New York.

Weitzmann, K. and H. Kessler (1990). *The Frescoes of the Dura Synagogue and Christian Art*. Washington, DC.

Wellesz, E. (1960). *The Vienna Genesis*. London.

Wessel, K. (1969). *Byzantinische Emailkunst vom 5. bis 13. Jahrhundert*. Recklinghausen.

Wessel, K. (1970). *Die Kultur von Byzanz*. Frankfurt.

Wessel, K. (1975). Manuel II. Palaiologos und seiner Familie zur Miniatur des Cod. Ivoires A53 des Louvre. In *Beiträge zur Kunst des Mittelalters. Festschrift für Hans Wenzel zum 60. Geburtstag*, edited by R. Becksmann, 219–229. Berlin.

Wharton, A. (1988). *Art of Empire: Painting and Architecture of the Byzantine Periphery*. University Park, PA.

Wharton, A. (1995). *Refiguring the Post Classical City: Dura Europas, Jerash, Jerusalem, Ravenna*. Cambridge and New York.

Whittemore, T. (1942). *The Mosaics of Haghia Sophia at Istanbul: Third Preliminary Report: The Imperial Portraits of the South Gallery*. Boston.

Wiedemann, T. (1989). *Adults and Children in the Roman Empire*. New Haven.

Wilpert, J. (1917, 2nd edn). *Die römischen Mosaiken und Malereien der kirchlichen Bauten vom IV. bis XIII. Jahrhundert*. 4 vols. Freiburg.

Wilpert, J. (1926). Early Christian Sculpture: Its Restoration and Its Modern manufacture. *ArtB* 9:89–141.

Wilson, R. (1983). *Piazza Armerina*. Austin.

Wilson, R. (1990). *Sicily under the Roman Empire: The Archaeology of a Roman Province, 36BC–AD535*. Warminster.

Wright, D. (1980). The School of Princeton and the Seventh Day of Creation. *University Publishing* 9:7–8.

Yannopoulos, P. (1975). *La société profane dans l'empire byzantin des VIIe, VIIIe, et IXe siècles*. Louvain.

Yannopoulos, P. (1991). Le couronnement de l'empereur à Byzance: Rituel et fond institutionnel. *Byzantion* 61:71–92.

Yenipinar, H. and S. Şabin (1998). *Paintings of the Dark Church*. Istanbul.

Zanchi Roppo, F. (1969). *Vetri Paleocristiani a figure d'oro conservati in Italia*. Bologna.

Zanker, P. (1979). Die Villa als Vorbild Design späten pompejanischen Wohngeschmacks. *Jahrbuch des deutschen archäologischen Instituts* 94:460–523.

Zanker, P. (1995). *The Mask of Socrates: The Image of the Intellectual in Antiquity*. Berkeley and Oxford.

Zeitler, B. (1999). *Ostentatio Genitalium*: Displays of Nudity in Byzantium. In James (1999), 185–201. Aldershot.

Zeldin, T. (1994). *An Intimate History of Humanity*. London.

Index

Page references in *italic* type indicate figures. Page references in ***bold italic*** type indicate plates. All historical people are listed by first name. Fixed art such as mosaics and wall paintings are listed under their location; movable objects are listed under media, such as ivory, manuscript, metalwork. Iconographic scenes, including Christ, the Virgin and saints, are listed under iconography.